Lipman
1975

THE GIRLS
IN
THE
OFFICE

———·———

by

JACK OLSEN

Simon and Schuster · New York

FIRST PRINTING
SBN 671-21156-0
LIBRARY OF CONGRESS CATALOG CARD NUMBER: 74-185771
DESIGNED BY IRVING PERKINS
MANUFACTURED IN THE UNITED STATES OF AMERICA

for Su

AUTHOR'S NOTE

Through the two years of researching this work, I tried to function strictly as a *tabula rasa*, as Christopher Isherwood's "camera with its shutter open." In the recorded interviews I avoided discoloring the discussions with my own prejudices and opinions, and I remain reluctant to abandon that non-directive approach in this brief note. I hope the reader will find that the Girls in the Office speak eloquently enough in their own behalf and that the familiar legalism *res ipsa loquitur* applies to each of their autobiographies.

Beyond that, the reader is entitled to know that the Girls in the Office are real people, that they are single, that they all work for the same company in New York City and that they consented to unfold the details of their lives on condition that their true names and identities be fully concealed. I have complied gladly with this wish, and I have changed *all* names except those of historical personages. To the fifteen women who gave so patiently of their time and energy, I offer gratitude most profound.

JACK OLSEN

Rollinsville, Colorado

The Girls

———•———

THE GIRLS
IN THE
OFFICE

Alexandra Oats, 38

———•———

Alexandra Oats is about the only girl I know in The Company who seems perfectly content. She maintains a lot of outside interests, and she works at them, keeps them up. She's got a good job in The Company, and she doesn't take any guff from anybody. She's established a niche for herself, and she seems happy. She's not too smart, maybe that's it.—Florence DuValle

• I •

PEOPLE SAY I'm tough, I'm cold, I'm this and that, and I just let them go on talking. If I was as tough as some people say I am, I wouldn't be running an office full of girls; I'd be a lady wrestler, or a bull dike, or a hard-hat. Of course, we all idealize our own images, as Karen Horney says, and I guess I'm no exception. I don't think I'm tough or cold at all, but I do think I'm fairly smart, or hip, or something like that. In the old days they'd have said I was street-wise, but what I really am is company-wise. I've been around here since I was twenty years old—with a short time out for marriage and divorce—and I've learned the hard way that you can let this company chew you up and spit you out or you can turn it to your own advantage. You can stick out your hands and let The Company put a lot of goodies in them and then kick you in the mouth, or you can hold your hands back a little and keep your distance and enjoy the whole scene. I don't exactly call that brilliance —it's more like self-preservation.

I started as a secretary and I would still be a secretary if I hadn't made a very quick study of the secretary's role in New York. Most of the bosses don't want secretaries at all, and very few of them need secretaries. What they want is servant girls, and that's what they try to turn you into. Make the coffee, answer the phone, run errands—like a servant. I don't go for that and I never did. To me, that's from the 1890s.

When one of these straw bosses around here starts pulling that crap on his secretary, he's really just trying to increase his own status. It's like climbing out of a pit of quicksand by stepping on somebody else's head. You debase the secretary and you show what a great, powerful leader you are. I'm convinced that's how it works in most of their minds.

There's never enough real work for any of the secretaries around here, but you just watch what happens when Mr. X goes to Mr. Y's secretary and asks her to do some inconsequential little thing. Mr. Y comes storming out of his office and he says, "She's *my* secretary!" And the girl herself gets all upset on her boss's behalf. Maybe she's been sitting there doing crossword puzzles for two hours, but she's not there to do work in the first place—she's there to enhance the prestige and the status of Mr. Y, and the less real work she does, the more she enhances.

You'll notice a pattern about the secretaries in this office. Very few of them are the beehive type, the girl from the Bronx who graduated from high school and led her class at business school in typing and shorthand and filing and can run that office like a dynamo. She's the perfect secretary—but she needn't apply here. With her local accent and her lack of college background, she never makes much of a status symbol, so she's not wanted. Most of the bosses around here are turned off by a girl like that. They want the miniskirted little thing that just graduated from Sarah Lawrence and she's wearing Gucci shoes and she's already made six trips to Europe, and her shorthand and typing are from nowhere. We hire a constant supply of this type. For a while the bosses were going one step beyond that and hiring girls from England, and you were nobody in New York business circles unless your telephone was answered by an English accent. These imports didn't know

American ways, American style, even American punctuation, but *everybody* had to have one. The vogue is over now, but there's several thousand of those girls still on the job in New York, still answering the phone with an Oxford accent, and still screwing up the American language. They'll write, "Our company *have* decided. . . ." or they'll tell somebody on the telephone, "I'll have Mr. Throttlebottom knock you up about four o'clock." It all sounds so cute to the bosses, but meanwhile those girls are spreading a hell of a lot of confusion.

If a girl doesn't catch on to the real pattern of secretarial life around here, she's finished fast. And most of the girls *don't* catch on. They sit on their backsides for four or five years, getting lazier and lazier, more and more spoiled, taking longer and longer lunch hours, drinking, chasing men, becoming frustrated, complaining, and finally goofing off, because they don't realize from the beginning that *they have no real job*. They're just decoration. God help them if they stay too long at the fair. They'll just get cast aside. That's the way it is in these so-called glamorous companies, and maybe it *has* to be that way. Prestige and status are what it's all about. At least three quarters of the New York executives think the same way, play their prestige games the same way. And *they're high-salaried executives, aren't they?* So the game must work, at least for them.

Well, I never accepted this routine, and also I was a little lucky. From the beginning, I worked hard—and my first boss *allowed* me to work hard; he even broadened my responsibilities to make my job more challenging. He's no longer with The Company, which is food for thought. He lost out in the politics. The guy who replaced him has two secretaries, and each one does about ten percent of a normal day's work.

Through the years I've always worked hard, and I've slipped from the grasp of more than one boss who wanted to make me into an errand girl or a status symbol. Now I have responsibility, and I still work hard. I'm usually at the office at eight-thirty, and I seldow leave before six-thirty. I've accumulated a little prestige myself, and I use every ounce of it to make people treat me fairly. I don't always win, but I never stop pushing. I'm management, so I've had to keep out of the Women's Lib movement; I don't even express myself on the subject around the office. But I'll tell you confidentially that the movement is badly needed. You would think that of all people in The Company, I would be one of the most fairly treated, but it's not true. Men who do my job in other departments get more money than I do. When I find out, I scream my head off. But it's hard to find out. Once I did a favor for Buddy Bowers, a guy who has my exact same job in another department, and he said, "Now what can I do for you in return?"

I said, "Well, you can answer one question. How much money do you make?"

Whoops! That surprised him. Like that was one question Buddy Bowers didn't want to answer. But he was stuck. So he said, "Twenty thousand plus." I figured him for twenty-one thousand. I made eighteen thousand. I went right straight to the manager and I told him I wanted a raise to twenty-one thousand. He said, "You're putting me in the middle. Why should you make more than others with the same job?"

I told him what I knew about "others in the same job," and he countered that one fast. "Buddy's been with The Company two more years than you," he said.

"So what?" I said. "When the President of the United States gets elected, they don't say, 'Well, you've only been in politics for six months, so we'll give you less money.' He gets the job and he gets the money."

"Let me think about it." He thought about it for a few weeks and then raised me to nineteen thousand five hundred, which still isn't fair, but it's an improvement. After the raise, I went to him with another complaint.

"Listen," I said, "I want to start going to a few conventions. I can show you twenty guys out there that have less important jobs than mine, and they're always running off to conventions. Why shouldn't I go?"

He said, "You know the answer to that, Alex, so why do you ask?"

"No, I *don't* know the answer!"

"Well, I'll tell you then. We don't invite women to our conventions because the guys like to be together and get drunk together and maybe play around a little, let their hair down, and it'd be uncomfortable for you."

"Now isn't that just lovely?" I said. I was really annoyed. "Tell me one thing, will you? Why should I be penalized for the misbehavior of the men? It makes no sense!"

"Well, we'll see what we can do," he said.

That was a year ago. Since then I've been to a convention at the Hilton in San Juan and another at Phoenix, Arizona. That's maybe half as many conventions as most of our men have gone to in the last year, but at least it's a start. And I don't get in the way of the boys' night out. When they're in the bar or chasing *senoritas* all over the terraces, I'm out getting a suntan, or visiting a local museum to learn something. I'm trying not to get in the way, so I don't wreck it for other girls who'd like to go on some of these junkets, too.

You have to learn quickly that the super-talented, super-creative geniuses in our company are different from other men—or at least they *think* they're different. Really, it's mostly in their minds; they're *not* that different. This company is set up to glorify the men, and a woman can buck it but she also has to face it and behave accordingly. For years I did most of the party-arranging on our floor, and I did it with an eye toward pleasing the men. That meant ensuring the presence of young females, plenty of booze, and an atmosphere conducive to playing around. Sometimes I felt like the chief madam in a whorehouse, even though I myself stayed aloof from the fun and games. I'm glad that those days are ending. The other day we had a little "pour," and it lasted for about forty-five minutes, and when almost everybody had left one of the older men in The Company came up to me and said, "Remember how the parties used to last all night and we'd all wind up in somebody else's apartment and be late for work the next morning? It's too bad those days are gone." I felt like saying, "How ridiculous for a gray-haired old crock like you to be talking like that!" But I didn't.

Lucky for my own mental health, married men have always turned me off. When I got my divorce, the married men came after me in packs. Every divorcee experiences this, especially at The Company. I think the psychological reasoning is simple. The divorced woman *knows how to do it;* she can't pretend she's innocent or naïve. *She's done naughty things,* and if she'll do them with one man she'll do them with another. Honestly, I think that's how their childish reasoning goes.

But I never fell into that trap. With married men, it's wham bam, thank you, ma'am. I don't know from my own experience, but that's what the other girls in the office have told me. Personally, I think that girls who make a career out of married men are masochists. They do nothing but suffer—because that's what they *want* to do. There's *no* way to make the extramarital-affair scene work out.

Some of the girls say it's hard to meet single men in New York. Well, I agree. But it's not impossible. And anyway a girl should be able to develop some inner resources; she shouldn't have to be dating a different dashing bachelor every night of the week. I will agree that New York men are weird in many respects. They'll make very few motions toward you, and if you make the slightest motion toward them, they'll run like hell. You can't call them up or be aggressive; that turns them off. It shouldn't, but it does. So you stay home a lot and wish you were out.

One day I was riding on a train, and I don't usually talk to people on trains or planes, but somehow I got into a conversation with a man from Uruguay. He gave me his card and told me that he was a sculptor and he had known Che Guevara and he hated the big U.S. oil interests in South America and blah-blah. He carried on for about an hour, very animated, very interesting. He knew Rubirosa and Allende and he'd been married to a very wealthy woman from Argentina and blah-blah. Then he began dropping names in the polo circles, in the society circles, all the *right* names. When we reached New York he asked for my phone number and he insisted that we had to see each other again and he would call me.

Three weeks later I gave a dinner party, and I called him up and invited him. He said he'd come, but on the day of the party he begged off, and like I've never seen him since. That's weird, isn't it? Like what is this? Why would a man act that way?

But these New York men are from another planet. They're the main reason that the swinging-singles myth is pure hokum. A girl can't swing as a single around New York; she'll just turn off all the men. I mean, she might get taken to bed a few times, but she'll never find anything meaningful or real. A woman can invite men out and consciously attempt seduction, but she'll soon find that New York men can't accept this. You try it a few times and then you quit. That kind of single-female life really doesn't exist, although certain writers and editors have found it profitable to *pretend* that it exists. The mass media would like us to think that there's such a thing as an aggressive, swinging single woman, but they've just confused a lot of the single girls in New York. The girls try to relate themselves to what they read, and they can't bring it off, and then they think that there's something the matter with them. They don't realize that they're trying to live an unrealistic fiction.

· 2 ·

BUT THAT doesn't mean that you have to be miserable at The Company, or in New York City. I don't believe in falling down and playing dead the first time something unpleasant strikes me; I believe in enjoying life and trying to make something out of it. If I lived on a desert, I'd collect sand. There's always *something*. Like in New York, I collect experiences, scenes, and this is the place to do it. My friends and I consciously seek out weird and interesting places to collect—gay bars, lesbian bars, places like that. Could you do that in Springfield, Mo? It's fascinating!

One night we went into a gay bar, just to see what it was like, and I got the shock of my life when I spotted a man from the office. He was a closet queen. Nobody knew. When he saw me, he pretended that he'd just dropped in for a beer, but obviously he was well known in the bar. He said, "Well, hi, Alex! Gosh, I just dropped in for a beer. Got taken with a real thirst all of a sudden, you know?" But then all the other queers in the bar began cozying up to him. I felt so sorry for him. Later I heard that he was worried I'd say something around the office, but I keep the office separate from my social life, and of course I didn't say a word.

The homosexual scene is fascinating in New York—strange and bizarre. Sometimes it's not an easy study. Usually I try to go to homosexual bars with a date—that way there'll be no mistake. But homosexual bars don't dig heterosexual couples. The other night two couples of us went into a lesbian bar in Greenwich Village, and the atmosphere was tense. The bartender was very slow about taking our orders, and when Bill made a crack, we didn't get anything else to drink. The bartender announced that I was underage and he wouldn't even look at my ID. He was off by about twenty years and he knew it—but they'd all wanted us out of there from the beginning.

I seem to pick up information about homosexuality wherever I go. I had seen this man around town, and then I ran into him at a party, a very handsome, ballsy type of man. He always said he was an actor, and he always talked a lot about his ex-wife and his eighteen-year-old son, and he came on very masculine. But after we'd had a few drinks that night he admitted that he was a homosexual and he agreed to tell me all about homosexuality if I'd tell him all about my marriage. So we talked till seven in the morning. I asked him how come he always seemed to have a beautiful woman on his arm, like a chorus-girl type, and he said there were lots of girls like that who enjoyed dating homosexuals. Talking to him made me realize that there must be a lot more like him in New York, men that you would never suspect, or men you'd think were very active with women. There's absolutely no way to spot them. Like this guy, they come on all balls, the rugged, domineering male caricature.

He told me that he had a lover, a man, that he'd lived with for twelve years, but in addition to that he was very active on the street. He figured he had about a hundred men a year in New York City. He said that's nothing unusual. He meets them on the subways, at the Y, in bars. He taught me some of their language. Ever hear of an eight-oh-niner? That's a guy who swings both ways. He goes to the Y and picks up a homosexual, and then he calls home to his wife and says he'll be on the eight-oh-nine for home. Some homosexuals get a special kick out of picking up eight-oh-niners.

Rough trade is what you meet on the streets. Male-prostitute types. Then there's the meat rack. That's the guys who stand around in Washington Square Park. There's also a meat rack out on Fire Island. Out there, the meat rack's a fence that the queers lean against. The first time I ever heard about the Fire Island meat rack was when I was a house guest of a homosexual out there. Some more guests came in from Cleveland, and he said, "Jesus Christ, all they want to do is see the meat rack!" I thought he meant a walk-in refrigerator, and I said, "I want to see the meat rack, too," and he laughed.

Another phrase I learned was "fruit fly." That's the very attractive model type, the young starlet type, that doesn't want a guy to touch her. She goes out with homosexual men and then other homosexual men find out about it and after a while they feel free to call her up. She knows the score and she knows the scene and they'll go to parties together. If her homosexual date makes a score, she'll just cut out on her own and no hard feelings. It's a symbiotic relationship.

Then there's the Mother Goose: an older woman who likes young gigolo types around her, Italian race-driver types, men that are usually queers. Some of the Mother Goose types are married, but their husbands are getting old and don't want to groove anymore. Or their husbands will let them go out with homosexuals. That way the queers get to meet certain people, go to certain social functions, that they'd miss out on otherwise.

Now I ask you, where else in the world could you pick up on things like this? I really enjoy accumulating information like that, not just on queers but on *everything* about this crazy mixed-up scene called New York. People think I'm nuts, *but I actually like it here!* I think it's the big apple! There's only a few other cities in the world like it. Tokyo is like it. Even before I got off the plane at Tokyo Airport I felt the power, the energy, in the air. New York has the same dynamic quality. Chicago and Los Angeles and St. Louis and places like that—they don't have it. They're just multiples of Springfield, Missouri. The only thing that Chicago has going for it is Hugh Hefner. L.A. has nothing at all. San Francisco is the deviate's paradise, but after New York it seems like a small town to me.

The energy of New York is what turns me on. It's like a big wine vat, mixing and bleeding and fermenting, bubbling. I used to like to sit in Grand Central Station and pretend I was waiting for a train and just watch the people walk by, try to guess their lives. Now you can groove on things like this, pick them up and make them a part of your life, or you can live in your own little apartment and act as though the city is nothing but a big menacing jungle and you'd better not come out at night. Personally, I'll take the chance. And when I do have to stay in my apartment, I don't lack for things to keep my interest up. I built a whole hi-fi system out of kits; I have a collection of antique clocks; I love to cook, and I've got about five dozen cookbooks on my shelves and all sorts of great things to eat like white Piedmont truffles and shallots and frozen steamer clams and snails and anything I want. It's all available in markets a few blocks from me.

So I'm content. I'm not on cloud nine, but I'm content. I like my independence. I like the hum of this city. I can hear it in the middle of the night—a low, persistent hum that most people's ears tune out. I wake up to it and it makes me feel secure. And I like the way New York keeps you off balance. I *enjoy* that! Why should every day be like every other day? In New York you never know what's going to hit you.

The other day I was looking in the window of Tiffany's and a woman came up behind me and started shouting at me. "You home-wrecker, you whore, you this-and-that and blah-blah!" I turned around, and I'd never seen this woman before. She was about fifty years old, neatly dressed, looked as though she'd just got off the train from Scarsdale and was on her way to do some shopping. I didn't know what to do, so I walked off as fast as I could, but the woman kept after me. "You housewrecker, you bitch!" I finally reached the subway station and I dashed down the steps and got away. After a little while I sneaked back up the steps and there was the woman! Only now she had another woman cornered, and she was shaking her finger and saying, "You home-wrecker! You bitch! You blah-blah!" I hurried away in the other direction, and I had something to talk about all day.

Certainly there's a crime problem here, and certainly it's a serious one. But people managed to survive back in the days of the Thuggees and the pirates, didn't they? I'm not suggesting that this is any way to live, or that the situation shouldn't be corrected, but I *am* suggesting that it doesn't make the city unlivable. Right now New York City's crime problem is ten percent reality and ninety percent paranoia. It's overreaction. I overreact myself. One night I got off at the wrong stop of the bus line and I had to walk a few blocks to get home. It was late, and as I started walking I noticed a big black guy walking along the sidewalk behind me. I started walking faster, and *he* started walking faster. It made me so nervous that I decided to walk out in the middle of the street. Then I heard him call out in this gentle voice, "It's okay, lady, it's *okay*." So I went back to the sidewalk. Later on, I said to myself, it was kind of stupid of me to get into that position, so from then on I began taking taxis home at night.

Of course there's some crime that's highly unpleasant, and it's time Mayor Lindsay hired himself a couple of thousand cops to meet the problem. Right now you can't get a cop to do anything, he's so overworked. A friend of mine was mugged in broad daylight on Central Park West, and when a beat cop finally arrived he told her she'd have to go report the mugging to the precinct station about twenty blocks away. Well, the mugger had taken her purse and she had no money, so she asked the cop to lend her the bus fare to the station. He said no.

I was robbed myself last month. They broke down the gate in front of my apartment on East Thirteenth Street and took a TV and several other things. The police didn't display much interest in the case. They came and snooped around for about five minutes and then they took my name and left. After they'd gone, I discovered a crowbar and a shopping bag under the bed, and I was real excited. Evidently the robbers had carried the crowbar in the shopping bag to get into the place, and then they'd discarded it after they got in. I called up the detective on the case and I said, "I think I've found something important."

And he said in this bored voice, "Yeah, lady, what is it?"

I told him, and he said, "Yeah, well, okay, lady. Tell you what to do. You keep that crowbar as a souvenir. Okay, lady?" and he hung up. So I still have the crowbar. It probably has the burglar's fingerprints on it, but who cares? That's what I mean by not having enough cops, or at least not having enough cops who care about their work.

One place that could use a few thousand more cops is the subway, although I'm no longer an authority on the subway, since I've refused to ride it for three years now. I just got sick and tired of being felt up each morning on the way to work and each evening going home. Every girl in New York has to develop her own technique for handling this problem. Mine was to turn in the general direction of the feeler and holler, "Keep your hands off, creep!" Somebody'd always say, "Who me?" and I'd say, "Yeah, *you*, you pervert! You know damned well who you are!" I might have victimized a few innocents, a priest or two, but something had to be done. One day I was sitting on the subway and two men were standing in front of me. One dropped a newspaper, and the other made a great flourish out of bending down to pick it up. As he was getting back up, he came real close to me and opened up his overcoat and *ba-whoom!* The whole penal area just hung right out, for my benefit. I *know* the other man saw it, but he didn't make a move, and that annoyed me more than anything. When we pulled into the next stop, I jumped up and ran out the door, and that was my last trip in a New York City subway.

So now I take the buses. There seem to be fewer of these "flashers" in the buses. On the other hand, there are far more constipated grouches. So many elderly people in big cities are grumpy and miserable to deal with, and you can't avoid them on the bus. They're just *begging* for something to get sore about. Yesterday I worked my way through a pack of people till I got to the back of the bus, and here comes a man about sixty. He stands next to me for a while, and then somebody gets up and this old guy almost knocks me down to get the seat. An elderly lady got mad about it, and she turned to me and said, "He's no gentleman," and blah-blah. The man looked up and said, "That's right, goils, I'm no gentleman."

So I said, "Well, you can have the seat if you want it, but just don't push me down to get it."

The old lady turns to me and she says, in a German accent, "Did you ever find an American man who vas a gentleman?"

"Yes, I have."

Now that made *her* mad, and she stopped talking to me. So for the whole rest of the trip I had to put up with these two old grouches sending out these bad vibrations at me. Well, that's New York. You have to take the good with the bad. That's the price you pay for living here, and to me it's worth it. I would die if I had to live any place else. I said that to Bettye McCluin one day, and she said, "Yeah, well, you'll die here, the way things are going."

"Well," I said, "I'm happy to take the chance." I *am*, too. New York is *it*, the big apple. As somebody said, everything else is Bridgeport.

Peg Kern, 36

———•———

Of all the girls in the office, Peg Kern is the nicest. She's very friendly, she's helpful, and she works hard. She's a case of one who's been with The Company a long time and worked her tail off and got nothing for it. It's not fair. There should have been a payoff. Unlike most of the others, she at least made the attempt to get ahead, and she didn't show resentment when others did better. When I got a promotion, Peg went out of her way to warn me that others might be resentful on her behalf, because she'd been in line for the same promotion. And she told me that she was glad to see that the job went to a hard worker like me. She was trying to ease my feelings, and I was grateful for it. She wished me only the best. She's one of the most active Women's Lib beefers, and I think she has every right to be. Most of the Women's Lib crowd are lazy and good-for-nothing, but Peg Kern has earned the right to be heard. Around the office she's very bubbly and bouncy and smiling all the time. Maybe it's pretense, maybe she's really miserable that she's in her mid-thirties and she's unmarried and unfulfilled. You never know what goes on behind those smiles.—Bettye McCluin

• I •

WHY DO people come to New York in the first place? I've heard a dozen reasons. It's the city of the finalists, and you're nowhere till you make it in New York. Or it's the big apple. Or "everything happens in New York." There's a little truth in all the expressions, but the main truth is that people don't go *to* New York; they flee *from* their home towns. Most Americans would rather live in hell than stay where they were brought up. Too much is expected of people who stay in their home towns; in New York you're your own person. The druggist and the bus driver and the minister—they're not all looking over your shoulder studying your morals. You're free.

I got my first taste of New York just after I finished college. My fiancé was graduating from Columbia, and I came to the big city from my home town in Oregon to look for a job and be with him. I stayed a few weeks, but only one day stands out. It was snowing, and we walked from Eightieth Street all the way down to the Village, and it seemed homey and fun. Snowfall in New York diffuses things, makes softer edges, makes the city look beguiling. That night it snowed like a bandit. The taxis and buses stopped, and the city was quiet. All the way down Second Avenue the city looked like something from Movietone News. The sounds were muffled; the garish neon lights were diffused into blobs of soft color; the dog dirt that litters the sidewalks was covered up. That night New York seemed so gay and free, a lot of young kids my own age having fun and screwing and leaping around. And all in good style and the best of taste.

The trouble was that my fiancé and I were having trouble. His family put too many strains on us. We figured we'd get married and I'd work while he went through law school, but his father stepped in and announced that he could not consent to any such arrangement unless I agreed in advance to pay one hundred percent of the room and board. He seemed so highhanded about it, and what annoyed me was that Don was taking all this seriously. I thought he should tell his father to go fuck himself—although I wouldn't have put it in just those terms, not back in those days—and we should have made our own plans and stuck with them, and the parents be damned. But Don and I had all these long scenes about the father and mother and it began to seep through to me that he cared a whole lot more about them than he did me. We had a short—very short—discussion about just living together, without getting married, but that didn't sound right to either of us. Maybe we were the last of our generation to worry about the morality of living together.

When Don began telling me exactly what kind of job I could accept and what to wear when I went job-hunting and how to wear my makeup and everything else, I began to realize we weren't for each other. I loved to play piano in those days—I had played for twenty years, ever since I was three—and I was about as close to a professional as any amateur you ever heard. I figured I could make a hundred dollars a week playing in supper clubs. But of course Don wouldn't hear of that. "You might as well be a whore" was the cute way he put it. So one night I got mad and I said, "Look, you made me quit the piano, you made me quit this and you made me quit that, and now I'm quitting you!" Very dramatic. But I was young.

So I hauled myself back to Oregon, back to the old home town, and back to the old homestead. The trouble was, my home town was a different place now. I had been through college and I didn't know the people at home anymore. When I was a little kid it was a sweet, naïve place—you could go downtown on the bus when you were twelve years old and it was a big deal, and you'd take your lunch and fifteen cents and go to the movies and stay all afternoon. But by the time I came home again there were ninety-nine new factories in town and the place had become cosmopolitan, or pseudo-cosmopolitan, and the whole social life was different. Which would have been fine, except that my parents hadn't changed *their* values or what they expected of *me*. So I couldn't live in an apartment by myself; that just wasn't done by single girls. I couldn't stay out till four in the morning because that was too risqué, too "fast." And I couldn't go away for three-day weekends with other kids my age—"decent girls don't do such things!" About the only good thing that happened in that year was my parents didn't charge me room or board, so I saved enough money to buy myself a little Karmann-Ghia and it added a lot to my life. In fact, it was just about the only fun I had.

I never could get that lovely snowfall on Second Avenue out of my mind—although I'd long since gotten over Don—and after a year I knew I had to go back to New York. I was strangling at home. Nothing was happening. I loved my parents—deeply—but I had to breathe. So I pulled my money out of the bank, kissed them goodbye and headed east, right across the snowpack. On the way I stopped off at a big new supermarket to buy some tidbits for the road—milk and cookies—and the cashier said, "Miss, you've won! See the red star on your bill? You've won!" I said, "What have I won?" She said, "A basket full of groceries!" Well, it took me almost a week to drive to New York, and I lived off that basket of groceries the whole time. I considered it an omen.

In that first week in New York I walked through a pair of shoes looking for a job. I ran into some old friends from college, and most of them were still unmarried and having a wonderful time—drinking, screwing, running around. It all looked good to me, but first I had to have work, and there didn't seem to be any around. I went to live with my old college roommate and her boy friend, but that didn't seem right. Kind of crowded, and things like that embarrassed me then. About four days after I moved in, one of the biggest companies in New York let a couple of hundred people go, and together we made up a cadre of the unemployed. I'd see the same faces at the unemployment bureau and at the employment agencies, and I made some good friends out of that adversity. But there was no work, *nothing!* I had a letter of introduction to one of the supervisors at The Company, but I didn't want to use it. It smacked of using "pull," and I didn't want to get a job that way. But after three weeks my money was getting low, and about all I had left was my Karmann-Ghia and an empty basket of groceries. So I called The Company and asked to speak to this particular supervisor. It was my first great revelation about the bullshit of New York. He said he'd be glad to see me after lunch. Well, where I come from, lunch is thirty minutes, from twelve-thirty to one, and if you're really irresponsible you can push it another five or ten minutes. So I said, "What time is lunch over?" and he said, "Three o'clock."

Fine. I arrived at the reception desk at three o'clock sharp and he wasn't in. Mr. Storns, the hot-shot supervisor, that son of a bitch, left me sitting in the reception room for forty-five minutes. And when he finally did call me in to his office, he said that he'd forgotten that I was out there. He didn't forget! Don't kid me! He just didn't get back from lunch till quarter of four. That's the way you treat underlings. He's still the same way now. If you're an underling, you practically have to sign up a week in advance to get into his office. But if you're above him in the hierarchy he'll walk through a wall to kiss your ass.

So we talked for a few minutes, but what he found out about me I'll never know. I had transcripts of my college record and letters from a few people back home telling what a wonderful girl I was, and some samples of the work I'd done in my year at home, but he didn't want to see any of that. He displayed a lot of interest in my legs, but I wasn't applying for a job as a model, so I couldn't see what good that would do. Finally he said, "I think you should have a talk with the chief of our trainee pool." At that time, the chief of trainees was a woman of about sixty-five, and the minute I walked into her office I could see she was tight. "Come in! Come in!" she said, like I was a visiting emperor. "Sit right down there and tell me all about yourself!"

I handed her my portfolio and sat right down, but she put the portfolio aside and didn't seem especially interested in my fascinating tales about life in Oregon and my wonderful career at San Diego State College. She kept that plastic smile on for about three minutes, and then she said, "Well, dear, if you want to get a start in this glamorous company, why, we'd love to have you as a trainee, and we'll promote you because you seem to have good credentials." I don't know how she knew; she still hadn't looked at any of my credentials. I was a little put off by this, but I thought, "Well, you'd better go along with it; this is the way things are done in the big city."

She gave me the name of a company official on another floor, and off I went for an interview with another woman. This one was smashed to the eyeballs. The chief of trainees had been a little drunk, too, but at least she could frame sentences and refrain from slobbering. But this new woman was far gone. She had a tough,

strident voice and a tough, aggressive manner. Any second I expected her bright red wig and her huge falsies to fall off and reveal
a man. She was about fifty, and she was brittle and hard and sterile-
looking. Her lips were two straight lines. She told me about all the
people she knew in my home town and my college. Every time
I'd mention a name, she'd say, "Yeah, I know him! I know that old
shon of a bitch! I usesh to get drunk with him in Portland!" I
sat back and watched her and studied her, and I was fascinated.
You see a couple of dames like those and if you have as much
ego as I have, you say to yourself, "Hmmm, these two old babes
have managed to make it. They've gotten ahead in this company,
and if *they* can, *I* can." And I'll have to admit I was impressed by
the place itself. The building. The smell of things. Everything
was steel and plastic, and where I'd come from everything was
wood—old, smelly wood that showed each stain for forty years
back. Here I was bathing in all this fluorescent, indirect light and
looking at all these fancy desks with easy posture chairs and separate
air-conditioning and heating units in each office and messengers in
neat red smocks running in and out like courtiers to a king. And out
the window there was a view of the river and the tugs and the
barges rippling by. You'd have had to be a corpse not to be impressed by it. But then I came back down to earth fast, because
the old bag was saying, "We'll be able to start you at seventy-five
dollars a week as a trainee."

I blinked and tried not to show my shock. By this time I knew
enough about New York City to know that seventy-five dollars
would barely keep a girl in nylons. I couldn't go on living with my
college roommate and her boy friend forever, so I said, "Gee, uh,
well, uh, I don't really think I could manage on that kind of
money."

The hospitality and cordiality went right out of her voice. She
stood up, swaying a little bit, to let me know that the interview was
over. "You think about it!" she said. A few days later I called her
back and told her I'd thought about it and didn't want the job,
thank you very much, but I'd like to try some other line of work.
The other line of work was waitress at a department-store restau-

rant. I held that job for one week, or long enough to find out that with tips and salary and all, the take-home pay was about forty-five dollars a week, or just enough to starve in the big city. Then I tried sewing in the garment district. It was piecework and I wasn't too good at it. One week I cleared seventy-four dollars take-home—by working twelve hours a day for six full days. My eyes were bugged out a half inch from leaning over the work. My money was getting lower and lower, and I was desperate. To share expenses, I had moved into an apartment with another girl from the garment district, but what she meant by sharing expenses was that I paid the rent and bought the food and she shared expenses by living there. And by moving her boy friend into the place at the earliest possible opportunity—about the third night we were together.

I was just about ready to abandon New York City—and how I wish to God I had!—when I got a note from the tough woman at The Company. "Would you drop in and see me?" it said. I went to her office and she was sober—it was ten o'clock in the morning— and she said, "I've been reviewing your background and we feel you'd make a good trainee. We can give you ten dollars more than the minimum. Eighty-five dollars a week."

By this time everything had changed. Eighty-five dollars sounded like a fortune to me. She went on, "This is a way to get a foot in the door of a very important company, a blue-chip company. Why, most girls'd jump at the chance! And once you get that foot in the door, you can become *anything* you want. The rest is up to you." She said she wanted an answer in twenty-four hours —there were plenty of other girls dying to get the job.

I went straight to a phone booth and called this elderly friend of my father's, and I laid out the whole thing to him. He was in the same business as The Company, though on a much smaller scale, and he knew the score. He told me all the pitfalls and problems, and at the end he said, "Peg, I think you should give it a try. But for God's sake, don't stay more than a year. That's a great company, sure, but it has a reputation as a tough place for a woman."

I was hired just before the Christmas vacation, and in the first five days I went to five office parties! I didn't realize till later why I was such an instant social success. I was young meat! Socially, The Company is built on a steady supply of young meat. I was young and single and funny and stacked—I was something new. They embraced me! But this is New York, and this is the way New York is personified. When you're thirty you're through.

The work was nothing. I put on a red smock and wandered around to these offices, delivering messages, things like that. A little typing. Some filing. Nothing that the Jukes and the Kallikaks couldn't have handled as well. And toward the end of each afternoon someone would bring me the word that there was a party on the fifty-third floor, or down in the sub-basement, and I was expected to attend. Why not? After the third consecutive party, I said to somebody, "Listen, if this is the way you people live, I'm going back to Oregon, because I can't take it. I can't keep up with it." This guy laughed at me and said, "Oh, well, it's Christmas. This is different." And I thought, "My God, Christmas! What a time to be acting like this!"

The big game was making passes. *Everybody* did it. One of the first came from this kindly, silver-haired old man. He was probably fifty, but at the time fifty seemed ancient to me. I could visualize his varicose veins and his flabby stomach, and I was repelled by the whole idea. He was very decent and refined about it. He said, "Let's have dinner together some night." And "Let's have drinks together." And "Let's go someplace else. It's too crowded here." Thank God he took no gracefully. Some of them didn't. The worst was an assistant supervisor named Dick Springen. I'd seen some minor-league operators, stupid and doltish, but he was the champ. He'd say, "Come on, baby, let's fuck!" The amazing thing about it was that this used to work with some girls. *Sick* girls. Then he'd beat them up. A wonderful guy. A real Casanova. But in those early days at The Company I wasn't sleeping with anybody, let alone him, so I was spared the ordeal. I turned him down politely. He'd clutch me and breathe these whisky fumes into my ear and say, "Well, when are we gonna fuck?" That was his idea of romance.

· 2 ·

AT FIRST, I wasn't very good at drinking. Back in Oregon, they drink a lot of bourbon, drinks like Seven-and-Seven, drinks like rum and Coke. But the New York drink was Scotch, and I was still getting used to the medicinal taste. This kept me from getting too drunk and enabled me to sit back and watch the way the others behaved. But about the third or fourth consecutive party, I did take a drink or two too many, and I got into all kinds of trouble.

They had a grand piano at this party—nothing was too good for The Company, and the supervisor who gave the party got it into his head that only a grand piano would do for this superior group of human beings, so he rented one for the occasion. By about the third or fourth round of drinks a fat woman sat down at the piano, whirled the seat up about two feet so she could reach the keys and began assaulting us with this horrible combinaton of singing and playing. All over the room, people were wincing! The woman had no rhythm, she had no voice control, she stabbed at the keys and only once in a while hit the right ones, and all the while her left foot was stretched out to reach the loud pedal, so that she seemed to be sitting at some kind of a grotesque angle. It was like watching a fat praying mantis play the piano, except that I'm sure a fat praying mantis could have played better.

One of the men told me that this woman had been studying piano and voice for years and that she lived in the hope that somebody would discover her and whisk her away from The Company, where she had a menial job, like mine. I noticed a greasy little man hovering around her as she played, and somebody told me that was her manager. "Her manager?" I said. "She has a manager?" I thought I was hearing things. But she did indeed have a manager. He was probably jollying her along and taking money from her on the side, but at the time this didn't occur to me.

Around midnight I had drunk too many Scotches. I had full control of myself physically, but my judgment was impaired. The fat woman was taking a break, and I was standing at the piano idly running through a one-finger version of the release from "Fly Me to the Moon." A supervisor came over and said, "Oh, do you play?" and I made the mistake of saying yes. He sat me down on the stool and—stupid me—I began playing. Well, I *can* play piano, and I can sing a little. I would class my singing as slightly better than average —certainly better than the screeching that had been coming from that witch—and my piano-playing as far better than average. As I said before, my piano-playing is almost professional.

I gave "Fly Me to the Moon" the full treatment, and when I finished there was an outburst of applause. Probably they were all relieved to hear a melody again. Then I swung into "All the Things You Are," and the party reassembled around the piano, and everybody began having a high old time. I must have played for an hour or so, answering requests for just about anything except the Bell Song from *Lakme*, and then a couple of supervisors asked me if I'd join them for a drink at Twenty-One. I was pretty drunk by this time and I agreed to meet them at the elevator bank. Just as I got there the pigmy woman and her greasy manager showed up. She was crying—the mascara ran down to her shoes. Her manager started yelling at the top of his lungs. "You bitch!" he said. I had been feeling pleasantly drunk and thinking to myself, "Well, maybe this isn't a half-bad place to work, after all," and now this guy was yelling at me and the woman was sobbing hysterically. "You bitch!" he kept yelling.

Finally I said, "What are you saying that for?"

He said, "You bitch! You knew what you were doing. You up-staged this artiste! You ruined her! You wrecked her career!"

And I'm standing there saying to myself, "What is this, a business office? What career did I wreck? Did I wreck her career as a typist?" I just looked at the guy. I really didn't know what to say. Finally I said, "I'm very sorry, sir. But I didn't mean anything bad." How naïve I was! What a dumbhead! "I didn't mean it," I said. "If I did something bad to the lady, I'm very sorry."

He kept calling me a bitch and making these accusations about ruining her career. I got upset, and I began crying. I cried all the way to Twenty-One. I sat in there and bawled into my food. One of the supervisors kept saying, "Peg, Peg, don't cry. Peg, stop crying! Come on, now, pull yourself together." But I felt like the biggest shit in the world. To this day I feel like a shit when I think about that party, because the manager was *right*. I *had* annihilated this poor mixed-up woman. I'd ruined her big night. That poor Florence Foster Jenkins of the office—she was going to be *discovered* that night, and her manager was there to make sure it happened, and then this dumb bitch from Oregon had wrecked the whole thing! But what did I know? I thought that offices were places where you worked.

But how I worked! I bought the whole phony ethic. I saw my future as a dizzying succession of raises and promotions and new titles, until one day I would become a supervisor myself because of my hard work and enterprise and dedication to The Company and the job. One of the supervisors asked me to do a little extra daily chore for him, to help him handle his own job, and I gladly accepted. To do this extra work, I had to show up thirty minutes early in the morning, which made me exceptional. Most of the other employees, even some of the trainees, would wander in around ten or ten-thirty, but I didn't care how sloppily they wanted to run their careers. I was going to go right to the top. Well, if not to the top, at least to a position of authority. I worked late at night, sometimes almost *all* night, taking on a lot of extras to make an impression. My job was menial, but I tried to build it into something. I sent memos to the executives. Some of them laughed; some of them rewrote the memos as their own and submitted them to the manager and drew a lot of praise. They never bothered to mention my name, but that didn't trouble me. I was already becoming dedicated. If my memos helped The Company, that was reward enough. One of the supervisors used to come into the trainee's room each morning and say to me, "Hi, Sunshine, what's new today?" We'd sit and talk, and he'd get an idea or two and take them into the staff meetings later as his own. I found out about it, and I was honored. I was interested, I was enthusiastic, I really thought I could make it! The other girls used to say, "We'll never get anyplace around here. We're the wrong sex." I told them they were crazy. I kept feeding ideas to the supervisors. A couple of supervisors got promoted on *my* ideas. One of them sent me a box of candy. I was so thrilled I wouldn't even eat it. I let it sit on my bureau at home, like a trophy.

But if I was blind about the way the promotional system worked at The Company, I was not so blind about the extracurricular activity that was flourishing around me. At first I was shocked. I'd seen a small amount of adultery when I was in college—and I'd participated in some of it, mostly with my fiancé—but at The Company they were carrying sexual activity to new heights. It was the number-one interest of almost everybody, married and unmarried. I was shocked, but before long I just learned to accept it. How long can you stay shocked at something that's so common, at something that's the number-one hobby of your very best friends? I remember that it took me a while to get over the fact that there were people who went over to a hotel and made it at lunchtime. At first, I was absolutely astounded. I'd never heard of anything like that. I talked about it to one of the men, and he said, "Why not? Some of the men go out and get drunk at lunchtime, and some of them go out and get laid. It's perfectly sensible. Who're they hurting? They're not taking any time away from their job. They're not taking time away from their families. So who's getting hurt?"

I couldn't tell him who was getting hurt then, because I hadn't learned yet—the hard way. Who was getting hurt was the other woman, the poor fish that agreed to meet the guy and let him relieve his anxieties at her expense. A woman is just not equipped to run out and jump in the sack and then run right back to the office routine as if nothing's happened. A man can do it. I believe they call it "getting their ashes hauled," as if the male body produces some kind of refuse that has to be discarded, and the place that you discard it is in a woman—that's the way men think. Is it any wonder that men get all mixed up about women, that they begin to think a woman's dirty or a whore as soon as she gives in to them the first time? Women just don't function like men at all—they don't need to get their ashes hauled, but they do need love, and you can't squeeze in much love from one to three in the hotel across the street.

Springen, the repulsive assistant supervisor, used to go out at lunchtime and get a whore. One day he walked into the office just ahead of this big, rawboned, ugly, black whore. They came into my office and he said, "Peg, I haven't got enough money to pay this broad. Can you lend me ten dollars?" I was so flabbergasted that I gave him the ten dollars. He was completely drunk, and in the middle of the workday! He handed her the money and she said, "Thanks a lot," real sarcastically, and he wandered back toward his office. You can imagine what kind of a job he did the rest of the day. But he was one of those employees—and we have a lot like him—who really don't have much to do, and three or four smart subordinates are always ready to cover up for them. Like so many of our employees, Springen could take off six months and nobody would know he was gone. Except we wouldn't see any big black whores chasing him up and down the halls for their money!

There were still parties, but naturally not as many as at Christmas and New Year's. Throughout the whole company there would be two or three honest-to-God parties a month, plus another five or six pourings for this or that occasion. So you could keep meeting the same freeloading crowd over and over, if you wanted to. At first I went to a lot of the parties. I was still the same dumb, naïve girl from Oregon, and I was fascinated, like the snake and the snakecharmer. But then I got tired of being patted on the ass. One specialist named Red Johnson was always feeling me up and telling me how he could make it fifty-three times a night, and how would I like to try him out. Like so many of the specialists—and a few of the supervisors—Red was a talented person, but he was just hung up on sex. When I could calm him down and keep him off his favorite subject, he was interesting. He taught me a lot about The Company. He'd had any number of chances to be a supervisor, but he regarded most of them as a bunch of untalented climbers. He told me he'd rather make twenty thousand dollars a year as a staffer than forty thousand dollars as a supervisor, because as a staffer he could keep his self-respect and not have to lick ass. I respected him and I admired that attitude—and I made the mistake of letting him take me home in a taxi one night. My roommate was sleeping—I figured it was safe, so I invited him in for a drink. I'd hardly shut the door before he put this big clutch on me, and I said, "Oh, *really!* I'm not interested, Red, you know that." I used the tone of voice you use on preschoolers, and he backed off. When he quietly left after a few drinks, I congratulated myself on keeping his friendship and my own self-respect.

Two or three days later, I began to hear rumors around the office. Red wasn't exactly telling people that he had made it with me, but he was dropping some very broad hints. I said to my friends, "Jesus!" I said. "Look at me! Do I look like I've slept with that man?" For a while I was furious. But then I said to myself, "Well, he obviously has to do this, because he's done it for so many years. He doesn't know how to do anything else. He has to go on pretending he's the great lover. He talks about how many times a night he can screw a woman. And whether he makes it or not, he has to run around pretending that he has." It's funny. Ten or eleven years have gone by, and Red's close to sixty now, and he's *still behaving exactly the same way.* He's screwing this friend of mine—or trying to—and going around telling all his pals about it. And I don't know why she puts up with it. I try to talk to her about it and she denies that it's happening and at the same time he's telling everybody that it's happening five times every Friday night. I don't know. He must have awful doubts about himself. I sometimes wonder who emasculated that poor devil!

Somehow I managed to keep men like Red at a distance, confine it to a conversational relationship. Only one person managed to slip a little too close to me, but he did it by sheer lunacy and energy. He was the head of the typing pool on one of the shifts—not a much better job than mine, when you considered that there was hardly any future in it—and he developed this mad letch for me. He was married, and I had never crossed *that* line, so I tried to turn him off whenever he started clutching. Not that I could blame him for cheating on that man-eating wife of his. I once heard her say, real loud, at a party, "Now, Everett, you have to remember: *I'm* the one with the education!"

When he realized that I wouldn't date him, I wouldn't have a drink with him, and I wouldn't let anything get started, he began shadowing me. I'd go to the bar for a drink with my girl friends, and he'd show up. I'd go to a pouring on another floor, and guess who'd managed to get himself invited? I'd go to the ladies' room and just as I'd be walking out of the ladies'-room door, he'd be walking down the hall. It was spooky. He'd get drunk and call me at home, late at night, and I had to be polite—he could have made it difficult for me around the office—and sometimes he'd threaten to beat down my door, if he got drunk enough. The next day, he'd apologize mawkishly.

One night I was invited to a get-together at an apartment rented by one of the supervisors and his girl friend. They'd long since passed through the afternoon hotel scene and gotten themselves a little digs of their own, where they spent a night or two a week and a couple of afternoons. Everybody knew about it—except his wife —and nobody seemed to care, and, really, they were a lovely couple and very pleasant company. Naturally, Everett showed up a few minutes after I walked in, but I managed to overlook that. He stood over in the corner giving me his dying-swan look, and I smiled at him and went about my business. Pretty soon somebody discovered that Everett was missing. We looked around and found his coat still in the closet. The door to the bathroom was locked, and one of the men knocked on it and called, "Everett?" There was no answer. "Everett!" the man said. "We know you're in there." Still there was no answer. The supervisor came over and said, "What the hell's going on here?" He told Everett to open up the door or he'd kick it in. The door opened an inch or two and there was Everett's pasty face peeping out. The blood was dripping from his fingertips onto the rug, and I just about passed out. The supervisor said, "Peg, you and the other girls get out of here. Get out right now!" So we did. The next day I found out that Everett had made a few nicks in his wrists, not even enough to require medical attention, and after a few days he was back on the job, wearing long-sleeved shirts to hide the scratches. What an actor!

Just as a matter of self-protection, I decided to stop going to the office parties and build my social life somewhere else. I had met this young intern named Christien, as rich as Croesus and good-looking in a Rock Hudsonish way, and I began dating him, though not going to bed with him. I liked him, but not all the way, and he liked me enough not to press it. Anyway, he lived in some kind of residence hall at New York Hospital and I was living with this insane roommate that I mentioned, the one who let me pay all the bills and spent most of her time screwing a fat buyer from the garment district. It was not an idyllic situation for romance. Most nights I slept in the bathtub—there were two beds, but Janette and Oliver Hardy—I always called him that—were usually grunting and pumping away in one of them, and I didn't want to be so close to all that action. I'd pile up some pillows and blankets in the tub and try to pretend I was sleeping when they'd come in to go to the toilet. Oh, it was lovely! I'd drop these broad hints about cooling it a little, but that couple didn't understand hints, no matter how broad they were. Christien and I talked about it and he kept telling me to just throw her the hell out, but I couldn't do that. She was so dumb—she'd have starved if I'd thrown her out. But then one afternoon I sneaked home from the office at about four o'clock, just to get some sleep in a real bed, and there they were stripped and chasing each other around the room when I walked in. I was furious! It seemed so unfair to be doing something like that in the middle of the day while I was downtown earning the money to keep the place going. So I said, "Janette, get your stuff and get the hell out of here. I can't take any more of this. You're not gonna treat me this way any more." I was so mad I was almost crying. She said, "Oh, Peg, I can't leave now," and the fat buyer said, "Come on, Peg, give her a break."

"I'll give you three days," I said. "By Monday I want you out of here." I went over to meet Chris for dinner, and he wanted me to stay with him that night at a friend's apartment. But I didn't want to. I'd never slept with him, and I still wasn't interested. Around midnight I went back home, and nobody was there. I unmade one of the beds and drifted off to sleep, and about three in the morning I was awakened by these rhythmic sounds. It was Janette and Oliver Hardy again, in the other bed. I fled to the bathroom, and that morning while Janette was asleep, that disgusting Oliver Hardy got up and said to me, "You'd better get out of that tub and fuck me!" I looked up and I said, "You miserable, fat, awful, bald, fat, awful, terrible son of a bitch! If you don't get out of here, I'll kill you!" I ran into the kitchen and got a butcher knife, and I said, "Janette, you get that miserable son of a bitch out of here or I'm gonna drive a knife through him!" It was nine in the morning, and I'd have been perfectly happy to kill that fat slob and take my medicine.

You should have seen him get into his clothes, that yellow-bellied snake! He was still tucking his shirt in and pulling his pants up when he hopped out of the place with this terrified look on his face. "Now just calm down, Peg," he said, and I stood there running my finger across the edge of the blade. And what do you think that miserable son of a bitch did the next week? He started calling me at work and saying sweet things like "When are you gonna come over to my place and fuck me?" Awful! I'd call Christien and say, "What am I gonna do?" And Chris told me to just hang up the phone on him, and pretty soon he stopped.

Well, two weeks after the big scene Janette was still living with me and still driving me up the wall. She had weird habits, not to mention Oliver Hardy. She had a sloppy figure, but she had long, beautiful, coal-black hair. She used to get up at five in the morning and stand in front of the mirror stark naked and brush it *for one hour*. I'd wake up and see her and I'd say to myself, "It's showtime, folks!" and pretend not to see. Later I'd tell Chris, "She's flipped her gourd! She's gone bananas! She did it again this morning." And he'd tell me just to ignore her, and she'd go away. But she didn't, so I did. I scouted up two new roommates and the three of us moved into a place in Greenwich Village. But I am just not lucky with roommates. One of the new ones—Sarah—was wonderful, but the other was another albatross. Her name was Lucretia—Lucky for short—and she came from Indiana and she was a walking version of the Chinese water torture. She was an unemployed would-be actress-singer who couldn't act and couldn't sing and was a huge pain in the ass. Any other normal person out of work would go looking for a job, but Lucky's policy was to stay near the phone so that one of her many agents could call her up about parts. The agents never called, but she never got tired of waiting. So since she was around the place all the time anyway, she fell into the job of preparing the food and taking care of the apartment, which was only fair, since Sarah and I were putting up all the money. The trouble was, Lucky began to see herself as some kind of housemother. She judged us and criticized us. If we didn't come home till four in the morning, she'd make some smart-ass remark. She'd call me up at the office and say, "What time will you be home for dinner?" And I'd say, "How the hell do I know?" And she'd say, "Well, how can you expect me to make dinner for three when I don't know what time you're getting here?" in a real fishwifely tone. So I'd get sore and I'd say something like "You can expect me when I goddam well get there!" and hang up.

If I had a date for dinner—and by now I was beginning to date fairly frequently outside The Company—Sarah and Lucky were supposed to get lost, but Lucky never did. She'd eat her own TV dinner and expect to be invited to join my date and me for ours. Then she'd sit around and ogle my date—because all she essentially wanted to do was get married. This happened three times before Lyman, a lawyer friend of mine, got sick of it and said he'd never set foot inside this apartment again. He said, "I can't stand a woman looking at me with all that energy and force!"

She never let up, that Lucky. One day she called me at the office and in this hysterical, shrieking voice she said, "Peggy, you've done it again!" I said, "What's the matter?" She said, "You've thrown out the grease pan. How many times do I have to tell you, you're *not* supposed to throw out the grease pan? I'm standing here with a skillet of hot grease, what'll I do with it?" I screamed back, "Stick it up your goddamned ass!" and then I realized that everybody in the office had heard me. I hung up the phone and turned to one of the other trainees. "Now I understand what it's like to be married to a kvetch," I said. "It never stops." But I was thoroughly embarrassed.

Pretty soon my girl friends from the office began dropping up just to get a look at her, because they'd never heard of anything like this. I used to show them her "joy machine," the great delight of her life. It was a douche that came in a box. This was before the hand vibrators became popular with the do-it-yourself crowd. I tell you, that girl used that thing more than anybody could possibly need. She was *married* to it! And it was the weirdest looking thing. It came in a silver box with a cameo on the outside, and inside was a long bakelite probe with tubing attached to it and a hot-water bottle on the other end. She'd hang this thing up on the hook on the back of the bathroom door, and it would *always* be there. Whenever Sarah and I brought home a date, we had to rush into the bathroom and take the joy machine off the back of the door. For Lucky's birthday, I made up a joy machine out of an old cigar box and all this tubing, but she didn't get the joke. She said it was in very poor taste. That didn't help relations around the apartment. Then she burned up one of my nightgowns. She used to light matches when she went to the bathroom, to get rid of the smell. She didn't want anybody to think that any such odors could come out of *her.* We'd kid her when she left the bathroom. "Smoking again, Lucky?" She'd get mad and flounce away. "It's okay, Lucky, you can smoke in front of us. We don't mind!" She'd draw deeply on her practically limitless vocabulary and say something like, "Oh, *real class!*" or "Fun-*ny!*" One day she lit one of those matches and my new nightgown went up. That certainly did mask the smell!

To put it in a way I'd never have dreamed of putting it back then, she was the world's number-one fuck-up. The total *nebbish.* She couldn't do anything right. If she even *looked* at the toilet, it'd overflow. Then she'd blame us and somebody else would have to solve the problem—usually one of Sarah's or my dates would do the dirty work. Or we'd come home with a date and there would be a note on the door. "For your information, garbage goes in the paper bag, not in the commode." Get that: the *commode.* She must have been the last living American to use a hot-water douche bag and call a toilet a commode!

The absolute end was the incident of the sheets. My mother had asked me what I wanted for my birthday, and I told her I needed new sheets. So Mother sent me four percale sheets and four perçale pillowcases. I hadn't even opened them up yet. They were in my closet on a shelf. I came home one night to change the sheets and my sheets were gone. I pulled down Lucky's spread and sure enough—there they were. Brand new, still smelling like the dry-goods store back home in Oregon. I got in such a rage that I tore those sheets into nine thousand pieces. My own good sheets! When Lucky got home, I was sitting there waiting. It looked like there'd been a terrible battle. I said, "See those sheets? I tore them up to show you something. That's what I'm gonna do to you if you ever touch anything of mine again!"

She behaved herself for about a week. Then I came home one night to find one of her dates marching out the front door of the apartment with three of my favorite books under his arm. "Where are you going with those, Buster?" I said.

"Oh, it's okay," he said. "Lucky said I could borrow them."

I knocked those books out of his hand and stormed inside. Lucky was sitting there in one of Sarah's muu-muus. I went straight to the bookcase—we had a bunch of orange crates all decorated and painted and made into a shelf for about a hundred books—and I began dumping them on the floor. Then I stepped on the crates and broke them into splinters. I ran to the door, flung it open, and hollered at Lucky. "There's the door! Either you're leaving or I'm leaving, Madam!" She started to cry, playing on my heartstrings, and she said, "Oh, Peg, I can't leave. Boo hoo. I have no place to go."

She was right. She had no place to go, and she couldn't leave. So she didn't. One week later I moved into a place of my own. I couldn't afford it, but it was that or the nuthouse. I figured I'd make up the financial difference in sheets and nightgowns.

· 3 ·

In a crazy little apartment on Horatio Street in the village, I began the pleasantest period of my life in New York. It was a matchbox of a place, with a circular staircase winding up to a sleeping loft, and the downstairs a single room with a kitchen at one end and a bedroom-bathroom at the other. In the bathroom there was a bidet and a stained-glass window that cast cool shadows around the room, and at one end there was a hot-coil affair that went on at the snap of a switch and sent out warm rays. As if that wasn't cozy enough, there was a walk-in fireplace in the middle of the big room. It didn't get used much—firewood costs an arm and a leg in New York—but it made a delightful decor. My dates and I used to curl up in front of the cold fireplace and drink brandy or hot toddies and pretend we were in some baronial estate along the Thames.

I was so happy in that place. I wasn't disillusioned at the office yet—I felt I was going someplace, slowly but surely—and I'd come home to my new apartment with a feeling that I was in the loveliest city in the world and working for the most glamorous, interesting company among the most fascinating people. The finalists. The ones who were too bright, too scintillating, too talented for second-class cities like Chicago and Los Angeles. Looking back, I wonder if I *really* believed that silly idea. What a job of autohypnosis! But now I realize that getting along in New York is ninety percent autohypnosis. You have to believe that you're in some kind of fairyland, and you have to keep telling yourself that there's no other place like it. Because if you stop hypnotizing yourself and just look around at the *real* New York, at the tawdry, dirty city full of tawdry, dirty people, you'll break up fast, and you'll be very happy to get back to Sioux Falls or Yellow Springs, Ohio, or wherever you started.

But I knew none of this in those days, and I thought I was really happy. I was lapping up New York, in the traditional manner of girls just in from the boondocks. There were very few tears. The city presented some problems, but they were part of the scene, and I accepted them in return for the good times I had. For the first time I began to know myself, and respect myself, and to *like* myself. I was hanging around with a crowd of university people from Columbia. There were a few undergraduates, but most of them were grad students, working on master's degrees and Ph.D.s, and a few instructors and one or two assistant professors or associates. There were the usual bores among them, but for the most part they were an interesting crowd. We used to meet at an upper-Broadway bar and drink till late at night, and nobody ever worried about getting home safely. The big crush of hopheads hadn't quite descended on the city yet, although it was on its way. I used to walk all around the streets by myself, day and night, and never worry about anything, the way you can walk around Paris and London now without fear. I can remember one night having a fight with one of my boy friends and getting drunk and walking down Eleventh Street and having to sit on somebody's front steps. Then I threw up. I leaned over this car, and a man came along and said, "Miss, could I help you?"

And I said in this pathetic, little childish voice two octaves higher than normal, "Could you just walk me down the street?"

He said, "I'd be more than happy to, miss. I believe you've had a little too much to drink."

Little Miss Marker said, "I surely have, sir. And I just had this terrible fight with my boy friend."

"Oh," he said. "Well, that's certainly too bad."

He took my arm and walked me to my apartment, took my keys out of my purse, opened the front door for me, walked me up the stairs, opened my apartment door, handed me the keys and said good night. Can you imagine? When I sobered up and realized what had happened to me, I was both pleased and scared. What a stupid thing to do, even in those days, because even then the city was starting to turn bad, and you had to be crazy to let a strange man see you to your door.

It seems like I was always wandering around in those years. I tried a few one-night stands, but I'm just not made for them. I'd wake up in the morning and hate myself. I seemed to draw my satisfactions from the job, from the fascinating evenings with all those hypereducated Columbia people and from gobbling up the city at night. I almost always wound up alone, on the streets. I remember meeting this charming and beautiful young man and deciding that probably I'd take him home and go to bed with him, but as the evening wore on and he couldn't stop talking about his dissertation on the hydrographic aspects of a cell or something like that, I realized that he was just a self-centered bore and I only let him take me to the front door of my apartment building and sent him home. So there I was sitting on my front steps at three in the morning, feeling pleasantly drunk and wondering what to do next, when of all things this dachshund wandered up and sat down next to me as though we'd been personally acquainted for years. The two of us sat there, and then I said, "Dog, are you lost?" He didn't say anything, but he nuzzled up to me and I remember saying, "Dog, I'm lost, too. I just sent that young man home. I'm not sure I did the right thing, but probably I did, don't you think?" And he looked up at me as if he agreed, but then he probably would have agreed with anything I'd said, because I'd had a lot to drink and I was very drunk, and he must have known it.

After a while I fell in with a young, energetic East Side crowd, and we had very busy social lives. Back ten or twelve years ago the East Side was full of crazy, funny people. We'd have a few drinks and decide to buy standing-room-only at some Broadway comedy, and then we'd go and break up the place with our alcoholic ad libs. Or we'd get grocery carts and see how many people we could stuff into them and wheel them into a bar. I think the record was eleven, counting people stacked vertically like a high-wire act. In those days you went into the East Side bars for hip companions and fun. Nowadays they call most of them "singles bars," and you go in them to recruit for a one-night stand. How awful! When I was hanging around those bars it was different. Maybe you *did* wind up in the sack, but first you had a lot of conversation, and you established some kind of rapport and friendship.

I took up with an assistant museum curator, and he used to sneak off early on Tuesdays and Thursdays and we'd go around doing crazy things. Then I got a crush on a guy I met at Fire Island, but it was like all those Fire Island affairs—when I saw him in the city it just wasn't the same. Some men are only interesting if they have sand in their feet. But there were always more men and more crushes. I met a composer, a stockbroker, a musician, a professional bowler, a crazy Frenchman, and fell in love with them all, one at a time. I took a few lumps, too, but I bounced right back up. I was in what behavioral scientists call the "pair-formation" stage, or "pair-formation" process, and it seemed natural and enjoyable to me. For every night that I cried there were ten nights that I laughed. Any night now I was going to meet the great love of my life and be whisked away to the altar. How did it all work out? Well, I'm thirty-six years old now and I'm not married. Does that answer your question?

Now that I look back on it, everything would have been perfect if I'd left The Company early on. I had seen enough to suspect that the place was wrong for women and especially wrong for me. But I refused to accept the evidence of my own eyes. I'm such a plodder. I keep making the same dumb mistakes. I was smart enough to see that The Company presented problems for a young woman like me, but I was so ego-ridden that I knew I'd be the one to overcome them. Others might suffer and be beaten down—and I could see the victims all around me, lushing and screwing their way through life —but it could never happen to old Peg the strong lady. *Ha! Ha!*

Maybe I would have left, but I got promoted. It was peculiar. I'd hardly seen Mr. Storns since the day a year before when he'd let me sit in the reception room for forty-five minutes. As a trainee, I had nothing whatever to do with Storns; my superiors were the two women who'd hired me and a few straw bosses who ran around looking important. But there was Mr. Storns summoning me to his office and announcing with his usual pomposity that I was being promoted to assistant, a good job and one that I thought I'd earned six months before. "Well, thank you very much," I said, and he said, "Don't thank me, young lady. You're going to learn to hate me before it's all over."

"Why?" I asked.

He got up and shut the door to his outer office, where his long-suffering secretary sat with her rabbit ears. He said, "I feel responsible for you, and I want you to do your best."

"I have no intention of doing otherwise."

"I'm the one that got you your job here, and I'm the one who's gonna look stupid if you do a poor job. So I'm gonna make it tough on you."

"Why?" I asked.

"Why?" he repeated, as though I was some kind of an idiot. "Because it'll reflect against me if you don't do well! Can't you see that? And if you do anything that reflects against me, I'll break you, do you understand? *I'll break you!*"

I thought to myself, Why, you poor sniveling little baby, where's your rattle and your Pablum? Is that all the confidence you have in yourself? I just stared at him for a few seconds, and then I said in this trembling voice, "There's one thing you'd better not try with me, Mr. Storns. Don't try pushing me. If I make a mistake, it's gonna be *my* neck, not yours. And I dare you to try to make anything out of it!"

He sputtered and fumed and fussed and little specks of spit came flying out of his mouth. "You can't say a thing like that to me!" he said, and I said, "I can say what I want to you, you frightened little turd. *I'm* responsible to *me*, that's all. And if you think you can break me, I goddamned well defy you to try!"

Storns was speechless. He just looked at me, and I walked out. He's never tangled with me openly since then. Oh, he's tried to break me, break my spirit, sure, but always by the back road. He's a back-road son of a bitch. He's sneaked around and knifed more personnel in the back than anybody could count. But here's one he won't knife. I'm as tough as he is, twice as tough. He's all talk. I'm not. A lot of years have gone by, and Mr. Storns has been promoted quite a few times, but he still slinks back into his office when he sees me coming down the hall. I'm onto him, and he knows it.

At first I was kind of a rotating assistant, working with whatever supervisor needed extra help that week. It didn't take me long to learn that there were two kinds of justice around The Company—justice for the men and justice for the women. One week my supervisor made a mistake and over my objections kept insisting that he was right. I argued and finally gave up—for the moment, he was my boss, and he was a good guy and I liked and respected him. When the error was discovered, there was hell to pay, and I was called on the carpet by the old bag who had hired me a year before. "If you were an experienced assistant," she said, "I'd fire you." I don't know how I held my tongue, but I did, at least long enough to storm into the office of the supervisor who'd made the mistake. The second I walked in, he said, "Peg, so help me God, I told her and everybody else that it was my mistake and not yours." And mad as I was, I could tell that he was telling the truth. He was that kind of person, and he had enough job security and faith in himself to take the blame for mistakes of his own. "Well, it's very simple then, isn't it?" I said. "If you told her it was your mistake, then she had no right to chew me out, and I'm going right back in there and kick her ass!" Oh, how I wish he'd let me! Instead, he ran around the desk and locked the door. "Now sit down and calm yourself," he said, but I was still raving mad and I told him to let me at the old bag. "That bitch!" I screamed. "I don't care who she is. She's not gonna chew me out for somebody else's mistake. I'm gonna punch her right in the mouth!"

He opened the door, ducked out and locked me in. I hollered, "Let me out!" and he said through the crack, "You'll come out when you shut up and cool down." So I stayed there for an hour or so until the mood passed. Too bad. If I had punched the old bag, I'd have been fired, and that would have been the best thing in the world for me.

Instead I mucked along. No, that isn't fair. I did better than "mucked along." I got along well with the supervisors. They liked my work, and a few of them really shoveled it on me. I loved it. I loved being respected by them and depended upon by them. One of them let me write a short report for him, subject of course to his final changes. He changed about two words and submitted it to the general manager, but he couldn't let it go at that. He began telling everybody around the office that I'd written "the best goddam report ever written by a twenty-four-year-old kid with nice tits." Imagine! But I took it as a compliment, and I waited for the old bag to add a little praise of her own. Instead, she called me in and sat me down. "I see you've written a report," she said.

"Yes," I said proudly. "But just a little one."

"Well, you listen to me, and you listen good," she said, and she gave me a look like John Wayne dressing down some cowardly corporal in the Wild West. "You're not to write any more reports, you understand? *Supervisors* write reports, and you're only an assistant. You learn the job of assistant, and until you get that job down pat, I don't want you writing anything but your name!"

Don't ask me how, but I managed to say, "Yes, ma'am," and leave without any further trouble. I was still euphoric about the report, I guess, and not even that vicious bitch could bring me down. But as the days went on and I discussed the matter with assistants who'd been there far longer than I had, I began to see it in a different light. The fact was that supervisors write reports, as the old bag had said, and *supervisors were men.* Assistants did *not* write reports, and *assistants were women.* The sexual breakdown could not have been sharper, at least in those days. Nowadays it's changing, thanks to Women's Lib, but very slowly. The old bag acted as a slavemaster on this masculine-feminine plantation. If she saw some pushy broad, like me, moving a half an inch into the domain of the men, she came down on them with all fours. That was the system, and she worked well within it, and that was why she held such a good job. While she was helping to keep women like me in our places, The Company was hiring men right off the streets as supervisors and specialists. Women couldn't aspire to either job, unless they'd been on the premises for twenty years or so, but men were hired right in for both jobs. And some of them were outlandishly untalented. There was no apprenticeship, no looking-over period. Bang! One day they were walking the streets looking for work, and the next day they were full-time workers or supervisors, superior to everyone in skirts. They say we women don't try hard enough, that everybody has an equal chance, and they know that's bullshit.

It only takes a few years of this to break the average woman's spirit. Just look at the idiotic males that have been brought in to boss us around! Why, one was hired a few weeks ago, and already he's known all over the building as "The Loon," because that's what he's crazy as. There are twenty women on our floor alone who could do a better job, but they won't get the chance. And "The Loon" will never be fired, either.

Well, it was three months before I overstepped the bounds and wrote another report, this time for a different supervisor, a lazy one. I wrote it only after he promised on a stack of Bibles that he wouldn't tell anybody. We had to sneak the report in as his work. Can you imagine? Skulking around to accomplish a challenging piece of work, not being able to take or enjoy any credit for it, and for one reason: because I was a woman, and a woman had her place.

· 4 ·

WELL, I know the score around here now, but I still put on the same smiley front. I try to look happy and maybe help others be happy. But it's not always easy. The other day Storns said to me, "What the hell's the matter with you?"

I said, "What do you mean?"

He said, "I haven't seen you smile all day."

I said, "Well, I don't have anything to smile about. If you can tell me something that'll make me smile, I'll be happy to smile for you. I'll even laugh. But right now I can't find anything that's particularly funny or amusing, and I'm allowed to have those days, too."

He laughed, and he said, "No, you're not. You're supposed to be Little Mary Sunshine."

I said, "Well, damn you and everybody else, you'd better get it through your heads. I'm allowed to have my off days, too."

The truth is, everybody's having more and more "off days" in New York. The city's become such a hassle. You can't even walk down the street, minding your own business, without something unpleasant happening to you. Listen to what happened to me just the other day. I don't need glasses, but like most New Yorkers I wear shades to keep the dirt out of my eyes. But the other day something got under the shades and I couldn't get it out. My eye ran and ran, and I couldn't see, and I got very upset about it. The company doctor sent me to Manhattan Eye and Ear Clinic, but before they'd even look at me they wanted fifteen dollars. There I was, holding my eye, trying to blot out the fluid, and feeling through my purse for fifteen dollars with the other hand. I gave them the money, but I said to myself, "What a bunch of shits!"

Then I went back into this green room and sat on a bench with two or three others holding their heads and their eyes and coughing. Now the nurse comes out and she says, "Read the eye chart!" She says, "Read the eye chart!" She must be joking! I have something in my eye and it's hurting desperately and I can't even open the eye, and she tells me to read a chart. So I read with the good eye almost to the bottom, and then she says, "Read with the other eye!"

Well, right then it hit me: I was a cow in a slaughterhouse, and they were saying, "Here, old cow! Do this! Old cow, do that! Go there!" Everything by the book. Because they have to handle so many people they can't individualize. After reading the eye chart, I sat there for forty-five minutes. The doctor finally came out and put some stuff in my eye and took something out. You know what it was? A piece of steel! *Steel!* It had blown out of one of those stinking buildings. I thought to myself, "Where else in the world can you walk down the street with your eyes protected by sunglasses and have a piece of *steel* fly into them?"

Only in New York.

There is absolutely nothing left in this city that isn't a hassle. Going to your dry cleaners is a hassle. They lose your clothes *and* your laundry. You go to another dry cleaners and he does the same. Or the grocery. The other night I walked in to get a quart of milk, and there were fourteen people ahead of me in the "express" line, all with enormous bundles of food. I took the milk back and went without. I didn't want somebody to bang me in the ass with a grocery cart for the ninety-ninth time. But all the stores are just plain bad. The aisles are narrow, the service stinks, they don't even smell right. Markets used to be one of my favorite places to go in and sniff around. But these just smell like antiseptic, or mold. The pickle barrels are long gone. It's more than I can bear.

This morning it was a hassle just to walk around the city. It was a holiday, and all the people were in from the suburbs and kids off from school. I could barely get across Fifth Avenue. Down by Radio City Music Hall there was a crowd of people all snaked in and out of the police lines waiting to see Albert Finney in *Scrooge*, with all their bawling little kids and the whole scene, and I thought, "Isn't that revolting?" For the ninety-nine millionth time there they are, the creeps from out of town. I've seen them standing there in the rain and the snow and the sleet, with the kids wailing and wondering what it's all about. They've ruined the drugstore across the street. You can't even get a pack of cigarettes in there when the ants are in line. If you want a cup of coffee, forget it. The ants are lined up three deep in the drugstore.

And why are all the people there, waiting? To see *Scrooge?* To see Albert Finney? No. They're there so they can go back to Steubenville, Ohio, and brag that they went to Radio City Music Hall. That's why they'll stand out in the ice and sleet for two hours waiting in line. They're trying to get a leg up on the neighbors.

It used to be that I could get coffee out of machines in the building, and I didn't have to worry about fighting the crowds at the various take-out places. But now all our coffee machines are hopeless. They're filled once in a while, but they're never cleaned. There are always puddles of sticky coffee or hot chocolate on the floors in front of them, and where the coffee comes out of a little tube you can see this gray-brown substance, leftover mold from the syrups and juices of the last several months. It's a wonder there isn't an epidemic of food poisoning around the building.

What puzzles me is not the people who own the coffee machines. No, sir! Anybody will get away with whatever you let him get away with. If they don't *have* to clean their machines and service them and can still make a profit, why, who can blame them? What puzzles me is the bigshots of The Company, the meticulous company in its tall shiny building that everybody stands at the bottom of and says, "Now *that* is success! *That* is progress!" They should see the progress inside! This gleaming citadel that attracts people from all over the world, the finalists' headquarters—its executives are so lacking in decency and pride that they allow decaying coffee machines to litter their corridors, and nothing is done about it. The machines aren't even any good when they *are* serviced. You put in a dime, dial hot chocolate, and out comes chicken soup. Or a combination chicken soup and chocolate. And the bacteria are thrown in free. Now tell me—if you were an executive of this wonderful corporation, wouldn't you go around the different floors, take a look at these machines, and call up the companies that own them and say, "All right, goddam it, either take care of these goddam machines or get 'em the fuck out of here." Wouldn't you? But they don't. The executives snap their fingers and their secretaries make them fresh-brewed coffee. They don't have to deal with the machines like us underlings.

And it's beginning to cost so much money to eat lunch! If I find a restaurant that's reasonable, I have to stand in an enormous line. And the situation's going to get worse when all those new buildings are finished in midtown. Why, they estimate there'll be twenty-five thousand new people in the Standard Oil and McGraw-Hill buildings alone, and that area's already congested. Where are we going to eat? You walk into one of these midtown places, expecting to have a few cocktails and then be ushered to a table for a nice lunch. Ha-ha. The people are bellied up to the bar six deep, waiting. The other day one of the girls and I thought we'd try a new place, so we went to this little hotel restaurant off Sixth Avenue and we thought we were dreaming. The bar wasn't crowded; there were vacant tables, and nobody appeared rushed or anxious or grouchy. She had three drinks and I had two, and the bar bill alone was nine dollars! That's why the place wasn't overrun yet. They can get away with prices like that because there's so many people crammed into this area. Why, a dollar and a quarter is the cheapest you can get a Scotch in mid-Manhattan. And Bloody Marys go for a dollar thirty-five to a dollar seventy-five. And the food! It's priced out of sight. No wonder so many of our executives have been skipping lunch. They go down and drink at the bar, get slightly swizzled, and spend maybe half what they'd have spent for lunch. They'll get cirrhosis, but they won't go broke at a restaurant. We went to a cheap-looking Italian joint for Sunday brunch the other day and it cost eight dollars apiece for eggs and a drink. *Eggs and a drink!* If you go the whole luncheon route at most of these places, it'll cost you ten or twelve dollars. Even if you stay at your desk and call up one of the take-out places, you'll spend three or four dollars for a couple of sandwiches and a milkshake, and who the hell wants to sit at his desk and eat anyway?

This city has a million ways to get to you. You jump out of bed and face the bright new day and put on your makeup and a smile, and wham! Some little thing sets you off and ruins your whole day. Yesterday it was a taxi driver. I told him where I wanted to go, and he spits out, "You're kidding!"

I said, "No, sir, I'm not kidding. Please drive me there!"

The address I wanted happened to be about twelve blocks crosstown, and the taxi drivers hate to go crosstown. We'd gone about three car lengths when we had to stop in the traffic, and he began this non-stop harangue. "If I'd a known you were goin' crosstown, for Christ's sake, I wuddna picked you up! I just come back from crosstown. I don't wanna go crosstown; I wanna go uptown or downtown!"

"Very interesting," I said, trying to read my newspaper.

"Why'n't you people learn to use your feet again?" he snapped.

"What do you mean by 'you people?'" I asked. "Who're 'you people'?"

"You clowns that take taxis crosstown. Don't you know us drivers don't wanna go crosstown?"

"That's exactly why we don't tell you where we're going till we get in."

"There oughta be a lawr against that."

"Yeah, there ought to be a lawr against people like you, too," I said. "You just want to make money. If you wanted to go uptown so bad, why'd you stop for me at all? Why didn't you just lock your bloody doors and put on your bloody off-duty sign like all the other bloody drivers?"

"Aw . . ."

"Aw, just shut up and drive me where I'm going!" He didn't shut up; he kept on talking the whole trip, but I ignored him. Now isn't that a lovely way to start a day? In a screaming session with a man you've never seen before and you'll never see again? And they expect me to be smiling when I hit the office!

I haven't ridden in a subway for years. It would take three men pushing and three men pulling to get me into a subway car at high noon at Grand Central Station. Anybody who thinks this city is civilized has never see those filthy, rotten, dusty, musty, dangerous subways. The last time I rode one at rush hour I encountered not one but two feelers, and not long before that I had run into a flasher. Luckily he was working on somebody down at the end of the car, not me, or I'd have kicked him where it would do the most good. But feelers and flashers are the least of it in the subways. The real danger comes from the hopped-up psychos that hustle the subway riders for their drugs. These guys are out of their heads, and anything goes. Last winter a man I know got drunk and went into the subway at about two in the morning. He was just standing there, waiting for a train, trying to sober up a little, when this guy bumped into him, grabbed his shoulders, lifted his wallet out and shoved him down on the tracks. On the tracks, with the third rail and all! Luckily no train was coming, and luckily a man way down the other end of the platform heard him yell. They finally found one of those little stairwells and helped my friend out. Another few minutes and he'd have been run over by a train or electrocuted.

And for what? For a wallet with eight or ten bucks in it. That's the whole problem. The atrocities these criminals are willing to commit are way out of line with the returns. If you were walking around with a half a million dollars in your pocket, you might expect to be knocked down or even murdered for it, but these guys will break your skull for fifty cents and a couple of tokens.

They've lost all sense of proportion. Their need for narcotics is so great that nothing else matters, including *your* life. They're not just robbers, they're lunatics. And everybody that takes a step in this city, no matter when, no matter where, is at their mercy. The day is gone when a man would step up to you on some darkened street corner, pull a gun and say, "Give me your wallet or I'll kill you," and you gave him your wallet and that was the end of it. You can't even be robbed gracefully in this city.

At lunch today I asked where my favorite waiter was. "Oh," the manager said, "he got mugged last night."

"Oh," I said. No big deal. Just an everyday and everynight occurrence. "What happened?"

"Nothing out of the ordinary," the manager said. How many of his waiters had been mugged going home late at night? At least three that I knew of. "The old boy was walking down Seventh Avenue to get the subway to go home to Brooklyn, and they slit his throat and got his wallet."

"Oh," I said.

"What'll you have?" the manager said. "The usual?"

You might guess you'd at least be safe in your home, but you're not. I walked into my apartment one night and a light was on that shouldn't have been, and then I saw that the whole place was a mess. My piggy bank had been thrown against the wall and shattered, and every drawer had been dumped in the middle of the floor. The robber had gone through my suitcases, my kitchen drawers, *everything*. He'd made an afternoon of it. I found out later that five of the six apartments in the building had been burglarized that same day. The cops came and looked around, but they made no effort to solve the crime. Crimes like that aren't solved any more; they're only *recorded*, so that the FBI uniform crime reports can keep going up and up every year and J. Edgar Hoover can show how much he's needed. The cops have turned into statisticians. "How long have you lived here, lady?" "How old are you?" "What's the value of the loss, lady? Now make it a good high figure. Remember your insurance!" Naïve me, I was waiting for a detective team to be assigned to the case—after all, there must have been *some* evidence to work on in five burglarized apartments —but no detective ever came, just a cop in a blue uniform with a very busy pencil. "Aren't you gonna dust for fingerprints?" I said.

The cop lifted his head from his notebook and smiled as though I was slightly bananas. When he was leaving, he said, "Well, I'll tell yeh, lady, be sure to sock it to the insurance company good. Everything you lost, plus a little more, yehknowwhatImean? And don't forget this is a tax loss. Okay, lady? Good night, lady." That was it. *Dum-ta-dum-dum.*

At the office they've got armed guards on each floor now, to keep the hopheads from carrying out the typewriters and televisions and desks and air-conditioning units they used to get. Even with the guards on duty there's a theft every day or two. The place is like an armed camp, and still the burglars hit! A few weeks ago a friend of mine lost her wallet in the building, and then she got a call from a detective in San Diego, California. One of her credit cards had been used to rent a truck, and then the truck had been used to hijack a liquor store! I said, "Congratulations. At last you've entered the big time."

It all adds up to one thing: New York is a painful place to live, a terribly painful place. The pain has accelerated in the last two or three years, and people are acting weirder and weirder. I've got a theory about that. How do you stand pain? Basically two ways. You can blot it out with an anesthetic or diffuse it with a counterirritant. Booze is an anesthetic, the most popular one in medical history. And a messed-up life is a counterirritant. If your whole life is in a turmoil, if you drink too much and smoke too much and run around too much and get involved with a whole sequence of troublesome people, you're better able to stand the pain of the city. A man will risk his marriage, his whole family's future to go to some slimy hotel for ten minutes of ecstasy with a streetwalker. Why? Is he madly in love with the girl? No, but during the ten minutes of his passion he's forgotten everything: the dirty streets, the murderers in the alleyways, the telephones that don't work and the insane drivers that run you down and the whole long list of horrors that New York has become. Of course, by messing around with the whore he's also risked more pain, more counterirritation, until he's all mixed up in one big hurt and throb. And so New York winds up with the highest rate of alcoholism and infidelity in the world, which in turn leads to more alcoholism and infidelity, and soon you're in a frenzy, a maelstrom of inhuman activity. Love? I realize I didn't mention love, and the reason is that it hardly exists here. Love requires a better setting. People in New York don't love. They fuck.

This city is a trap, a sea anemone that beckons you to come near and then you can never get away. You're right in the middle and you can't get out. The money's good; you'll never get anything close back in The Dalles, Oregon. The people are about the same, but you get so entwined in them that it's hard to get away. You're right in the middle of this sea anemone, and you're being digested. For women, the solution is marriage, but I haven't seen that in my future for a long time. God, if the right man came along I'd marry him in thirty seconds!

Some people try to compensate by throwing themselves into their work, but the office social scene is just not normal. Anyway, it's all changing now. The group that used to assemble at Santana's Bar doesn't exist any more, and the new kids coming in don't go there. In fact, the new kids hardly drink. They must be getting their kicks out of marijuana and things like that. The Company is throwing fewer parties these days. We're in a depression right now, although nobody uses that word. So the new kids don't have the same kind of company social life that we used to have. The place is getting more like a regular office. "Good morning, Miss Smith." "Oh, good morning, Mr. Jones." It's less inbred. I don't know exactly why, except that maybe young people are getting smarter over the years. And colder. And less pleasant. I'll take the old days, with all their perils. Some of these young punks that come in here have one thing on their minds: money, lots of money, and they'll cut your throat to get it, just like the assassins in the street. In my day there was a code among trainees, among assistants, among specialists and supervisors and everybody. No matter how ambitious you were, you didn't knife one another. Go out and knife somebody else, but not somebody on your own level. Now that code is gone. Listen to this—no, wait a minute. I'll have to have another double Scotch to tell you this story.

This kid, Bettye McCluin, came to work here as a trainee, right out of some la-de-da college in New England. And from the minute she walked in the door she began pushing. And pushing! I don't *like* being pushed! I might think you're the greatest person in the world, but if you shove me, I'm going to hate you and I'm going to kick you and it doesn't matter *who* you are.

Now this shit of a Bettye McCluin has absolutely appalled me! She's done almost everything I can think of. I haven't even spoken to her for a month or two. I'll never speak to her again. She's done nothing to me—she doesn't have the guts—but she picked on the weakest of all the assistants, Alicia Nemerow, and really gave her a rabbit punch. Well, I wasn't surprised. I hadn't liked Bettye McCluin from the beginning. The others said I was too tough, too harsh on her. Give her a chance, and she'll be all right. Ha-ha.

When we were gone on vacation, this bitch Bettye McCluin moved in and took over one of Alicia's permanent assignments. She did it by working on Storns, the jerk who thought he'd hired me. And Alicia is so fucking unsure of herself, she let it happen. She sat still for it. And after it happened, Alicia comes to me and she says, "How come we don't invite Bettye McCluin to our luncheon group once in a while?" I said, "Forget it, Alicia. She's not coming. I'll never go to lunch with you girls again if that bitch comes along." Alicia said, "It wasn't her fault Storns gave her that assignment. She's my friend. She wouldn't do anything dirty to me." I said, "Fuck that, Alicia! I don't believe a word of it."

We got the true story in bits and pieces. Miss Fucking Shit McCluin had gone in and asked Storns for a new assignment to add to her power and importance. She suggested that he give her one of my assignments, one of Mary Rizzo's or one of Alicia's. Alicia being the weakest of the three, Storns gave her that one. I'd have put a knife in her fucking back if he'd given her one of mine! And so would Mary. But he wasn't afraid of poor little Alicia.

No, McCluin wasn't sleeping with Storns, she was just using her feminine charm. She was having an affair with another one of the specialists, but what the hell good's that? He was a nothing; he couldn't help her out. So she made goo-goo eyes at Storns. This was a first for him, an absolute *first*, and he fell for it. Meanwhile, she's cultivating all the other men, too, and none of the women will talk to her. Miss Fucking Shit! What a way to get ahead!

I'll tell you, she's Sammy Glick. She's a rattlesnake. She learned it all from that jerk she's sleeping with. He never paid for a fucking thing in his life. But she doesn't know how obvious it is to all the rest of us. We *all* hate her. She's even got her hooks into a couple of the assistant managers, because that's the way to get to the manager. It's so obvious, it's disgusting.

One of her tricks is to go around pretending she's having intimacies that she's not having. The other day she asked Sam Johnson if he'd ride home on the subway with her. Poor defenseless thing, five-eleven in her socks, she needed protection on the big, bad subway! Why, if any mugger ever tangled with her he'd wind up like a Colonel Sanders chicken! Sam was puzzled, but he said okay. She left the office on his arm, and the next day she put the word out that Sam Johnson—one of the most absolutely faithful men in the office and one of the most talented—had made a pass at her, but she'd refused because she didn't want to hurt Sam's wife or his baby. Isn't that sweet? I guess the idea is to show how much charm and power she has.

Lately she's been cultivating the men harder than ever, because none of the women will talk to her. She fucked us all, and she did it because she thought we were all so fucking dumb, but now she's finding out how dumb *she* was. So she stages scenes, as if to show the men that we're all victimizing her. The other night she's down in the Santana crying and saying to Dick Springen, "Everyone dislikes me. Everyone's mean to me. I can't help it if I cry now and then, because everyone is bad to me." She tells Springen so he'll go to the manager and tell him how vicious we all are. *She's out to get every one of us!*

How do you stop something like this? The only way I know is to sic a couple of bad people on her. Give her a couple of bad throws, that's all. We're working on it. Alicia doesn't have the balls to do it, but I do. I'll get her! I always used to think that justice wins out automatically in things like this, that people like her end up destroying themselves, but I've seen too many cases where it didn't work out that way. Justice takes too long, and too many innocent victims fall along the way, like Alicia. So we have to screw Miss Fucking Shit before she screws us! *Somebody's* got to get her! What are they all waiting for? Are they all stupid? The men around her won't do a job on her, they lap it up. She's got them flattered out of their heads. What if I had behaved like that? Why, I couldn't have stood myself!

Some of the girls say I ought to feel sorry for her, that she's coming to a bad end. I say screw that! She's already hurt one person who was too weak to defend herself. How many more'll she get before she's through? She's got to be stopped! I'll stop her! I'll kill that girl before I'm through! *I'll kill her!*

Well . . . I'm sorry I get so excited. I used to be able to drink a few Scotchs and not let it show like this. The whole trouble is, I still take The Company too seriously, and the city, too, for that matter. The Company *matters* to me. Fairness matters to me. The old friendships and affections matter to me. There's a new generation waiting in the wings to take over this company, and I don't like them one bit. That Bettye McCluin, she's one of them. They're the ambitious ones, but underneath their ambitions they're cold as ice. There's nobody left who can really get emotional about The Company, about the product, about the people. These new ones— they don't really laugh and they don't really cry. Everything's for effect, you understand? They're automatons, and they're going to annihilate the real feelings that we used to have around here. The honest-to-God camaraderie—the belief in the product—the caring. They're engineers. There's not a poet among them. No feeling, no passion. They have fewer office affairs. I'm not condoning office affairs, but I don't think it's a new morality that's keeping these new people from running around. I just think they're too cold-blooded to have an affair. They play the percentages, and you play percentages with your brain, not your heart.

I don't know how I'll ever fit in with this generation that's taking over The Company, but I'll goddamned well try. I'm not about to quit! I used to think that there was no future for me at The Company and no future for me in New York, but then I realized that I would just keep rising to the challenge until I'm knocked down for the absolute last time. I have this enormous ego—I believe I can overcome anything, and I will. They'll have to make me a supervisor. I've waited too long, and now I've figured out how to do it, and it's got to work, and fuck all the people who get in my way!

The Company is everything to me. I'm serious about it. It's my whole life. But I'm not taking any more horseshit. I may have to quit just to make my point. But then I'll come back. And you know why I'll come back? *Because I'm going to make them pay!* That's what I really want and I'm going to get it! Make them pay. *Make them pay!* Don't fool with me, Company! I've been around too long! *Don't fool with me!* I've taken enough. I've been patted on the ass, patted on the head, patted in my ribs, and *fucked up!* But let me tell you something: As far as I'm concerned—I mean this!— The Company is where I *have* to be. New York is where I *have* to be.

I wish I knew why.

Bettye McCluin, 25

———————•———————

McCluin is the number-one hate among the other girls. At first I paid no attention to her, but then she back-stabbed Alicia Nemerow in the dirtiest way. Everybody hated her for that, and I began thinking about hating her myself, trying it on for size. But my hatred didn't last long, because, really, she's so funny! She's so obvious it's laughable! I love to watch her play up to the men. What an operator! It's like watching a junior-high-school drama. Why, one day she was having a long talk in the hall with one of the supervisors, Buddy Bowers, and the whole time she was stroking his tie! Up and down, stroke, stroke, stroke! But the men around here are all so dumb—they think she's got a special crush on every one of them.

She does so many things that I haven't seen since high school. For example: She shares Fred Storns's habit of never speaking to you unless you're of some use to her. You walk by and say, "Hello, Bettye," and there's no answer. The first time she did that to me, it irritated me no end. So I yelled, "Good Morning, Bettye Mc-Cluin!" She turned around like she'd been stabbed and she said, "Oh, good morning! I didn't see you!" Baloney! The liar! I just said very coolly, "Exchanging greetings in the morning is only civilized. I regard it as the minimum in politesse," and I stalked away. For a while I stayed highly annoyed at the girl, but then I said to myself, "Why hate her? She's welcome to her way of life. You can't hate anyone so pathetic." Hatred is emotion, and emotion is idiocy. So I've stopped hating Bettye McCluin. She'll come to a bad end. The only trouble is she may cause some terrible damage before she's through.—Stephanie Grant

When I first got there, one of the other assistants took me aside and said, "Whatever you do, don't listen to Bettye McCluin. She's the worst worker in the office. She makes more mistakes than anybody, but she gets by with them because she sleeps with the supervisors!" I thought, "What kind of a remark is that to make about somebody I don't even know?" Then I got to know Bettye, and I found her to be a tough, abrasive, honest and outspoken chick. I like her. I really do!—Mary Adams

· I ·

I KNOW they don't like me, and I know that I'm not imagining things. At first I thought that maybe I was acting paranoid, but then it became obvious. So who cares? I don't like them either. I've never gotten along particularly well with women. I never had girl friends. Even when I was in finishing school I didn't have them. I'm not *good* at having girl friends. They're a pain in the ass. In college the other girls said I was a snob, so they went out of their way to snub me first. Like they said I was a haughty bitch and they didn't want to talk to me because I'd made it so obvious that I didn't want to talk to *them.* I never understood how I'd made it so obvious, but this sort of thing happened to me enough times to convince me that there must be something to it. I must have been incapable of pretending that I liked girls. I don't. I'm completely at ease with men of any age, any walk of life. But girls bug me. Like who needs them?

I was brought up in Chappaqua, New York, which is an exurban community about thirty miles north of New York City, on the Harlem division of the Penn Central. The main fact of my childhood was my father. Without telling you exactly what he does, let me just say that my father controls the purse strings of so much money that it's painful to think about. Not his own money—although we always ate well—but tons of money that he can distribute just about wherever he wants—to colleges, to scientific pursuits, to charity organizations, to businesses, *anywhere*. My father commands respect, and since he and I were closer than any father-and-daughter combination I've ever seen, *I* commanded respect as well, from childhood on.

Like when I was trying to pick a college. I flew to Boston to check out a few of the New England schools, and I was met at Logan Airport by the dean of students of a university. A chauffeured limousine took us to the campus, and I got the grand tour. I was wined and dined. But I was much more attracted to Smith, and that's where I went. Disliking women as much as I do, Smith was a mistake, but I didn't know it at the time. There was a lot of hypocrisy there—all that crap about being young *ladies* and so on. It made you want to gag. In my sophomore year I began coming down to New York a lot, not seeing my parents, but getting lost in the city itself. I'd come down on the Trailways bus and wander around and then go back on the Trailways bus. Nothing much happened till my senior year, but for the first time I learned my way around New York City and learned to like the excitement and the pulse of the place. All through my childhood it had been just somewhere to go with the oldies on special occasions, but now it was something of my own.

In the summer before my senior year my father got me a job at Universal Studios, guiding the people from Indiana in their white socks and Instamatic cameras. I'd be showing them through the underground corridors and here would come Hugh O'Brien strolling along, and the tourists would like knock each other down for a better look. You couldn't drag them away. They were dying to see somebody famous, and they loved it when I'd pull them together into a confidential little knot and say, "See that white-haired man coming toward us? That's Tobias Smollett, the famous author," and they'd ooh and ahh and stare, and their trip would be a success. You had to play it a little cozy. I was very much into literature in those days, and I'd point out Joseph Addison and Simon Daedalus and Richard Feverel and all sorts of important Hollywood writer types. Of course if I'd said, "See that man? That's William Shakespeare," then two or three of the people in the crowd might have caught on. But only two or three—that was their mental level. Celebrity freaks, all of them. Me, I wasn't so impressed by celebrities. They'd been hanging around our house for years, trying to separate my father from money. Celebrities bored me.

I graduated third or fourth in my class, with like nothing but the highest grades in every subject except phys ed, which never appealed to me. As a child I'd had rheumatic fever, and one result was that while I grew tall, like the others in my family, I was always scrawny and weak. Even now I'm five feet eight and I only weigh a hundred and ten pounds. The other girls say I should have been a model, but the very idea makes me want to throw up. There's not enough money in the world to make me into a model, with all that dreary posing and running around begging for work. I never had to beg for work, and I never will.

From my senior year on I had big eyes for The Company. My father and I both. To begin with, it's an impressive place. When you go in for interviews you walk on rugs three inches thick and you are met by receptionists with English accents and you get the feeling right away that you have to have a Ph.D. to work in the place. Even the elevators are exciting. They're electronic and so automatic that it's unreal. You feel like you could step into one of those whispery elevators and tell it to take you to Philadelphia, *and it would.* In the elevators are these fabulous people, high-fashion women and men with talent oozing out of every pore, brilliant people doing exciting things, flying off to Marrakech, wheeling and dealing, talking softly: *the top finalists.* And everyone knew that salaries here were the highest in town and working conditions the pleasantest. "First class is the only class for my baby," my father said to me, "and The Company is first class all the way." I agreed.

My father gave me an "in" with The Company, and I had a very nice series of job interviews. Not interviews with personnel directors but with actual supervisors and managers who were running actual departments. I never had to fill out a personnel form or see a personnel interviewer. Most of the people were courteous and respectful and helpful. This eliminated a lot of the pain of job-hunting and enabled me to do some picking and choosing that most

job applicants can't do. I chose a department of The Company that
turned out a product that interested me personally. There was no
opening when I first went in for an interview with this fabulous-
looking young woman named Alexandra Oats, but less than a week
later something opened up. Miss Oats called my father, told him
that the job paid one hundred thirty-one forty a week and said The
Company would very much like to have me. So exactly seven days
after my commencement at Smith I began working for The Company. I had my own desk with my own in-box with my name on it,
and a telephone that rang only for me. I knew that Daddy had
influence, but I was still flabbergasted. And I was very impressed
with myself that I merited all this. I was also very impressed with
Miss Oats. I thought she was much younger than she turned out to
be, and it staggered me that someone so youthful could be in a
position to hire and fire at The Company. I went home and told my
father that I had met this fantastic young girl with long beautiful
hair and miniskirts and she was like the boss and she wasn't more
than twenty-seven or twenty-eight years old. Later I found out
that she was more like thirty-seven or thirty-eight, but I was still
impressed. The other girls called her the hatchet woman and hated
her, but I thought she was terrific, competent, intelligent. She
knew where she was going and she knew how to get there.

Unfortunately, I didn't stay as impressed with some of the others
at The Company. I mean, my father hadn't sold shoes for a living,
and a few of the big bosses expected me to fall over at the very
sight of them and were surprised when I didn't. Very few men
measure up to my father, but then I guess all girls feel that way. As
for the women in the office, it turned out that they looked better
than they were. I'd ride on the elevator and see these girls with
their hair tied back with yarn and their paisley silk dresses and their
Gucci shoes, but it didn't take me long to find out that most of
them had whisky on their breath and were all dolled up to create
the impression that they were awfully important, when in fact
they were a bunch of nothings—and malicious little gossipy nothings at that.

Of course my own relationship with the girls in the office wasn't helped by the fact that I had skipped right over the trainee period, and most of them had had to spend the better part of a year as trainees—running errands, delivering messages, going out for coffee, stuff like that. I was spared that ordeal, and some of the other girls hated me for it. It was as though I had gotten into a sorority without being initiated. Never mind if you're intelligent, if you've had a very superior college experience. If the other girls suffered, *you* have to suffer. And if you don't, they hate you for it.

My father had given me this big lecture about how to get ahead in The Company. He knew lots of the top officials personally, and he'd been dealing with them for twenty-five years. He told me that the "business lunch" was all-important and never to pass one up. He said, "If people ask you to join them for lunch or a drink, by all means go." He offered me extra money so that I could afford these kind of lunches, so I could go out and learn something at the lunch table. My very first day an assistant named Alicia Nemerow asked me if I'd like to have lunch with her and her friends. I was very nervous. They seemed so much older. They knew what they were doing around The Company and I didn't, so it made me uneasy. But I went.

All they talked about was the office. Mostly they griped and bitched—and drank. I wondered how they talked when they were alone together, when a stranger like me wasn't there. I had the distinct impression that it must be a pure gossip bee on most days. They sat there for two and a half hours, and they consumed a lot of drinks, and when I whispered to Alicia that it seemed odd to go out and get loaded and stay away from the office so long, she laughed and told me I'd be happy to take these long lunches before long, that they were the only thing that broke up the day and made the day tolerable. I thought, My God, if your job is so intolerable, then why not quit? Later I learned that their jobs weren't intolerable at all, it was their attitudes that were intolerable. No wonder they drank a lot! They weren't doing their work, and the more they drank, the less work they did, until some of them were drawing salaries—good salaries, too—for coming to work and doing nothing and spending long hours griping about how awful The Company was.

Well, I didn't like Alicia's group at all. On top of everything else, they frightened me. I've always been very intimidated by females who are older than me, and all of these girls were. Not only that, but they were *together,* on the same wave length, and they knew each other's idiosyncrasies and manners. Like I felt I was sixteen years old and had braces on my teeth and wore funny shoes.

The next week I went out to lunch with another group of girls from the office—I call them "the nuns." I liked them just as little, and they were even less interesting, if that's possible. The nuns were not as together or as alike as Alicia's gang, not as homogeneous, nor were they as lazy as the other group. They were the workers, the drones, the harmless drudges. One or two of them were very hostile, and one or two were very withdrawn and detached, and I felt completely out of place with them.

I only went to lunch with the girls in the office two or three times, and then I figured I'd learned what I was supposed to learn, and I quit going. Also, the girls quit asking me. What I had learned from these lunches was: nothing. Like *nothing.* But my father had told me to go, so I went. As soon as I stopped going, I became branded as a snob—just like college days. And from then on I was alienated from most of my female co-workers. So to handle the lunch-hour problem I started staying at my desk for lunch and studying work charts and pamphlets. I soon discovered that I had things in common with Miss Oats. She stayed in, too, and sometimes we would sit in her office and talk. Miss Oats kept herself separate from the other girls, and I didn't blame her.

It was Miss Oats who tried to explain the men of The Company to me, but much as I admired her I never could buy her total explanation. She billed them all as super-talented geniuses who had these terrible pressures and tensions and had to go out and blow off steam once in a while. She said it didn't matter how much boozing and philandering they did; when it came right down to getting their work done, they were the best in the world. There never was an instant when I completely agreed with her, though I didn't let on.

To tell you the truth, I was astonished at what was happening around me. I'd heard about the men at the office, but I'd always thought the stories were hyperbolic. Now I was seeing for myself that, if anything, the stories had been understated. I'd never been exposed to anything like the luncheon drinking thing, and I still find it intolerable, three years later. Just when you're trying to get something done, the whole office empties out for three hours starting at twelve o'clock, and if you have something to ask one of the supervisors and you haven't asked it by noon, forget it. For the next three hours you're not going to get anything done, and chances are that when he comes back he'll be drunk and unable to function right. A supervisor named Jock Harris used to infuriate me! After lunch he'd fly into completely unjustifiable rages, and it was a long time before I understood that he was just plain drunk. The worst afternoon of the week was Friday, because then I was exposed to people at the tail end of their week and at their drunkest. It was so frustrating! Friday was an important day for us, the most important of the week, and it was agonizing to try to get an intelligent decision out of a supervisor at four-thirty Friday afternoon, *when it counted the most.*

But apart from their drinking, I was pleasantly surprised by the friendliness of the specialists and the supervisors. I had expected The Company to be more hierarchical, more formal, but within a week I was taking naps on Buddy Bowers' couch and being invited for talks with others. So many of them seemed to take an interest in me! There was an executive named Tom Lantini who was especially attractive, all smoothness and ease and style, and he used to sit and talk to me and give me tips on getting ahead at The Company. He looked so *good* for his age. He must have been forty-four or forty-five then, but his skin was always tanned and smooth, and his muscles still seemed to dance under his skin. If there was anything wrong with him, it was only that there was something kind of feminine about him when you got up close. But I didn't get up close.

I was as pleased by the warmth of the men as I was turned off by the coolness of the women, and it's still that way. As much as anything else, my work habits annoy the women. I don't take the three-hour lunch hour; I don't go out and get stoned and let it interfere with my work, and I do my work quickly and efficiently. I'm at my desk at nine A.M., and I don't leave till six or later. I was brought up on the Protestant ethic; I still believe in it. You get a week's pay for a week's work. You should be as capable of doing your work at four in the afternoon as you are at nine in the morning. You *owe* that to your employer, and he owes you a decent salary. And believe me, the salaries at The Company are decent!

It didn't take long for word to get out that I was pushy. I'll admit it. If pushy means determined to get ahead and willing to work hard to do it, sure, I'm pushy! But I push hard and honestly. I'll admit that I seem to have a way with the men, and this doesn't hurt me on the job. But that's not the whole story. A lot of the girls in the office would like to think it's the whole story, but it's not. For example: I'd been there about six months when Alicia Nemerow and Peg Kern went on vacation together and Fred Storns gave me an assignment that Alicia's been handling *on a trial basis*. No promises had been made to her, and the truth is she hadn't been doing a very good job. I asked Storns if the assignment would be mine regularly, and he said it would. But right away word went out that I'd sucked in with him and stolen Alicia's assignment while she was gone. The poor little thing! But I never took anything away from Alicia. Storns had let her have the assignment for a while and he'd told her he would think about making the appointment permanent. But then he gave the job to me. Of course, he did all this in his inimitable stupid fashion. He never went back to Alicia and explained anything to her. He just posted the assignments and there was my name next to a regular job she'd thought would be hers. So that made her mad, and it made her friends mad on her behalf. But instead of hating Storns for it, they hated me, which is not very fair. After all, he's the one who fucked up.

It made matters worse when he assigned her one of my old departments, giving her a feeling that she was progressing backwards in The Company, which maybe she was. For a while she was doing my scut work, my garbage work, but that was Fred Storns's idea, not mine. She came into my office one day and said, "Bettye, I know it isn't your fault that it worked out this way, but I'm very upset and I think that Fred has been very unfair and he handled this thing very badly." I could see she was trying not to cry. She said, "There's no reason why he shouldn't have let me have that assignment. Or at least he could have had the decency to discuss it with me, to give me a fair chance." She told me that she was going in to complain to Storns, but she wanted me to know that she wasn't complaining about me personally, that she knew I had nothing to do with what happened. I said, "Alicia, I'd go right in there with you and tell him to give the assignment back to you if it's gonna upset you so badly, but I think it would be a very bad idea. Because Fred won't change his mind, you know that. He'll only get his back up, and it'd just make things worse for both of us." We had a long talk, and I think Alicia wound up not going in to see Storns at all. There really would have been no point in it, he's so bullheaded.

Not long after that incident I refused to take part in an early Women's Lib-type situation, and that ended it for good between me and the other girls in the office. What happened was this: Two assistants had been in line for the same promotion. The female of the two had been with The Company for nine years; her work had always been first-rate, and she was highly qualified for the promotion. Her competitor for the job was a man six years younger, with three years less experience, and with a lot less on the ball, at least as far as the rest of us were concerned. So naturally he got the job.

The other girls blew their cool and began circulating a petition. This was in the days before women burned their bras and marched around Manhattan shouting obscenities at the construction workers, but in all other respects it was a Women's Liberation scene, even before the phrase was known. The petition accused The Company's executives of being male chauvinists and exploiting women and all the other stock clichés of a few years later. You can imagine how I felt about it. I had a good job; I was being treated well by the executives, and I had very little to complain about. So I refused to sign. I didn't feel like I was being persecuted, and anyway I'm too selfish to take on a cause. I can't march around and sign petitions on behalf of the poor persecuted women of The Company when I'm not being persecuted myself. How could I spit in the face of the men who were doing their damnedest to help me? Why should I jeopardize my own chances of getting a better job? To sign the petition would have been to say to all those men that their efforts in my behalf had meant nothing to me.

After the whole thing had blown over, hardly any of the women would talk to me, but I had become the fair-haired girl among the executives. Even the manager began to smile at me and say hello to me in the halls. This more than made up for the cold shoulders I was getting. I'd never had a chance of making friends with the girls anyway. And I couldn't have cared less what those little shits thought of me. One smile from the manager was worth a hundred lunches with those awful broads.

What I'll never understand is why so many of them are kept on salary, why they're just not fired. They sit at their desks day after day and do nothing. It *infuriates* me. The lazy assistants don't bother me so much, because I'm not competing with the lazy assistants. I'm already ahead of them, because I work. The lazy assistants are going no place, and they know it, and they don't seem to care about it. The greatest part of their energy goes into bitching, and what little energy is left over they put into their jobs. It's all right with me; let 'em bitch. They're like old ladies who love their symptoms.

The women who bother me the most are not the lazy assistants but the lazy supervisors and specialists and others higher on the ladder. I *am* competing with them. They're holding jobs that I want. We have one that has worked on a project for the last year. I could have dusted off this project inside of two weeks, but she's made it last a year, and nobody seems to care. In fact, she has one of the nicest offices in the building, with a view of the river and a carpet three inches thick. She goes out to lunch each day at noon and comes back at four, reeking of liquor. She's pimply and unattractive, and I happen to know she draws about fifteen thousand dollars plus all the extras. When I see her, I get so mad I could spit! What I could do with that woman's job!

People like that should be fired on the spot, but the union protects them, and that's one reason I don't believe in the union. Once there was a time—before I was even born—when unions were needed to protect the workers. But that day is gone. Nowadays the unions only serve to protect incompetents, to make it more and more difficult to recognize merit. I firmly believe that if I were someplace where there was no union I'd have done better financially. The way it is here, everybody gets a raise after a certain stipulated length of time, and that includes the incompetents as well as the hard workers. The money that is used to raise the incompetents has to come out of the salaries of the hard workers, and that's ridiculous. When I went to the manager about a merit raise, he was very pleasant, but he put me off. He pointed at a lazy assistant who earned more than I did, and he said, "As long as I have to pay her more than she's worth, I have to pay you less." I had to agree with him. And I appreciated the implied compliment.

· 2 ·

SEXUALLY, I regard myself as the essence of normalcy. I mean, I have orgasms, I'm not promiscuous, I waited till I was twenty-one to start, and I feel fine about the whole thing. I did make the classic mistake—having an affair in the office—but I'm over that now and I think I learned my lesson. I may have another office affair, but I'll have a better idea how to conduct it the next time.

I give Desiderio Ruiz-Azorbal a lot of the credit for my normal sex life. Desi is thirty-one years old and one of the few Puerto Ricans who managed to pull themselves out of the *barrio* by sheer force and intelligence. He works on Wall Street, he makes about eighteen thousand, and he was my first and best lover. I'd fought the boys off for years before Desi. It wasn't that I thought sex was dirty or wrong or anything like that. It's just that I wasn't comfortably ready to do it and face its repercussions, and I hadn't met the right man. I wasn't a virgin by conviction; I was a virgin by circumstance. There was no morality involved. I didn't think that virginity was some kind of elevated status to be preserved for as long as possible. I just hadn't found the one man to get me started.

I met Desi on one of those weekends away from college, in my senior year. He was with another girl, but we were attracted from the beginning, so much so that the hostess came over to me during the evening and told me to keep my hands off Desi, that he was going steady and people were noticing us peering into each other's eyeballs. So I put him out of my mind until I ran into him again at another party a few weeks later. This time we made a date, and on the date he did all the right things. He cooked a lovely dinner with chicken and wild rice and wine, and he took me to see his old house in the *barrio,* and we went for a long walk on the lower East Side and shared Italian ices at a place in the Village. We talked about everything imaginable, including sex, and I told him right off that I was a twenty-one-year-old virgin. Maybe this slowed him down, or maybe he was just being cool, but it was three weeks before anything happened. Then I got four days off from school, and I moved right into his apartment for the long weekend. I had strong physical feelings about him, but I could wait, and so could he. In fact, we almost waited too long. On my last night in town I was dressing to get the train back to school, and I was depressed about it, and Desi said, "Look, why don't you stay over one more night, and I'll drive you back tomorrow morning?"

The idea appealed to me. By now I knew I was in love with him. I didn't want to leave him at all. We opened a bottle of wine and listened to Berlioz and fell asleep about two in the morning, and when we woke up on Monday morning we had intercourse. He was very calm, very slow, very patient, and very nice. It wasn't particularly good, but he said it would get better. It hurt. But underneath the hurt I felt good about it. I was pleased with myself that I was doing it at last and that I seemed to be making him happy. Around nine o'clock he telephoned his office and said he wouldn't be in. I was very impressed by that. He didn't say he was sick or his grand-mother had died or anything like that. He just said, "Alice? Tell Bergen I won't be in today." Then he drove me two hundred miles back to school.

I saw Desi whenever I could get away from Smith, and I kept on seeing him when I went to work at The Company. I *still* see him, but it's become a frustrating arrangement in a way. He won't marry me. The first indication of this problem came when I was still in college. I wanted to start taking the pill, because I figured I'd enjoy sex more if I was safer. But he wouldn't let me. He said that taking the pill would imply a kind of permanent relationship that he didn't want to discuss. So for about six months we just lived dangerously, without pills or anything else. Then I got mad and I said, "Look, it's my body. Like I'm the one that's gonna get preg-nant, not you." And I went to a doctor and began taking the pill.

From then on I felt freer, less inhibited and less worried about sex. I became a completely whole nother person, and our sex became very good. Desi is young, strong and imaginative, and so am I, and we developed a real fun sort of attitude about sex. Silly things, like going furniture shopping and coming back to my apartment with a new kind of easy chair and then putting it to the highest test that a couple can put furniture to. Which we thought was a great kick, and we'd be running around the apartment laughing about the fact that this chair was better for screwing than that chair. We had a very good playful kind of attitude about sex. It wasn't something that had to happen at the end of the day, in the bedroom, with the lights off.

You can say what you want about New York being an ugly, sordid place, but that first winter after I got out of Smith it was anything but an ugly, sordid place to me. I was getting along well at The Company, and Desi and I were seeing a lot of each other. We'd come to my apartment and light the fire, and we'd turn on the hi-fi and turn off the lights and look out the window. Like maybe it'd be snowing, and New York is lovely when it snows. We'd see the other buildings with their lights lit up, all frosted and cool, and we'd have that storybook feeling about the people that were making all those lights go on in all those windows. Or we'd go to Desi's apartment, in the back of a high-rise facing another high-rise, and he had binoculars and we'd sit up half the night watching the crazy things that went on. Sometimes it would be cold, and he'd turn on the oven and we'd wrap ourselves in blankets and drink wine and watch people get whipped and spit water on each other and all kinds of macabre things. It was like that movie *Rear Window,* only we never saw a murder. Everything *but* a murder.

If you wonder why Desi and I never got married, well, I wonder too. He just doesn't seem to want any entangling alliances. I'd marry him tonight! But it'll never happen. It's not progressing. We see less and less of each other. And the worst part of it is that I do love him and I would give anything to be married to him, but I don't even dare mention it to him. He'd just say, "If you don't like it, get the hell out!" and lead me to the door. Once I made a very slight scene, crying, and I said something like "You don't love me enough," and he said, "That's right, I don't!" I said, "You're never gonna marry me," and he said, "No, I'm not!" He's so cool. He will not rise to hysteria. So I said, "I can't stand this any more, it's not going anywhere, it's making me unhappy," and he kissed me good-bye and walked out the door. Two weeks later I called him and we were together again. Sometimes I think it's an endurance contest we're in. Maybe some morning he'll wake up and find he prefers me to all the other girls, but I don't know. It's been three years now and he still shows no signs. The other night he was over here and we had intercourse the same way we've been having it all these years—except that he was drunk and it was slower. He was *so* slow. Not leisurely slow, but slow and frantic, wanting to have an orgasm but not being able to. So it went on for a long time, and when it was finally over he said, "You okay?"

"Sure," I said. I was fine. I don't get all uptight about sex anyway.

He said, "I'm sorry I was so slow. If I'd known I was coming here I wouldn't have drunk that much."

I said, "Desi, it's *okay!*"

He said, "Are you sure?"

I said, "Sure, I'm sure. Besides, when you've been drinking like that it lasts a long time and I like it to last a long time. So don't knock it."

He said, "That's good, because I don't want you just to feel like a receptacle for my outpourings."

I had to laugh at that silly expression—receptacle for his outpourings!

He said, "Don't laugh! The situation is serious. I'm thirty-one years old and I'm a drunken old man. What am I gonna be like when I'm forty?" I just had to roll over and hug him! There's this whimsical, little-boy attitude about him that turns me on so thoroughly, but then he'll dress and leave and maybe I won't see him for a couple of weeks. Or if I make a mistake and mention love or marriage, I might not see him for a month. So that's what I mean by a frustrating arrangement. The very thing that I want the most is the very thing I don't dare mention.

Desi told me a long time ago that we should never consider that we were going steady, and we should never turn down a chance at a date with someone else. I didn't like this idea, but as usual there was no arguing. But apart from him, who was I supposed to date? The only other men that I knew well were the men in the office, and the trouble with them is that they tend to spoil you for the guys on the block. That's one of the very bad things that happen in this office. Every day you come into contact with men who are intelligent and talented and sophisticated, several cuts above the people you would normally meet and date on the outside. Desi was an exception, of course, but by now I realized I couldn't depend on his company for the rest of my life. So I started looking around, and the pickings were lean. And I soon came to realize that there's a big myth being perpetuated about the single girl in New York. Helen Gurley Brown is the number-one propagator of the myth. She teaches that there's a wonderful, swinging, single life to be enjoyed in New York by single girls, and she's full of crap. There is *no* big pool of glamourous single men here, and there are damned few interesting single men at all. This is the city of the finalists, and the finalists are almost all married and mostly older.

The few single men have a buyer's market. There are X number of Helen Gurley Brown-oriented chicks running around looking for men, and the single men can practically write their own prescription for what they want. That's one of the reasons that Desi's the way he is. On any given night he can take his pick of dozens of girls. The other singles are the same way. And when you consider that a large part of the male singles pool is made up of dullards and homosexuals, you find that life is very bleak indeed for the single girl. That's why there are so many office affairs. That's why half the single girls in New York play around with married men. An affair with an interesting married man is better than a romance with a dull single man or a scintillating fruit, take my word!

The worst thing is that everybody reads all that Helen Gurley Brown stuff and thinks that we single girls are having a wonderful time. All my friends from Chappaqua, for example—they think I'm the luckiest thing alive, to be single and working in New York City. They don't know what a typical week's dating is like. I had a blind date last night with a very, very nice guy, attractive, pleasant, twenty-eight years old, with a decent job. And I was bored the whole evening! All day long I'd been listening to the married men in the office tell about their trips to Rome and London and Paris and watching them swing their big deals and listening to the imaginative ideas that crackled out of their brilliant heads, and now I was bored by this very nice twenty-eight-year-old guy with the decent job.

Most of my friends wouldn't believe that I have to accept blind dates, but in New York you don't have much choice. You accept what you can get! I seldom hear from my blind dates again. Maybe it's because I'm usually bored by them, and when I'm bored I make it very apparent. I'm not good at creating conversation. I lack the social graces, the little hypocrisies. If I don't like the wine, I don't gush about how good it is. I say, "This wine stinks!" And if I feel like going home, I'll say so, even if it's ten o'clock at night. And I'll tell the guy good night at the front door.

I hate to tell you what a typical week's social life is like. Tomorrow night I'm going out with a schoolteacher. He'll bore the crap out of me, I just know it. But I keep hoping. Saturday night I'm going out with a guy I knew in summer camp. He runs a restaurant now, and if you're interested in how to make *Wiener schnitzel,* he's a fascinating date. A couple of nights ago I went out with the owner of some parking lots. We had a seafood dinner in Brooklyn, danced in a nightclub for an hour or two, and then went back to my place for the mauling scene. I sent him home for a tranquilizer. A couple of nights before that I dated this graduate student at NYU and we smoked grass at his pad. I smoke grass fairly often; sometimes it's good, sometimes it can be very bad. A few times I've noticed it's made me paranoid, but that's not often. On the whole I'd say it's a far better high than a liquor high. I recommend grass to my friends, especially in New York, where it might make the difference between another boring evening and a fairly decent time.

But contrast any of those evenings with one of my rare evenings with Desi. God, what a difference! Desi and I don't go out, we don't go dancing or to Brooklyn for seafood. We have a fire, some drinks, listen to music, sit and read, make a couple of gigantic cheeseburgers and eat them in front of the fire with some cheap wine, and then sip some more wine or maybe smoke grass for an hour or two, and finally fall into bed, all peaceful and nice, and make love. The perfect evening. The most fun of all. How can my dates measure up to evenings like that? Of course, if this city were full of men like Desi, it would be different. But they're so rare it's hopeless. There are some guys around the office who fascinate me, guys I know would make great companions like Desi, but they're married, and that's a dead end. I know that now. So I just hope for a miracle, and all my old friends think how lucky I am to be single in New York.

· 3 ·

As FAR as office romance is concerned, I can't say I didn't have plenty of warning. My father told me that all the married men on the floor would be lusting after my body and to avoid them at any cost. He said it would be okay to be companionable with them, to accept their invitations for lunch or drinks, but to draw the line right there. He told me some harrowing tales about friends of his who had *not* drawn the line and who had wound up regretting it for the rest of their lives. Daddy didn't really have to tell me all that; I knew it instinctively, but I thought it was all sort of apocry-phal, that he was referring to the bad old days before times had changed. I couldn't believe the cliché that certain things went on behind closed doors at the office and that certain people got ahead in the horizontal position. But I soon found out that Daddy had been absolutely right. The married men in the office practically knocked down my office door! They couldn't believe it when I repelled their passes! Apparently fresh young things like me were supposed to roll over and play dead for the executives, and I had a hard time keeping them away. Of course, a lot of the married men were just flirts, and a lot of the passes were just talk. But not all. There were some extremely serious passes made at me, including the candy-and-flowers number, and the mysterious unsigned notes, and the urgent phone calls to come down to the bar in the afternoon and sip a few drinks, away from the crowd. There was even "The Breather," and I have reason to believe that he was one of the men at the office. The Breather used to telephone me at home and never say a word. He'd just breathe. I'd say, "Who is this?" and he'd pant. I'd say, "What are you trying to do to me?" and he'd pant some more. If I hung up, he'd call right back, and he'd do this several times a night. It went on for several months, and then he started calling me at the office. As soon as I'd walk in the door of my office the phone would ring and he'd be on. That night when I came home the phone would ring as soon as I stepped inside. That's what made me think The Breather was from the office, because he knew too much about my movements, and I figured he had to breathe at me because if he talked I'd recognize his voice. I called the telephone company and the police, but they couldn't do anything. The whole thing went on for several months, and then it stopped as suddenly as it started. Who knows who The Breather was? Maybe he's the man I eventually had an affair with!

A lot of the adultery around the office began at office parties, and some of the girls even theorized that this was the true purpose of the parties. We're having fewer now, but three or four years ago there was a party almost every week, on one floor or another, and the married men would call their wives and tell them they were staying in town overnight and then go to the party and make a selection.

Before I'd gone to my first party I was terrified by the whole idea of standing around drinking and talking with the people I worked with. I refused to go to the first party that came up, but then afterwards Alicia Nemerow told me it was a bad thing not to make an appearance and have at least one drink. She said some of the men had commented on my absence. I went to the next party, but my knees were shaking. I was afraid that I wouldn't find anybody to talk to, and I'd look stupid standing there all by myself. But I got over that fast. I learned how to turn the men's lust against them. I'd pretend to be interested in one of them and I'd get him to talk to me for three hours and let him think he was making a great successful pass, and then I'd turn around and leave! It worked great, and I never lacked for a talking companion at an office party. I did it just the other night, with a supervisor named Buddy Bowers. I knew good and well I wasn't going to let him take me home, but he was fine company at the party, taking care of me and flattering me at the same time. The same men will do this chore for you over and over again. Their egos are so huge that they can't believe they'll keep on striking out, even though they do.

Of course, there are hazards. No one can be totally sure of herself, least of all me, and I have to be careful of certain vulnerabilities. At one party I found myself talking to this brilliant young supervisor named Sam Johnson, and we began to find that we had a lot in common. After about three hours of dancing cheek to cheek, we went back to my apartment and made a fire. Then we stared deeply into each other's eyes till about five in the morning, and then to my disappointment he got up and went home. I would have adored seeing him again, even though I knew he was married, but he didn't ask me. A few weeks later he showed up at another office party with his wife—and she was very pregnant! I was really shook! I was very, *very* shook and I got drunk that night and went to see Desi. I was floored by the idea that Sam Johnson would do a thing like that when his wife was pregnant. Up to that instant I'd had no real feeling about her as a person. I mean, she was nothing. But now she was A Pregnant Lady, and her husband was trying to screw around behind her back because he couldn't screw around with her. It also annoyed me that he hadn't told me she was pregnant. In all that staring at each other, he'd never chosen to mention that fact. I don't know why it annoyed me so much, but it did.

After that, Sam and I became friends on a more platonic basis. When his wife was in the hospital having the baby, I invited him over to my apartment for dinner, but purely as an act of compassion. I could tell that he was uncomfortable all through the dinner and later when we turned down the lights and watched television. But nothing happened, and it's just as well. For purely selfish reasons, an affair with a married man who has a newborn baby is not a smart thing. No matter how much he might pretend to be interested in you and disinterested in the new baby, you'd know where his real interests were. And no woman wants to play second fiddle to a baby!

After that experience I did a lot of thinking about what I'd done. It embarrassed me that he'd put me into the position of being on the make for him. Nothing had happened, but if it'd been up to me, a *lot* would have happened! But on both the occasions when it might have, he lost his guts. I wondered why I'd ever let the thing get started in the first place. Going out with married men is something I don't do, something that is definitely not in my own personal code of ethics. So why'd I do it? Well, I was flattered by his attention. Your ego gets far more flattered by a married man than by a single one. The married man is risking something. Also, the married man is much more likely to compliment you on your appearance, and I enjoy this. I also have a very dangerous tendency when I'm bored to get myself involved in bad things, even if I *know* they're bad. A bad scene is better than no scene at all, and right at the stage where Sam Johnson came along, Desi wasn't paying me much attention and I guess I figured a relationship with a married man would be better than nothing. So I walked right in with my eyes open—and then Sam wouldn't make a move!

The trouble with that experience is that I learned nothing from it. I didn't get clobbered good and hard, so I was like wide open for the next glamorous, intelligent, interesting married man who came along. He came along about a week after Sam's baby was born, at a time when all my defenses were down and I was craving attention, *any* attention. His name was Ernie Rhoades, Jr., and he was one of our specialists and very talented. He had a wife and three children at the end of his commuter run in New Brunswick, New Jersey, and he had a long record of infidelity, which I didn't know at the time. I had worked with him on a report several months before, and he had been all business. I hadn't found him the least bit attractive, nor him me. If somebody had told me that later on we'd be getting together, I'd have laughed, which may say something about where my head was when the pass finally came.

I was sitting in my office on a Friday afternoon working up some figures when my telephone rang and it was Ernie Rhoades, Jr., calling from the Santana Bar. He sounded drunk, but that was nothing out of the ordinary on a Friday afternoon, and I figured that he wanted me to do some chore for him, carry out some modest assignment. But it turned out he wanted me to come down and have a drink with him. I told him to call me again in an hour and maybe I'd join him. That gave me an hour to weigh the pros and cons, and during the hour I got very curious about the whole thing. So I said yes when he called back.

When I arrived he was completely loaded, which I found partly annoying and partly cute and amusing. He gave me this fantastic come-on about how did I get so beautiful and how did I get so slim and sexy? It was very unclassy, but my ego was going through a bad trip at the time and I found myself enjoying it. So I had a drink, and another drink, and a few more, and with each one I enjoyed the flattery more, and with each one I lost a little more of the sense of consequences of what I was doing. Then he asked me would I like to go with him on a weekend business trip to Baltimore the next day. I had enough sense to say no. That was a little speedy for me, even after all those drinks. He said he had to go and he would call me and let me know when he was coming back and we'd have dinner together. I said fine.

On Monday he telephoned, and we began this routine of having lunch together every day and drinks together every evening after work. It was very pleasant, just what I needed. There was a lot of interesting talk and a lot of sexual play—hand-holding, the eyes bit, staring at each other for hours, and lots of teasing remarks like "Just wait till we get our chance." It was very intense and nice in a B-movie kind of way, and I was enjoying every second. It was summer and hot as hell, and my sister had moved in with me for a month, and Ernie was all involved with his wife's relatives, but we kept telling each other that our night would come and how wonderful and exciting it would be. I wouldn't make the hotel scene or even talk about it; it would have been too sordid for this smoldering and beautiful affair we were having. How thrilling it all was! That's the best stage of a romance, before anything physical has happened, when you can still get turned on by an illicit meeting in some Greenwich Village bar, or call each other on the interoffice and whisper meaningless suggestive remarks. He'd say he was going to give up his awful middle-class existence in New Jersey and run off to the woods with me, and we talked for hours about quitting The Company and living in a commune together. He'd say, "It's worth it to me. I'll dump my wife and kids and there'll just be you and me, you sweet young beautiful thing." Sick? It got sicker as it went along. The whole thing was like a month-long tease. When he went out of town, I'd get long-distance telephone calls and these fantastic letters, and I was going out of my head with the intrigue and the fascination of it all.

At last our great night came. My sister had gone back to Radcliffe, and Ernie had told his wife he was going to Chicago on business, and we met in the Village for dinner and drinks, knowing full well where we were going to end up. He had more than the usual number of martinis during the dinner, and by the time we got back to my apartment he was drunk, but that was nothing unusual. He was drunk most of the time anyway, and I simply attributed it to his horrible middle-class existence and figured the drinking would all end when we began our new life together. It puzzled me a little that he had chosen this night, of all nights, to get sloppy drunk, but I was so excited at the prospects that I didn't worry.

We went inside and he kissed me. I put on Simon and Garfunkel's "Sounds of Silence," and Ernie opened a bottle of wine and poured it, and the two of us sat on the floor listening to "Hello, darkness, my old friend" and those other great lines by Paul Simon. I lit a couple of candles and turned off the lights, and I waited for him. I wanted him. I was convinced that I loved him and that this was the great romance of my life. For the moment I had even done something that I thought was impossible: I had forgotten Desi. All I wanted was Ernie Rhoades, Jr.

He kept pouring wine, and I turned the record over and put on still more records, and he stayed drunk. After about two hours he swept me up in this muscleman grip and started staggering across the room with me. I said, "Where are we going?"

He said, "To the bedroom."

I said, "Put me down! What's wrong with the rug? We're very comfortable on the rug."

That must have disturbed him. He was nearly forty years old, and he came from this generation that does it in the bedroom, in the dark. The rug's dirty and perverted. That attitude always annoyed me. In the first place, if you're feeling sexy when you're on the rug, it turns you off to get lifted up and taken into the bedroom and have all the lights switched off and all the preparations made—

like it's already time to play Monopoly after all that. What's wrong
with the living-room rug?

He said, "Come on, we have to go into the bedroom."

I said, "No, Ernie, that's ridiculous! There's no *reason* to go into
the bedroom."

He lay back down on the rug and poured some more wine and
sulked for a while. After another hour or so he grabbed me and
kissed me, and then he began ripping at his clothes and almost tearing them off. I soon found out why the hurry. He had barely
pulled his pants down when he climaxed on my rug. The dumb ass!
My first instinct was to laugh—it was all so ridiculous! But I'm glad
I didn't, because he was taking the whole thing like the last act of
Hamlet. He was all repentant and apologetic, and he's lying there
with his face turned the other way and he won't even look at me!
Mr. Contrite! I tried to tell him that it was no big deal to me, not to
worry. I'd been well schooled by Desi, and I could appreciate the
fact that sex was not the end of the world and that it could even be
very funny. And if you can't laugh about sex at the times when it *is*
funny, you're in bad trouble. After all, we'd had this month-long
tease, and it had been very intense, and it was no surprise to me that
it was all too much for him and he couldn't control himself when
the time had come. I said, "Look, Ernie, there'll be other times!" I
said, "Look, you're being very silly. It doesn't matter. These things
always start out bad, they always get better." I didn't know what I
was talking about, but he was lying there sniffling and beating his
breast, and I had to do something to calm him down. He finally
dozed off, and I went into the bedroom and slept alone.

Ernie stayed at my apartment for three days, and the sex didn't
work at all, but I still wasn't worried. I told him, "Look, let's laugh
about it and try again some other time. And it'll work!" And he'd
put his head in his hands and berate himself.

Well, it went on that way for several months. I thought I loved
him, and I was ready to put up with anything, even his premature
ejaculations or his inability to have an erection. Love had to find a
way! And he was persistent about it, I'll have to give him that.
He'd try and try, half the night, until I'd be quite content to quit

and listen to music or talk or smoke or take a walk, anything but those incessant attempts to get it up. I told him, "Look, it doesn't *matter*, I love just being with you. If you'll stop trying so hard, everything'll work out." What I didn't realize then was that he didn't enjoy being with me nearly as much as I enjoyed being with him. That's one reason the sex was so much more important to him. He was using me, but I didn't realize that till much later.

Soon I figured I knew Ernie Rhoades, Jr., pretty well, and the better I knew him the less I was certain that I wanted to spend the rest of my life living with him and the wreckage of his marriage. He had very strange feelings about himself. He seemed to think it necessary to see himself as a very unusual person. He thinks that he's the only person at The Company who had blue-collar, stiff, straight, cold parents. And he's not! He's really very ordinary for his age. He thinks that there's something very unusual and significant about the fact that he married young and that he went into the service at an early age because it represented structure and authority. He thinks that all this is peculiar to him, and it's all his parents' fault. He *hates* his parents. He thinks that his own coldness, his own inability to be open and honest and verbal with people, is something that he absolutely can't help because that's the way he was raised. And I'll be damned!—lots of people were raised that way, and lots of them broke out of the mold. But he indulges himself in all these myths, that everything's his parents' fault, that he's a very unusual and sensitive person, when really he's very commonplace.

I soon found out that he's terribly psychologically oriented, but in a Psych One sort of way. He would go on for hours about why the sex was no good between us, and he'd come up with these banal Psych One explanations. He'd say it was an incest thing because of the difference in our ages and that subconsciously he was thinking of me as his daughter. One night he woke up in my bed and called me by his daughter's name, and that really spooked him. From then on all he talked about was incest. He also noted that I was very close to my father, and therefore I was making a surrogate father out of older men. I'd say, "Ernie, I don't think you're my father, I think you're *you*, and I *love* you!" And he'd say, "Yeah, well, you don't know anything about psychology or you wouldn't say that."

He finally developed a comfortable theory about our sex problem. He admitted that he had often been unfaithful to his wife, and he figured that his inability to have sexual relations with me was a new kind of subconscious fidelity. He'd lie in bed and talk about it for hours. Then he'd roll over on top of me and try to do something, and he'd work at this till he was drenched with perspiration, and then he'd say, "See, it must be my own peculiar way of being faithful to my wife."

He also did a lot of gratuitous lying, something else that was new to me. Once he'd established the fact that I was very gullible, he began lying all over the place, just for the fun of it. He hated everybody at the office, and he'd meet me at a bar and he'd say, "Well, I walked right into the manager's office and told him to stick the job up his ass." And he'd carry on like this for a couple of hours and finally tell me it was all a lie. Why? I haven't the slightest idea. Or he'd leave my apartment and he'd say, "I've got to get away for a couple of weeks. I'm going up in the woods someplace. I'll send for you tomorrow." And the next day he'd be at the office! It was all horseshit! And then he'd laugh at me for believing him. It was like some kind of power thing with him—he derived pleasure and power from convincing me of some outlandish thing and then laughing at me later.

After a while I got to wondering *what* to believe. He began doing the classical number about his wife and how she didn't understand him, and how he was trying to get up the courage to leave her. He'd tell me how much he loved me and give me this very heavy stuff about how he was going to go straight home and pack his bag. But then he'd come back to the office the next day and tell me that she'd cried and he'd lost his guts. One day he came in and said, "It isn't that I love her or anything, but we were married in college and she's never had to take care of herself. I couldn't leave her now; she wouldn't know what to do with herself."

As the affair went on, I began to fall apart slowly. Like I became even thinner than usual and I smoked my head off out of sheer nervousness. Those night-long discussions would have worn down a horse! Understand, it wasn't the lack of normal sex that bothered me. I could always take sex or leave it alone. It was his *attitude* that was killing me. We would try and fail, and then he'd keep on trying for two or three hours, and then he'd pace the floor for another two or three hours trying to figure out what it all meant. By now I'd long since figured it out. He was always drunk and he was thirty-nine years old, that's all it meant! Nobody could have a normal sex life in the condition that he kept himself, and with a mind all crammed with theories from Psych One. But he'd go on and on, reacting and overreacting, and I'd begin to react to his reaction. And we'd both walk the floor until dawn and stagger around the office in a trance the whole next day.

Don't ask me why I still loved him; these things are beyond explanation. You love someone or you don't, that's all. And I still did. One night I almost saw the happy ending. He was at my apartment and he said, "I have to call my wife and tell her I'm gonna be late." He makes the call and it's obvious that she's hassling the hell out of him. He gets off the phone and he's furious, and now he doesn't want to go home at all because he knows he'll be hassled some more when he gets there. And he's sick and tired of going home to be hassled. So he says to me, "The hell with it. I'm staying here from now on."

I said, "Fine. I'm glad you finally made up your mind."

He said, "Call her up and tell her I'm staying here."

I said, "What?"

He said, "I'm afraid to tell her. I want *you* to tell her."

I was flabbergasted. I said, "Come on, Ernie, for Christ's sake, make the call. Act like a man!"

That turned out to be the wrong thing to say. He flounced around and sulked and even cried a little, but he wouldn't make that call. So I got on *my* high horse. I said, "Now listen here, Ernie Rhoades, you can't expect me to do your dirty work for you! You can stay, but only when it's your decision, and only when you're ready to face up to it, *to all of it!*"

"What does that mean?" he said.

"It means that you get up and get the goddam hell out of here till you're ready to take the consequences of your actions and tell the people that have to be told. It means it's time for you to be a big boy and make a decision to stay and stay for the right reasons, because you *love* me, not out of some childish anger or out of guilt or some other stupid reason."

He got up and went home to his wife, and I lay there for hours thinking about how ironic the whole thing was. Here I was in the middle of a full-fledged affair with a married man, and *I wasn't even getting any sex out of it!* I mean, like what are these things for if they're not sexual liaisons? And I got to thinking how annoying the whole pattern had become. We'd be charged up in the morning, Ernie and I, and amorous all day long, and everything would be fine until it got to be almost bedtime. Then he'd get drunk and not be able to perform, and then I'd have to listen to the Rhoades lectures on psychology half the night. I began to realize for the first time how much he was using me and how little real feeling he must have for me. He really didn't enjoy being *with* me, at least not the way I enjoyed being with him. The attraction was that his marriage was a disaster and I was young and interested in things that he thought were *good* things, *young* rejuvenative things, as opposed to the idle interests of his middle-class life—bridge and golf and country clubs. To him I must have seemed the potentially archetypal hippie chick, and I was going to furnish him with a second childhood. But as the affair ground on, he discovered that I wasn't that different from any other girl in her mid-twenties, that I was just another version of his wife fifteen years ago in a lot of ways. I wasn't all that much different from her, and I wasn't going to turn out that much different as a housewife. And now that he was beginning to see this, now that I was becoming less appealing to him, his wife was looking better, because soon after the scene at my apartment he began telling me what a fine person she was and comparing her to me, to my detriment. I put up with that for a while, and then I began noticing another phenomenon of our affair. He was taking me to meet older friends of his, or running around to bars with older friends and then summoning me to appear on a moment's notice. He was showing me off, as a pretty ornament! It impressed his old buddies that he could drop a dime in the phone slot and twenty minutes later this chick would show up, and not just another chick, not just some two-bit whore, but a young, lissome, talented woman with a good job and some style and some brains. What an ego trip I must have been for him!

Well, I have a certain amount of soap opera in me, and I kept this thing going long after I should have, long after I knew it was never going to get any better. I guess I need a little bit of intrigue to keep me going, which is kind of a spooky thing to realize. One night Ernie brought some LSD to the apartment and said we should drop it. I said, Why? He said some of his friends had cured sexual hang-ups with acid, and we could at least give it a try. I hated the idea, and I told him so. I feel that the normal, unstimulated, undoctored, undistorted human body works the best. He stomped out the door when I refused, and by one of those lucky coincidences Desi called about five minutes later, and I told him of course he could come over. I hadn't seen him in a month and I hadn't been to bed with him for three months, and by this time I was wondering if I was still normal. You go through something like my ordeal with Ernie Rhoades, Jr., and pretty soon you've convinced yourself that it's all your fault. Well, that night with Desi I found out that nothing had changed. Sex was as enjoyable and as normal and as pleasurable as ever.

So now it was time for the breakup. I don't remember if I still thought I loved Ernie or not, but I knew one thing for sure: that it was going nowhere, and I didn't intend to drag it out any longer. For a few weeks I saw both Ernie and Desi, and then one day I just announced to Ernie that it was over. He didn't seem to mind. By this time he had reworked that wonderfully malleable mind of his, and he had done a very common thing. All the while we'd been seeing each other he'd cast me into these different molds, turned me into all the things he was looking for: this great young, beautiful, free-spirit type person with fresh, healthy attitudes. But now that it was over he had reconverted me into the archetypal middle-class housewife type, early phase, who was only trying to trap some man into a home in the suburbs. The truth, of course, was that I was neither of these caricatures—the hippie chick or the chiffon-curtain type. I was something in between that he never knew anything about, because he'd never had any sense of *me*, Bettye McCluin, the real person. It was always Bettye McCluin as he wanted to see her. As a result, when our affair was over he had no affection for the real me, and it hurt, because I still had affection for the real him. I had gotten to know him, and I wanted to keep on knowing him. But whenever I went near his office he became very nervous. He made it plain he had no desire whatever to talk to me or be near me. I'd come in and sit down and say "How are you?" and he'd say, "Fine," and then there'd be this awkward pause and he'd say, "Well, gotta get back to work now, see you later." It upset me for a long time, until I finally sat myself down and told myself, "Look, he's a very sick man. If he had abandoned his wife and children and run off with you, which he might have done, you would have been very sorry. You would have been *sorrier* than sorry. So forget about it and be glad it didn't happen."

One good thing was that our affair never became office gossip. At least I don't think it did. The others might have surmised something because there was a period when Ernie and I went out to lunch together every day, and they might have drawn some dirty little conclusions from that. But as Desi says, "You don't really know unless you're standing there holding the towel."

I was reminded of Ernie the other day when I came across a copy of *The Sensuous Woman*, by "J." I thought the book was hilarious, one of the funniest put-ons ever written, but certainly not to be taken seriously. Desi and I talked about it later and we came to the conclusion that if you're having a successful sex life you don't need to be told all these mechanical "secrets" that "J" tells you. Somebody who needs to be told these things is just going to be horrified by the attitudes expressed in the book, the cold, precise, train-yourself thing. But there was one part of *The Sensuous Woman* that struck home to me, the part that told how you can tell if people are good prospects for lovers or not. "J" wrote about the people who do the great pretense number, with eyes and hands, all the trappings and aura of a great sexual thing, and she said that you can pretty fairly jump to the conclusion that these people are fakers and the sex thing is not going to work with them. And I realized that that was exactly what had happened with Ernie and me. We had constructed this very heavily charged electric thing— and there was absolutely nothing underneath it. It was all tissue paper, and when you tried to put it to practical use, it just tore to pieces.

The funniest thing happened later. Two or three months went by, and he hardly said a word to me, and then one Thursday afternoon he walked into my office and said, "I've been trying to call you all day."

"Well, I've been in and out of my office," I said.

He looks at me with these great soulful eyes, and right away I can tell he's been drinking all day. He says, "How are you?"

"Fine, Ernie, how are you?"

"Would you like to have a drink?"

"When?"

"Whenever you want. Now, if you want."

"Well, it'll have to be soon, because I have a date at seven."

He gave me this superior disdainful look, the great-old-man-laughs-at-sweet-young-thing-with-date look. "Oh, come on," he said.

"Okay," I said, "fine. Let's have a drink."

Down at the Santana he ordered a double martini and guzzled it down and ordered another. He asked me if I was sure I had a date, and I said yes, I was very sure.

He said, "Well, what are you doing tomorrow night?"

I said, "I have a date. Why?"

He said, "Oh, well, I was thinking of spending the weekend at your place."

I played it very straight. I said, "Why, Ernie, what would give you an idea like that after all these months?"

He said, "Well, first of all I think I treated you very badly. And secondly, I remember those times we spent together and how much fun it was at your apartment. And I've been thinking about you a lot. I took my wife to a Princeton game the other weekend and I didn't enjoy it at all, and I said to myself that I was getting just what I deserved, because I'd promised to take you to a football game and then I never did. And it made me feel guilty and rotten."

What a line he had! Even at this stage of the game I enjoyed listening to his line. But then I had to tell him that I still had a date and of course he couldn't spend the weekend with me. He persisted with his line the same way he used to persist with the sex, and finally I told him I'd think about it and let him know the next day, Friday. In my own mind there were two thoughts racing back and forth. One was that I wanted to keep the option open, just in case I *did* decide to let him spend the weekend, which was extremely unlikely, and two was that I enjoyed the possibility that he would go to all the trouble of making up an excuse at home and bringing his overnight bag into town and then have to spend the weekend in a hotel by himself. I admit it: I acted on a combination of self-interest and malice.

That night I had the most curious dream. I had gone to a play about homosexuals in prison, a beautiful, scary play called *Fortune and Men's Eyes*, and in it was this queer named Queenie, six feet tall, stocky build, borderline between strong build and fat build, and kind of going to pieces around the face. All through the play Queenie was trying to make this young, effeminate, poetic type and having fights with a stud in a cowboy hat. I went home to bed and immediately began a dream in which Ernie Rhoades, Jr., was Queenie. I have no idea why. There was something about their eyes, something about how insistent they both could be, something similar in their aging physiques. In the dream it seemed perfectly logical that Ernie should be a drag queen. When I woke up Friday morning I had this squirmy feeling, because I knew that from now on Ernie would always be Queenie to me and I had to go into the office and face him on a personal basis.

Well, I should have been an actress, because I have a great sense of the theatrics of these things. By now I was certain that Ernie had no real feelings for me and that he was not even capable of being nice to me around the office. He had been using me, period. So now it would be an eye for an eye! I stood in front of my mirror making up my face and giggling about what I was going to do. I wanted him to be lusting after my body, so I deliberately left off my bra. When he saw me jiggling around the halls with all the young assistants drooling after me, it would make him lust all the more and improve my revenge.

By noon he hadn't even come in. He strolled into his office at four P.M., and I bounced right in and said, "I don't think you'd better stay tonight."

He couldn't have acted more bored. He said, "Well, I wasn't sure I could stay anyway." I turned around and walked out. That son of a bitch! He wouldn't admit that he was the least bit bothered! He had to have the last satisfaction. Later on one of the young guys in the office asked me if I had a cigarette, and I said no, and then I told him to wait right there. I strolled past Ernie's office and saw that it was empty, and I stole a pack of Winstons right out of his desk and handed them to the other guy. It gave me a certain satisfaction. I'm such a sick thing! Then I sat at my desk and thought it all through for the absolute final time, how if I ever let Ernie back into my life I'd be sorry for about seventeen different reasons, because he'd pull the same shit-ass stuff all over again. I said to myself, I need you like another hole in my head, and I said to myself, Fuck it. I haven't spoken to him since.

Well, I suppose I should say that I learned my lesson and I'll never make the same mistake. Like "Daddy, I promise!" But I'm not so sure. Of course I'm a whole lot smarter. I'll keep my eyes open in the future for that kind of foreplay stuff, which I'll be very suspicious of from now on. Foreplay is fine for about an hour, but when it goes on for a month, that's a pretty good sign that something's very wrong. Another thing: If I do have a repeat performance, I don't think I'll try so hard to talk myself into thinking I'm in love. If I have another office affair, it'll be for fun.

At the moment I can't see anybody that I would be likely to have an affair with, but then logic doesn't rule these things. I have to say quite honestly that I'm attracted to a few of the married supervisors, but I'm just as glad nothing's happening. They'd probably wind up being perfect bastards, like Ernie Rhoades, Jr. I'm good friends with a couple of them, and that's enough for now. I've never had more than a few good friends.

I really don't know what's in my future. I wish I knew. I'd like to get married, but I'm not sure I'd want kids. I don't feel qualified to raise children, and the last thing I'd want would be the responsibility of fucking up another human being. That's not my thing, and I have no hangups about having kids or not having them. If my husband said, "No kids," I'd say, "Fine. No kids" in about two seconds. I think my husband's and my life together would be more important than having children. I'm selfish, and I think that I'm the most important thing. I don't need to make myself immortal by having children.

Professionally, I'm as ambitious as ever, but I'm becoming a little more frightened about the prospects. I don't think I'm a very good pusher or office politician. My edges aren't that sharp yet; I don't like to climb over other bodies. I look at some of the losers around here and it gives me the creeps. I have a strange rapport with Phyllis Brown, one of the secretaries, and I shudder when I think that I might end up like her. Whole periods of her life seem to pass in drunken amnesia. Every once in a while she'll wander into the office and I'll get the distinct impression that she really doesn't know where she was the night before. Right now she's involved with a supervisor in the office. He's married and has a family and he's a devout Catholic, so you can see the wonderful prospects she has with him. She also had a one-night affair with Ernie Rhoades, Jr., and some matinees with Red Johnson and several other supervisors and specialists. Sometimes she seems bright and efficient and able, but other times you see her sitting at her desk with her head in her hands. She makes me want to cry.

I look at her and at some of the others and I say to myself, "What's to keep you from ending up like them?" Well, what's to stop me? Sure, I'm getting further professionally than girls like Phyllis Brown, but I may also wind up just as sharp around the edges—and just as single. I mentioned this to Desi the other night, but he said he didn't want to hear my troubles. He's a New York man. It's no skin off his ass if I wind up miserable.

Phyllis Brown, 35

———•———

Phyllis Brown overreacts to almost everything—she goes through life shrieking. A long time ago her best friend met this marvelous man, and pretty soon the two of them decided to get married and move to England. Well, Phyllis had depended on her best friend for almost everything—because Phyllis is like a little child, and she had made a mother out of the friend. But it wasn't enough for Phyllis just to be unhappy about losing her substitute mother. No, sir! She went around screaming that the man was really no good, at least he wasn't good enough for her friend. She got very uptight about the whole thing! She'd get drunk and start crying and say, "What am I gonna do without my old friend?" At that time Phyllis was almost thirty.

Of course, the men around The Company would make anybody overreact. One night Phyllis gave a party while she was in the middle of her affair with Tom Lantini, one of our executives. And goddam if Lantini didn't show up with a new girl friend! And poor Phyllis—it blew her mind! It ruined her own party! And Lantini's date knew that something was going on, too, but she didn't know exactly what. You could feel the tension. Phyllis had this hysterical look on her face, and the girl friend had a look of quiet desperation, like "I know he's sleeping with one of the girls at this party, but which one?" And pretty soon it became obvious which one, because Phyllis had this awful dying-cow expression and Tom was dancing with everybody at the party except her. Once in a while he'd give the new girl friend a smooch, in front of everybody, and Phyllis would practically collapse. I felt like kicking him right in the balls—if any! He was so sick, so arrogant. He knew that he had Phyllis psyched, and he knew he had the girl friend psyched. Later

I realized that Phyllis had a flair for attracting cruel and vicious people like him. She's made it a career.—Alexandra Oats

· I ·

I'M JUST about the only native New Yorker in The Company. I've never known anything *but* New York, except for a few trips. I was born and raised in the Bronx, way up in the two hundreds, where it's green and there are a few parks to flee to and the colored haven't taken it over completely. I went to one of those high schools that had so many students you couldn't really get an education. They just *processed* you. I've always said that my education stopped at the eighth grade because there were a thousand in my class in high school and we were just like a herd. You didn't have to study anything to pass your subjects, but then you didn't learn anything, either.

I was a dutiful child. Oh, yes, dutiful *and* obedient. My mother was cold and my father was stern, and it seems like I spent my whole childhood trying to reach one or the other, especially my father. But he was an almost unreachable man. He seldom changed expression, and he was seldom pleased with anything. I had two big brothers and a kid sister who was just like my own daughter, and none of us could satisfy that man. I'd trim the hedge and weed the front yard and edge along the sidewalk, just praying that my father would say, "What a beautiful job!" But he seldom did. I was always working in the house, polishing, scrubbing, anything to make an impression. The others gave up early, but I never did. I never made the impression, either. The only times I ever really reached my father were when I did something wrong. Once I decided to clean the screens, but when I took one of them out it cracked along the edges—from old age!—and I couldn't get it back in the wooden frame. I was so afraid about what my father would say, and finally I decided not to tell him at all. My mother said, "You've *got* to tell him! He'll see it!" He came in and I said, "It was a little loose and I was just trying to clean it," and he blew up and made me to go my room. And I was trying to do a good job! Another time I fell in the snow right in front of the house and my brothers and I thought it was so dumb and funny; I just sat in the snow laughing and they just kept looking out the window, laughing. But then my father got all annoyed over such a silly thing! I also remember bringing one of my first watercolor paintings home from school and showing it to him. It was a painting of a cat, and I'm afraid it had at least five legs and a growth of mustache like an eighteen-nineties barber. My father looked at it as though it smelled, and he said, "That's the stupidest thing I ever saw!" It hurt my feelings. But he was a wonderful man. When you grow older and look back, you see the fine qualities in your parents. There were always terrible pressures and tensions on the poor man. He was afraid he couldn't support us on his civil-service salary; he was afraid we couldn't own a car; he was always on the edge of being a failure. I guess he *was* a failure. Well, he couldn't take it out on the Mayor of New York, so he took it out on us. Who can blame him?

I hated being a teenager. My mother and father didn't keep up with things; they hadn't the slightest idea what was going on in the world, and neither did I. When I was sixteen I was as mature as a ten-year-old. My older brothers had begun dating, but I never dated a single boy in high school. Not one! I never even kissed a boy in high school. I remember one very persistent boy from 211th Street. He wouldn't take no for an answer, and I'd finally have to threaten to scream. He'd say, "Phyllis, you're the cutest girl in the school. Come on, give us a kiss!" and he'd begin to maul me. Well, I may have been the cutest girl in the school, but I was terribly retarded. I didn't begin acting like a grownup till I was well into my twenties—and then it all happened *too* fast.

High school went by like a long, sad, bad dream. I didn't go to my junior or senior prom. I wore no lipstick or eye makeup—my father would have sent me to the priest if I had painted my face. I was not permitted to wear anything so immodest as a bra. My mother kept me in undershirts. I may have been the only teenager in New York City history to go through high school wearing undershirts. Underneath, I had a nice figure—I still do—but nobody could tell. Maybe that was the idea, to keep the men from getting interested in me. If so, the plan worked. But it didn't keep me from getting interested in *them*. All through school I had these mad, silent crushes. I'd sit up and write poems about the boys I was in love with, and then I'd flush them down the toilet. My father would have killed me if he'd known. I was too afraid to make any gestures toward the boys I loved. Maybe that stems from my relationship with my father, which is an awful thing to say. But all through those years, males frightened me. And obsessed me at the same time. My childhood was a sick, sick time.

But I'm not trying to say that my childhood is the cause of my unhappiness. That's making excuses, and I detest people who blame everything on their childhoods and their poor parents. Some people are just born to be unhappy, and there's no point in blaming it on anybody else. I usually say that my failure to go to college was the turning point in my life, and sometimes I find myself trying to blame that on my parents, on the way they refused to lift a finger or even encourage me to keep up my schooling. But that's not fair, that's ridiculous. If I'd really wanted to go, become somebody, if I'd had a genuine motivation, I'd have made it. Abraham Lincoln didn't go to college, but he went out and learned a few things. And he turned out all right. So I can't blame things on my not getting an education.

I was seventeen when I graduated from school, and I was still lost and immature. Some parents try to help their children start looking for work, introduce them around, give them a little support, but my father never had the courtesy to do that. On my own, I had to go to the placement bureau at my high school and say, "I've got to get a job."

They sent me to a department store in Manhattan, and the store gave me an intelligence test and turned me down. I said, "What's wrong with me?"

They said, "You wouldn't want to be a sales person. You tested too high on intelligence."

I said, "Well, I need a job and never mind my intelligence."

So they put me to work sorting mail at twenty-seven dollars a week. Some job! You took bins and bins of mail, as much as you could handle. You had to raise your hand to go to the ladies' room! I was very quick at the work; I even enjoyed it for a while. I didn't know any better; I wasn't complaining. About ten generations of New York City girls like me had gone through ordeals like this one and never knew it hurt. I was following tradition. When they gave me a ten-minute break, I took ten minutes, not eleven. I was a "good German"! I'd probably have been great under Hitler! I do what I'm told.

I worked on that job for one year, until I was bored out of my head, and then I took a test with a manufacturing company in Newark and scored so high they not only hired me, but they began sending me to night school to learn typing and shorthand, two of the subjects I had neglected to learn in the Bronx. I'm not bragging, but I'll tell you how good I was as a secretary. Within one year the night school announced that there was nothing more for me to learn, and I began to get better and better secretarial jobs in the company. The men competed for my services, and I kept working for bosses higher and higher on the executive ladder. After four years with the company I was secretary to the president. But I also had made a terrible mistake in my private life. I had met an older man, unmarried, and very handsome in a mid-Thirties kind of way—slick hair and red waistcoats and argyle socks. Before I met him I had had a few dates with men of my own age and I hadn't enjoyed them at all. But this man was different. I loved being with him. One night I said to myself, "This is the great love of my life." But I was so inhibited—I wouldn't even let him kiss me. Then I began taking a drink or two, to loosen myself up, and then I became *too* aggressive with him, talking about marriage all the time. I came on too strong—that has become one of my worst failings—and it didn't appeal to him and he got sick of me.

I used to make that long train ride from Newark to Manhattan and up to the Bronx—as a dutiful child, I was living at home and paying room and board—and there'd be tears in my eyes the whole way. The man I loved wouldn't even speak to me any more, let alone take me out. So after nearly five years with the manufacturing company I quit, I just couldn't stand being in the same building with the man I loved. I *had* to get away. The day that I cleared my desk and left for good I sobbed and sobbed. I couldn't accept the fact that I would never see him again, and yet I had no choice. One of my girl friends at the office led me to the train and put me on, and I never went back. Even today I dread the idea of going anywhere near Newark—but then Newark isn't the same as it was then. *Nobody* wants to go there now.

When I left, I was twenty-four years old and still a virgin. Then I got a job at The Company as a secretary—and that was my downfall! I had never seen anything like The Company before—let me tell you! And I doubt that The Company had seen too many young girls like me. I had coal-black hair down to my knees—I wore it in a bun when I went to business—and I looked extremely mature and grownup, but I was still the same infantile person I'd always been. All of this seemed to intrigue a supervisor named Terry Jacobsen. He absolutely would *not* let me alone! He was always hanging around my desk, writing me notes, sending me flowers and candy. When I'd leave to go down on the elevator, he'd somehow wind up in the same elevator, and he'd demand that I go out with him for a drink. Just as firmly I'd tell him no, but that wouldn't keep him from repeating the performance the next day and *every* day.

Anyone would have relented after persistence like that, and I finally did. I let Terry take me to the bar for a drink, and drink has always been my undoing. After three or four martinis I began to see that he was a very interesting man, ten or fifteen years older than I was but still very interesting. The next day I was beside myself. I was mortified about going drinking with him! I called him up and I said, "You're not going to ruin my life this way! I'll quit The Company if you don't stop pestering me!"

He said, "How am I ruining your life?"

I hung up on him, but this only made him more persistent than ever. As the weeks went on he began giving me advice, offering me a helping hand, playing the role of the concerned and dear friend. He was on the telephone every hour, asking what he could do for me. I would tell him to let me alone—I remember screaming at him once, "Just stay away! You're making me upset!" But whenever I did anything like that, he just redoubled the pressure. Then I made the mistake of going out with him again, and for the first time in my life I felt the touch of a man's hand on my body. Years later Terry said to me, "When I first saw you in the office you were at a point where you were so old you were ready to explode! You were so repressed, and you needed to find something about life!" Well, he was right, I suppose. But you can imagine how chagrined I was when I found out he was married. The first man I ever had any physical contact with, and he was married! Not only that, but now that he had felt me he was making me feel that he owned me, that he controlled my life. He seemed like my father to me, taking over, telling me how to breathe, ordering me around. I didn't like it, but I didn't know what to do about it. I was still a virgin, but it was almost like being in white slavery.

One day when he called and announced where we were going to meet for drinks that night, I started to cry, and I said, "We're *not* meeting for drinks tonight or any other night!" and I picked up my purse and quit. It was summertime, and I fully intended to stay away from The Company and Terry Jacobsen for good. The Company sent me the money that was coming to me, and they were very nice about it. One of my bosses explained to Personnel that I'd had sort of a minor nervous breakdown but that I was such a good secretary that it would be a good idea to keep tabs on me and try to hire me back when I calmed down. So off I went, to spend the summer in a bungalow at Spring Lake, New Jersey, with a bunch of female assistants and secretaries I had met at The Company.

What a world of difference there was between them and me! They were sophisticated girls, Vassar and Wellesley types. That summer I saw bare-breasted girls for the first time in my life! They must have thought I was the strangest person in the world, a nobody from nowhere. I'd just sit over in the corner and stare at those bare-breasted girls running around! All they ever did was chase boys and talk about boys. It seemed odd to me, odd but fascinating. In the daytime I walked in the sand and sunbathed, and gradually I began to forget my terrible experience with Terry. Then I met another older man—a thirty-five-year-old bachelor—and fell madly in love with him. He didn't reciprocate. All he said was "Look, call me when you're back in New York City and you have a place of your own."

I was beside myself. I *had* to see him again. I said to myself, "This is the end of the world!" I finally decided to take him at his word, so I packed up my things and went home to the Bronx to tell my mother and father that I was taking an apartment with a girl friend in Greenwich Village. My father said, "Once you leave this home you can never come back!" I left anyway, and I returned to my old job at The Company. I waited for the telephone to ring. And waited! Not long afterward I got word that my summer romance had married somebody else, but by then I was pretty much over him. He was just another of my numerous crushes. It always seemed that I couldn't live without my loves, but then I'd wake up and be over them. This sort of thing still happens to me, and I don't know why.

One day I looked up from my desk to see Terry Jacobsen standing there. "Well!" he said. "Welcome home!"

"Where have you been?" I said nervously. I'd been back with The Company for three months and hadn't seen him once.

"Overseas sales trip," he said. "Japan." That was one thing about the men of The Company—you never knew what glamorous adventures they were going to have from week to week.

He seemed more mature and calm—God knows he should have been; he was almost forty years old then, and if a man doesn't show some maturity by forty, you might as well give up on him. As for me, I wasn't the slightest bit more mature. I had two speeds—stop and go. I either detested a man or was madly in love with him, and if I was madly in love with him and had a few drinks in me, I'd maul him and fall all over him and just annoy him completely. That happened several times. Drink always had that effect on me, still does. Drink was finally my undoing with Terry Jacobsen. One night he was walking me to the subway when we decided to have a martini. We wound up having about six martinis, and then we went to another bar for old-fashioneds, and we finished off the evening with numerous brandies and Cointreaus. When I woke up at three o'clock in the morning and realized I was completely undressed in a hotel bed, I was like a madwoman.

"What happened?" I said. "*What happened?*"

Terry jumped up and pulled the covers around him. I'm sure he was as shocked as I was. "Nothing," he said. "Nothing. You were drunk, and when I realized you were a virgin, I never touched you."

"Oh, my God!" I said. I grabbed my clothes and began pulling them on. I kept repeating, "Oh, my God!" I was certain that I had committed adultery, and I was absolutely mortified. I couldn't get to a priest quickly enough. "Listen!" I said. "We've got to find a priest! I've got to confess right away!"

He said, "But, Phyl, *nothing happened.* Honest to God! I wouldn't lie about a thing like that! Can't you tell that nothing happened?"

I said, "No, I *can't* tell. Come on, we've got to find a priest!"

He was still buttoning his coat when we stumbled through the lobby and into the rain. I was crying hysterically, but thank God there was nobody on the streets to see me. St. Patrick's Cathedral was closed; at least we couldn't wake anybody up. We began going up and down the West Forties looking for a church, and we went all the way to Hell's Kitchen before we found one, a little parish church sandwiched between two tenements. I'm afraid I was almost screaming when we went inside, and an elderly priest appeared in an old-fashioned nightshirt, frantically working on the button of his collar.

"Father," I said, hiccuping and crying and reeking of drink, "Father, a horrible, horrible thing has happened!"

The priest said, "What horrible thing is that?"

"Father," I said, "it's the end of the world for me."

"What's the end of the world, dear child?"

"Father," I said, leaning on a pew to keep my balance, "I've committed the sin of adultery!"

The priest stared at me through his rheumy eyes. He almost looked disappointed, as well as tired and bored with the drunk in front of him. Terry had taken a seat in the back of the church, but he rushed forward now and stuck his hand out to shake hands with the priest, and in a halfway drunken babble he said, "Now just a minute, Father. It's not that way at all. I'm not a Catholic."

"What does that have to do with anything?" I asked.

"I mean, *nothing* happened, Father. I mean, I didn't do anything, but she's afraid that I did."

"I'm *sure* that you did," I said, crying loudly.

"But I didn't! I swear I didn't! Father, I took her to a hotel room, it's true. But when I found out she was a virgin I didn't touch her. Father, that's true." Terry was acting as though he was going to be tried and flung in prison.

The priest didn't look any happier. "Stand out in the vestibule, please," he said and brushed Terry away. He led me to the confessional.

"Bless me, Father, for I have sinned," I began. "This is the first time I've been to confession since—"

"But, Father, it's unfair! I didn't lay a hand on the girl!" It was Terry, knocking on the confessional.

"Just step outside, please," the priest said. He sounded as though he'd had quite enough of this four-A.M. drunken charade. "Now go on, my child," he said to me.

"Father," I said, "I have committed the sin of fornication. At least I think I have. At least I went to a hotel room with this man."

"The man says nothing happened," the priest said impatiently.

"Well, when I woke up in a hotel room with a married man—"

"A married man?"

"Yes, Father, and I was sure that we had committed adultery."

"Well, personally, I doubt it," the priest said wearily, "but the Lord knows, and the Lord will forgive you. A hundred Hail Marys and a hundred Our Fathers. Now I would like a word with the gentleman."

The two of them talked for several minutes out in the anteroom, and I think Terry put ten or twenty dollars in the poor box, and then he took me by taxi to my apartment, grumbling all the way. When I got home I tried to figure out if I was still a virgin, but I couldn't tell, so I cried all through the Hail Marys and Our Fathers. I felt awful the next day.

I don't know how to explain it, but from then on Terry Jacobsen held a strong power over me. I told myself that it was because he had seen me like that in bed, all naked and drunk. It was as though he had seen into the real Phyllis Brown, the wanton, adulterous, sinful Phyllis Brown, and therefore the other Phyllis Brown, the naïve and scared and virginal one, could never fool him again, could never use her virginity as a defense again. Not that I lost my virginity right away. It took many more months of heavy drinking and hysterical scenes and reproaches and recriminations, but now Terry Jacobsen was like a tiger on the trail. He knew he was going to get me, and he knew he could afford to be patient and slow about it. That first night in the hotel room had paved the way and made it inevitable. Because what's the difference if you think you've done it and it turns out you haven't? You might as well have done it!

For several months we drank together and went to hotel rooms together and he wouldn't even touch me. I wouldn't always know for sure, but he would always tell me later, "Nothing happened." One night he said, "I never laid a hand on you, and I never will." I became more and more under his power; I even began to think I loved this old man, this man that waiters and ushers sometimes mistook for my father. "A table in the corner for your daughter and you, sir?" "Where would you and your daughter like to sit, sir?" It went on all the time. How disgusting, now that I look back on it! And me dancing like a puppet on a string!

One night I lost my virginity, and I didn't even know it, I was so drunk. I blocked it all out. If I know I'm doing something bad, I can do this. Blank it out entirely. This is how I keep my sanity, probably. I haven't the slightest idea how it happened; I don't *want* to remember. But I wish it hadn't happened. Not only because he was married but because it was all so cheap and sinful. I wouldn't want anyone else to have to do it this way. It certainly wasn't normal; it certainly wasn't pleasurable. Lying drunk and practically unconscious on a cheap hotel bed! This is not the way that young girls should act, losing their virginity on a smelly mattress, underneath the flabby skin of an old man. And a married old man! Wrong! All wrong! I hate to think about it.

When I remember it now, the whole thing infuriates me. But I don't blame Terry. I think he truly cared for me as a person. Our relationship went on for years, off and on, and even today, ten years later, he still calls me and says, "There isn't a day that I don't wonder how you're doing and what you're up to." He's a widower now and semiretired, and he still says he wants to marry me. Once I told him, "But I'm not *interested* in you now. I don't care for you now." And he said, "But you're the only woman I've ever really loved." And I said, "No! I have no interest in you at all. I more pity you now." The truth is I realize now that I don't especially like him. I've met so many more fascinating people at The Company. He just happened to be the first, that's all, and so he seemed interesting at the time. Now I know better. But he never quits trying, even now when he's in his fifties. Last year he called me and asked me to vacation with him at Virginia Beach. I said I didn't want to, and anyway it would be too indiscreet. He said it didn't have to be indiscreet, he had a cottage of his own, and I could come there and do whatever I wanted, no strings attached. *But there are always strings attached.* My life was at a low ebb then, and I went to the cottage, and he began pawing me as soon as I arrived. I jerked away from him and I said, "I don't even want to be under the same roof with you!" which was mean of me to say. He can't help himself; he says he's madly in love with me, and maybe he is.

· 2 ·

THERE HAVE been quite a few Terry Jacobsens in my life—I wouldn't want to try to count how many—and sometimes I try to figure out what happened to me, what made me spend most of my adult life sneaking around with men who already had wives and children. Sometimes it seems that I've *never* had a date with an eligible bachelor. In all honesty, I can only think of three or four normal dates in my entire life! My social life is almost always the same: a few drinks in a quiet bar with a married man, usually a married man from The Company. Then maybe dinner, or maybe not. Then a few more drinks at my apartment. Then bed. Or more often than that: a telephone call from a married man; he's on his way over; I dash around and tidy up the apartment; he arrives, we have a drink or two and a talk and then we go to bed. It's that way night after night. On nights when the married man isn't here, the bottle is. I can't seem to sleep without a few drinks.

Do I consciously choose married men, or do they consciously choose me? I don't know. I do know that the married men at The Company are extremely *active*. When I first went to work there I couldn't understand it. When they found out that I was single and available, it was like an avalanche. If I hadn't been all involved with Terry Jacobsen, I honestly believe I could have had a date every night of the week with any one of twenty-five married men in the office. They're all so willing! They're all on the lookout! There isn't a married man around who wouldn't invite a girl out. Truly! That's the way men are, at least in New York City. And New York City is a married man's city. The single men just aren't available; they must all live in caves and come out from four to five A.M. and then sneak back into hiding. My girl friends ask me, Why go with married men so much? They say there *are* single men around, and they accuse me of not trying to meet any singles. Well, my girl friends are just plain nuts on that subject! I *don't* meet single men. Where do you look for single men when you're thirty-five years old? I can't stand these singles bars and these so-called "mixers"—I get invited to a lot of them, but I don't go. The last thing I want is to be seen standing around a group of strange men and wearing a "help wanted" sign across my chest. Why, it borders on walking up to a man and propositioning him! What decent girl would do a thing like that! You might as well say, "Hey, let's go to my apartment and do it." Disgusting!

In my dream world, a girl should meet single men without having to try. They should just *appear*. But of course they don't. Well, who cares? I'm beyond all that now. It doesn't matter any more whether I meet single men or not, just that I meet *somebody*.

I don't remember exactly when it was that I found myself becoming attracted to the married men at the office, but it was not long after the Terry Jacobsen thing began to cool down. It was at least nine years ago, and I've been seeing them ever since. I don't see how you can avoid it. As I said, they're all on the prowl. And you get to know them so well, and they get to know you, and soon you know them better than their wives do. One of them said to me the other night, "You seem to know so much about me and The Company and all the things I'm interested in," and I said, "Well, why shouldn't I? I'm always picking somebody's brains from The Company. I'm picking the brains of the most brilliant people in New York!" And that's the truth. All day long I'm working side by side with the most interesting people in the world. That's what's wrong with me! They're so interesting that I hang my hat and myself on them, I live my life through them!

But I'd be interested in them even if they weren't so bright. Because they're so nutty! So unpredictable! You never know what's going to happen, and even though you'll get hurt now and then, you'll still have these crazy memories to look back on. Which is better than nothing.

For five years now I've been seeing one of the brightest men in The Company, maybe *the* brightest man. I'm crazy about him! He's all energy and brilliance and flair. He'll run the whole show some day, if there's any justice! For five years we've staggered around New York City together, drinking and talking and making love. We're not making love any more, but thank God we're still seeing each other once in a while. Thank God it's not completely over.

I met him at a company dinner, one of those affairs that used to go on regularly and help to bring us all together—as though we needed bringing together! He was seated next to me, and we talked all through the dinner. He told me his name was Tim Bolte and that he was thirty-one years old and that he was divorced. We both drank a lot and even before the dinner was over we were holding hands and looking deeply into each other's eyes, and the heck with everybody else at the table! He said he'd been married years before, practically as a child, and that he had two young sons, but his ex-wife and sons lived in San Francisco and he didn't see them any more. He seemed like one of those characters from fiction, all tragedy and comedy intertwined. He'd say these outrageously funny things, but I could see that he was capable of deep sadness, too. He had suffered, and so had I; maybe that's what drew us together. Later that night we went to my apartment for a nightcap, and he kissed me and said, "Phyllis, I have found the love of my life." He was mean to say that to me, because it opened me up to him. We saw each other constantly for a few days, and we went to bed together, and he admitted that he was still married and lived with his wife and sons in Bedford Village, north of New York City. I cried for hours, but he told me not to worry. He said it was just a marriage of convenience; he didn't love his wife; he loved me, and we would work things out.

Well, of course we never worked things out, as you might have guessed. Not only was Tim Bolte thoroughly and completely married and devoted to his family, but he was even more thoroughly married and devoted to his job. He would come to my apartment so tormented by the problems of his job that he looked ready to explode. Then he'd get a few double Scotches in him and start spilling it all out, and some nights I'd have to sit there and listen to him rage for five or six hours. One night he got so upset I had to help him down the stairs. I've never seen a man cry like that. But he's a very complicated man. He was saying that too much pressure was on him, and he said, "I'm doing it *all!* Everything! Half the people in the department can't even function. It all ends up on *my* shoulders." And he'd put his head in his hands and be wracked with these deep sobs. Then he'd pull himself together and he'd say, "I wouldn't mind if somebody'd just *acknowledge* what I'm doing. But they're incompetent upstairs too. They don't have the slightest idea what's going on! So there I am in the middle, doing it all, and getting no credit for it!" I finally dug out of him what had happened. Someone had been promoted over him. The man had been there three times as long as Tim; he had "come early and stayed late," as the saying goes, and his reward was to be promoted over Tim. "And he's not qualified to shine my shoes, Phyllis! Everybody knows that!" I agreed with Tim and tried to console him, but it was no use. He cried so loud I thought he'd wake up the other people in the building. I said, "Tim, Tim, you've got to stop it. I've got to get you out of the building!"

He wouldn't even shut up on the way down the stairs. I said, "Tim, you've got to be quiet. The superintendent will hear you!" and I said, "Tim, you can't let your wife see you like this!" I walked him around the block about ten times and finally put him on the train to Westchester County. He looked a mess, and I often wondered what his wife thought when he came home like that. I doubted that she understood the turmoil this poor, talented man was going through.

Of course, he does crazy things, he gets crazy ideas. Not that he's twisted or anything, but he's under so much pressure. One night he announced that he wanted me to go out and meet his wife and sons. I said, "Tim, you ninny, that'd never work! You'll give me a couple of drinks, and you know me after a couple of drinks!"

He said, "No, no, it'll work. You're all very dear to me, and it's time you met. You don't have to tell them *everything* about us."

"But, Tim, you know I will! You know I can't keep quiet when I've had a few drinks!"

"Well, I'll be the bartender," he said, "and I'll see to it that you only have one or two. And I know you'll like my wife! She's a wonderful person, and so are you."

But I flat refused to do anything so ridiculous as go out to his house. He *does* love his wife, and no doubt about it. I'm convinced of that. But he happens to enjoy me, and I enjoy him. I learn so much from him! And we have such rapport. I sit for hours listening to Tim Bolte talk about the colonial life of the army ant, and I'm hypnotized! And I honestly think he enjoys talking to me. He must!

But an unpredictable, inconsistent man is going to hurt you once in a while, too. He does some very strange things to me, but it's only because he's a character, he's so brilliant. Not that he means anything, not that he means to be cruel. He sometimes makes dates with me and doesn't show up. He says he'll meet me for a drink and then I'll sit there till midnight and he won't show up. Or he'll call up and say he's coming right over, and I won't see him till the next morning. And then I forgive him. He doesn't do it intentionally. He's just different. Lately he's been showing me off a lot, but I don't mind. He'll go out with the boys and then he'll telephone me and order me to join them. I always do. He introduces me around. I think it makes him feel good to be able to introduce me around, like some kind of bauble on his chain. But I love him so much, I do it.

No, I don't think he loves me, at least not the way I love him. He doesn't make love to me any more, but he does to others. I know he does, because he tells me about them. He torments me about them. I never had an orgasm with Tim, or with anybody else, for that matter. I'm one of those people who just don't have orgasms. Does that make me a freak or something? I don't think so. I enjoy sex. I have to have it. But I just don't have that physical reaction at the end. And I know this always annoyed Tim, and I know it's the main reason we stopped going to bed.

Now he likes to sit around my apartment and tell me about his other girl friends. The other night he told me there was a young girl in another department who practically had orgasms just by looking at him. I said, "Oh, really? How nice!" He said he took her home and gave her three orgasms in one night. He said she was so excited that she could hardly get out of bed the next morning. I said, "Don't give me that!" It really hurt my feelings. I made it my business to take a look at the girl he was talking about and she was wearing a miniskirt and long boots and she had a bad complexion. I said to him, "Why, she's nothing but a hippie, and she's got some kind of skin disease!" He just laughed. He's so strange. He's got fantastic problems.

One night he telephoned me and said he was coming up, and pretty soon he stumbles in with his old pal, Red Johnson. Johnson is another of the unsung geniuses in The Company, and when he and Tim get together for a drinking session and start telling each other how unfair the business life is, they can get pretty drunk. On this night, they were hardly able to stand. They both sort of fell into my apartment. I poured drinks for them and a double for myself, and pretty soon I'd caught up, and we were all three sloppy drunk. Then I looked up and Tim was gone. He'd just slipped right out of the apartment, and I was left alone with his buddy at two in the morning.

Really, I didn't know *what* to do. Red Johnson is a married man, and he started right in asking about my relationship with Tim. I didn't think that was any of his business, drunk or sober. Then he started talking about sex and kept on about sex, sex, sex for two hours. It was very plain to see what he wanted, but I couldn't see how he expected me to respond. When I finally got rid of him, I was upset and drunk. I thought that Tim was using me as a convenience, that he was setting me up with his friends. I didn't understand. Now that I've thought it over, I don't think that he meant it that way at all. I think he meant it all in good faith. My friends say differently, but I think he meant it all okay.

The morning after, I woke up in a terrible state. All I could think of was why would Tim set me up like that? And with a married man, too! The only conclusion I could reach was that he was trying to get rid of me, trying to unload me on somebody else. I called up my best friend, Kit Michen, and I told her all about it, and I said, "He just tries to humiliate me! He must have no respect for me at all!" And she said, "Look, if you ever see Tim Bolte again, you're crazy! If he calls you and you let him back into your apartment, you're crazy!" I said I would never see him or anybody else again; I was going to slash my wrists. This wasn't the first time I'd threatened suicide. It's something that's always on my mind. I think about it often. I tried to throw myself under the wheels of a car one night—at least that's what they told me the next morning. My friends stopped me. Suicide is never very far from my mind. Sometimes I think I'll just sit in the bathtub and let my head slip deeper and deeper till it's under the water and I'll quietly drown. Just sit in the bathtub and go to sleep. But I won't do it. I'm a coward.

Anyway, Kit and her husband came over and sat with me, saw me through my latest ordeal, the way they always do, and a few days later I called Tim and asked him what he meant by setting me up with Red Johnson. He said, "Why, I didn't mean anything, Phyl. I was just drunk and decided to go home, that's all."

"You don't understand," I said. "You don't see how it looked. I took it as a terrible insult."

"Oh, Phyllis," he said in this conciliatory, sympathetic tone. "I didn't mean it that way a bit!" And he didn't. He really *didn't.* Because he's not thinking to hurt me personally; he just thought I wanted a good time. He thought that's the way I was. He doesn't realize that I love him and only him. He thought that I might enjoy a night in bed with Red Johnson, that it would be good for me. I also think that he did it a little bit out of spite, because I wouldn't have orgasms with him. But how could I? I didn't have orgasms with *anybody.* I tried to explain this to him, that he must have a few secret hatreds against me, but he disagreed, and that night he came over to the apartment and told me his latest troubles around the office, just as though nothing had happened, and then he borrowed a hundred dollars and went home. He forgot all about the hundred dollars later, but I don't care. He's worth a lot more than that to me. We haven't done anything sexually in months. I still want him; some nights I want him so bad that I make advances. But he's inadequate with me; I think I *make* him feel inadequate. Sometimes he tries, but he can never do anything, and then he'll say, "It's just because at heart you're too good and decent." We'll wait awhile and then try again, and once again he won't be able to do anything, and then he'll say, "You're just too good and decent, that's the reason."

So lately I've been resigning myself that the sexual end of it is over. Sometimes it worries me, that I'll lose him completely, but still he calls me and we have drinks and we rattle around the bars together just as though we were both in our right minds. A couple of weeks ago I said, "Maybe it's good that the sex is over, Tim. I'm just as glad. We have a nicer relationship the way it is now. It'll never be anything more than it is, and I'm not asking for anything more. I just want to know you all the rest of my life."

He said, "You always will."

· 3 ·

OH, BUT isn't he grand? Don't you get a *grand* picture of him? Believe me, there are not that many Tim Boltes in the world. I should know. I've had love affairs with dozens of married men— don't ask me how many; I would hate to have to count them. A Tim Bolte comes along about once in a lifetime. There was one other man that I loved amost as much, Roger Hanley, but that romance was all mixed up with my father and my father's death and so many sick, disturbing things that it pains me to talk about it.

Roger was also married and also a minor executive of The Company, and we went together for about two years, a long time ago, and I thought I loved him. He was another one of the driven types that seem to thrive in our company. He would absolutely crush your skull if you got between him and a promotion, or between him and another little addition to his power—more money, maybe, or more responsibility. He was under better self-control than Tim;

he didn't get drunk and cry, but he was just as disturbed in his own cold style. He'd plot ways to accidentally turn up at the bar at the same time as the big boss, so they could have a drink or two together. He even went out of his way to ride on the same commuter train and happen into the same club car. He'd send memos to his superiors, modest, clever memos that subtly tried to make the point that he knew more about The Company and the product than anybody else. He was *totally* devoted to getting ahead. I was an adjunct, and so were his wife and children. But I enjoyed him. It was like dating a lion in a Brooks Brothers suit.

Don't ask me how to reconcile Roger Hanley's religion with his philandering, but he was a very devout Methodist, and he had some very peculiar ideas about God and religion. He used to make sacrifices, enter into bargaining sessions with God. He'd pray, "Dear God, if you give me that raise, I'll quit drinking." Then he'd quit drinking and if God didn't come through on the deal after a month or so, he'd start drinking again. I watched all this with amusement, but then he made an announcement that wasn't so amusing. He came to my apartment one night and told me that he felt he had to give up something big in order to get promoted, and I asked him what he was going to give up, and he said, "You!" And wouldn't you know it, within about two weeks he was promoted. That ended us! He felt that there was a direct relationship between giving me up and getting the promotion, and for a long time I couldn't talk him out of it. I said to him, "Didn't I make you happy all the times when you weren't doing so well and your job was even in jeopardy? Didn't I stand by you?" I told him how hypocritical it was, not sleeping with his wife all that time, sleeping with me, and then giving *me* up as a sacrifice. I said to God in my own prayers, "Isn't he being very selfish?" But I guess people use God for their own benefit. The man had gotten a nice promotion, and he was paying his debt to God by staying away from me.

Months and months went by before we started up again, and then it was on a random basis. He would come up to my apartment and take me to bed and then race home as fast as he could, I guess so God wouldn't see him. He explained one night, "I've decided that it's all right for us to sleep together, but that's all. No going out. No running around town. But we can be good friends."

"Do we always have to be good friends in my apartment?" I asked.

"Yes," he said. "It has to be right here."

I said, "Why do we always have to be good friends within these four walls?"

"Because I could never be seen with you," he said. I thought that was a lovely little explanation. Our affair dwindled after that, although it continued off and on for nearly five years. Most of my affairs have dwindled off and on for long periods, and most of them have overlapped. I have a need for men—it's an awful thing to say, but it's true—and if one man isn't seeing me often, then I'll see several men simultaneously.

Well, you find out who your *real* friends are when something terrible happens to you, and something terrible happened to me after Roger and I had almost broken up entirely. My father died. Poor man! He wasn't yet fifty years old, but he'd never been strong, and he'd always had to work so hard to support us all.

He lingered for about six months with cancer. Horrible! He had the little bag attached to his side and all the suffering. He called for me, but I wasn't there when he died. I should have been; I *could* have been. But it upset me too much to see him so sick, and it upset him, too. He was too proud. I'd come to see him, and he'd say, "No! Go! *Go!*" So I'd leave quickly, because I knew my father better than anybody else in our family and I didn't want him to see me in tears. We knew he was dying, but he didn't know, and I didn't want my tears to give it away. He died at three in the afternoon. Isn't it awful? I *could* have been there, but I let him die in a hospital with a lot of strangers around. I let him die alone.

I insisted on doing all the arranging. I did *everything*. The priest said, "You're not supposed to be doing this; the funeral home is." I said, "He's *my* father." I was trying to arrange to have a Mass said and then a quick burial. But the priest said, "You can't arrange these things. You're not the funeral home."

I said, "That's right. I'm not a funeral home. But *I want a Mass said for my father!*"

The next day was Saturday, and the priest said they couldn't squeeze in a Mass; there were weddings scheduled at our church all day. I said, "Well, tough! My father went to this church for forty years, and now you can't say a Mass for him?" I was really distraught. I got into a taxi and I began going around to all the churches in the Bronx, and finally I found one that would have the service the next day, but it had to be in the morning, because the cemetery only worked a half day on Saturday and they had to have the body by noon.

I prepared my father myself. I pressed his suit. I put the tie on him that he loved, one that I'd given to him. I wouldn't let the funeral home touch him. My brothers and sister and my mother wanted him in a closed casket, but I insisted that it be open. I wanted people to see my father. All his life he'd gone to everybody else's funeral; why shouldn't they come to his and see him once again? I even arranged a wake, though only three or four people could come on such short notice.

When it was all over, I was a wreck. I sat in my apartment and cried for two days. My friends called and tried to comfort me, but I'd just have to hang up on them. Somebody sent a doctor to see me, but I told him to go away and let me alone. I drank a bottle of Scotch to get through each day and another one to get through each night. It was awful.

The death of my father meant so many things to me, and one thing in particular. I'd always had my own view of heaven and hell, not as faraway places where you went if you were good or bad, but something very different. I didn't believe in the traditional hell. I don't believe you'll be consumed in fire; that makes no sense. But I believe there's a hell, and here's what it is: Hell consists of floating around in space looking down at your miserable relatives living their miserable lives. When you are in hell, you can see *everything* that your survivors do; you are *forced* to see everything they do. That is the *real* hell.

Long before my father died I told my friend Gloria Rolstin that I would never have anything to do with men after his death. I said, "I could never subject my father to watching anything like that."

Now he was dead. Roger Hanley called me after two days and said he'd heard that my father died, and could he come over and offer his condolences? We had a few drinks, and then we went to bed. He wouldn't take no for an answer, and I was too drunk to know what I was doing. I felt terrible when it was over. I thought how it was just like me, making decisions and never carrying them out, and then I thought about my poor father, and I said to myself, "Well, he knows the truth about me now, and there's nothing I can do about it." I told Glo what I'd done and she said, "Fine, *fine!* You lasted two days." I still sleep with men, and I know my father still sees it. I wish I could stop. I wish I could relieve him of this agony, but maybe it doesn't make any difference any more. Now he knows what I am, and there's no way that I can take any of it back. When I tried to explain all this to Roger, he just laughed and said I should see a psychiatrist. I made an appointment, and I cried through the whole hour, and then I had to pay the man forty dollars. He'll never see me again. I can cry at my apartment for nothing.

· 4 ·

SOMETIMES I'M just mad that God made us the way he did, with all our frailties and needs. Why does sex have to be done the way it is? Why can't we just hold hands and have babies? It's unfair. Everybody makes such a big thing about it. Men feel terrible because they can't have an orgasm, and women feel terrible if they can't, and you open the magazines and see endless stories about this. It annoys me that I have a need for sex. I enjoy it, and I can't even have a child! There's something wrong with my insides. Oh, what I'd give to be able to have a child! I'd have one in a minute, married or not, but of course I'd have to have feelings for the father. I can't bear to go to bed with a man I don't have feelings for. Men are different. Most of them can go to bed with anybody, any time.

Sometimes in my calmer moments, I think that sex isn't all it's cracked up to be, and a lot of people agree with me. We have married couples in The Company that have orgies together and watch dirty movies with other couples. They certainly can't be too thrilled by their mates if it takes all that to get them interested. Sex is overrated. It's a big hangup. But I *need* it. I *need* people, which is a terrible thing. And to keep people around me I'll go to bed with them, not so much for the sex as for the person, to keep him interested in me. I don't have to go to dirty movies to be interested in a man. Quite a few men have tried to take me to dirty movies— they're showing all over Manhattan now—but I've never enjoyed them. I laugh all through! You never see any young people at the dirty movies, just an occasional older couple and a lot of filthy old men. The young people are home doing it; they don't have to sit there watching others do it on a screen.

It's all so sick, having to get yourself charged up like that. But then most of the men I know are inadequate sexually, even some of the ones that are known as great lovers. Oh, I could tell you a few things! But then what is a great lover? Is there any such a thing? Is a great lover a man who strokes your arm for ten minutes instead of five? Personally I think techniques are immaterial. It takes two people to enjoy each other, and if you don't have a mutual feeling, you don't have *anything*—no matter what techniques you use. And if you do have a mutual feeling, then you have *everything*, no matter how dumb and clumsy you are. I've seen men practically hang from the ceiling of my apartment to try to get started, but if the feeling isn't there, nothing happens. Sometimes I turn men off, and usually it's because of this habit I have of throwing myself at them. I don't mean to, but I'm terribly honest. If I love you, I'm going to knock you down! I don't believe in hiding my feelings like a hypocrite. But men don't like that. One of them said to me, "I don't come to see you any more because you make it too easy for me."

I said, "Well, the hell with you!" which was a terrible thing to say. I said, "You told me we couldn't go halfway, that it had to be bed or nothing. And now you tell me I made it too easy for you!"

So I stagger along, messing up my life, trying to hold onto a few old loves like dear Tim Bolte, trying not to lose *everything* I've had. That's one reason I don't ask much of men. I don't make them take me out. I don't like to dance or go to nightclubs. If I like somebody, I like to be *with* them. I've never asked much from anyone. If I like you, it's enough that you come up here and be with me. Sometimes I misjudge and get into trouble. Men have hit me three or four times. I understand why. They get upset at the office, or their wives frustrate them, and they have to take it out on somebody. And once in a while I'll get a little pushy or a little whiny and a man will haul off and smack me. It's usually my own fault. I don't stay mad at them. Most of the men I see are married, and married men are under such heavy pressure, you have to be reasonable with them. One of them said a funny thing the other night. He's known me for quite a while now and he's begun to know my habits, and he said, "Phyllis, just tell me one thing that's been puzzling me. How come you prefer married men?"

I laughed. "What gave you that idea?" I said.

"Well, it just seemed to me that going around with married men is the life you want," he said.

"No," I said. "This isn't the life I *want*. This is the life I've *got*."

I used to rely heavily on certain friendships, men *and* women, people that I could always count on, but now I'm beginning to wonder. I do like people, I like them *too* much, but I've begun to think that a lot of them can't be trusted. Especially the women. They say they're your friends, but they're only posing. Women talk about me behind my back, I know that for a fact, and some of the worst gossipers pretend to be my friends. Men don't gossip about me, but women do, and you can't even count on your best friends to stick up for you. One night I was on the subway and I'd had something bad for dinner and I'd drunk too much and I got sick. The girls in the office found out about it, and a few days later Florence Du-Valle took me to dinner, and after a few drinks she said, "I've been told to ask you something."

I said, "What is it?"

She said, "We've decided that you should cut down on your drinking."

I said, "Who's 'we'?"

She said, "All of us, your *friends*. We also want to know if you're pregnant. If you are, we want to help you."

Can you imagine? They all presume that *they* can tell *me* anything they want; they're the adults, and I'm the thirty-five-year-old child. These are friends? You go around thinking that people understand you and then something like this happens. To me my personal relationships with men are my own personal business, strictly between me and the man. These gossips have no right to try to make me feel awful about it. But they're a bunch of single biddies and they haven't got anything else to do. They're just sick because they have nothing else to think about. All right, I have made mistakes, and love affairs don't last. But you *try*, you have to keep on *trying*. And you don't want your so-called friends coming to you later and asking how can they help you. That's debasing and insulting.

After a while you begin to wonder if you have a single real friend. For years now I've hung around with a married couple, Kit and Bill Michen, but lately they have begun to act strange, and *they're my best friends in the world*. Bill is an advertising manager for one of The Company's departments, and Kit works a few blocks away in the front office of a modeling agency, and they have the cutest cottage on the beach at Brielle, New Jersey. All week long they put up with New York City, and then they dash down to Brielle for the weekend, and about half the time they take me with them. It's worked like this for years, and we always got along fine, and Bill and Kit were two of the first people I'd call if I got into any trouble, and vice versa—not that they ever needed me much, but once in a while Kit would want to cry on my shoulder over something or other, and my shoulder was always available.

But a year or so ago those weekends at Brielle began to get peculiar. The Michens have no children, and maybe they have no sex life, either, because they seem to spend more and more time questioning me about mine. And like a dope, I answer them! They also spend a lot of time filling me up with drink, which is very easy to do, and filling themselves at the same time, which is something new. The result is that we stagger around that cottage for hours at a time, three drunken people, and I begin to wonder what we're doing in Jersey. You don't have to drive all the way to Brielle to have a drunken weekend!

Well, I didn't know where all this was heading, but I found out a few weekends ago. We got down there on Friday night and all got drunk, and I was awakened at ten the next morning by Bill standing over me offering me a Bloody Mary. He and Kit were drinking Scotch, but I like to maintain the pretense that I don't drink hard liquor in the morning, even though there is plenty of hard liquor in a Bloody Mary.

All day long they fed me drinks. The Bloody Marys turned to luncheon martinis, and then we skipped lunch and began drinking French wine. Kit threw some frozen pizzas on for dinner, and we sipped Chianti with them and then settled down to plain Scotch and water for the evening. I was game. It had been like this for weeks now, and nobody ever knew me to turn down a drink. I think I would die without the stuff!

Sunday was a repeat of Saturday. On Sunday evening we were sitting around and Kit said, "You know, Phyllis, you're more like a man. You must have been a man in your last incarnation. Not that you're a lesbian or anything like that. But you do things like a man. You take the active role in the courtship, and that's a role that men like to play themselves."

I said, "When I like somebody, I can't stop myself. When I like somebody, I want to do everything to please them."

She said, "That's stupid."

I said, "Maybe it's stupid, but I can't stop myself."

"You're weak!" she said in a very loud, annoyed voice. It sounded as though she was on the verge of losing her temper, so I stayed quiet. Then Bill said, "What's the latest in your sex life, Phyl?"

Well, ordinarily that would be a horrible thing for a person to ask, but the truth was that I'd always confided in Kit about every step of my sex life, and then she'd go home and tell Bill, and they knew everything there was to know about me. I don't know why they *cared;* maybe they didn't have a good relationship of their own, and they had to do a little living through me. The point is I'd never had any secrets from them, and I didn't keep any now. I told them about my latest dates and how things were going with me and Tim Bolte and all the others, and the two Michens sat on the edges of their chairs listening. Then Kit said, "How come you're not mentioning Ernie Rhoades?"

"What about Ernie Rhoades?" I said. Ernie was a specialist at The Company, a very nice and confused guy, and I hadn't been to bed with him in four or five months.

"Oh, come off it!" Bill said. "We know you've been going to bed with Ernie every chance you get," only he used the gutter word for sexual intercourse.

"No, I haven't!" I said. I was honestly shocked, both at how wrong he was and at his nerve.

"I don't know why you're giving us the Miss Innocence routine," Kit said. "Everyone knows you sleep around."

"And everyone knows who with," Bill said.

I started to choke up. I couldn't understand this onslaught. "Please!" I said.

"Shut your mouth!" Bill said, and he got up and stood over me like a gorilla. "There's one more thing we ought to tell you while we're at it."

"Yeah, tell her about the pants," Kit said thickly.

"Those red pants of yours that you've been pulling up all day," Bill said. "Don't you think you could get a pair that doesn't keep falling down? Don't you think you could get a zipper that works?"

Kit said, "We're sick and tired of watching you expose yourself all day long in those pants. If you want to know what I think, I think you wore them on purpose."

I said, "These aren't even my pants! I borrowed them. I'll never borrow another pair of pants in my life!"

"Well, if you do borrow some," Bill said, "make sure they cover up your crotch the next time!"

I felt like saying, Why all this interest in my crotch? I'm not interested in *your* crotch! But I kept quiet. I just couldn't understand. I went into the kitchen and poured myself a drink. "Look at her!" Kit said. "She gets her own drinks now."

"Oh, Kit," I said, "I've always gotten my own drinks here. Is it wrong all of a sudden?"

"It's *always* been wrong!" Kit said in a loud, irritated voice. "And while we're at it, when you went shopping with Bill today, I had to make your bed. Is it too much to ask that you make your own bed?"

"No," I said. "It's not too much to ask."

It was quiet for a while, and then Bill began to mumble drunkenly. A lot of the words I can't repeat, but he was making remarks like "I can't stand a woman like you" and "You're just not our type of person; you sleep around and we all know it," and "You're an insult to this house, an insult to my wife." He just sat there in a drunken stupor, getting himself all charged up, and when Kit left the room to go into the kitchen he hauled himself to his feet and stood over me again. "What kind of a whore are you?" he said, which was a terrible thing to say to me. "Get out! We don't want you here! You're a disgrace!"

What could I do? It was the middle of the night and I was fifty miles from my apartment and I didn't even know where to go to catch a train. So I just sat there and waited for him to calm down. But he didn't. "*Get out!*" he shouted. When I didn't move, he pulled me up and began shaking me. I was crying by now, and I said, "You're not even a man! How could you treat anybody like this?" With that, he reached back and punched me in the mouth. I was so confused I didn't even feel the pain. It kept going through my brain: Why did he *hit* me? Why did he hit *me?*

I ran into the kitchen and told Kit, "He hit me! Bill hit me!"

Kit laughed. "Nobody hit you, Phyllis," she said. "Just calm down."

I was almost hysterical by now. "Look!" I said. My lip was bleeding, and my hands were bloody from touching it. "Look!" I held out my hands.

"Don't bother me, Phyllis," Kit said. "I'm busy."

"Your husband hit me!"

"My husband did no such thing."

It was like a scene from a mental institution, me standing there with blood dripping from my chin and her wiping a dish and pretending that nothing had happened. Then Bill stormed in. "She's got to get out of here!" he said. "I can't spend another night under the same roof."

"I quite agree, darling, but I'm afraid she'll have to stay," Kit said. "There's no train."

"Well, keep her the hell away from me," Bill said and went back out. I just dragged myself into the guest bedroom and shut the door and poured a few more drinks from my private flask. I hardly slept all night. These were my best friends. I couldn't imagine what was going on.

The next morning we were all supposed to get up at dawn and drive back to the city and go to work. I expected that the whole bad dream would be over, and everybody would be contrite and apologetic. When I walked into the kitchen in my dressing robe, the two of them were there, and neither said a word to me. *What had I done?* Then Bill began making a big pretense of doting on Kit. He said, "Kitty Lou, honey, would you like me to mix you a Scotch and watuh?" in this broad Southern accent, and Kit answered, "Why, sho enough, honey, that would be just scrumptious, mah dahlin'."

After he made drinks for both of them, he turned to me and said, "Pray tell, Kitty Lou, who is this woman?"

"You remember, don't you?" Kit said. "It's that awful person that comes to drink our liquor."

"Oh, yes," Bill said. "Well, I can't even sit in the same room with that woman."

He headed for the living room, and I said, "Bill, you didn't *have* to invite me."

"No," he said. "I didn't *have* to, and I won't make the mistake again."

I looked closely at both of them, and they looked horrid! I suppose I did too. They just looked *pathetic*. My poor dead father looked better in his casket! When I saw this, I was ready to forgive both of them. I said to myself, "What children! How sad! What a man to be married to! How tragic if this is the way they are!" Bill had settled down with the paper, and the pages were rattling as he tried to control himself. Kit was pretending to be busy in the kitchen, and I knew that if she didn't stop soon she'd drop every dish in the place. I wished somebody would say something apologetic, and the whole nightmare would be over, as though it had never happened. I understand that people get strange when they drink, and I don't like to lose my friends no matter how peculiarly they act.

But nothing nice was said. "Get in!" Bill said roughly to me when it was time to drive back to town. "You sit in the back!"

They stopped at a café for breakfast, but nobody invited me to join in. Almost as an afterthought, Kit said, "Do you want me to bring you out a hamburger?" I said no. For the rest of the drive they were sickeningly lovey-dovey, practically necking on the parkway in broad daylight. I got out at The Company building and they didn't even say goodbye. "See you later!" I said, but they didn't answer. I started to say, "Thanks for a nice weekend," but even in hypocritical New York that would have been too much.

As usual, I turned to my other friends to try to help me figure out this new crisis. Gloria Rolstin told me to drop them cold, never to go to Brielle again. "They're using you as a toy!" she said.

Alicia Nemerow insisted that Bill Michen must be madly in love with me. "It's so obvious it's pathetic," she said. "Bill's crazy about you, and Kit knows it. But they can't admit anything. Bill's hostile toward you because you make him jealous, sitting around there telling them all about your sex life, and Kit's hostile toward you because she's not getting it from her husband and he's madly in love with you. They must have no sex life at all, if they have to borrow from yours! A situation like that was bound to explode sooner or later."

Well, that only happened a few weeks ago and I haven't talked to Kit or Bill since. But if I know myself, I'll end up forgiving them. I still think it was just a case of alcoholism, of temporary insanity, and then in the morning they were too ashamed to admit what they'd done. I don't think they're really bad people. They were always nice to me before. Nosy about my sex life, yes, but decent to me and generous about inviting me to their place. How can I stay mad at them?

· 5 ·

A THING like that makes you wonder who are really your friends. Sometimes I think that the essential fact of life is that everyone of us is alone. Friendship is a myth; companionship is a legend. Lately I've tried not to depend on others so much. I'm trying to learn how to go it alone. That's going to be my thing. *I've got to go it alone.* The only ones you can trust are the children, and where do you find them? Children make the *biggest* fuss over me, which is ironic when you consider that I'm sterile. I've always wanted children close to me. Sometimes I take my little nieces and nephews and cousins to the movies, Rockefeller Center, places like that, and they just fall all over me. They *love* me! I've thought about adopting children, too. Just the other day Gloria said, "Phyllis would be a wonderful mother," and I would! I *would!* Believe me, I *know* I would! But nobody'd ever allow me to adopt a child. If I even went in and asked to adopt a child, they'd treat me as though I was *non compos mentis.*

So what's the use? If I had met and married some eligible young man, I'd have been able to have all the children I wanted; either I'd have had an operation to correct my condition or I'd have adopted some children. But marriage eluded me. I never even came close. I played the game at The Company, and I got caught. Thirty-five years old and no one in sight and a company-wide reputation as the married man's delight! Marriage would have been the answer. Last night I was having drinks with one of the specialists and he said, "You know, Phyl, you're always feeling sorry for yourself, and you oughta cut it out."

I said, "You've got your nerve! You've got a wife and two lovely daughters *and* a girl friend on the side, and still you go around complaining. I don't have *any* of those things, but I'm not allowed to complain at all. But I *do* have to sit around and listen to *you* complain. Well, sure I complain once in a while. And I have every right to."

He said, "Oh, yeah? Well, I'm married, so what? You can be married and still be miserable."

I said, "Really? Well, *just give me the chance!*"

People who don't know me well look at me and think I'm pretty normal, well adjusted. I keep smiling, and I'm friendly. But underneath if you get me in my bad periods I can be nasty, because I really didn't ask for this kind of life. But I'm not a nasty person at heart, although more and more I find myself taking out my unhappiness on others. I don't know what people think when I turn on them like that. Maybe they think I'm getting old and grouchy and feeling sorry for myself. My sisters-in-law look at me and they say, "What does she have to be grouchy about? She has a grand and glorious life in the city!" They chose to marry, and now they say they'd love to be in my shoes. When they say that to me, I think to myself, Maybe they have something there. I guess I do have a good life. I've got friends, I've got a good job, I make enough money to get by. Sure, there are things that I can't do, but there are things that *everybody* can't do. Maybe I'm lonely, yes, but maybe I'd be lonely if I was married, too! Maybe getting married would have been a bigger tragedy than I've got!

What I'd really like is to bear a child. I went to a doctor to see if my insides could be straightened out so I could have an illegitimate child, but he said the operation was very complicated and they couldn't be sure it would work anyway. Even at that, I almost went ahead with it. But then I considered how old I am and how difficult it would be, and I finally gave up.

But the idea still comes back strong once in a while. I'd name the boy Timothy or the girl Jennifer. My friends say I'm just talking big, but I could carry off an illegitimate child beautifully. I could be a good mother. This is what I wanted the most, all of my life. My only consolation is my young relatives. I have *such* a good time with them. Of course, that can't go on forever, though I'm sort of hoping it will. When I'm fifty, they'll be about twenty or twenty-five, but I can still take them out, can't I? Why not? When I'm sixty, they'll be too old to go out with me, but sixty is a long way off. I'll probably be dead by the time I'm sixty. I hope so, anyway.

You would think that the consolation of my life would be my job. Lots of old spinsters throw everything into their work and lead pretty good lives. But I'm not one of them. My job is boring, and it gets more boring every day. I don't have the slightest interest in any product The Company turns out, and my boss is thirty-two years old going on seventy-five, if you understand. He's about as interesting and as inspiring to work for as the chief of janitors. If there's one thing that this company has a surplus of, it's fascinating men, but I don't happen to work for one. But he's ambitious and he'll probably be here for forty more years, and I'll be stuck with him. Ugh! What a prospect.

The truth is that my little niece Miranda, who is ten years old, could do my job, that's how tough it is. People think that we New York City career girls are engaged in such challenging pursuits, but they don't realize that most of us are bored stiff. I get to work at nine in the morning and I work till five-thirty, and it's eight and a half hours of sheer, painful monotony! My boss is one of those busy-seat workers. He actually spends time making up things to do, so he'll look busy and get a promotion. He dictates this bunch of nothingness to me all day long. He dictates long memos about what he's going to do the next day and the next! On any given week I can pull a piece of paper out of my desk and show you in black and white my boss's entire schedule for weeks to come. He even dictates information on what he's going to *think* about the next few days! This is lunacy, and it is also monotony. If there were something momentous or interesting about his memos, I'd welcome them. But they're strictly make-work. And even then there's not enough work to occupy the time. I read the papers. I look up at the ceiling. I file my nails. Some lunchtimes I get drunk, but he's always nice about it. Lately I've been getting drunk more and more at lunchtime. I'm losing ground. I should be able to get some satisfaction out of working at a glamorous place like The Company, working together with all those intellectuals, but that's another thing I've learned: *Nobody's* really working together, believe me! Every business organization, every company, including this one, it's like a pirate ship. The knives keep flashing all the time, along with the smiles. How can you take any satisfaction out of so-called togetherness in an atmosphere like that?

I don't know. I can't even get any satisfaction out of my sleep. I have terrible dreams. Sometimes they're so real that I think they actually happened. I never have erotic dreams—too bad!—only scary ones. Dogs are always biting me in my dreams. I only ever had one dog as a child, and he ripped some muslin curtains and we had to get rid of him. But why do I always dream that dogs are biting me, or knocking me down?

My father has been dead for five years, but I dream about him a lot. He comes up all the time, and I wake up babbling to myself. Then I turn on the light and I say, "Well, he's not even *here*, so what are you worried about?"

For the first time in my life, I've begun to have trouble getting up in the morning. I pull the covers over my head and I say to myself that I just want to stay here in bed all day, or sit around the apartment and sew and cook and do things and not go to the office at all. But then I hear the horns honking in the street and I get up when I hear that. I'm still the dutiful child.

I don't know what's going to happen to me in the future. I don't have a dime. Scotch costs eight dollars a bottle; everything in New York costs a fortune, and I don't really make enough money to maintain my Greenwich Village apartment. I'm never sure where the money goes—just that it's gone. I have no bank account; I've borrowed against my salary for years, and I live from hand to mouth. Looking at me, you wouldn't believe it, but it's true. I'm a *poor* working girl in every sense, at a hundred and twenty-one dollars a week. Sometimes I worry about where it's all going to end; sometimes I drink and forget it. One thing I know for sure: I can never retire, I can never stop working. There'll never be the money for it. This isn't fair. I shouldn't have to worry about my old age. I should stop worrying. I could die tomorrow, and then all the worry would have been for nothing. It seems unfair. And even if I don't die tomorrow, I'll wake up one of these days and discover that I'm old. *Old!* Wrinkled and unattractive and veined. *Ghastly! Horrible!* Then I'll have to learn to face a life without men. I'm already trying, but it's not working too well. I think about it all the time. *A life without men.*

Sometimes I get strange thoughts. I wonder how it would feel to have a truck run over my foot. I dwell on that. Sometimes I think about suicide. There was only once when I was really going to kill myself. No, maybe two or three times. But I could never do it. One day I got very drunk in the office and I told my girl friends that I wanted to commit suicide. They told me to stop talking like that and they began watching me. But I really didn't have the courage anyway. They say cowards commit suicide, but I think it takes courage. The last time I decided to commit suicide I was all alone, no one to watch over me, and I tried desperately to find an alternative. I thought if I could just have some children, some young people, around me, I'd be okay. So I called Odyssey House and Phoenix House to ask if they had any young kids that I could take to the zoo or something. They said they'd look into it. They haven't called me back yet, but I haven't killed myself either. I think I got drunk instead.

If you want to know my best guess about my future, I think I'm going to be murdered. That's not so farfetched as it might sound, living in New York City. I'm convinced of it: *Eventually I'll be murdered.* Sometimes I get drunk and forget to lock my door or double-lock it. I've just been lucky so far. Some mornings I wake up and find out I've been sleeping in an unlocked apartment all night. And I do such dumb things. Some nights I'll come in and open my door, leave the door open and then turn on the lights. That's one of the stupidest things you can do in a jungle like New

York. That's how a girl up on Seventy-second Street got murdered —one of the most horrible murders I ever heard of. She was a schoolteacher and she'd just come here from Iowa. Either she didn't close her door or she left it unlocked, because the murderer just walked right in after her. She was stabbed and beaten and strangled and the knife was left in her. There she was: a lovely little girl from Iowa. She hadn't been here six months, and she wasn't a pick-up or anything like that.

Something like that will happen to me: I'm almost counting on it. Then it'll all be over, and I can rest.

Stephanie Grant, 28

———•———

I don't pretend to understand Stephanie Grant, and neither does anybody else around here. Certainly she's an eccentric. I don't think a soul knows what she does when she leaves the office. She's very secretive. Once Alicia Nemerow saw Stephanie out on a date, and Stephanie was very upset that she'd even been seen. People aren't supposed to know what she's doing. She's a private girl, a beautiful loner. She'll go all the way to Philadelphia to see a play by herself, if that's what she happens to want to do. She takes Russian lessons for no particular reason—just because she wants to take Russian lessons. She once told Alicia that she likes to eat gourmet meals at a tastefully decorated table, and one of her biggest pleasures is to make herself a dinner like that, all alone, and light the candles and enjoy herself. She's a very strange and lovely girl.—Bettye McCluin

Stephanie Grant is the big enigma around here. She does her work and goes home. She doesn't go to the office parties. She's a very, very decent person, but she's also a little peculiar.—Florence DuValle

• I •

I LOVE New York. I absolutely love it! New York and I are best friends. I understand the city very well, and the city understands me. We are forgiving of each other. If New York were to ask my hand in marriage, I would gladly consent. But then I have lived with Indians in Latin America. I have gone all the way down to the bottom, down so far that I didn't think I would ever get back up. I have not been pampered and mollycoddled all my life. Therefore my preparation for New York was better than most.

I was born in Monterey, California, to a couple of struggling artists with very definite ideas about life and living. They were strong people, and to me they seemed like a god and a goddess. Both had had awful childhoods, and they decided to bring me up in an ivory tower, away from bad influences. We never lived near people, always out in the tules away from town. My life was lonely and isolated, although I didn't realize it at the time, and I didn't care. Through most of my early childhood I had no other kids to play with, because there *were* no other kids where we lived. I played with lizards running up and down the wall. My parents were the kind of people who could find value in a pebble, and they taught the value to me: the design, the texture, the feel of it, the whole world in a rock, or Tennyson's universe in a wildflower.

My mother had a physical condition that made her short of patience, short of temper. She let me run as I pleased, so long as I didn't stray too far. I built a treehouse and practically lived in it, only coming home to eat and sleep. I kept bugs for pets. I was supersensitive; the death of a sparrow would make me cry all night, and I would stay depressed for months. In adolescence I felt like Alice in Wonderland in that enormous hole. I had the same hopeless feeling. But there were also times of elation and joy. My childhood was not uniformly grim. It was more like a patchwork of highs and lows.

You might suppose that being artist types, my parents would have been liberal and outspoken on subjects like sex. But where I was concerned they were the exact opposite. They taught me *nothing* on the subject. And since I lived practically to myself and had almost no social contacts, nothing is exactly what I knew about sex. Of course I accepted my parents' attitudes. They would look at my classmates and say, "Those Jones girls are so cheap, they wear lipstick." They didn't mean it literally, but, being a child, I took it literally. I remember when we were sightseeing in San Francisco, and a Negro couple came walking down the sidewalk, and they were so happy together that the man just picked the girl up and whirled her around. My father reached around the seat and turned my head with his hand and said, "Look! Look over there! That's the opera house!" Without saying a word, he'd given me the idea that such horseplay was bad. I lumped it together with the remarks about lipstick and fast women and put it all under a category of my brain marked "Not for me."

In candor, I was a freak of a child. My grandmother showed me a picture of me taken when I was seven. I looked like a monster, unkempt and disoriented, almost deranged. A colleague of mine at The Company ran into somebody from Monterey a year or so ago, and the guy said, "Oh, you know Stephanie Grant? What is she doing now? She must *really* be weird!"

When I was in the seventh grade a strange thing began to happen to the other girls at school. They started wearing straight skirts and lipstick and going to town to watch the boys play baseball. I couldn't understand this. They had turned into something else, something different, and the threads of communication I had with them were broken completely. By this time I knew the biology of sex, but that's all it was: biology. It had nothing to do with feelings or emotions or the changes in the girls at the school. I knew nothing about romance.

Life was just about the same till my senior year. I paid attention in class, I was polite to my classmates, and when the school day was over I went home to my treehouse. If somebody looked at me crosseyed I was upset for a week. I was an eighty-pound bundle of nerves, and the only place where I felt truly at home was up in the tree with my bugs and my lizards. In that setting there were times when I could even be happy.

In my senior year an amazing thing happened. A boy answered my prayers by asking me to a basketball game. I had been praying to God for several months for something like this. "God," I would say, "if you'll just give me one person to invite me on one date, I will never ask you for another thing." I didn't particularly believe in God, but desperate situations call for desperate measures.

The boy's name was Don Mahoney, and he was a fascinating person. He had wit and imagination, and he saw life in a wonderful

colorful and creative way. We talked all through that first basketball game, and then we started seeing each other constantly. I had
never been out with a boy, and now I was going steady! We did
silly things like staying up till midnight and walking through town
looking at the store fronts and chasing each other around the park
till all hours. Don Mahoney made me happy, and I began taking
better care of myself. I brushed my hair and began using light cos-
metics. I didn't go back to the treehouse much, except once in a
while with Don.

It never occurred to me that my parents' attitude toward me and
Don was peculiar. They were letting me do just about anything
with him. They never complained when I came in late, and they
didn't object when I tried to make myself look pretty for him. Of
course they knew he was a queer, but they didn't bother telling me.
Why, I didn't even know what a queer was! I thought I was having a nice, normal high-school romance.

After we had gone together almost a year I thought it must be
time for him to kiss me. I was no expert on love and romance, but I
had done a lot of reading, and it seemed to me that the standard
timetable called for a kiss or two at this stage. But hinting didn't
seem to reach Don, and I began to wonder if he liked me at all, or if
I was just some kind of buddy to him. One night I decided that the
time had come, and I pushed him against a wall and gave him a
massive bear-hug-type kiss like I'd seen in the movies. He twisted
and squirmed, and when he finally tore loose from me he staggered
away like a drunk.

I walked around by myself for a while, trying to figure things
out, and when I got home it was after midnight. The telephone
rang and it was Don's whiny mother. She was crying, and she said,
"Where's my *Donny?* He hasn't come *home* yet and it's my *birthday* and I'm all *alone!*"

Something cracked in me—I was stupid and sixteen and repressed and all that, but somehow I knew that there was a connection between this woman's possessive mewling and the way her son
had treated me earlier—so I said, "You shut up and you leave him
alone!" It was pure instinct speaking. I said, "You let him be a boy!

Let him go where he wants! You have no right to keep him from being a boy!" That was the end of my first romance.

A few months later I became the dumbest girl ever admitted to the University of California. One of the students came right out and told me.

"You are the unhippest chick in history," he said. "You should be put away!"

Except for my dates with Don, I had almost never been with people other than my parents. Most of my life had been spent completely alone, and I knew none of the code responses of young people. I didn't know what to *say*. Like when somebody comes up to you and says, "How you doing, kid?" you're supposed to say something back, you're supposed to know a code answer. But I didn't make the proper responses because I didn't know them. I would have given anything to know them! I used to stammer around and the girls would walk away as if I was one of the weird sisters, making Birnam Wood come to Dunsinane, and then I'd go back to my room in the dormitory and write in my diary, things like "I built a wall so that nobody knew who I was. Nobody knew who my soul was." My diary was a survival thing, but it was also demented and destructive.

As the semesters went on, I felt myself swirling down and down! I wanted desperately to be like the other girls, but I couldn't bring it off. I always answered the wrong way, and they always thought I was crazy. I'd go back to the dorm and my heart and my whole insides were hurting. All I could think of was "It's wrecked in there! My insides are wrecked! It's all cold and clammy in there." I told myself that I was alone, and I would *never* be able to talk to these people.

Once in a while I'd find myself at a mixer, and once in a while I'd meet some strange guys who wanted to dance, and then we'd talk. We had these disturbed conversations! I used to lie about myself, give a different name and tell them that I didn't go to Berkeley, that I was a typist or a messenger in town. I figured they were probably doing the same thing: lying about themselves. It just seemed a logical thing to do. It enabled me to learn a few things.

Even to this day there's nothing I like more than a party where I don't know any of the people and they don't know me.

I know it sounds hard to believe, but right up to my junior year of college I did not understand sex or romance. I didn't have the biological impulses, or if I had them I suppressed them. I couldn't understand what it was that boys wanted. I was dumb, *really* dumb. One night a very nice boy took me to his room at a frat house, and and after a while he turned off the light. I couldn't understand why. Then he put me on a couch and started talking to me. When he began pushing me down very gently, I said, "Why are you doing that? I don't understand!" I pulled myself back up to a sitting position and resumed our conversation where it had left off. Later he pushed me down again, and I said, "What's that about? What do you mean by that?" And he said, "Do you mean you really don't understand?" and I said, "No, I don't." He took me home, and I never saw him again. I understand he became a priest.

But nobody could stay *that* dumb at Berkeley, and by the end of my junior year I had learned a little about fitting in. I learned some of the code responses and code reactions and made a few friends and began acting a little more normally. When I graduated, another girl came up to me and she said, "Stephanie, I want you to know we're all proud of you. You've improved *so* much. When you first came here we thought you were crazy. But you're really a great kid now."

Later, I realized that I'd killed myself in college, literally killed my soul. I killed the lonely little kid that I'd been all my life. By copying the others and trying to be something I wasn't, I'd made myself into something I no longer recognized. I hated myself. I needed a purgatory, and I found it quickly. I joined a group of kids that were going off to South and Central America to donate two years to the starving Amerindians. Some of the group were scheduled to stay together and work in the larger villages; some would go off completely alone and live with the Indians almost *as* an Indian. I volunteered for the solo job; I thought it might help me regain my integrity.

Now I will tell something peculiar about psychiatry. The agency had us all screened by a psychiatrist, and the girls were coming out of the sessions one by one and complaining that he'd asked them if they'd ever had physical relations with a girl and things like that. About a third of the girls were rejected on one ground or another. Well, by this time I knew what society regarded as normal and what society regarded as weird, and I went in there all briefed with the right answers. After ten minutes the psychiatrist said, "You're completely normal," and approved my assignment.

Well, of course I was *not* normal and I was *not* ready for anything so taxing as moving into the middle of an alien culture and trying to fit in. I had just done that at school, and I was not ready to do it again. There was nothing at all wrong with the Indians; they were just different. They looked at life entirely differently from the rest of us. To begin with, they thought I was nuts for coming there. By definition, I had to be nuts to leave the rich land to the north and join them in their suffering. You might think this would have bound me to them, but it did the opposite. It caused them to reject me as abnormal.

They also made strange assumptions. They assumed that any man who spent more than five minutes in my hut was sleeping with me. One day a visiting sociologist came through our village and he stopped and visited me for a few hours. We had a perfectly lovely afternoon, talking and playing the guitar and sipping a bottle of cheap wine he had brought. But when he left, my reputation was destroyed. It turned out that the Indians had asked him how I was in bed, and he'd answered, "Fine." He *had* to say that, because it was assumed that anyone who spent all that time closeted with a woman had to be sleeping with her. Either that or he was the world's biggest liar, or a queer. So to protect his future usefulness with the Indians, he told them I was fine in bed. He explained it to me afterward, and I didn't get mad about it. By this time I understood. What great training this was for New York!

The visits from my colleagues were rare, maybe five or six times a year. The rest of the time I was dying of loneliness. I tried to work among the Indian children, to make friends with them, but I got nothing but grunts and grouchy expressions in return. I lived for the sound of a jeep that might be bringing visitors who spoke English. One day four girls from the program showed up, and I was so thrilled. I said, "Come to my hut, *talk* to me," and they said, "No, thanks, we're just on our way through," and they gunned the motor and took off. I cried all day. My anxiety was growing. I used to wake up at night screaming, and run out the door and into the woods in my pajamas. I had developed a terrible paranoia, because the Indians did not believe in locks—putting a lock on my door would have been a hostile act—and I slept in fear that somebody would come in and I would have no defense, because my hut was separated from the main village by a hundred meters and no one would hear me if I screamed. I lived like that for months and months, in loneliness and fear. I couldn't even take any consolation from my old friends, the bugs and the lizards and snakes. Too many of them were poisonous.

One day I was visited by a half-breed Indian who called himself "Joselito," "Little Joe," even though he was nearly six feet tall and must have weighed two hundred pounds. Joselito was the classic Latin American middle-man. He was neither Indian nor white, but he had learned to move between both worlds to his own advantage. I had heard long ago that my predecessor, another girl from California, had been driven out of the village after she refused to sleep with Joselito. He had mounted a vicious gossip campaign, and since he spoke the Indian dialect perfectly and the girl could barely say yes and no, he succeeded in having her removed. I wondered if he was going to begin the same assault on me. I said no when he asked me if I wanted to go for a ride in the jeep he had blackmailed out of the provincial leaders. His jeep was the badge of his superiority; everybody else walked, but Joselito proudly gunned his jeep through mud holes and across stream bottoms and everywhere else, and the Indians were in awe of him.

For a long time he persisted in coming to my hut in the evenings and trying to strike up a conversation. But he didn't click with me. He had the instincts of a genius but the intelligence of a dolt. He reminded me of an animal, and I'd never been exposed to anyone like him before. One night he was especially persistent about taking me for a ride. "No, thanks," I said. "I'll walk. I'm *supposed* to walk. like everybody else."

A few days later he told me that the whole village was talking about me. I said, "Why should they be talking about me?"

He said, "They've been saying dirty things about you."

I was shocked. "Why should they do that?" I said. "All I do is try to help them, and then I go home."

"Well, they're talking anyway."

Joselito was clever. He kept needling away at the subject until he almost had me on my knees. Finally he promised to tell me the whole story if I'd ask him in for dinner.

After more teasing over dinner, he came out with it. "One of the chiefs saw you walking on the side of the road at night," he said, "and he thought three things. One, if you don't go in Joselito's jeep you must be looking for one of the Indian men to pick you up. Number two, if you're not driving in Joselito's jeep, you are not a friend of Joselito's, and any enemy of Joselito is an enemy of the tribe. And three, anybody who has the use of a jeep and prefers to walk must be crazy."

From then on I always took the jeep when it was offered to me. I told myself that I couldn't be any use to the Indians unless I learned how to see life through their eyes. I didn't realize it at first, but that was a hopeless task. Matters only seemed to get worse. Then I found out why. When I persistently refused to sleep with him, Joselito had begun the same whispering campaign that had eliminated my predecessor. He spread all sorts of sinister tales among the Indians, and of course he told them that he was sleeping with me. I thought it all out, and I decided that the simplest way to handle the problem was to let him have his way. So I lost my virginity in a steaming jungle hut at the age of twenty-two. Emotionally, I felt nothing. It was strictly politics. I figured I may as well be educated, and it might do me some good with the Indians at the same time. Going to bed with Joselito had no deep, dark overtones for me. I hadn't been taught that sex was a fancy, forbidding thing or even that it was bad. It was just something you didn't think much about. It was nothing, or, rather, it was undefined. For most people it's something dirty and you do it behind the barn. For me it had no definition at all, except the definition of procreation, a biological process. That's the way I was brought up. I wasn't worried about having babies, because Joselito had told me many times that he was sterile. He said, "Don't worry. I'll take care of it, and you'll never have to worry about getting pregnant."

So I did what he wanted. I would cook his dinner and then I'd take care of his physical needs. I did exactly what he said, too. He was a clean fellow, for all his inner corruption, and nothing that he asked me to do bothered me psychologically. I had so many other psychological problems in the village that Joselito's demands seemed minor ones. Toward the end I even enjoyed the sex, a little, although I continued to detest the man.

But maybe another layer of my mind was hating the whole scene, too. I don't know. I'm no psychiatrist. I began to get deathly ill. I had menstrual periods for months at a time and cramps that would keep stabbing at me for weeks, until I'd sit in my bed and scream and scream and scream. I got so sick I couldn't even walk, and after a year with the Indians I had to be carried out of there on a litter and flown into the nearest town in a hospital plane.

Back at my parents' home I went to bed, still moaning, and I stayed there for four months. There were times when I was so sick and exhausted that I could barely move my thumbs. Solitaire was my only recreation, and I would exhaust myself by playing a game or two. I got out a notebook and I began writing everything down, and I discovered that I had been living a pack of lies, deceiving myself about my own innermost thoughts. For example: I used to wake up at three in the morning and scribble in the book till five. One morning I wrote, "I hate staying awake like this," but then I thought about it awhile and I crossed out "hate" and wrote in "love." It was a period of finding out what I really liked and really hated, and I reached some firm conclusions about myself. So did the doctors. Three or four were called in, and they made all kinds of tests, and they were unanimous in the verdict: There was nothing physically wrong with me. It was all in my head. That was a shock! I bought a book by Karen Horney and tried to figure things out. Slowly I began to gain some mastery over my demons. I read *Neurosis and Human Growth,* and within four days my pains were gone. When they came back, I willed them to go elsewhere. I learned to control them. When I'd have a stomach cramp I'd say, "Go to my thighs," and literally my thighs would start to ache. Then I'd say, "Go to my knees," and I'd feel the pain in my knees. Then I'd say, "Phooey, I don't want to have pain in my knees! Go out of my knees!" and the pain would be gone. I promise you— that is the truth!

· 2 ·

LATER ON I figured out the role of the Indians and Joselito and my pains and suffering in my life. I figured I'd gone all the way down and hit bottom, and from now on everything would be up. Working with the Indians was growing up by fire, trial by fire. Now I figured I'd been tried and tested; I felt I knew myself, and I believed in myself. I was no longer the lonely little girl in the tree-house. I was a strong woman, and I was ready to act like one.

So I got on a Greyhound bus and headed for New York. I'm not sure why I chose New York, but one reason was that I wanted to get as far away from my childhood as possible. If I was going to start a new life as a mature person, I wanted to start it in a new location. When I got to Manhattan, I checked into a cheap hotel, looked up a few friends from college and asked them flat out, "What's the most fun job in New York City?"

One of them suggested working in Harlem with the underprivi-leged, but I said, "No, thanks. No more saving souls for me. I've *had* that. I want to live a selfish life. Tell me a good selfish job." She told me to try The Company. I said, "Why, I don't know a single thing about The Company or its product," but later when I thought about it I realized I didn't know a single thing about *any* company or its product. My friend had told me that The Company was where everybody in New York wanted to work. If you worked there, you had automatic social prestige and all sorts of privileges and good pay and wonderful hours. I didn't want to be a social butterfly, but everything else sounded good, so I hauled out my degree in history and wangled a job as filing-clerk trainee, salary seventy-four dollars a week. It was an illogical thing for me to do, but I have always enjoyed doing the illogical thing.

For several months my job was pleasantly routine, but life on the outside was difficult. I was thrilled by the energy and the vitality of the big city, but I couldn't seem to find the right place to live. My cheap hotel was a disaster. The people there looked sick, crazy. Strange animals congregated in the lobby. There were nymphomaniacs, lesbians, people on welfare, people running away from their lives. I stayed four days, and then I began chasing down want ads in the newspapers. But the places I could afford looked so dirty and dangerous. There were garbage cans all over the sidewalk, cracked streets, filth on the pavements. Fire escapes ran up the fronts of the tenements, and they were all so ugly and frightening. I would go to look at a place, and the neighborhood would look so menacing that I wouldn't even dare to walk down the block to the address. This went on for weeks, until I finally got New York City real-estate patterns through my head. Housing is strange in New York City. Middle-class people live in lower-class housing. Upper-class people live in middle-class housing. There is *no* upper-class housing. The so-called upper-class housing along streets like Fifth Avenue and Park Avenue would be called middle-class anyplace else. As for the lower-class people, they live in dungeons. They live with rats. They can't afford what would normally be classified as lower-class housing. All the available lower-class housing is taken up by people with middle-class incomes.

This was something you had to learn to survive in New York. You had to learn that even though you might consider yourself a firm member of the middle class, you were going to have to live in a tenement, because at New York prices that's all you could afford. When I got that through my skull, I began walking around the upper East Side looking for a place. At first it was frightening, but

I soon got used to the filth and the noise and the alarming people running up and down the sidewalks. On a salary of seventy-four dollars a week, I couldn't afford more than ninety dollars a month for an apartment, and I finally settled on a studio apartment, a single room with a bathroom at one end and a kitchenette at the other, for ninety-five dollars. It was a sixth-floor walkup.

For a year or so—before it became too dangerous—the apartment served me well. It accustomed me to the big city. It made me realize that I could survive very nicely in the middle of all this confusion. It taught me to sleep with an enormous high decibel count in my ears. A half block away there was a place where Nazi-style meetings were held almost every night. Men would get up and shout into a bullhorn about Jews and kikes and Aryans and non-Aryans. It sounded like Munich. Then other people would heckle them, and pretty soon there'd be singing and yelling and whistling. Everybody had a fine time, but I counted this mostly as a minus because I didn't like excitable people like that. I liked quiet people. But I stayed on. By this time most of my time and attention were taken up by The Company. I wasn't doing well at all.

It had only taken me three months to be promoted from filing-clerk trainee to assistant, but I think when they gave me the promotion they didn't realize who I really was. At this point in my life, what did I know? I knew my treehouse back in Monterey, I knew the strange folkways of a jungle Indian tribe, and I knew the tiniest bit about men and life. As far as business was concerned, I knew *nothing* whatever about it. The businessmen I met at The Company were the first businessmen I had ever seen! It was like getting to know a wild tribe of Berbers in the Atlas Mountains. They were *that* much different from the other human beings I had known. Other people had had lifetimes to get used to businessmen; they were surrounded by them, raised by them, related to them, but I was meeting them for the first time. It's hard to describe how they puzzled and amazed me.

They were imposing, frightening. At first I couldn't say two words to any of the supervisors, *and yet my job consisted of working closely with them.* You can imagine how smoothly it went.

Some of them seemed very bright and talented, and they always gave me the feeling they would scold me if I made a mistake. They were like slavemasters, austere, frightening giants. Some of them were cold and unyielding; these were the ones I couldn't even say hello to. Once I rode up in the elevator with two like that. They asked me something and my mind went racing ahead and I could see where their questioning was leading and I blurted out about three answers at once. I could see I'd made no sense at all to them. They gave each other this look that said, "Well, what did you expect from *her?*" I know they couldn't wait to get off the elevator to talk about it. I've never been able to talk to either of those two men, and they're rising higher and higher in The Company. Nothing that I say to them ever turns out right. God help me, some day I'll figure out *something* to say to those two men. I don't dislike them, I just don't understand their code, and the responses.

On top of knowing nothing about businessmen, I knew nothing about business, how things work, and here I was in a job that required me to help things run more smoothly for *businessmen* in the *business* world. It was laughable, to everyone but me. I worked twice as hard as anyone else, learning my job. I overdid everything. If I wrote a short report, I would go over it five times for errors, then go out to lunch and come back and go over it five more times. My only working pace is top speed, and I worked that way for six months on my new job as assistant. But there was just too much to learn. And I wasn't getting along with my colleagues. The first night I was on my new job there was a big party, and right away I got the impression that this was a really dirty place, an indecent place. It seemed like everybody was mixed up with everybody else. I thought: "I'm keeping out of this. This is *not* the social life for me. I've come here to work."

One day a supervisor named Alexandra Oats called me in. She said the other supervisors had been complaining about my work. Several of them had said, "Never assign that Stephanie Grant to me again!" One supervisor had said, "I absolutely *refuse* to work with her. We've hired some crazy people, but this is the craziest!" Miss Oats said to me, "I can see the beginnings of a good assistant in you, but you're a long way off. You make fewer mistakes than anybody, but you're so completely unprofessional."

I asked her what she meant by that, and she began a long speech about getting along with one's fellow workers and "fitting in." She said, "You walk around the halls as though everybody else in The Company smells. And that doesn't go over." How could I tell her that I didn't think anybody smelled, that I was just nervous and lost in this peculiar new world? Finally she said, "I'm putting you on six months' probation. Unless you change drastically, you might as well consider it six months' notice."

"Well, I *want* to stay on here," I said. "I *like* it here. Tell me what to do."

"Get a little social," she said, patting me on the arm. "We've got a lot of nice people around here, and they have a lot of fun together. Give it a try. They won't bite you."

I knew that her suggestion was *wrong*. I had an instinctive feeling about separation of office and private lives, but I was desperate, and I was frightened. I knew by this time that it was almost impossible to get fired at The Company, and yet I had only six months to go. Where would I work next? I had a terrible dread of employment agencies and personnel directors, and I wanted to stay right where I was in the worst way. Besides, who would hire me after I got fired from a company that never fired anybody? What a stigma!

At that time a group of about ten or twelve of the younger employees hung around together. At least once a week, usually on Friday night, they'd meet at the bar and drink and stay together till four in the morning, when the bars closed. A few would pair off and disappear into the night, and the whole group was kind of incestuous—there were all these pairings and repairings and romances and breakups *and never a single marriage*. Marriage wasn't what that group was about. I knew very little about the girls in the group, except that they behaved peculiarly for business girls. One of them, Doris Crosby, would come into work two hours late and then tell everybody, "I don't remember anything that happened after eight o'clock!" She always said it with a certain pride. I had heard college men brag about their hangovers and all the awful things they had done the night before, but never a businesswoman. I concluded that there must be very little to her life if she had to come in and act proud of getting drunk at least once a week. She acted as though it was all a gay, mad whirl, and she was the happiest girl in New York, but I'm sure she wasn't. She persisted in doing her charade right in the office. She was trapped in the New York single-girl myth, and she wouldn't admit it to herself or anybody else. Poor thing! I have nothing but sympathy for her. I don't feel like pointing at her and saying, "She's dirty." I accept her as a human being.

One night after I'd been told I was on probation, I decided to check out one of these all-night jamborees. I drank with the crowd and talked, and everybody acted as though they were quite pleased with me. One of the men said, "You know, of all the assistants you're the only one I don't understand. I know about the sex lives of all the other girls, but I don't know about yours, because you keep your mouth shut. And I *want* to know about yours."

Later he came over to me and struck up another conversation, and just before closing time, when I'd had six or eight drinks over the long night, he bothered me again. "Let's go someplace," he said. I knew what *that* meant.

"Where's your girl friend?" I said. I'm very scrupulous about other girls' boy friends. I never want to steal a guy from another girl, because I have a bond with other girls, a bond for strength, and I don't believe in violating it.

He said, "My girl and I aren't going out any more."

"The hell you aren't!"

"No, we're not!"

"Listen," I said, "I don't go with anybody who's got a girl friend."

"I don't have a girl friend any more," he said. "We've broken up. That's a fact."

I mulled it over. "Okay," I said. "If you're a free man, maybe we can communicate."

"Where?" he said.

"At my apartment in about an hour," I said. "I'd rather not leave with you."

All the time I was thinking, Well, I'm not social enough, but maybe if I can just talk to this young man we can click, maybe he's a good man. I'd never heard him say an interesting word, but then I hardly knew him. Some of the other girls had been telling me all evening what a perfect pair we'd make, and in my slight state of inebriation I got the idea that they might be right. *In vino non veritas!*

At my apartment, it developed that we could not communicate an inch. He seemed like a child, an insecure baby. I felt like he needed a mother, that I could have taken him and led him to adulthood, but I didn't want to. I'm beyond that. I don't need a son until I have a real one. The sex that night meant nothing, because I couldn't relate to him as a human being. It was like relating to a wall. The whole thing made me unhappy, not because the sex was boring but because the whole rest of it was so dull. There was such a lack of rapport.

When I woke up the next morning he was gone and I had a lot to think about. Mainly I thought that maybe I'd been wrong, maybe we'd both had an off night, what with the drinks and all. So the next time he asked me for a date I accepted, just to find out.

On the second night, we had to start all over, from the very beginning. He sat down in my apartment, and I said, "Who are you? I mean who are you *really?*"

He said, "Do you always quiz the men in your life?"

"It doesn't matter what I say to other men. I'm asking *you. Who are you?* Tell me who you are!" I wanted to know what he believed, what he stood for, what he thought. Does he eat wild mushrooms? How does he cook them? What kind of music does he like? *You* understand.

Well, he couldn't answer. He didn't know who he was. He had no sense of personal identity, and he had no personality. He was barely human. About all he told me was his draft classification and the number of siblings he had. I began to realize that I had been completely right the first time, that underneath that dull exterior there was a dull *in*terior, and I knew that the sex was going to be terrible again and that that would be the end of it.

After a while he moved over next to me on the couch and began rubbing me up and down my body, like a masseur. I said, "What's this?"

He said, "I've read Masters and Johnson since I saw you last." He had gone home in a state of shock and rushed out to buy Masters and Johnson on sex! Somewhere in there it must have said that a woman loves to be felt, and he was just following the directions. It was *so* funny! He had the old idea that dexterity makes sexual prowess and that you'll really be a lady-killer if you learn all thirty-two positions. He still didn't understand that sex was communication between two people, and he thought he could make it work out right if he didn't waste any time talking to me, but just started this Swedish massage up and down my body. I could almost hear him counting as he did it: hup, two, three, four!

The one thing that I'm proudest of is that I didn't laugh, because that man would not have been able to stand anybody laughing at him. He would have dissolved right into a puddle of oil on my rug. It would have killed him! So the sex went terrible, and I felt very badly about it. The next time he asked me for a date, I said no.

Word must have got out that the unapproachable Stephanie Grant had now joined the human race, and a few days later a roly-poly supervisor with about as much sex appeal as a sunburned oyster began pestering me. He asked me to have a drink with him so many times that I finally had to say yes, and then he began his routine. "Come on," he'd whine, "just let me hold your baby finger."

"Stop acting silly," I would say, but he never let up. Finally I let him hold it. Big deal! A grown man complaining and whining to hold my baby finger! Then he insisted that we go to dinner, but I said, "No, thanks. I don't go out with people from The Company. The Company is where I make my living."

A few days later I found out that he was very much married. The next time he asked me for a date in the hall, I said loudly, "I never go out with a married man," and stomped down the hall. He called after me, "Oh, let me explain. It's not that way. We're almost separated!" Sure, he was. It's a wonder he didn't say he was sterile!

I've never had any office romances at all except that little tiny one at the beginning, but I've come to know a lot about office affairs—or at least I think I do. In my opinion, most of the affairs are not romance at all. They're masochism, sadism, parisitism and infantilism. A lot of them spring up when one of the men starts weeping on the shoulders of one of the women, telling his troubles, and she understands him very well because she's in the same office working with him all day long. Well, I head that situation off by *never* letting them weep on my shoulder. If somebody comes into my office and starts singing the blues, I walk out. I have no interest in company gossip to begin with. I turn those cry-babies off like turning a switch! One night I went to an office party and a specialist trapped me in a corner and began telling me how terrible his life was, how nobody understood him, and how he loved talking to me because I had such a sympathetic ear. When I extricated myself I said, "Excuse me, I'm going to the ladies' room," and I grabbed my coat and went down in the elevator. He doesn't speak to me any more, but that's no loss.

So many of these specialists and supervisors are little boys in grownups' clothing, scared to death about the big leagues around them. You'd be surprised; some of the highest-ranking people in The Company are just little boys. One day an assistant manager took six or eight of us girls to lunch and started telling us who he didn't like in The Company. Right out! Unleashing his little-boy emotions in front of everybody! Didn't he know that these enemies of his were sure to find out that he'd been talking about them in public? How juvenile! This was the same boss who used to invite the more childish assistants and specialists to his apartment for marijuana parties. A fat old man, staging pot parties! He had another cute little habit that has destroyed a few people. He would pick out a favorite, usually female, and elevate her far beyond her talent. She'd wake up one morning and find herself in a supervisory position that she couldn't handle. And then the great man would lose interest in her and she'd start drinking or running around and eventually come to a bad end. I guess it gave him a feeling of power.

At first I respected a supervisor named Fred Storns because he seemed a lot like me. He kept his private life out of his business life, and he worked something awful. Night after night when I'd be working late I would see Storns's light on down the hall. I asked a few of the girls about him, and one of them told me, "He's one to watch out for. He's very powerful; everybody's afraid of him. He's mean. He makes no small talk. It's all work with him. Now you be careful of him!" Strangely enough, I found this a good recommendation for Mr. Storns. Goodness knows we had enough playboys around the office; it was a pleasure to know that we had at least one supervisor who didn't engage in small talk or play around.

But then I got to know the real Fred Storns. I was assigned to help him on a project. He called me in and outlined my duties and told me the project was very important, and when I started to leave he said, "Oh, by the way, Miss Grant, there's one more thing." I turned around and faced this steely glint in his eyes. "If you make a mistake on this project, you're gonna hang!"

By this time the dark clouds had begun to roll away from me and I was feeling more secure. My six-month probationary period was over, and I had learned my trade. So I said simply, "If I make a mistake on this project, Mr. Storns, you're gonna hang *with* me!" and I walked out. Since then I've gotten along fine with him, although I don't like him one bit. It's fine to be all business, but there's nothing wrong with a little courtesy and mutual respect at the same time. Storns has never learned that.

· 3 ·

OVER THE last seven years I've learned that there are two kinds of workers at The Company: those who work too hard and those who don't work at all. There doesn't seem to be any in between. I've always done more than my share, and I'll continue to. I happen to enjoy the job of assistant at The Company, and it doesn't even seem like work to me. It's challenging and interesting, and every day I thank my stars that I passed through my trial and became one of the more respected assistants. I've reached the point where I do my own assigning; I don't have to go in on my hands and knees to somebody like Storns and beg for some project that I'm interested in. I look at the project list, and I pick what I want, within reason, of course. When the other girls are working on three or four projects each, I'll be working on six or eight. Right now I'm working on nine, and there's not another person in the whole company who could tell you exactly what all nine are. So to that extent, I've become my own boss. I love it this way. I feel wanted and needed. I get a good salary and I have wonderful working conditions, and I work hard so that I'll continue to deserve them. And there's not a single thing to keep the other girls from having the same kind of rewarding lives—except themselves. They blame The Company, when the real fault's within their own silly heads. Then they go to Women's Lib meetings and union meetings and blast The Company.

In my opinion, the Women's Lib and the union people are the laziest louts in the place! Most of them are *proudly* lazy; they run around bragging about what they get away with. I know some who actually fill their handbags once or twice a week with supplies from the stockroom! They regard this as a right!

I laughed at the Women's Lib thing when it started. I do what I like and I handle my own problems; I don't need to go out and burn my bra. If I want something, I go after it, and I usually get it. I don't want very much, it's true—I don't give a damn about money or status. In fact, I'm against money. I'm also against the union. They say I must be a member; they say it's to my advantage because I'm underpaid and exploited. Well, I'm twenty-eight years old and I live alone and I work forty hours a week for twelve thousand dollars a year and I come to work pretty much when I please and go home when I please and take three or four weeks' vacation a year. Does that sound like I'm underpaid and exploited? All this emphasis on money is ridiculous. I don't even know how much I make a week, and I don't care. I have enough to get by, and that's plenty. I work a lot of overtime, but I never put in for it. I don't need the extra money. The union girls say I'm crazy for not taking my overtime, that I'm not getting my fair share. But I don't *care* about my fair share. I just care about living happily, and I *do* live happily. In a happy, full, exciting life, there's no time for scrounging around for the last thin dime. If you're doing that, you're not living happily, no matter how many dimes you bring in! I lose money on my income-tax return every year, but it's worth it to me not to have to do all that penny-pinching, trying to figure out every single deduction. I can use the time to better advantage.

I'm against the union and I've always been against it. It's just a way of spreading the money around where it doesn't belong. The union sent out a notice that we gained psychiatric insurance in our last contract, and now we're going after dental insurance. That burned me! I don't think that The Company—and that means me and the other employees indirectly—should have to pay for any-body's dental bills.

I went around to Peg Kern—she's one of the shop stewards—and I said, "What's this business about asking for dental insurance? I've got perfect teeth! Four cavities in twenty-eight years! What do I want with dental insurance?"

She said, "Well, others need it."

"Why?" I said.

"Because it's a big amount of money," she said. "Last year my dental bills were four hundred dollars."

"Well, that's *your* problem," I said. "It must be some stupid idiot that made this demand for dental insurance."

She said, "I *beg* your pardon. You're insulting me."

"Why?"

"I'm the stupid idiot that brought it up."

"Well, why should *your* dental bills be *my* problem?" I asked.

"They're not *your* problem," she said. "They're *everybody's* problem. We're going to demand dental insurance, and we're going to get it."

"Well, lots of luck," I said. "Please accept my resignation from the union."

Really, I get so impatient when I deal with girls like Peg. And she's a long way from being the worst. At least, she *works*. Some of the others spend their time bitching and griping and never raising a finger in honest labor, and if you ask them about it, they'll be only too happy to sit down and assault your ear on how The Company has ruined their lives. That is the worst lie of all, and if I were the chairman of the board I'd come down here with a huge broom and sweep out about five hundred of those liars.

Their favorite theory is that The Company exists to exploit them and abuse them and even, in a symbolic sense, rape them, simply because they're poor, frail creatures of the opposite sex. Well, I can't go along with any of this fancy theorizing. Of course, I've never worked any place else; all I have to compare The Company with is the Indian tribe I worked with a long time ago. But I *do* have eyes, and I *do* talk to people from other companies, and I have to say that the girls in our company are the luckiest girls in New York City and maybe the luckiest in the country. They don't know when they're well off. I've even heard some of them complain about the easy working hours. Well, The Company won't fire you if you come in at eleven and leave at five and take three hours for lunch, but so what? That doesn't mean you *have* to come in at eleven and leave at five. The Company very seldom fires people. Is that bad? I like to think it's because of a certain corporate compassion that's fine and decent and honorable. The Company is very indulgent with people who don't produce, or people who get sick, mentally or physically, but how in the name of common sense can these girls count that as a minus against The Company? They're like ten-year-old kids who wet their pants and then run in and say, "It's Mommy's fault! She *lets* me do it."

The biggest lie is that old one about The Company being set up to catch young girls and make them available for older men. What rubbish! Whoever dreamed up that idea ought to be writing for *Mad*. The only young girls that wind up in any kind of trap are young girls who walked in with their eyes wide open. They got exactly what they wanted—and what they deserved. I've grown sick and tired of hearing girls like Peg Kern and Phyllis Brown and Samantha Havercroft blaming all their troubles on The Company. The Company wasn't up in their apartments throwing them into bed with married men. The Company wasn't force-feeding them all that liquor that they drink. The Company hasn't made it mandatory for everybody to take three-hour lunches and come back falling-down drunk. Sure, they give parties at The Company, but nobody's ever been dragooned into going to one. I've been with The Company almost seven years and I've been to exactly three parties. You're not forced to go, and it's not held against you if you don't. That's just an excuse some of the girls use. They say they didn't want to go to the party, but they felt they had to, and they didn't want to have all those drinks with their supervisor, but they felt they had to, and they didn't want to wind up in bed with him and threaten to break up his marriage. It all just sort of happened; it can't be their fault; it must be The Company's. What a joke!

Nobody can deny that The Company gives you the freedom to destroy yourself, but it also gives you the freedom to have a very enjoyable, creative business life, to add dimensions to your life. Take away the one and you take away the other. Instead of beefing all the time about what The Company does *to* them, these girls should be thankful for the salaries they get, for the freedoms they enjoy, for the opportunities The Company gives them, for the dignified way they're treated. They should be on their knees! If I had my way, most of them would be on her way to a certain Indian tribe south of the border.

The other big legend that I hear circulated around the halls until

it bores me stiff is the legend that there are no single men in New
York, and therefore the poor girls have to have affairs with married
men. That's as much baloney as the idea that The Company is mean
to them. How would you classify me, ugly, ordinary, or pretty?
Something between ordinary and pretty, right? Certainly I'm no
beauty queen, and yet I've never lacked single dates in New York
for a second. In my early days at The Company I was going out
with seven different single men seven nights a week. And not one
of them knew who the others were! It was a gay, wonderful time,
so happy and so simple a life! I could enjoy it to the fullest for one
reason—I wasn't looking for a husband. All I was looking for was
interesting men, interesting evenings. I found lots of them—and
lots more found me. One night I'd go out with an advertising man,
and the next night with a jazzman, and the next with a banker or a
lawyer. The ad man would take me to Charley Brown's and I'd hear
all that silly ad-man talk about running ideas up on the flagpole and
seeing if anybody salutes. The jazzman would take me to the Village Vanguard or to hear Bobby Short or to Slug's, all these funny
places, and keep me on the edge of my seat learning about jazz.
Each one of these men had something to teach me, something interesting and unique that was his alone.

Did I say there were never any problems? Why, of *course* there
were problems, but you can't expect to go out with seven or eight
men and not have an occasional problem. The main problem was
with the egos of some of the men. New York men tend to be a little
weak on the ego side, and you have to be constantly aware of it.
They don't seem quite sure that they're men, and they seek reas-
surance. Some of them become so repulsive about it, you don't
want to reassure them, you just want to send them home. I'll give
you an example.

At a party a young businessman talked to me for an hour or so,
and then we were both interrupted by another young businessman
who seemed especially pushy about getting in our conversation.
The first man soon left, and the second man said, "He's my main
competitor in business."

"Oh?" I said.

"We're at each other's throats all the time," he said.

He seemed immensely interested in me, and as we talked he seemed reasonably interesting, and I agreed to go to dinner with him. He took me to Lüchow's, and in the course of explaining something to me he began writing on the tablecloth with a pen. I had never seen that in my whole life; I was shocked! I said quietly, "Please don't write on the tablecloth!"

He said, "All businessmen write on tablecloths."

I said, "Well, I've never seen it before. Please don't! It's very hard to clean ink out of a tablecloth, and somebody will have to do it."

"You're acting silly," he said.

I insisted. I said, "I don't think there's anything silly about it. I think it's cruel to make somebody else have to work unnecessarily."

He said, in a slightly louder voice, "Well, just don't you worry about it. They get paid well for cleaning tablecloths! They're probably glad I do it."

I sensed an extra note of aggravation in his voice, so I shut up, but he kept on, getting louder and louder. Soon he was half out of his seat, shaking his finger at me and telling me off so loudly that everyone was watching. "Don't make a scene!" he said, and then he kept on making a scene. I couldn't understand! What had I done? Every time I opened my mouth to defend myself, he shouted me down. After a while it began to seem like a ritual killing, that he was symbolically trying to kill me right there in Lüchow's, in front of everybody. So I said to myself, "Don't even talk!" And I kept quiet till he calmed down.

As we walked out after a lovely dinner, he made a great show of throwing a scrap of paper on the floor. I had to keep quiet, but I felt like saying, "Now why drop that paper on the floor? Somebody will have to lean over and pick it up." But I kept quiet. He would have said, "That's what they're paid to do."

The next time he called I turned him down. I had figured it all out in my own childish way. I realized that he was a complete materialist, that his original attraction to me was because one of his competitors had been talking to me. He was the kind of person who would almost kill to rise in his materialistic world. He moved in on the competitor so he could show me off and rub me in the man's face. At the restaurant he was writing on the tablecloth and dropping paper on the floor to assert his doubtful masculinity. He was the big, powerful businessman, and the lackeys around Lü-chow's could clean up after him. And of course when I objected to this sick show of masculinity, I was castrating him. That's what made him so unreasonably angry.

A few weeks after I refused to go out with him he showed up slightly drunk at my apartment. Right away I realized that he was there to prove that he was a man, and I knew right away that it was a case of conquer or death for me. So when he started making advances I said "good night!" very loud, and he said, "Don't say it so loud, you'll arouse the neighbors." I said "*good night!*" again, but he refused to leave. I said, "Okay," and I walked outside and left the apartment. I went down to the bottom landing and waited in a dark corner. When he passed me I couldn't resist saying, "Good night!" He just kept on going. That was one of my earliest adventures with American men, and it taught me a lot. Later I went with a foreign-born man with an equally fragile sense of his own masculinity. His own personality was shattered and incomplete and therefore he had an extra emotional investment in his car, a solid black Porsche 911S. It was his life. I was with him one night when an old lady backed into him and put a dent in the side of the car, and he almost went crazy! It was as if a part of his own *persona* had been rent. He cried out in pain! I comforted him, but I never went out with him again.

You just can't let yourself get involved mothering men like that. Mothering is just what they want. I don't mother men any more. I got over that in high school with Don Mahoney. Nowadays I don't have time to help little boys grow up or find their masculinity. When one of them starts bossing me around and acting like King Kong, I just haul off and say, "Whoa, there! If you're looking for somebody to push around, you've got yourself the wrong girl!" And if they start telling me their troubles, I do the same thing. I have great sympathy for some of the men in New York, but I don't like the sort of relationship that grows out of letting men cry on your shoulder. It takes away their masculinity, and then they're forever trying to get it back—at your expense. They have to prove and re-prove it every day. That's sick, but it's also very common.

Another trouble with New York men is that they make the perfectly normal enjoyable act of sex carry such a heavy load. They use sex to get back at their mothers and fathers and to shake off the frustrations and annoyances of their lives, and to prove to themselves that they're real he-men, that they're really *somebody*, and to show how much power they have, how much humiliation they can heap on a girl in bed. They use sex for everything except what it really is: the ultimate in normal, happy communication between a man and a woman. How sad!

To me, sex is a very simple, sweet thing. It's a part of life, and one of the big problems with sex is that it was ever given a name: s-e-x. It should just have been called "life" or "part of life." Sex is just another way of getting to know a person. It should be a very normal thing, like with the Polynesians. When they feel it, they do it. When a woman gets to know and like a man, sex should be a part of their relationship. It's another way to know him, another way to express yourself, and he himself. The more you can give of yourselves to each other, the better.

Thank goodness I have one semisteady boy friend who doesn't have this New York attitude about making sex perform so many different jobs. Sometimes we have a very active sexual life together, and sometimes we can go a month without it, if that happens to be the way we feel. With him, sex is a reaching out, a joining together. It's not a gimmick to prove that he's a man, to prove that he can run around thrilling women and thrilling himself with his big masculine organs. He knows he's a man, and even if he goes out into the business world and gets kicked in the teeth all day long by vicious bosses and stupid clients and all the other cruelties of the big city, he still knows at the end of the day that he's a man. He doesn't have to knock *me* down to prove it.

I call him a *semi*steady boy friend because we've agreed that for personal reasons he and I can't get married and therefore I should have a normal dating life. By normal I mean dating eligible and interesting single men. Where do I find them? All over! You have to beat them off with a club. You can't help finding single men, if you don't panic, if you relax and take it easy, and if you don't go searching around for a husband like a lioness on a hot scent. New York men can smell out a husband-hunter from a mile away. They hate aggressive women and they hate women on the make. If you just stay cool, they will come on the run.

So many girls have said to me that it's hard to meet single men in New York City. One of my friends left New York and went to Miami for exactly that reason. She *swore* she couldn't meet single men here. Well, she was one of the panicky type. On her second date she'd start measuring the man for a bathrobe and slippers, and on her third date she'd find herself stood up. She hadn't learned the essential trick, which is to remain a little aloof, keep your dignity and *relax*.

When I go to New York parties I can walk off with almost any single man I want. To begin with, I dress a little more casually than most of the other women. I wear less makeup, and I try to look more nonchalant about my attire. The other girls are standing around dressed to kill, and they look ridiculous. They overkill, and the guys are off in the corner laughing at them. They gravitate to me because I at least look like a human being. I also try to remember that men are shy, a good deal shier than most girls think. So at parties I go around and talk to every man who's my height or over. That way I find dozens of single men that are dying to meet single girls, but they're just too shy to make the overtures. Some of them are wonderful men, wonderful human beings, sitting around with their knees shaking. So I go around and start talking to them to see if anything clicks.

Another way to meet single men—and men with class—is to go to the concerts in New York. I have met some of the most fascinating single men at concerts! They just follow me right out the door! One night I went to hear Horowitz with a girl friend of mine, and during one of the intermissions a man walked up to us and said, "I've been watching you girls all evening, and I've just come to New York and I'm a lawyer and I want to get to know somebody and could I have your addresses?"

I said, "How do we know you're not a murderer?"

He said, "Honest, I'm not. Look at me. Do I look like a murderer?"

Honest, he didn't. He was just a lonely lawyer who wanted to meet some girls. I gave him my first name and my telephone number and he called the next night. Now here's what I mean by relaxing, by not panicking. Did I rush right out on a date with him? Not on your life. I did it at *my* speed.

"I can't go out with you," I said. "I really don't know who you are. You might be a pervert."

"Oh, come on," he said.

"And another thing," I said. "I don't like to meet people at concerts. It's too much like a pick-up."

He argued and tried to twist my arm, but I wouldn't give in. At last I said, "I'll tell you what. You call me in six months and maybe I'll change my mind."

Well, that's exactly what happened. He called me in six months and I went out with him and had a perfectly lovely time. And he was *fascinated* by me. He told me later he'd never had a woman twist him around her finger like that, and he asked me to marry him. I hadn't twisted him around to be cruel or to play games. I did it because New York men *must* be handled like that. The woods are full of women who fall all over them. You've got to stand up and be yourself if you want them to notice you.

It's a shame—there are so many attractive women wandering around this city helplessly, desperately, looking for single men. They're told they're not supposed to meet people in bars. They're told they're not supposed to meet people on the subway or at concerts. That's foolish! In the game of dating there are no rules. The old rules about being properly introduced and all that nonsense have been passé in New York City for three decades, ever since World War Two. You live by your own wits; you meet people any way you can, you make up your own rules—and nobody censures you. That's why I love New York, because you *can* make up your own rules. What on earth is wrong with giving a lawyer your home phone number and dating him later? My grandmother would collapse if she knew I'd done that, but it isn't my grandmother who's trying to get by in the big city, it's me, and I've got to do things my own way, at my own speed.

· 4 ·

BUT PEOPLE say, "How can you stand New York? It's so *dangerous!*" Well, it is, and it's getting more dangerous every day. When I lived on the East Side, our whole building just seemed to go downhill overnight. One day it was a decent place to live, except for the Nazis screaming their heads off down the block, and the next day it was Murder Incorporated. I always dated the beginning of the trouble from the time our superintendent left, and the owner put a sign in the window: "Super Wanted." That told the thieves that the building was a soft touch, and things began to happen. A girl was attacked right outside my door, but we all ran out and the man took off. She had made the foolish mistake of opening the front door while a strange man was standing there, and of course he followed her right in and up the stairs. When she got to the cul-de-sac at the top, he started in on her. She said later that she hadn't said anything to him when he followed her "because I didn't want to be rude." So she almost got raped instead.

A few days later the girl next door to me woke up at three A.M. and saw a foot coming through her window from the fire escape. She jumped up and shouted, "Don't you come in or I'll call the cops!" As she stood there watching, the foot slowly withdrew back to the fire escape, a rope came inching down from the roof, and the man climbed up and got away.

Two weeks after that I woke up at two A.M. to a strange sensation that somebody was looking at me. It was midsummer and I was sleeping naked and my two windows were wide open. I looked out toward the fire escape and saw a red flashlight poking around out there. Then the beam came in the window and focused on me. I slid out of my bed on the far side and cringed behind it, and the flashlight went out. I crawled on my stomach to the telephone and told the police, "There's a man on my fire escape!"

The cop sounded annoyed. "Lady, do you want me to come for *that?*" he said.

"Yes," I said. "I certainly do!"

After a while two cops showed up and started telling me that I was a nervous hysteric, that I ought to get a roommate. They laughed at me. Literally! When they left, one of them said, "Don't worry, lady, you didn't see no red flashlight. You just had a nightmare. Lay off them pickles at bedtime!"

A few days later I talked to one of my neighbors, and she'd seen the same red flashlight on the same night. We tenants pieced together all the information we had, and we came to the conclusion that we were up against a rooftop crime syndicate, a gang of thieves working together on the roofs. Such syndicates are common in New York City, but our neighborhood was supposed to be a safe, family neighborhood, and there weren't supposed to be any rooftop societies here.

The knowledge that there was a whole group preying on us made me nervous, and I called the precinct station and asked for some advice. "Listen," I said, "I'm a girl living alone and I want to know how to protect myself. Somebody said I should get an ammonia gun, but that blinds a man. I want something that's safe."

The cop hemmed and hawed around. "Well, lady," he said, "I really don't know what you can get."

"Isn't there some kind of gas gun?"

"I don't know, lady. Most of them things are illegal."

"Yes, I know."

"Maybe you could carry a hatpin."

The conversation went on for three or four minutes, but the policeman didn't have any new ideas and it was plain that he wanted to get off the phone and back to his card game. Finally he said, "Well, lady, what can I tell you?"

"Apparently nothing," I said, and I hung up.

Just about that time our landlord talked a detective into looking around on the rooftop, and he found definite indications of a crime syndicate up there. Among other things, there were X's chalked on the frames on certain windows. The detective said this evidently marked the places that were easy to enter. He also found cigarette butts and footprints where the robbers had waited for lights to go off. As if we needed any further proof, a lady in a downstairs apartment was knitting in front of her fireplace when suddenly there were four or five explosions right in her room. It turned out that somebody had chased a robber across the roof of our building, and the robber had flipped his pistol down the chimney and into her fire.

Pretty soon I came to the realization that there was *no* police protection on the upper East Side. I realized that you could no longer depend on the New York police except maybe to get cats out of trees, or to get somebody to lower his radio. They'll go to a little effort on a murder case, at least if there's any publicity in it, but in between the cat in the tree and the horrible murder, police protection in this part of New York City doesn't exist.

When I came to this realization, I decided to move to another part of town. I had a friend who lived on the West Side—near the locale of *West Side Story*. The neighborhood had a reputation for being dangerous, but my friend carefully explained to me that it was far safer than the East Side. "Statistically," she said, "most of the murders occur on the West Side and most of the robberies on the East Side. But eighty-five percent of the murders are family murders, and you don't have any family here. But you do have things that people can rob. So logically you're much safer over here, even though this seems to be more dangerous." I agreed with her reasoning, and I soon found a lovely studio apartment way over by the Hudson River in a neighborhood that would scare most people to death. It took me a while to adjust, but I'm completely adjusted now. I installed a special lock. I put grates over both my windows; they're in a Dutch-grille pattern and they look pretty while they're protecting me. With my apartment secure, I learned how to secure my person. I often work late, and it's scary going home to a depressed neighborhood at two in the morning. The first thing I did was tell each cab driver, "Look, I'll give you an extra dollar if you'll walk up the stairs with me and watch me go through my front door." Most of them would say, "Aw, that's okay, lady. I'll do it for free," and I'd say, "Now, listen, this is a business deal!"

To protect myself on the street, I bought a pepper spray—I still don't know whether it's legal or illegal, and I don't care—and I carry it right in my hand whenever I'm walking in the neighborhood. Sometimes people stop me and ask me where they can get one. I got mine at a drugstore in New Jersey.

I enrolled in a course in karate, thinking that I'd become so powerful that I could repulse full-grown men with a flick of my fingers, but I soon learned that karate didn't work that way at all. I'm convinced that a full-grown man is a match for any woman, no matter how many black or purple or pink belts she has. Besides, I found out that most of my fellow karate students were the exact people I wanted to learn to defend myself against—blacks and Puerto Ricans—and after I got to know them in my karate course I began to lose my fear of them, and therefore I lost my motivation for taking the course in the first place. So I dropped out after reaching the first level of accomplishment. It was good exercise.

I've found that the best defense against muggers and people who attack on the street is simply to walk fast and purposefully and try not to look sexy at all. When I walk, I go at top speed with my chin jutting out and my feet flying almost at a jog. Some of my friends get goosed on the streets now and then, but nobody can get close enough to me to do that. Fast walking turns them off right away. Number one, you look crazy. Nobody in New York walks that fast. Number two, if you're walking fast a mugger practically has to run to catch you, and this makes him too conspicuous; he'd rather wait for the next customer.

Also, I don't wear skimpy miniskirts on the street, and I don't go wiggling down the streets like a chorus girl. I know a girl on the East Side who's been attacked on the street four times, once during the height of the rush hour. I laugh at her. She wears super-short skirts and hot pants, and from the rear she looks like a sack of cats going to the river. Subconsciously she's *trying* to be attacked, and she's gotten her way often. As for me, I have never had the slightest encounter on the streets, and until some of the Olympic sprint champions turn to crime, I probably never will.

The only thing that worries me now is that I've become familiar with my neighborhood and I've lost my fear of it. Once the fear of the unknown is gone, you drop your guard, and I may be making that mistake. You can't drop your guard in New York City; you'll wind up on a slab in the morgue. Every once in a while I'll pick up the newspaper and see where somebody was stabbed to death within a few blocks of my apartment, and that straightens me out for a while. But it's hard to keep your guard up permanently. You have to keep yourself in a constant state of paranoia. They used to consider paranoia a dread mental illness, but it's become normal in New York. You have to have it to survive. Listen! Hear those shots? That's normal for this neighborhood. One, two, three, four, five. Six shots! He's emptied his revolver, and there's probably one less man around here now. Slaughter on Tenth Avenue. That's little old New York for you! Never a dull moment!

It's funny how so many sweet and innocent girls accommodate themselves to this jungle and even learn to like it. When I saw the subways for the first time, all I could think of was the cattle cars that took the Jews to the ovens in Germany. I swore I'd never ride one! But now I ride them often. I *have* to. People think I'm crazy when I put my fingers in my ears as the train's coming in. I don't care how many are watching and giggling at me. When that terrible sound of metal on metal comes out of the blackness, squeaking and grinding and caterwauling at me, I *have* to cover my ears. Anyone who can stand that sound has already lost a lot of his hearing, or his sensitivity, and you can't give away that much sensitivity and still be the same person.

There are times when I think that we actually are bringing up a different race of people here in New York, people that are at home with things that would kill anybody else. I know from my own experience that the kids are much different here. There's very little

of that childish innocence and sweetness that you encounter elsewhere, even among the rich children. They learn too much too
young. One day I overheard some kids on the landing of my building. One was saying, "Now you be the mugger and I'll be the detective," and another time "You be the abortionist and I'll be the
lady." They were making games and casual play out of things that I
didn't find out about till college! Ten-year-old girls! And they routinely use language that I won't use to this day. These kids lose the
delight of growing up. They're little adults at ten. Gnomes! I often
wonder what kind of adults they'll make.

Well, the nice thing is I can retreat into my lovely studio apartment and get away from it all and order my own life in my own
way. I've learned to be like the Japanese. There's no place in the
world uglier than Tokyo, but inside the doors of those crowded
houses there are lovely little worlds of flowers and pebbles and
even trees. I can see a tree through my back window. I think it's a
mimosa; it has lacy leaves and pretty pink flowers. I have a tiny
terrace of my own, and I'm going to start a grapevine on it and
maybe grow some Chateau Stephanie 1971! I have a deep feeling
about living in this place. People complain about New York, but I
say, "I don't live in that New York you're describing. I live *in my
apartment*." This is my world. Look over there in the corner. Look
closer. See it? That's a spider so small that he and his whole web
don't cover a half-inch area. I don't even know how he makes a
living, but he's survived there for two months that I know of.

To me, that spider is life, and I adore life in all forms. That
spider is my treasure, my pet. Why, he's just a pinpoint, but I
enjoy him! I remember an article by an Englishman in which he
wrote that Americans could never understand why he had no
screens on his windows and doors; all the bugs were getting in.
Well, I can understand why. I wouldn't think of having screens on
my own windows. Grilles, yes, to keep out the robbers, but no
screens to keep out the insect life. When something new flies in, I
get all excited, because it's life! I love all living things, with two
exceptions: mosquitoes and cockroaches. They can take care of
themselves; they don't need my sponsorship. When I was in the

poverty program I had enough of mosquitoes and cockroaches to last the rest of my life. But the others are beautiful. Once when I was taking a bath I saw a speck lowering itself from my skylight and it was a wonderful jumping spider. For a long time he was my favorite. When I was little I used to have a jumping spider, until my pet lizard ate him, and now here he was reincarnated in my apartment in New York! I put him in my hand and he jumped off, and I put him in a glass and installed him in one of my corners. But it must not have been pleasant because he took off. Let's hope my new spider stays longer.

I've watched my friends moving into bigger and bigger apartments, but I wouldn't mind staying where I am for the rest of my life. I don't see the point of sheer size. I pay a hundred and fifty dollars and I have everything a girl could ask for. Some of my friends pay up to six hundred dollars and still they're miserable. They seem to get no pleasure out of their apartments. It's all one big grinding chore. There's no charm.

My place is *all* charm, and I love working in it. I do things slowly, to make them last. It took me six months to get new curtains. I paint and repaint all the time, and I savor each step. It's pure pleasure; I can't understand people who think that painting their apartment is a chore. I install driftwood in corners, and I experiment with lampshades and the patterns and colors they cast. I arrange flowers and pebbles on my tables and change them frequently. I cook gourmet meals for myself and feed myself on a creamy white tablecloth with a silver service. Long ago I decided that I didn't want to disintegrate into an animal who came home each night and opened cans for dinner. Never! There's nothing that thrills me more than making a perfect soufflé for myself, and if it falls, who's to know?

I love walking into my apartment and locking the locks behind me and settling down in my own beautiful fortress. I've always loved being left alone, and in New York you can make your own life and your own rules. You don't have to know your neighbors; no Welcome Wagon will ever call on you. It's the perfect place for somebody like me.

So I make no grandiose plans. I used to wonder where I'd be in two years, but now I live strictly for the present. I don't think about the future at all. That's what starts anxieties: looking for security, looking for a husband. I hope to be married by forty, and I hope to have children, but I'm not going to get married just to get married. I'm enjoying myself too much alone!

For a while when I first turned twenty-eight I worried about the future, but then I said to myself, "Well, marriage isn't all of life. I can still live very happily and very well alone. And that will be just as true when I'm thirty-nine and not married." If I back off and view myself dispassionately, I have to say that I think I'm probably ready for marriage now. It's taken me till the age of twenty-eight to grow up for marriage. I've stopped the mad round of dating seven nights a week, and I seek fuller and deeper relationships now, try to get to know people better, and I may wind up marrying one of them. It doesn't bother me that it's taken so long. I won't panic. Right now there are three different men I could marry if I wanted to. One of them is a millionaire playboy, but he's entirely too lazy and too purposeless to suit me. When he left for a two-week holiday in Bermuda, I said to him, "Well, have a nice time pursuing your vocation!" He's a nice person, but I have a contempt for that kind of life. The second is a physicist who insists that Einstein's theory of relativity is wrong and he'll be the one to prove it. He's a charming person. The third is a fine gentleman, handsome, beautiful, impeccably dressed. But I find it hard to develop any feelings for him because he's like a chameleon; he changes his accent and his personality to fit where he is. When he came back from three weeks in England, he said to me, "It's a jolly good day, isn't it, luv?"

Maybe I'll make a choice from one of those three, but I doubt it. My overriding aim, far more important than marriage, is to keep my life simple. I love my apartment. I love my job. I love my love affair with dirty old New York City. I love people, but I've learned to live very happily by myself. If I go out three or four nights in a row, I begin to get desperate to have a couple of nights to myself, in my apartment, living a *simple* life. Maybe this is because I never had a friend as a child.

Peg Kern once told a friend of mine, "You'll never get close to Stephanie. Nobody ever gets close to her." It's true, and in a way I think that this is my strength. It saves me. The main thing I've learned is that life has its yin and yang, its sweet and its sour, and it's all part of the beauty of life. In my own life I look back on the bad and I realize it's part of a mosaic, and the whole mosaic is made more meaningful by the bad in it, the little discords in it, just as music is made more beautiful by an occasional false note.

That's how you have to approach New York. The good that's here is made more meaningful by the bad. I don't say that bad is good; I simply say it's a part of the whole, like the spider on my wall. It all fits together into life, and you can't have the yin without the yang. I accept both; I embrace both. I wouldn't take back a single line of my life, and I don't have a single complaint. There's nothing I would do differently. Sometimes I think I'm the happiest person in the world.

Jayne Gouldtharpe, 24

———•———

Jayne's a Freudian analysand and I find it hard to be friends with Freudian analysands. They work out life in their own terms. Like Jayne calls up when she wants something or she wants to go to the movies or she wants to meet one of my friends. She'll give me this big warm "Hello, Vanny! How are you?" and it's all on her own behalf. It has nothing to do with any friendly feelings toward me. And Jayne can be very pushy. She was pushy at a cocktail party last night. She kept asking me who she should talk to and what she should say. I don't see that sort of approach as useful. She kept asking me who was a celebrity, who was important, who was somebody? *I don't think Jayne really comes across truthfully or sincerely. I know a lot about her, but most of my knowledge came from mutual friends. Very little of it came from her. She pretends to be my close friend, but she doesn't tell me the truth about herself.*

I do know that she keeps busy sexually. She says she's only known a few men, but I know it's quite a bit more than a few. I happen to know some of them personally. One of them told me that she absolutely devoured him in bed. In fact, she scared him away. After they'd made it a couple of nights, he just stopped calling her. Her version of the story was that he was too selfish and she dropped *him. He was also my good friend at the time—but Jayne didn't know it—and he told me that she was amazing in bed, not fun amazing, but* scary *amazing, that she took off through the roof, like she was in another fucking world. She was like nobody he'd ever slept with before, and she nearly ate him alive. He said she really took over the whole act of sex. It confirms a theory that I've always had, that these mousy conservative-looking people are the real tigers underneath.*—Vanessa Van Durant

· I ·

IT's so exciting here! At a party I ran into my idol, my intellectual dreamboat—Philip Roth. Everybody was talking about *Portnoy's Complaint*, so I didn't feel I could discuss it with him—he'd be bored by the subject. So I decided I'd talk about the one book of his that really gripped me: *When She Was Good*. That book was ill received and sold poorly—it's only selling now because of *Portnoy's Complaint* and *Goodbye, Columbus*—but I identified completely with the female character. To me, she represented the paradox of American female life. She wanted to be a good feminine woman on the one hand, but on the other hand she wanted to be a ballbreaker, too.

I walked right up to him. I said, "Excuse me for imposing myself on your privacy. Excuse my bluntness, but I can't walk out of the room till I tell you how much I thought of *When She Was Good*. It was the best novel I've read in five or seven years."

He said, "Don't apologize for your bluntness." He was beaming. He said, "I *appreciate* your bluntness."

I said, "I identified with that character *so much*."

He thanked me, and he really seemed thrilled by my appreciation, and I was thrilled that he was thrilled, and I was so nervous that I completely missed my opportunity to get to know him as a person. It was overpowering, meeting Philip Roth in the flesh! My knees were knocking, I was stuttering, I lost all semblance of social poise, and that kept me from relating to him. The *ambiance* was perfect, but I didn't take advantage. He tried to make small talk with me, and I guess we talked for five or ten minutes, and then somebody else cut in and I left.

Now this is to show you what strange things can happen in New York. Not *two* hours later I was in the Doubleday bookstore on Fifth Avenue and who walks in but Philip Roth! I almost fell over. He recognized me and he said politely, "So! We meet again." I felt like giving him my phone number right away—I hear he's single and available—but I'm not very fast on the uptake and I missed my chance again. We chatted for a few minutes about *Portnoy's Complaint*. I said, "Believe it or not, and this is no lie, I'm reading the book for the second time, and it's just as hilarious as it was a year ago."

He said, "I'm glad you like it."

I said, "Like it? I *love* it! My favorite part is the last ten days when Alexander goes to Israel. I've been to Israel myself, and I could identify. I gave the book to my mother and father for their anniversary."

He looked aghast. He said, "To your mother and father?"

I said, "Sure, why not? We've always been a very broad-minded family, and literature is literature, right?"

We chatted on like that for maybe five or ten minutes. He told me he was teaching and I said, "You must be a *divine* teacher."

He said, "How did you find out?" and he laughed.

I said, "Anybody who writes a book like *Portnoy's Complaint* would *have* to be a divine teacher."

He said, "Well, the thing that I like the most about it is my students. They're very bright. They're so bright it's a pleasure to teach them."

After a while he excused himself courteously and for the second time in a single evening I'd missed out. He didn't even try to date me or anything. I think about it often. But then this is New York. I'll probably run into him again some time.

You never how who you're going to see in New York, and sometimes you'll walk right past somebody that's a big shot in the movies or TV or politics and then you spend the rest of the day trying to figure out who he was. Once I passed Barbra Streisand right on Seventh Avenue. At the time I had been playing her records morning, noon and night. I was really into her! She's fantastic. I dig her so much! And there she was walking along the street in this real businesslike style. I stopped and turned and watched her. Fantastic!

A couple of weeks ago I saw Ali MacGraw, and two years ago I saw William Scranton, and when I first came to New York I almost knocked Jackie Kennedy down with my bicycle in Central Park. That was an experience! I was with my friend, Mary Ellen, and we were cycling along early on a Sunday morning. Out of the corner of my eye I saw a woman in a car coat, and from the rear she looked just like Mrs. Kennedy. I stopped, and I said, "Mary Ellen! That's Jackie Kennedy!" The woman walked across a crosswalk and we came at her in the opposite direction, walking our bikes, and it *was* her. I got so excited I almost ran over her in the crosswalk. I actually brushed shoulders with her! I felt like I'd touched the queen of the United States. She has fantastic charisma and magnetism. Her features are out of place, like a Picasso painting, but she's still electric-looking. Running into her is an experience you'll never forget.

One day Melina Mercouri said hello to me! I was bouncing around the halls of Rockefeller Center and here came this fantastic-looking woman and I smiled at her, not realizing who she was. She smiled back, and she said, "Hello," and then she disappeared around a bend, laughing loudly. I thought for a few seconds and then I said to myself, "My God, that's Melina Mercouri!" and I went dashing around to see where she'd gone. But I couldn't find her. I'll never know what she was doing in Rockefeller Center, but she certainly did light up the place. That big robust laugh of hers, and that big toothpaste smile. She mesmerized me!

I'm not overly impressed by the celebrities in New York, but I do find them interesting. The only one that truly bowled me over was Truman Capote, but I chickened out with him, too, just like Philip Roth. I *really* wanted to talk to him. Both my parents are intellectuals, and I was brought up on Truman Capote tales instead of Bible tales. *The Grass Harp. Other Voices, Other Rooms.* My father used to say, "Truman Capote has absolutely nothing to say, but my God how beautifully he says it!" Of course that was before *In Cold Blood* and some of his later work. Now we all know that he has *plenty* to say.

Well, anyway, I went to a party and there was Jackie Kennedy's sister—what's her name?—Lee Radziwill, holding hands and practically necking with Truman Capote. I kept trying to get up the courage to say something, but they seemed so close and so fascinated with each other that I couldn't break in. Then she went off to talk to somebody else and he just stood there and I was the nearest person. I opened my mouth but nothing came out. I was tongue-tied! He seemed absolutely super-human to me. So I just turned away and talked to somebody else. My heart was beating real fast for a long time.

I suppose I should learn not to act like the tongue-tied fawning fan around people like him, but if you heard Truman Capote's name through practically every day of your childhood you'd be bound to get all nervous the first time you saw him standing right next to you. My mother said I should be used to celebrities after my childhood, but the celebrities I had known were of another order—artists, musicians, writers—and most of them were Midwesterners, regional celebrities. My mother and father were artists, commercial and otherwise, and very successful, and we had a busy salon at our home in Milwaukee. You never knew who might drop in—but *never* Truman Capote! Our family also had money—not on a level with the Whitneys and the Rockefellers, of course, but enough to place us firmly in the upper middle class. Socially, my family had looked toward the East for about five generations, but our roots were also deep in Milwaukee, and we found it convenient to stay there. Every Gouldtharpe on my father's side and every Brouilly on my mother's side had gone east to school, the men to Princeton, the women to Wellesley. Of course, I was supposed to carry on the tradition.

But my grades were a slight problem. I wasn't too highly motivated in private school, and I came out with only a fair average. Mother took me east to shop around for some kind of a junior college where I could prep for a year for Wellesley, and we stopped off at New York. I was captivated! I made a romance out of every dirty truck and every garbage can. It was all so visibly rich and interesting and exciting, and the vitality and energy almost knocked me down. Even the exterior of the city excited me. I saw these different shades of gray and black and white, almost like a big black-and-white photograph that had been lying in somebody's

attic accumulating a layer of dust for ten or twenty years. I imagined all the life that must be seething and crying out underneath
that gray surface, and the whole idea just exploded in my brain. I
was seventeen, and I had been to Europe three times, but I had
never seen anything so stimulating as this noisy city in its perpetual
motion.

So I went to school in Chicago! It was my mother's decision, and
I was stuck with it. The school was a crashing bore, and so was that
filthy, dangerous, windy city with its blocks and blocks of flat,
drab scenery and its crooked cops and its dirty politics. It depressed me horribly, and I did worse than ever in school. I flunked
courses that I had already passed in prep school! New York was on
my mind, and I finally decided to go there by one means or another.

I took the train up to Milwaukee for a heart-to-heart talk with
my parents. I cried and I cajoled. I told them that I was no longer
motivated toward higher education, that Chicago had killed it for
me, and that I just wanted to go out and get a job.

"As what?" my father said.

I hadn't thought of that. "I don't know," I said. "Anything but
school."

My father suggested that I enroll in secretarial school so that I
could pick up a few skills, and it worked out to be a good idea. I
went to school right in Milwaukee and after eight months I had
learned typing and shorthand and filing and office procedures. I had
no intention whatever of staying in Milwaukee—it seemed like a
miniature Chicago to me, and it had a shrinking population of
young people, and sometimes it seemed I would go weeks and
weeks without meeting anyone of my own age. So off I went to
New York!

My mother had given me the address of a classmate at Wellesley,
and I looked her up. It turned out that she was a big shot at The
Company, and she told me that by coincidence she needed a secretary in her department, and she sent me down to The Company for
typing and shorthand tests. I had heard a lot about The Company,
but I never dreamed that I would have a chance to work there. In

my eyes, The Company was the *ne plus ultra,* the living end, a super place to work. The *ambiance* was fantastic! Air conditioning and deep rugs and ladies' rooms that looked like the ladies' room at the Ritz in Paris, and all these chic, sophisticated people running around looking so busy and so productive. My head was swimming all through the tests, and I just knew I did awful! But when I turned in my last paper a messenger came up and whisked me to my mother's friend's office, just like that, and I was told that I was going to work for The Company at ninety-six dollars a week, starting the next day. I was amazed! I said, "Don't they want to grade my tests? Don't they want to see how I did on shorthand and typing? Doesn't anybody want to interview me?"

"No, my dear," Mother's classmate said. "You're just *perfect* for us."

I stayed impressed by The Company for a long time, but of course you can't stay totally impressed forever, although I still love The Company dearly. I'll say one thing: It's different from anything I'd ever seen in Milwaukee. The veneer is fantastic. On the surface, everybody is friendly and cooperative and charming. The Company tries to hire the most talented people in the world, and if it sometimes seems a little weird around here, you've got to realize you're working with the intelligentsia. The overriding impression that they gave me was that I was now part of a great source of energy, part of something grand and huge and meaningful, and so much bigger than I was. This in turn gave me great energy, and for my first year or two I gave that job every ounce of strength in me. I almost never went home before eight o'clock at night, and I ate lunch at my desk. Sometimes I was so busy I didn't have time to go to the john. But I felt extremely fulfilled, extremely rewarded. And I still do.

The only reason that I'm not working those ridiculously long hours any more is because I came to realization that there was more to life than the office, and I began dating and having a sex life for the first time in my life. During my first two years at The Company, I had hardly dated at all. When I did date, it was with strange, unappealing men, men with responsible positions with other companies, but dull! And I couldn't get interested in the men at the office. The married ones were often brilliant and fascinating, but they were off limits. The single ones were usually so married to their jobs that they were bores. They had no sex appeal for me. They talked all the time about their work, and they made a lot of loud noises, power-struggle grunts and groans, but they did very little real communicating. They didn't level with each other, and they certainly didn't level with me. For two years I found them that way, and the rest of the men in New York weren't any better. They all seemed terribly lower middle class. Maybe that's the snob in me.

I've been told that office people in New York engage in a lot of hanky-panky, but I must say I've seen very little of it myself. Of course, they're skilled at keeping it covered up. In my own department I worked closely with a couple of dozen men and women and never saw anything out of line. But on the other hand, three of the men have gotten divorces in my four years with The Company, and two of them married girls in the office, so something *must* have been going on! My only personal experience with office roués came at a party in the banquet room. I noticed that one of The Company's executives was standing in the corner alone, and I figured this was my chance to score some points. He said he remembered me from a telephone conversation, and he turned out to be quite charming. I mean, he was fifty-five years old and bald and slightly potbellied, but he talked interestingly, and he was a good dancer. We danced for two hours that night, and he kept telling me that I was delightful, I was fantastic, I was the most interesting woman he'd ever met, and so forth. I was naïve! I thought he meant it seriously. I was then twenty-one years old, and very much a virgin, and he seemed so sincere and honest, and a little shy and lost at the same time. But I did have enough sense to turn him down when he asked to take me home. "Well, how about a ride through the park?" he said. I said, "No, thank you," and I excused myself politely and took a cab home.

The very next day I saw him in the elevator, and he turned six shades of red! And it dawned on me for the first time that there had been sexual overtones the night before! That's how naïve I was. I'd thought it had been a pleasant, innocent evening; I'd never *dreamed* that he had designs on my body. But he must have, or why would he be so embarrassed in the elevator? That's how knowledge came to me—very slowly and painfully. I thought the whole thing over and I said to myself, "Well, there must be a lot going on around here, and I'll just keep myself out of it."

I had only one other fling with someone from the office, and it lasted for about an hour and a half. There was a very handsome, very young assistant who kept flirting with me, and I thought he was interesting in a juvenile sort of way and allowed him to take me to lunch. He spent the whole lunchtime knocking the other girls in the office! About the only nice thing he said about the girls in our department was that they all had great-looking legs. Which was true! Even the boss, fifty years old and overweight by twenty-five pounds, had a great pair of gams. But after he said that he began tearing them down. "That Alexandra Oats is a bitch!" he said. "Phyllis Brown is drinking herself to death. Samantha Havercroft is the easiest lay in town. Vanessa Van Durant is a nymphomaniac." I didn't enjoy this line of conversation at all. I wondered what he told the other girls about *me*. "Jayne Gouldtharpe has good-looking legs, but she's the dumbest broad in town." And I couldn't understand his preoccupation with all the defects of our women. I realized there was something funny about him, and I never went out with him again. It wasn't until a year or two later that I found out what was so funny about him. He was a queer, a closet queen. One of the girls saw him in a gay bar down in the Village, and he tried to pretend he had just dropped in.

One Monday morning after I'd been with The Company for about two years my desk telephone rang and a man's voice introduced himself as Scott Evans. "Are you in The Company?" I said. He burst out laughing.

"Don't you speak to anybody outside The Company?" he said. "I've heard about people like you."

He went on to tell me that a friend had suggested that he call me, that we seemed to be kindred spirits and he wondered if we might have lunch together. It seemed perfectly respectable to me, and that was the start of the most meaningful relationship of my life so far. Scott Evans was an extraordinary person, a cultured, intelligent, sophisticated person with a very keen mind. He was a businessman—typewriters—but he loved the world of the theater and the arts. I suppose you would call him a dilettante, but only in the best sense of that word. Within a month I had begun attending play openings, concerts, art-gallery openings, all the very best things in New York. He knew *everybody*, and they all seemed to like him and respect him. It was through him that I met the people who still sustain me—the social set that throws parties attended by people like Philip Roth and Truman Capote and—what's her name? —Lee Radziwill.

After that first month Scott and I went to bed together. It seemed like the most natural and healthy and normal thing to do. Every virgin should get started like that. I was so in love with him that it would have seemed abnormal *not* to go to bed together. But of course that was the beginning of the problem. I turned out to be a very sexually active person, and he turned out to have big hangups. Even while we were having wonderful times together socially we were having bad times in bed. Looking back, maybe the first night together was the only time the sex ever really worked. After that he just seemed too excited by me. But there was no chemistry on my part, and after a year or so I had to face up to the reality that I just didn't love him. He was wonderful to be with, the perfect companion, until the lights went out, and then everything was wrong. He was sort of impotent. I mean, he couldn't get it up, or, if he did get it up, it would go right down again. Sometimes the whole sex act was over in thirty seconds. I was simply not being gratified, not having orgasms, and the whole scene began to get very dreary. When you know that you're going to be left hanging, night after night, with *nothing* happening, it begins to get to you. You turn sour. Finally I told him I had to get away, and I flew to London for a week's vacation. There in London I put the thing into perspective, and I realized that the two of us would never work together, and the whole affair was headed no place. On the

way back from London I met a fabulous man named Tom Hardin
on the plane. We were seatmates for the whole six-hour flight in
first class, and by the time we landed in New York I was divinely
enamoured of him. I met him for lunch the very next day, and I
flirted outrageously with him, teased and enticed him. But Scott
and I were still going steady, and I turned down Tom's suggestion
that we meet that night.

This didn't keep Tom from calling three or four times a week,
and one night he caught me in a vulnerable mood. He said, "Come
on, let's go out together tomorrow night."

I said, "Okay, okay." I knew what was going to happen.

Well, Tom Hardin turned out to be the exact opposite of Scott
Evans. Scott was a wonderful person who was awful in bed. Tom
was a horrible person who was perfect in bed. We had identical
sexual styles, and we went at each other like cannibals on a desert
island. I had been conditioned for nearly two years to always being
disappointed, but from the very first date with Tom I was having
grand and glorious orgasms, oodles of them, multiple ones and
Technicolor ones and every conceivable kind of ones. That first
night together we made love till six in the morning, very compul-
sively. On our second date we went to bed about eight o'clock in
the evening, so we'd have plenty of time, and after the first orgasm
he turned to me and he said, "You're such a fabulous lay!" I
thought he was using dirty words—that's how naïve I was! I
propped myself up on my elbows, and I said haughtily, "What do
you mean by that?"

He said, "Relax! It just means you're good to make love to."

On our third date we made love for twenty-five straight hours!
We took a little time out for a nap and we ate a couple of English
muffins and cheese, but the rest of the time we were making love
non-stop. Twenty-five hours! I loved it! And he was back the next
night for more! We were young once. God! But we got tired, too.
Just exhausted. He would keep me in a constant state of excitation.
He would build the suspense in me. He would touch me, feel me,
and then kiss me, and the kiss would be more exciting than the
whole act of intercourse had been with Scott. He was the master of

anticipation, of suspense and nuance and tension and relaxation. It was so exciting!

But that was in bed. Outside of bed he was a sadist who had found a masochist—me. He was the most moody, bitter-tongued person I had ever seen. He worked in an insurance office on Madison Avenue, and he talked about his fellow employees as though they were Neanderthals. He would storm and rage around my apartment about them, and then take his annoyance out on me. After a few nights with him I would look forward so much to an evening with gentle, gracious Scott. And after a few nights with Scott I would look forward to an abandoned evening with brutal, sexy Tom. It went that way for a year. Scott kept applying the pressure for me to marry him, and Tom kept pleasing me in bed and making me miserable everyplace else. He did such strange things! One morning I made soft-boiled eggs, and they were perfect. I ate mine and I noticed that he left the yolks on his plate. I said, "Why are you leaving your yolks?"

He said, "Because of the cholesterol problem." Imagine! A cholesterol problem at twenty-seven! He *had* to be paranoid!

I said, "I can't stand seeing those beautiful golden yolks go to waste. Let me just scrape them off and eat them myself."

He said, "Please don't do that."

I said, "Just one more spoonful. To me those yolks are precious."

He got a crazy look on his face and he said, "I told you not to do that!" He grabbed my wrist and flung the spoon out of my hands against the wall, and he screamed, "I told you not to do that!" For five or ten minutes he was like a hysterical animal.

I said, "Tom, that's nothing to get so uptight about." But he kept on acting in this crazy, schizophrenic way. And I took it, because in those days I was terribly masochistic.

After we'd been seeing each other on the sly for six or eight months, we even began having a little trouble in bed, something that I'd never expected. The trouble was that he always had to have his way, in everything. One night I was asleep and I began playing with him without realizing it, and suddenly he was on top of me trying to make love! I said, "Oh, Tom, forget it! I'm so tired!" and he said, "Whether you like it or not I'm getting into you." A few nights later the situation was reversed; I wanted it and he didn't, and when I persisted, he threw me out of my own bed and told me to go sleep in the living room. Silly masochist me, I obeyed.

Sometimes we would have big fights, and he would stay away for a few weeks, and I would stop giving Scott excuses and go out with him. Scott never stopped applying the marriage pressure; he gave me ultimatum after ultimatum, and sometimes he would announce, "This is the end," and then he would stay away for two or three weeks, and I would get back with Tom. It was agonizing. But there were pleasant aspects, too. Scott gave me everything I wanted out of bed and Tom everything I wanted *in* bed, and if I could have kept it going that way I'd have been okay. But of course I couldn't. I began to feel that Tom was slipping away from me, that maybe he was even seeing somebody else. One night after we'd made love there was this tiny spotlight of moon coming through my window, and it fell right on his face, and I turned over and saw that he was looking at me with a hateful, vicious look, like an animal. I was shocked. I sat up and I said, "What in God's name do you have on your mind?"

He knew I had caught him revealing his true feelings. He turned and faced the wall and said, "Just leave me alone! Just don't touch me!"

I thought about it for a while, and then I said, "I think I've figured out your problem, Tom. You're really hostile about women, aren't you?"

I was surprised by the gentle resignation in his voice. "I don't really like anybody," he said. "*That's* the problem."

And then the whole thing blew up in a period of four days. Scott came up with umpteenth marriage ultimatum, and I turned him down for the umpteenth time. "Well," he said, "I can't go on this way. I can't live without you. I have suicidal thoughts. My work is suffering severely. I have to be with you on a permanent basis. You have to marry me."

"I'm not ready for it, Scott," I said.

"Is that final?"

"Absolutely final."

He got up and put on his coat. "If you won't marry me, Goldie," he said, "then we can never see each other again."

I was shattered. I had grown so dependent on Scott, and in my own way I loved him. I started to cry. "Why does it have to be that way?" I said.

He said, "Because I can't stand not having you all the time."

"Maybe things will change," I said.

"When they do," he said, "let me know," and he walked out. I cried all night. I called Tom, but he wasn't home, and I just walked the floor and sobbed and smoked three packs of cigarettes and didn't know what to do with my life.

Four awful, silent days went by, and then Tom came over for dinner. We were taking a shower together and he said, "You know, all we ever talk about is you. I have problems, too."

I said, "What are they?"

He said, "Well, one of them is you."

"What do you mean?"

"Well, I'm going to Italy tomorrow for a long visit, and my big problem is how to tell you that this is the last time we'll ever be together."

I was crushed. My whole life was built around two men, and now I was losing them both. "I can't accept that," I said. "You can go to Italy and still come back and see me."

"No, I can't," he said. "I can't, because I don't want to."

"Tom," I said, "you *have* to see me again. You *have* to feel *that* responsible."

He said, "Do me a favor, Goldie. Find a boy friend who's nice to you. Forget me. Don't worry about me. I have so many girl friends I don't know how to count them."

Two days later I asked for some time off and bought a plane ticket to Rome, just to be in the same city with him. But he wasn't registered at any of the major hotels, and I sat around the lobby of the Flora for a week, staring into space. I couldn't even walk the streets of my beloved Roma. A hotel doctor gave me some tranquilizers, the first I'd ever had, but they didn't help. I was in a state of paralysis. One morning I looked in the mirror and I found four gray hairs growing side by side on my temple. At twenty-three years old!

I hadn't been back in New York for two days when I saw Tom in a taxi. I checked around, and I found out that he'd been in town the whole time. I might have known! The story about Rome was a lie, but he was not lying when he said we were finished. He was a sadist dealing with a masochist, and the ultimate bit of sadism was to stand in my shower naked and tell me that we were through. Later I put it into perspective. I realized that Tom was the classic con man, the classic New Yorker. Con men can't have relationships that are too heavy; if they find themselves involved deeply, they show their fangs and run the other way. They're very spoiled men, and they get angry and uptight about genuine closeness, genuine love, and they dash off to some other chick. New York is full of this kind of man, because there are so many girls to fall at their feet and help them act out their aggressions. I *did* love Tom, I really did. I thought I would never find anybody else I could love so intensely. But he was always acting crazy, always getting underneath my skin. He was horrible, he really was. I had to go to Rome to get over him. I was heartsick. But in Rome I realized that I had loved him because of several negative things, because he was crazy and destructive and cruel and because he was so good in bed. No, I never loved him, it was just a sexual infatuation. I found that out a few months later when I saw him at a concert, and he saw me. He got up out of his seat as though he'd discovered a rattlesnake under there, and he ran out of Lincoln Center as fast as he could go pushing people aside in the process. And I thought, "My God, what a baby! He's terrified of me!" And I wondered how in the world I'd ever fallen in love with him.

· 2 ·

A MONTH after I got back from Rome I went with a horrible blind date to a jam session downtown. Times have changed; young people go to rock sessions and middle-aged people go to jazz sessions, and almost everybody here was over forty. Most of the men turned me off; I've never been partial to older men, or at least to men more than ten years older than me. After a while my date began to circulate—thank God!—and an ugly, hideous man came up to me and began chattering. He said, "I've been watching you for an hour and a half and I decided I had to come up and meet you." I looked at him and I thought, "What a nerve!" He was about five six, very thin and emaciated, bald-headed, with long, stringy gray hair in the back, as though to make up for the pate in front, and an ugly hooked nose and bad teeth. I thought, "Wow, what did I do to deserve this!" He looked about sixty years old, but later on I found out he was thirty-five. He face was wrinkled, his posture was atrocious, and his clothes were awful and tasteless.

He kept on talking to me in this deep, soft voice, and after a few minutes I realized I was paying close attention. He told me that he was a composer and arranger and that his name was Allan Magnesen and that he found my miniskirt too exciting for words. He said, "The best thing about that outfit is it shows your leg up to the thigh, and you have a fantastic body."

I was embarrassed, and I said, "Well, I'll never wear *this* dress again, if that's the effect it has."

He said, "Why? You've got a good body! Show it off!"

I can't explain this, but I began to turn on. This ugly, repulsive man was exciting me! I said to myself, "He may be ugly, but to me he's one of the handsomest men I've ever seen." And I'm usually so picky about men!

We talked about some of his experiences with girls and how he was getting tired of being psychoanalyzed by every woman in town, and about music, and some more about my dress and my body. It was sexual talk, and if somebody came on with me like that now I'd say, "Bullshit," and walk off. But for some reason he excited me. I'd been feeling sexually compulsive ever since the double breakup with Tom and Scott; I craved sexual fulfillment. Sex, sex, sex was on my mind all the time; I was lost, and now this ugly old man was getting to me. It's weird, now that I think back on it. Strange! The simple truth is I fell in love with Allan Magnesen on the spot.

He asked for my name and telephone number, and he called me in a couple of days. I was thrilled. He invited me over for dinner, and I accepted, and I went out and bought another sexy dress for the occasion. His apartment was in the Village, and it was stunning! *Quel ambiance!* There were oaken beams, walk-in fireplaces, sleeping lofts, a warm, aromatic kitchen with a Franklin stove, and a hi-fi system that filled the whole place with resonance. It was the home of a man of taste and a man of affluence, a man who liked the lights low and decor understated. The only trouble was that Allan was in a bad mood from the second I stepped in the door. He almost seemed to be looking for trouble, and I thought, "What a change from the other night. Why did he invite me at all?" He told me to sit down, brought me a drink, and then turned up the music so loud that conversation was impossible. After a few embarrassing moments another musician came in, and the two of them talked shop for two hours, leaving me sitting on the couch. It was interesting talk, but it left me confused. When the other musician left, Allan served a casserole and some wine and began picking at me in bitchy, subtle ways. When I started to clear the dishes off the table he said, "Now you're acting as though you're trying to convince me that you'd be a good wife." That made *me* feel belligerent, and I said, "Now listen here, I'm not interested in being your wife or anybody else's, and I'm not interested in taking any more crap from you, either!" And I started to head for the bedroom, where my hat and coat were lying on the bed.

He reached my side fast and put his arms around me and kissed me, and then he led me over to the couch. He pushed me down and held me and kissed me again, and he felt good, as good as I'd expected him to feel. I said, "I'm not very good for one-night stands, especially on the first date."

He said, "That's a lot of crap!"

I wrenched loose and jumped up. "I'm leaving now!" I said, and I went into the bedroom to get my things. He followed me in, and when I reached over he hooked my ankle with his foot and shoved me down on the bed. He was surprisingly strong, and when he got on top of me I fought him for a few minutes until the pressure became excruciating. Then I gave up. I said, "Well, okay," and we began.

It was great! He was a terrific lover for such an emaciated-looking person. He gave me one orgasm and then after an hour or so he gave me another one, and when I left I was crazier than ever about him. I said to myself, "Well, now I've got a new boy friend." I loved him, really and truly loved him! I said to myself, "He's great stuff! How lucky I am that he came along!"

Five days later he called and invited me for dinner again. Once again there was the wrong *ambiance* when I arrived. This time he had a female house guest, an old girl friend of his named Erika, and the two of them were billing and cooing all over the place. All during dinner and for an hour or two afterward, they hardly paid any attention to me. But around midnight Allan whispered, "Go to bed. I'll be there in a few minutes."

I was pleased by this. I didn't care how much he fooled around with Erika as long as he wound up in bed with me. I got undressed and pulled down the covers, and then I spotted several drops of blood on the sheet! You can imagine how I felt! When he came in, I showed him the stain and I said, "What do you have to say?"

He said, "Gee, I really didn't know there was a bloodstain there. I didn't know she was having her period."

I said, "Who are you talking about? How did this happen?"

He said, "It's just an old girl friend of mine. She comes around once in a while."

"Erika?"

"No, another one."

I felt like the whole bottom had dropped out of my life. I loved him so much, I was just *gone* over him! And now he was acting like these bloodstains were just a minor oversight, nothing to come between us. He was telling me that he had quite a few girl friends who "come around once in a while," but he said we didn't need to let that stand between us.

I said, "Allan, I can't stay here tonight, and if this is the way things are going to be, I can't see you any more."

He said, "Look, we've only just met each other. You can't expect me to give up my other women. That's the way I am. I have several women, and no one of them is so great that I'm gonna give up all the rest. And that includes you."

I said, "Okay, then I'm going."

Well, he sweet-talked me and turned down the light and changed the sheets and once again we made love. We climaxed twice, and it was good sex, and I was glad I'd stayed. But the next day I felt awful. All I could think of was how he'd humiliated me and disappointed me, and I knew I could never go back to him. I felt as though I'd lost something great, but I knew I'd only be killing myself mentally if I let him put me on his harem list.

He called me a week later, and he began that sweet talk again, and he told me that he'd gotten his hands on a chicken turbot and he was going to prepare a magnificent broiled dish with sauce *aioli* for me that same night, and we were going to have two bottles of Mumm's by his fireplace, and talk and make love all night. I was shaking with nervousness, and I didn't know what to say. So I said, "Yes." But thirty minutes later I called him back and told him no. I said, "I really can't handle it with all the other women, Al."

He said, "Well, I'm sorry that's the way you feel."

I wanted to break in and say, "Look, can't you see I love you?" But I didn't. Instead I said, "Allan, if you could just promise me not to see the other women."

"I can't promise," he said.

I gave him about five chances to make some sort of concession toward me, but he kept saying that he dug me and wanted to see me but he didn't intend to change his whole life for me. I said, "Well, it's final, then, Allan. I can't see you on that basis."

"I'm sorry," he said. "Let me know if you change your mind."

Four months went by. I saw no one, and all I could think about was sex, sex, sex. It reached the point where I just wanted to get laid, period. I was feeling sexual vibrations all around me, whether men were there or not. So I called him up on a pretext, and we made a late date. When I got there he was having a party, but he seemed so glad to see me that I didn't care if the whole town was there. He took me into a side room and he grabbed me and kissed me and he said, "Can you come and stay with me tomorrow night?"

I was surprised. I said, "Why not tonight?"

He pointed toward the living room, and he said, "Not tonight. There's somebody else tonight."

I said, "Which one is it, the redhead?"

He said, "Yes."

I said, "Oh, that's too bad for me."

I hung around the party for another hour or so, and when I went to get my coat and leave, Allan followed me into the bedroom and said, "Wait! Don't leave! There's been a change." He explained that his redhead had freaked out when she'd seen me. She'd caught the vibes right away and she knew that I was there to sleep with Al. So now she was acting difficult and threatening to leave early with another man.

I bided my time as the guests were leaving, and as I did I studied Allan more intently than I'd ever studied him before. He was making small talk with the guests, and I realized that it was very boring, very petty conversation. And I suddenly realized that he was essentially a stupid, boring, shallow person and that I'd never really noticed this before. All my emphasis had been on sex, sex, sex, and I'd never taken the trouble to see that outside of the bedroom Allan Magnesen was nothing.

When there was nobody left but the redhead and me, Allan motioned me into the bedroom, and I undressed and got under the covers and waited for him. I heard him smooching with the redhead, and then I heard him say good night to her, and then he came in and began making the same dumb small talk with me. The lovemaking turned out bad. I always demand that a man make love to me at least twice each night, and he wouldn't do it the second time. I hadn't had an orgasm, and I said, "You *have* to do it again!" But he didn't want to be bothered, and this made me realize how self-centered and egoistic he was. So I just *demanded* that he do it again, and I made such a federal case out of it that he finally did get it up and do it, begrudgingly, like he was doing me a favor. He didn't even ejaculate himself, and once again I didn't have an orgasm. The whole sexual scene had been a catastrophe, but it was a good catastrophe because it taught me something that I had never known in my naïveté. It taught me that sex is no good unless you love somebody, unless you really and truly dig them. There's got to be more than just soft lights and music. You have to *really* love them. This was a marvelous revelation to me. Up to then I'd thought that I could just taxi over to Allan's house and get laid and get my thrills out of it and then just get up and go home. But I no longer dug the guy, and that threw the vibes all off.

Since then I haven't made the same mistake. Five months have gone by, and I haven't slept with anybody, and I don't intend to sleep with anybody unless I dig him, unless I have deep feelings for him, and him for me. Because it just isn't any fun if you don't, no matter what you read in the magazines.

And something else hit me, too. I looked back and I realized that all three of the men I'd slept with in New York had been latent homosexuals in one way or another. Scott had a big mother hangup and all kinds of problems in bed with a female. Allan and Tom were just as screwed up, because they couldn't have normal relationships with a woman. They both had to berate women and put them down, and they both had to have a lot of women on the string. Women were *objects* to them. They couldn't relate to a woman, they couldn't talk to a woman, and above all they didn't want to get close, really *close*, to a woman. But when you saw them with men, they were energized! Great bolts of wisdom and clever-ness went flying about. They were relating like crazy! Then they would turn to a woman and start their regular line of meaningless chatter. "What a beautiful body you have, my dear!" To them, women are identical. "At night all cats are gray." Or that lovely line I heard in a play: "They all look alike when you turn 'em upside down."

At first I asked myself why I had been attracted only to latent homosexuals, and I considered the possibility that maybe something was wrong with me. But then I realized that it couldn't be me, because it was the male side of those men that I had been interested in and the female side that had turned me off. And after months of trying to figure things out, I realized something crucial. I realized that the problem of latent homosexuality is a New York City social problem and bigger than anybody thinks. The city is loaded with latent homosexuals, and most of them are frantically spending their time in bed with women, denying the truth about themselves.

I think the suburban culture has created this problem. To become a normal male, a male child has to have a male model to identify with. If he doesn't, he'll identify with the mother and become a homosexual. Well, look at the way life is lived in the suburbs nowadays. The father doesn't come home for lunch any more. He doesn't sit down to breakfast with the kids any more, or, if he does, it's all over in a few minutes, and he reads his *Wall Street Journal* the whole time. At night he catches the seven forty-four and gets home exhausted just before the kids go to bed, and on weekends he's so pooped out from the whole weekly commuting schedule that he pays little attention to his sons or—worse yet—he gets drunk. The result is that the sons are all mama-oriented. It's mama, mama, mama, twenty-four hours a day, seven days a week, and the latent homosexuals in New York are the result. We're churning them out by the millions. It's no accident that there's much less homosexuality in countries like Italy, France and Germany, countries where the father still dominates his household, the way fathers dominated their households for ten thousand years before suburbia sprang up.

The other disturbing thing about love in New York is the constant pressure to go to bed. Contrasted with other countries, the sexual pressure here is extraordinary. It builds up, date after date, until you can barely handle it. If you haven't gone to bed by the third or fourth date, he starts telling you that maybe you're frigid, maybe you should see a doctor, and you begin doubting yourself! I went out with a very interesting man and on our second date he began talking about going to bed. I said, "Forget it, we're not going to bed."

He acted as if I'd cheated him. In a silly, hurt, deceived kind of voice, he said, "If you didn't want to go to bed, why'd you accept a second date?" Well, at least he was an improvement on some of the men in New York. If you don't "put out," they wonder why you accepted the *first* date!

It's different in Europe. I've had a few small affairs in Europe and I can tell you that the pressure is much lighter there and the sex becomes much more natural when it does happen. I hate to generalize, but there's no other country in the world that produces the sexual pressure that we do. Sex exists everywhere, but it's only in the United States that you cave in just thinking about it. You feel sexual pressure before you get any real feelings for the person. The American man thinks, "This woman is attractive, so I want to sleep with her, and maybe I'll love her later." The European man thinks, "This woman is attractive, maybe I'll learn to love her, and if I do I'll sleep with her."

With Americans in general and New Yorkers in particular so intoxicated with sex, it's no wonder that it soon disturbs the female as well as the male. In my periods between lovers I used to feel that I was going to jump out of my skin. I felt like a heroin addict withdrawing. I thought sex, sex, sex, night and day. Why not? It's all around you in New York; the pressure is constant. And pretty soon the girl begins thinking like a man and seeing sex the same way. Everybody else is talking and thinking about it, so she starts talking and thinking about it, too.

It comes in all forms, this sex intoxication. A girl friend of mine was taking a night course in economics, and one morning she walked out of her apartment to catch a train to Katonah and found her professor sitting in the hall outside her apartment. He explained that he'd fallen in love with her, that he had to have her body, and that he'd been sitting out there all night! She quickly slipped out the front door, with him following, and the only way she avoided a scene was to let him take the same train and ride for two hours with her to Katonah. She calmed him down enough to get him to turn around and go back to New York. The main calming remark was that although she looked older, she was only seventeen, and since the professor was about fifty, he could easily see the error of his ways. But just for safety's sake, my girl friend dropped the course.

You never know where it's going to come up. What is an indecent exposer doing but reacting to the sexual intoxication of New York? Look at the "flashers" on the subways, or the "feelers." Even little kids are exposed to them. I walked past a man in Central Park the other afternoon and when he came abreast of me he lurched in my direction and I could see that his penis was sticking out. I ran, but then I remembered that two little girls had been walking a few hundred feet behind me in the same direction, and I panicked at the idea that they should see such a sight. I ran to Fifth Avenue, looking for a policeman, but of course there was none.

See that thick black curtain over my bedroom window? There's a reason. That window fronts on an alleyway, and when I moved in there was no curtain or screen on it. I used to love to lie in bed and see the little patch of blue sky out my window. It was so crystalline and lovely, and once in a while a puff of cloud would come over to excite me even more. Who needed a curtain?

Now see that window next to mine? It doesn't look dangerous in the least, does it? It faces away from my window and if anyone wanted to stick his head out that window and spy on me, he'd have to have a foot-long neck and a head that swiveled like an owl's. So I didn't worry. I walked around my apartment in the nude, and I made love with the window wide open, and I never gave it a second thought. I knew the man who lived next door; he was a teacher, a man of about sixty, and he was always pleasant and respectful when I met him at the supermarket. And he didn't have a foot-long neck!

One morning at dawn Tom was lying on top of me. We'd been making love all night, and now we were just resting, and I happened to notice a hand come slowly out of that next-door window.

I said to Tom, "Ssssh," and as I watched I saw that the hand held a pocket mirror. "Tom!" I said. "Don't move, but we're being watched!"

Tom jumped about six feet and grabbed an andiron. He was stark naked, and as he reared back to fling that andiron through the window, he looked exactly like the famous statue of Poseidon with his spear. I said, "Tom! Don't!" and I grabbed his arm and tried to calm him down. He was enraged! He wanted to call the police and he wanted to go over and beat the man up and a half a dozen other things, but I convinced him that the best thing to do was stay calm.

That night I wrote a note to my next-door neighbor. I said, "This is to advise you that I know what you're up to. I think you are aware of the charges I could bring against you. I hope that we can maintain our slight acquaintanceship, and I don't intend to bring this matter up again, *unless your actions leave me no choice.*"

A few days later I saw his hand come out the window again. He was shaking a dust rag, and when I called across to him, he said, "Oh, Miss Gouldtharpe, I'm mortified! I'm embarrassed! I'm upset! Won't you please come over and talk to me?"

I went over, and he poured me a drink. We talked for three hours, and he told me the whole story. It was really very simple. He planned to write a book about single girls in New York City. "I just wanted to know the ins and outs of your life," he said.

"How long have you been studying my ins and outs?" I said.

"About three months."

"Oh, how embarrassing!" I said, but as I thought about it I began to see the humor in the whole thing. This poor old guy, a teacher, trying to do his research with a hand mirror! I'm dying to see his book, but it hasn't come out yet. We talked and talked, and finally I confessed to him that I'd done some spying of my own. There was a handsome young man who lived across the avenue from me, and we used to spy on each other with binoculars. So I forgave the old teacher. He agreed with me that peeping was just another part of the sexual intoxication of New York. It's all so New Yorkish! It's fun! New Yorkers have these little games that help them survive, and peeping is one of them.

· 3 ·

AFTER THAT experience the teacher moved away, and I decided to make a study of my neighbors on the theory that I'd get along better with them if I knew what they were up to. Down the hall there were two beautiful models, and right next door to my apartment was a beautiful married woman who turned out to be a lesbian but a rather passive one. I grew to like her enormously. We started talking at a party one night, and after a few drinks she said, "You look so lovely tonight, I'd just like to grab you and hold you." She said, "When I really like girls, they attract me physically, and I really like you." Well, I could understand that. Some people are just very tactile. She said, "But I don't think you really understand what I'm talking about. I used to be an active lesbian, and I feel an attraction to you, but I'd never overstep the mark with you because you're my neighbor and I know you're straight."

Something about that remark endeared her to me, and we became good friends. She told me later that her father tried to rape her when she was eight and again when she was ten and finally succeeded when she was twelve. No wonder she hated men! She also told me to beware of the two glamorous models down the hall. "Stay away from them," she told me. "I know what I'm talking about. They're a couple of lesbians, and they're red hot for you."

I said, "I can't believe it. Why, they're two of the most feminine women I've ever seen!"

"They're bull dikes," she said. "Take the word of one who knows." I respected her antennae, and I broke off my friendships with the models. Maybe my lesbian friend is right. Those two models spend hours fawning over their pet Dalmatian, but I've never seen either one with a man.

My other good friend in New York is a strange girl named Vanessa Van Durant, who lives a few blocks away. Vanny is a peculiar case, and I bring her up because she seems to be one of the victims of this sexual intoxication that I've been talking about.

I hate to say it, but Vanny's really almost a whore. I think she's slept with over a hundred and fifty men, probably two hundred. That's quite a lot. I've slept with five or six. She has absolutely no discrimination, and her attitude toward sex is very distorted. She doesn't sleep with a man because of any great vibrations between them or because she really wants a particular man at a particular time. She sleeps with a man to relieve her own anxieties, the same way I take an afternoon nap when I'm depressed. Sometimes she'll go to bed with a man just to relieve the anxiety of being *with* him. She may feel completely ill at ease with him, but in bed she can handle the situation; she's right at home with the sexual relationship. She ought to be by now. She short-circuits all of her mental problems to her crotch.

I met Van through a mutual friend, Marvin Quinley. He used to come over to my apartment about twice a month and have these marathon conversations with me, usually from about eight at night till six or seven in the morning. There was no sex involved, but our friendship was intense. Marvin was fifty years old, but he treated me like a mother confessor, told me all his troubles and did a lot of crying on my shoulder. One of his troubles was Vanny. One night he said to me, "Do me a favor, Goldie. I'm worried about a friend of mine, Vanessa Van Durant. She has absolutely no girl friends in the city, and she needs somebody to talk to."

I said, "Marv, I don't need another girl friend. I have a very rich social life. I have more friends than I can handle." But he persisted, and I agreed to try to help Vanessa out. I got in touch with her and we decided to go to a rock concert together. It was a very boring and very strange evening. Here I was trying to help her, trying to give her one girl friend she could relate to, and she was giving me the cold shoulder. I don't know what her thinking was, but she acted aloof and grouchy. I called up Marv when I got home and I said, "Marv, Vanessa and I will *never* be good friends."

A few weeks later I got a postcard from Dublin, and it was from Vanessa. The postcard was warm and friendly and personal, and I began to wonder if I had misjudged the girl. When she came back to New York, we got together again, and ever since then we've been seeing each other intensely about twice a week. But we're not really close friends, and I don't think she knows this. I don't think she has the sensitivity to know it. She's cold; she doesn't pick up on complexities. She has a very narrow mind. If you try to explain something complex to her, you get to the end and she's sitting there looking at you with a blank face, or playing with the split end of one of her dark black hairs. She's very weird.

Sometimes I think she's just not smart, but then I'm not sure. She thinks she's terribly intelligent herself, and she must have something to base that feeling on. But when it comes to communications between people, she's got a very low I.Q. Sometimes I wonder how she holds her job. She's a kind of glorified messenger at The Company; they call her a public-relations assistant, but all she really does is carry The Company's news releases to newspaper and magazine and TV offices and then turn on the charm. With a job like this, you'd suppose she'd have a lot of sex appeal and personality, but she really doesn't. A man might be attracted very briefly by her overdone appearance, and the hair down to the waist, but as soon as she begins coming on, the feeling is lost. She thinks she's great with men, but she's awful! I saw her at a dinner party a few nights ago, and she didn't have a date, and she went after two men who were there alone. The chemistry, the dynamics that she was emanating toward those two men was very poor, very desperate, and very depressing to watch. She was trying to get laid, and it was *so* obvious. I talked to one of the men later and he said, "My God, we were practically bombarded!"

I suppose I should feel sorry for her, but she gives no signs of feeling sorry for herself. She acts like she has sex all figured out and she's having a wonderful time at it. Her attitudes are positively crazy! Like I told her once that I routinely invite my dates into my apartment for a drink or a cup of coffee after a date, and she acted shocked! She said, "Why, Goldie, that's just an invitation to get laid!"

I said, "It certainly is not! It's just good manners, common decency, good upbringing. You can't leave a man down on the street. That's uncivilized."

"When you invite him into your apartment at two o'clock in the morning," she said, "you're just inviting him to fuck. And if you don't, you're just teasing him."

"You're mad! It's just simple, polite feminine courtesy."

"Well, that's not the way I was taught. To me, it's just a screwing invitation."

"You've got a lot to learn."

We're always having conversations like that, and she's always revealing these weird attitudes. Meanwhile she runs around sleeping with every man in sight, to relieve her anxieties, and then she lectures *me* on proper social behavior. She prattles on and on in this super-fast manner, with no genuine feelings in anything she says. I feel sorry for her. I'm torn, because she's not really a friend and yet I agree with Marv that she needs somebody to talk to, somebody to help her get her head straight. She's got big eyes for my ex-beau, Scott, but he can't stand her. He says she's so obvious. She keeps asking me, "What went wrong between you and Scott? He seems like a dream to me." She can't fathom why we broke up. She calls him up and tries to get him to take her out, but he won't do it. I warned him about her.

Once I tried to put her straight about a certain evil man. I don't know how it all turned out, but I have my suspicions. This man could match Vanny neurosis for neurosis, strangeness for strangeness. I ran into him in a Chinese restaurant on Mott Street, and I thought I recognized him, and it turned out he was an old acquaintance from Milwaukee. I hadn't seen him in ten years, and when we bumped into each other in the cloakroom he suggested that we take a walk and renew old acquaintance. We hadn't walked a block before he took my hand in his. I thought that was a little peculiar, a little bold. Then he began talking about spending the night with me. I said, "What?" I was amazed. I said, "Why, Ted, I'm surprised at you! Besides everything else, I have a date later tonight."

He said, "Break it!"

I said, "Ted, I don't *do* things like that."

Soon we came to his car, and he drove me home and kept pressuring me all the way home to sleep with him. At my door he said,

"Okay, this is your last chance. Do we go to my place for the night?"

I said, "No, we don't."

"Okay," he said, "forget it!"

A few weeks later I was in a singles bar with a date, and there was Ted looking all morose in the corner. "Oh," he said, "we meet again."

I said, "Good evening, Ted," and I introduced him to my date, and we exchanged small talk for a few minutes.

Late that night I got a phone call from Ted. "Tell me something," he said. "If you can sleep with that fat old faggot, why can't you sleep with me?"

I said, "He's an old friend of the family, that's all. We just talk."

We began one of those patented non-stop two-hour telephone conversations that New Yorkers use to ward off loneliness. He updated me about himself, and I must say I was impressed. To begin with he *was* a handsome specimen—six feet tall, curly black hair, about twenty-eight or twenty-nine, with the charm of a cobra. He told me that he'd been a full professor at a Southern university, that he'd dropped out and gone into the record business, and that now he was making thirty thousand dollars a year and enjoying the single life in New York.

Inevitably, the conversation turned to sex, and he began coming on very strong again. He said, "You know, I've fucked a lot of women, and I'm really ready to settle down now. I think you'd be somebody good to settle down with. We're from the same background, and I think we're compatible."

"I think you're just tired," I said.

"Maybe so," he said. "In the last three months I've had about ninety women. I just go to places like museums and concerts and pick them up. It's so simple. Married women, single, divorced, all kinds of women. I just turn on the personality and they fall over. Of course, you have to know how to pick out a vulnerable woman. I pride myself on knowing how to do that." He said that he guessed he'd had about four hundred women in his two years in New York.

After we'd talked till three in the morning he suggested that I come over to his apartment for a drink. "No, thanks," I said. "I still don't think we're compatible. You're not my kind of person."

He said, "Oh, come on! I won't hurt you."

"No, thanks," I said.

Then he began an onslaught of personal invective, how he was tired of taking crap from people, and he didn't intend to take any from me, and how he had to beat up a woman every once in a while "to keep them in their place." Wow! I tried to speak in my most calming voice. I said, "Ted, you must know that's a very unhealthy attitude!"

He hung up, but a few minutes later he called me back. "I'm sorry I hung up," he said, "but you were beginning to give me some shit and I didn't feel like being shat on."

"I was only trying to help you, Ted."

"You can help me by coming over to my apartment right now."

"No," I said.

"God damn you!" he said, and he hung up again.

A few weeks went by, and I got this excited phone call from Vanny. "I've just met the most charming man in the world," she said. "I had my usual armload of packages and bundles and I was leaving a restaurant and this wonderful man offered to help me carry them home." She raved on and on about how nice he'd been, how handsome he was, how he had turned on the charm, and how he had tried to get invited into her apartment but she had made a date with him instead.

"What's his name?" I asked.

"Ted Cohn," she said, "and you might know him. He's from Milwaukee."

"I know him, Vanny!" I said. "Oh, Vanny, Vanny, *Vanny!* Let me tell you about him!"

I told her the whole story, and she thanked me. Later she told me they'd had their date, but he had turned her totally off, and she had no intentions of ever seeing him again. She said she found him totally repulsive. I think I know why. On the surface, they were made for each other, because they were both sexual athletes, using sex for a million different reasons, all of them wrong. But Vanny is a seducer, and so is Ted, and seducers don't like to be seduced. It takes the fun out of the game. That's my theory about Vanny and Ted. I've tried to discuss it with her, but as usual she doesn't get the point. She doesn't get any point unless she's slapped in the face with it.

· 4 ·

I WAS talking to Marvin about the sexual intoxication in New York City, and he told me that he had a simple explanation. "It's the noise," he said.

"The noise?"

"Yeah," he said. "The noise, and the people, and the aggravation, and the annoyance."

I said, "People go to bed together because of noise and aggravation?"

"Yes, indirectly. They get so worked up in this abnormal environment, and then they begin looking for something to take their mind off it, and the first thing that comes to mind is sex. Why is sex the first thing that comes to mind? Because as you walk down the street you see all these young broads swinging their asses in miniskirts. You look up on a billboard and there's a girl twenty feet tall overflowing her bikini. You pick up magazines and all you see is crotches and tits. You head for the movies and three out of four of them are rated X. You pass a bookstore and all the books are about screwing. You walk down Broadway and you see the topless go-go dancers, and you're approached by hookers, and dirty underground movies are showing on every other block, and I could go on and on. So what are you supposed to do to relieve all the aggravation? Play Parcheesi?"

Sometimes I honestly think he's right. At least about the amount of aggravation. I wouldn't leave New York for anything—I absolutely love it here—but it certainly has to be the world's capital of aggravation. Just the noise alone is enough to get you. Do you know, on Friday and Saturday nights I can't even have people in? We can't converse. The din coming up from Seventh Avenue is ruining my eardrums. I've been holding my ears in the subway lately, because I heard that it's a hundred and twenty decibels, far too many for the normal human ear, but sometimes I think it's at least that loud right here in my apartment when the traffic jams form and the big trucks go by. I've actually ordered three big plastic baffles for my front windows, but I know they won't do much good against all that racket. But at least maybe they'll enable me to stay in this apartment, to survive here.

I love New York, but sometimes it's like having a lover with bad habits. You love him so much you just put up with it. Everyone is so uptight here, and there are so many people here that they lose sight of the fact that they're dealing with people and they start treating each other like machines, without even the minimum amount of human courtesy and decency. Like my landlord, for instance. He's been trying to get me out of here, because if he gets a new tenant he can raise the rent. So he began sending me little notices about "two-dollar arrears." I wrote back that I would be happy to pay the arrears if he would just explain to me what they were. He sent me four more notices that I was two dollars in arrears. I hit the ceiling, and I tore the notices up. So he started eviction proceedings. I talked to a lawyer, and he said, "Look, spare yourself the aggravation. You're right and he's wrong, but pay the two dollars and get it over with."

So I sent in a check for two dollars, and it came back uncashed. "I won't accept your check," the landlord told me over the telephone. "I don't like your attitude." Right now I'm sitting around waiting for the next eviction notice. That landlord doesn't know it, but I'm mad now, I'm aggravated, and I'll take the darned case all the way to the Supreme Court if I have to.

But that's typical of what goes on in New York. I had a similar go-around with Con Ed, the electric company. They sent me a check for a hundred and thirty-one dollars and fifty cents, and I figured, what the heck, I'll go along with the gag, and I cashed it. Six months went by, and they began billing me for a hundred and thirty-one fifty. I called up and complained and screamed and hollered and they were very apologitic and removed the amount from the bill. A few months later they put it back on my bill and began dunning me again, and when I ignored them they shut off my electricity. I called them right up and I said, "Look, my mother's living with me and she's deathly sick and the doctor has to come three times a day and check on her, that's how bad off she is. And *you've* shut off my electricity!" They apologized and sent a man right away and turned my electricity back on. They took the hundred and thirty-one fifty off my bill for the second time and I laughed and said to myself, "The perfect crime! Well, if you can't cheat Con Ed, who can you cheat?"

Last week I got my new bill. The hundred and thirty-one fifty was back on. So maybe I'll pay it anyway. End of the perfect crime!

That's the sort of thing you have to learn to roll with in New York City. You can't let it get you down. When you live in New York you have to take special pains to survive, you have to *think*. You have to learn to do things imaginatively, uniquely, to do things on your own time schedule and not on New York's time schedule. For example, I never go out on Saturday night in New York. It's suicidal. You'll get crushed out there with all those people from Bergenfield, New Jersey, that come in for their Saturday-night dates like animals. You learn to go to the movies in the afternoon, never at night. You learn not to go to a movie opening unless you want to stand in line for an hour. You learn not to take the crosstown bus in the rush hour and not to ask a taxi to take you crosstown, because the driver will just aggravate you to death. If you remember such things, and alter your life style accordingly, New York can be a very pleasant place. Sometimes you find yourself having a dinner date at four-thirty in the afternoon, but what's wrong with that?

Which brings me to one of the reasons I like The Company so much. They're very wise up in our executive suite, and they know what New York is like, and they know what you have to do to live

here. They realize that we'll get a far more intelligent type of employee if we allow some special freedoms and allow our people to
make some adjustments to the city. Some of our employees are
always complaining, but they don't know how lucky they are. If
The Company wasn't so tolerant about working hours and lunchtimes and extra time off and things like that, we'd *really* be miserable. If we had to come to work right in the middle of the worst
traffic jams and go out and find a decent meal in exactly sixty minutes at lunchtime, we'd be up the wall! The Company is very wise
about its personnel policies. You know what I always say about
The Company? Some of the other girls hate me for it, but I always
say, "This is the greatest company in the greatest city in the
world." And I really mean that. Ultimately it'll be the *only* kind of
company that can survive in New York. With all the other aggra-
vations, nobody wants to work in a sweatshop.

But for the rest—I've almost had this single life up to my neck.
Falling in love, going to bed, falling out of love, meeting somebody
else, having orgasms, not having orgasms, the same patterns over
and over. There's going to come a point, and very soon now, when
I can't take the disappointments any more. Emotionally, I just can't
handle any more heartbreaks. In the single life in New York, the
negative outweighs the positive by so much. It would be different
if I could just go out and screw and not get involved, but I can't.
There has to be something else, there has to be love.

So now I'm trying to meet nice guys. I'm trying to stay away
from the destructive people, the Scotts and Toms and Allans and
Ted Cohns. I've learned and benefited from my experiences with
these people. Now my antennae are out for a different kind of man.
I have a good friend who's a psychology teacher in the Bronx and
she tells me, "You've just been punishing yourself with men, because you feel inadequate inside. Unconsciously you've been seeking out men who'll harm you." I realized that's been the pattern of
my life. But in New York it's so hard to meet any other kind of
man! You have to be on your guard every second. You meet the
cutest, the handsomest, the most intelligent man, and pretty soon

you find out he's Jack the Ripper underneath! They talk about women being destructive, women being ballbreakers, but in New York it's the other way around. The men are the killers.

My teacher friend told me, "It won't always be this way with you. The things that turned you on in Scott and Tom and Allan won't always turn you on. You'll grow, and you'll find yourself responding to a different kind of man."

So that's what I'm waiting for: the Change. I've hardly been going out at all. I haven't had sexual intercourse for five months. I don't have horny periods at all, but I do have a few erotic dreams. I'm happy with my attitude about sex, and I don't feel compulsive any more. I know I will never make love with another man unless I'm sure of his love for me. That's for the benefit of my self-respect. It's an intellectual decision, not an emotional one, and I'm going to make it work. I don't want to toy around with sex and diminish the beauty of it. I want it to mean something, to mean *everything*. And now that I've come to that conclusion, I feel a new wholeness in myself, a new integrity. Five months now! I no longer think of myself as a sexual object, or something to help a man reassure himself that he's a man. I am a person, not a *thing*. Men must relate to me as a person, not as a mother, not as a confessor or a gimmick to help them solve their psychological problems. When I meet a man who doesn't feel exactly the same way about sex and life, I discard him right away. So I'm not going out much. But I will be. And who knows? I might meet Philip Roth again.

Vanessa Van Durant, 26

———◇———

Vanny is not a woman, she's still a little girl. She's got little-girl problems, and a little-girl way of looking at things. Like a child, she doesn't catch nuances; she's off somewhere in a world of her own, and if you use the slightest nuance or subtlety of expression, she won't get it. If you tell her that you're so hungry you could eat a horse, she'll believe you. Literally. Not that she's stupid. I'm convinced she's really a bright girl, a bright child. She's obsessed with men, but I don't think she really sees them as men. I think she sees them as toys. All this used to be okay; she was very young and full of vitality and she had plenty of time to come out of it. But she's twenty-six now, and she's not coming out of it. I don't feel optimistic about her future.—Faith Stronberg

Vanessa's had a great education, and she has a pretty groovy father. But I don't think her relationships with men are too good. But she keeps trying, from one man to another. Her life is wall-to-wall men.
—Alexandra Oats

• I •

IT'S STRANGE to stay in New York on a holiday like this. The streets are empty, and there are very few women around. Mostly it's just men on the streets, looking for something. It's bleak out there, like a struck set. The subways are long hollow tubes with nobody in them, and it's scary to ride one of the trains. People who stay in New York on holidays get very upset. It's the atmosphere, all empty and gray and bleak. There are always a lot of suicides in New York on holidays. Losers. People who didn't get invited someplace and can't stand it. People who have no place to be invited any more. They go out on the streets to get some of that shoulder-to-shoulder warmth that New York gives you, and they find that nobody's there, and they come back home and turn on the gas. Holidays make you realize how much you depend on those huge crowds of people that you're cursing the rest of the time. Without the crowds, you're in a different environment, and maybe even a dangerous one. It's all *men* out there today. Men on the prowl. I think I'll just stay in till the party tonight.

Of course, the crowds *are* getting impossible. I mean, there are crowds and *crowds*. The other day I went to Grand Central at five o'clock in the afternoon and I couldn't believe it. First I had to wait for five subway trains, all full, and then I got on one because I was in the center of a crowd and I got pushed on whether I liked it or not. Luckily it was the right train. The people were all so rude! I turned to a man and I said, "Listen, this is 1971, and you don't have to push!" He looked at me as though I was weird.

Then I went to my bank for the second aggravation of the day. I asked for my balance. Like I *never* know my balance—and they told me they'd have to have a dollar first. Wow! That's the new rule. Every single time you want to know what the fuck you've got in the bank, you've got to cough up a dollar. Why, I can't afford to bank in New York any more! So I canceled my account.

Sometimes I get so mad about things like that, I decide I'm going to move to some other place. But I know that's ridiculous. My roots are so deep in New York I'll never get away. I've been other places and I just *perish* there. I rush back to New York for the music and the hassle and the stimulation on the streets. I love the tall buildings, I love the fuss and commotion and the culture: the rock music and the Beethoven concerts and the theater. My new game is ordering from the deli. Where else in the world could you snap your fingers and have somebody come rushing to your door with a prune Danish and a hot pastrami on rye? Why, you can even get a whole French dinner delivered to your door! *Quiche*

Lorraine, quenelles de brochet, petits fours, things like that. Try that in East Cornball Junction sometime! So that's my new game: snapping my fingers and having things sent up to me. Sometimes I even have the money to pay for them!

Well, let's see, what should we talk about? Personally I love to talk about sex, and I'm very good about talking about sex, because I *like* sex, I think it's wonderful. I was reading *Future Shock* by Alvin Toffler the other day, and he says that in this time of rapid change screwing is the one way of being sure of *something.* You might not win the person in the long run, and you might not even see him again, but if you can fuck at least you can make *that* connection. I agree. When you haven't got anything else, you've always got fucking. It's a consolation.

I've slept with maybe fifty men, more or less. I admit it: I'm a seducer of men. I do it consciously. My technique varies. Sometimes I just plain fuck them, or sometimes I do the whole number: making a dinner, laying a table, having flowers, dancing, whatever. At parties if I see a man I want to sleep with I may even be overtly sexy, open my eyes wide at him, flirt outrageously with him. I don't care what the other people think; it's the man's reaction I'm interested in, and getting him into my bed.

I realize that an attitude like this is going to bring certain problems. People have such hypocritical attitudes about sex, to begin with. There's a wide difference between what they do and what they *say* they do, as in the case of my friend Jayne Gouldtharpe, for example. She comes on like little Miss Junior League most of the time, but the simple truth is she likes to fuck, just like me, just like you, just like every normal person. The only difference is, I don't mind talking about it. God knows I've been talking about it to psychiatrists forever; why should I stop now? But the subject is so full of totems and taboos and weird prohibitions. Did you ever think about the vocabulary of sex, for example? Take the word "cocksucker." That's a bad word, isn't it? But how did it become a bad word? I realize that it should be an insult when one man calls another man a cocksucker, but what about when a man calls a girl that? They'll say, "You lousy cocksucker," as though they're using the ultimate insult, but cocksucking per se is not a bad thing. Of course, men will also say "fuck you," as though fucking was bad, when everybody knows that it's good. I don't understand the use of sexual terms as insulting terms. No wonder we're all screwed up. "*Screwed up!*" See, I'm doing it myself! There's another use of a sexual phrase to denote something bad. Our language is riddled with contradictions like those. Somebody should do a dictionary of them.

Well, you want to know how it all started.

Let's see, it started about two hundred years ago on one side of my family tree and God knows when on the other. Van Durant was originally spelled as one word or something like that. The name is Dutch, and my Dutch ancestors came here in the *Mayflower*'s wake. On my mother's side we can trace back five generations of New Yorkers and maybe more. We're not necessarily old-line New York aristocracy, but we are old-line New York *good* people, solid people, and well-to-do people. Once I was out with a guy and he was giving me some crap about class and social standing, and I said, "Listen, you creep, don't tell me about social standing. You're out with the great-granddaughter of the man who built this goddam building, so shut up!" In my family tree there are statesmen, famous lawyers and builders, big politicians, good people. My mother's grandfather was one of the men who helped build the New York Central Railroad and my paternal great-grandfather held a patent on an industrial valve that made him a fortune that he later lost in the stock market. He used to ride in a chauffeur-driven gun-metal gray Rolls-Royce, and even after he was forced to sell the car he used to borrow it back once a month and park it near the house for a few hours so nobody would think he was broke. The Van Durants are noted for things like that. One of my aunts serves nothing but Ambassador twenty-five-year-old Scotch at her parties, but as soon as the guests leave she goes back to the most horrible rotgut bourbon, about three dollars the fifth. That's all she can afford, and she enjoys getting drunk. She used to drink the Ambassador twenty-five *all* the time, but then she lost her money. That is a family trait, not being able to hold onto money. I swear it's in the genes. My mother and my father and my twin brothers and my aunts and uncles and me—there's not *one* of us who can handle money. And we don't wish to be taught! We're not ambitious; we eschew money; we can't get rid of it fast enough. That's why I never know my balance at the bank.

I had a difficult childhood, and I'm still not sure how I survived it. I grew up in the city, attending the fanciest private schools, wearing clothes from the best stores, and dying of insecurity and lovelessness. My mother and father were mismated, to say the least, and all they ever did was fight and argue and slash at each other with words and sometimes with other instruments. My father was a drunk right out of F. Scott Fitzgerald. He was a Dartmouth man who had learned basket weaving and beer drinking in college, and little else. He loved to pal around with the boys. He'd go to his brokerage office and work for about an hour, and then spend the rest of the day in clubs and bars. You can imagine the financial stability this brought to our life. My brothers and I would sit around waiting for him to come home, because we liked him to kiss us good night, but Mother would rush us off to our rooms when she heard his car pull up. She knew he was drunk, and she didn't want us to see him. The three of us kids had two favorite games: to count the number of times Daddy stuttered, and to count the number of times Daddy swore. *Because he only swore and stuttered when he was drunk!* It was a great game for kids. Fantastic!

When I was twelve, I was sent to a psychiatrist, but it didn't take, and I quit soon after I started. It was my mother's idea; she had just taken up psychiatry herself, and she thought it would be good for her disturbed little daughter, the one who was always making scenes. Now I realize it was natural and normal for me to make scenes when I was twelve. That was the only way a child could get attention from those two cold, hateful parents. There was so little communication and warmth in my family that I had to make scenes to register on them at all, to break through that constant sullen hostility.

When I was eighteen, my father turned to me and said, "Well, you can leave home now."

I was shocked! I was terrified! I said, "Do I have to? What are you talking about?"

He said, "Well, that's what *my* father told me when I was eighteen." Father was a little drunk, as usual.

I began screaming. I said, "No, no, no! I don't *ever* want to leave." And I didn't, because as cold and hostile as my family was, it was *my* family, and I was scared to death of the rest of the world.

He said, "Well, don't get excited, Vanny. I only said it because I thought you *wanted* to leave."

Well, he really did mean it, he really did want me out of there, I'm convinced of that. I'll *always* be convinced of it. So I wrote to one of the colleges that had offered me scholarships and accepted their offer, and instead of telling my parents and saying my good-byes and all that sort of thing, I just left them a note in the middle of one night and went away. The note said something like, "Good-bye forever. I will never see you again." That was me making a scene again. I *loved* to make scenes!

The college was Bryn Mawr, a very decent place if you can *stand* phonies, and I fitted in like a truck driver at a tea. I was heavy and sloppy and I felt it. I hated my body, I hated my complexion, and I hated my prep-school-girl wardrobe. I realize now that I wasn't nearly as horrible-looking as I felt, but for that first year I just sort of snuck around Bryn Mawr, fitting into no particular crowd and keeping to myself. My only social life consisted of a few dates with two fairies, one of whom let me alone and the other of whom took away my virginity when I was least expecting it. I guess it was one of those nights when he failed to score with the men in the neighborhood and I was the only game in town. So he screwed me, and it was no big deal, except that it felt unnatural, strange, bad, cruel, smelly, dirty, painful and awful. There was nothing *memorable* about it. I don't even think he particularly wanted to do it, and I was too terrified to enjoy it the least bit. They talk about penis envy, but what I had was penis fear. I said, "What's that?" and I shrank back against the wall like a first-year Brownie. I didn't want to see it, touch it, feel it, or have it inside me. I was terrified. "What are you gonna do to me?" I said.

"What's that thing gonna do to me? What *is* that hairy animal?" I found out a few minutes later.

In my sophomore year a very persistent boy began to chase me. He kept asking and asking and asking, and finally I accepted a date with him. The measure of my mental state at the time is this: I never, *never* liked that boy, and yet I wound up going with him and sleeping with him and becoming engaged to him. I had so little sense of myself; I just did what other people wanted, and *this* was what he wanted. I was the classic case of the other-directed person. The boy was gentle and nice about the sex. He said, "I don't want to make you a non-virgin, so you make sure you *want* to do it or we won't do it." He said, "Once you lose your virginity you'll want to keep on doing it and then you'll become a whore and I will have ruined your life." Wow! He didn't know that I was already a non-virgin, and I wasn't even positive myself, so I admitted nothing. When he finally took me to bed, I pretended that it hurt and that he had deflowered me. I didn't want to let him down. As you can see, he was a little fucked up on the subject of sex himself, and for weeks afterwards he insisted that we had to get married, not because we were in love, but simply because he had fucked me and he owed it to me. But by this time he was the last person I would have married, because he had begun to come on with these little cruelties, little insults and wisecracks that hurt my feelings and put me down, and I finally decided not to see him at all. It took a lot of courage for me to say so, because I was terribly uncertain and insecure in those days. But one day I just came right out and said, "No, I *won't* go to the Library Follies with you!" and he said, "You've *got* to!" And I said, "I don't got to do anything," and I left school and went to London to get away from him. I stayed there for six months, till my money ran out, and thank God I had a lovely affair with an Oxford student, or else I might have grown up to be a frigid woman. I also had a love affair with a priest, but we didn't sleep together.

When I came back home from London, I did a very difficult thing. I moved back in with my parents. I had no choice, and anyway I thought they might have changed after two years. They hadn't. I was twenty years old now, and I didn't have the slightest idea what to do with myself, so I just spent most of my time sleeping. My parents went up the wall! One night my mother said, "Well, Vanny, what do you want to *be?*"

"What do you mean?" I said.

"Well, you have to *be* something, you have to *do* something."

"No. I don't," I said. "I think I'll just sleep awhile."

Soon they had me back into psychiatry, but that was no help. The psychiatrist was awful! I would tell him eleventh-grade sex fantasies and he wouldn't understand them. Or I'd tell him something that was very sexy and he'd get embarrassed. Imagine an embarrassed psychiatrist! My parents must have got him at a cut rate —a discount psychiatrist. He would leer at me and say, "Tell me about your sexual fantasies," and I'd get mad and I'd say "Listen, Doctor, I'm having a very active sex life, and I don't need to have any sexual fantasies. I've got all the guys I want, and if I do have any sexual fantasies, they're not going to be about you, they're going to be about somebody who looks good!" One day he got so mad he threw a pillow at me. Wow! Some psychiatrist, huh?

After I'd slept and moped around the house for a few weeks, my father suggested that I go to secretarial school and learn a few practical things like typing and shorthand. I did, and I was a huge success at the school. I amazed myself! Right after graduation I got a job with one of the biggest banks in New York. What a let-down! It was a sweat shop, right out of the nineteenth century. They gave you *nothing.* They had the poorest personnel relations I've ever seen, and they were always on your back. They didn't know how to exploit people, how to make them love the company and put out for the company. They just *worked* you, like water buffaloes. If you were two minutes late, you heard about it. The office conditions were lousy. Desks were crowded together, and if you had a personal conversation on the telephone everybody else could hear you. You had to clean off your desk every night. If you were in the middle of a project and you had seven piles of papers set out on your desk, you had to file them away before you went home and start from scratch the next morning. The result of stupidities like that was that we all hated the bank and cheated the hell out of it. If we could steal a pencil, we were happy. If we could stay an extra two minutes in the john, or stretch the coffee break by a minute and a half, we were ecstatic. We were in a war, and the enemy was the bank that employed us. You can imagine how fulfilling it all was.

· 2 ·

IN THE back of my mind I sometimes thought about The Company, because The Company was sort of a tradition in our family. One of my great-uncles had actually been on the board of The Company about sixty years ago, and both my father and mother had worked there during summers at college. I had two cousins on the staff and an aunt working in the Honolulu office and all sorts of friends and distant relatives involved in The Company's operations. It seemed like a perfectly natural place for me to work, except for one thing: I had so little self-esteem, and The Company was the place where only the cream of the cream got hired. At least that's what I thought till I got up my courage and applied there for a job.

I was interviewed by a terrific and nifty and enthusiastic woman, and just about as quick as it takes to tell about it, I was hired as secretary to the manager of a new department. Wow! Like I was in heaven! I went home and told my mother and father, and they asked if I'd mentioned all the relatives who'd worked at The Company and I was very proud to tell them that I hadn't mentioned a soul, that I had gotten the job completely on my own. The truth is I'd been ashamed to mention my illustrious forebears. I already felt like a nobody, and I didn't want to be compared to my great-uncle and made to feel even *more* like a nobody.

My new boss was cute and funny and a perfect father figure. He was very nice and gentle to me, even when he was drunk, which was fairly often. He'd take me in his office and shut the door and breathe these alcoholic fumes on me, and he'd tell me how his wife didn't understand him and how frustrated he was in his job and how he sometimes thought about suicide. But he didn't come on sexually. He told me, "That's one thing you don't have to worry about, Vanny, at least as long as you're *my* secretary."

I really learned to love him, in my own way, and I worked very hard for him, sometimes covering his tracks and sometimes working extra hours to get something done that he'd been too drunk to finish. But after a few months his sloppy drunkenness did begin to wear on me. My father is a sloppy drunk, too, and I've got no tolerance for it day after day. So I went into my boss's office and I said, "Listen, you better shape up or ship out. I'm not gonna spend the rest of my life working for a drunk!"

He was astounded. He said, "Why, my own wife never told me anything like that!" He laughed. He seemed to think it was very funny, and he kept right on with his heavy drinking. But he kept on being nice to me, too, and I just learned to accept him for what he was. He did good things for my ego. He told me I had a good mind, which I'd never known until then. He was the first person who ever gave me a compliment I was able to accept.

At first I didn't know that he was playing around with the girls in the office. I really knew very little about sex, but I couldn't help notice that he kissed a lot of the girls at office parties, although he never kissed me. So I asked him why not, and he said, "Because I'm your boss," and then he kissed me. But that was the last time we had any contact till he left two years later, and then one night he called me up drunk and he said, "I'm not your boss any more, so I thought I'd come up and kiss you." I told him I was busy, because I was. There was a man in my bed at the time.

During those first years at The Company, I may not have been the greatest secretary in the world, but I was certainly the hardest worker. I did everything as perfectly as I could. I took on extra responsibilities, I broadened the job, I did everything that was asked of me and more. I felt scared and intimidated by the people around me. They were adults, I was a child; that's how I felt. I lived at home with Mommy and Daddy, and the outside world was a grownup, spooky place, and I was the only child in it, and to make matters worse I was still sloppy and immature and insecure. I still wore my school clothes, and one day my boss said, "Don't you have any clothes?" I said, "No, I don't!" The truth is that my school clothes hung on me and hid the fat. My school clothes were my security blanket in a world of intimidating adults.

After a while I tried moving into an apartment with roommates, but that didn't work out too well. I moved in with three other girls, and on the first Saturday I woke up and found them on their hands and knees. I had a lot of personal errands to run, and I said, "What's this?"

They said, "We're cleaning. We always clean on Saturday."

I put on my things and got ready to go out, and they said, "Where are you going?"

I said, "Out. I have a lot of things to do."

They said, "Oh, no you don't! *We* clean on Saturday."

I said, "*You* clean on Saturday." I got my things and moved out.

Then I found another roommate—a girl who worked with me at The Company. She was strictly a working girl, fat and bored. She came home, ate, went to bed, got up, and went to work. Even though she was fat, she sat around drinking beer and eating things like lasagna and spaghetti. She just didn't know any better. She turned on the TV the instant she walked in the door, before she even took off her coat, and then she'd sit there and watch the fucking tube till one in the morning. She never *didn't* watch Johnny Carson. It was just her way of life.

So what I did was go out. I became a street person, only returning to the apartment at two or three in the morning to sleep. I learned how to eat on the street and not go broke. Pizzas, hot dogs, tacos, hamburgers. My parents found out about it and sent me to another psychiatrist, but he was a mean guy and I dropped him fast.

The one good thing about my life remained The Company. It was the exact opposite of the bank I'd worked in. You get better money, better hours, better title, better working conditions, better *everything* than any other place in the city. If you go in to them and say, "I need two thousand dollars more a year," they give you three thousand! If you get drunk at lunchtime you just go down to the infirmary and sleep it off. If you have cramps, they give you great pills, with codeine and Benzedrine in them. You get long vacations, and good sick leave, and extra time off whenever you need it. It's the most comfortable fucking place in the world.

Of course this turns some weaker people into zombies. They can't handle a place like this. They lose their souls, their sense of themselves, and they become a part of the great machine. The Company treats you so nicely that it makes you feel guilty, and this makes some people work far harder than they normally would, and pretty soon the office is their whole life. I realized this very early, and I didn't fall into the trap. I cut down to an eight-hour day; I worked very hard and very efficiently, but at five o'clock I was through, and I didn't take the office home with me or go down to Santana's and drink with my colleagues till midnight. I had plenty of things going for me, but they didn't involve the office people, and they never have. With one exception. I went to an office party very early on, and I met a specialist named Ernie Rhoades, Jr. He was a good dancer, and I fell madly in love with him instantly. He had to go home to his wife that first night, but a few days later he called me and invited me to lunch. We both had about six martinis, and then he told me he'd reserved a room at a hotel down the street. I didn't particularly like the idea, but he wanted to make love to me in the worst way, and so I consented.

Well, the hotel room was about eight feet by eight feet, dingy and dusty and dark, and right away I was offended that he hadn't had the class to reserve a double room. He asked me if I'd ever slept with anybody before, and I said yes, and he said to take off my clothes. So I did, and he took off his, and we got into bed—and he couldn't get it up! I just sat there and laughed. I said, "That's what you get for only renting a single room, you cheapskate!" He looked so stupid, and pretty soon I was just embarrassed for him, and I dressed and left and never had anything to do with him again.

Very briefly I moved back in with my parents, but then we had this big scene after I stayed out all night, and I stomped out and fucked the first guy I could find, just to spite them. This was the first time I'd ever fucked anybody where I was using him instead of him using me. I snuck back to my parents' house and left them a box of bon-bons with a note attached to it that I was leaving them and they would never see me again. That was the last time I cut the umbilical cord, because I have never lived with them since. I stayed with friends for a while, and then I took an apartment of my own. I see my mother and father often, but I would never think of going back there to live. One reason is that I have a very busy sexual life, and I intend to go on having one, and they don't appreciate my attitude.

That first year at The Company was a big year for one-night stands. If you're looking for one-night stands, New York is the perfect place. Of course, one-night stands are terrible for you and a very bad indication of your mental health. They show that you've reduced your sights, that you're not looking for much or expecting much out of life. But I wasn't! I still didn't know myself. I was very insecure, almost desperate. I was so happy when somebody even spoke to me that of course I went to bed with him, without any consideration about whether I wanted to or liked him at all. I was always puzzled when I'd wake up in the morning and he'd be gone. I slept with Tom and Bill and Harry and Bob and who knows who else. I met a pianist at a party and took him home to bed, and when he left the next morning he said he would call me, but he never did. *And I don't know his name!* He's the only person I've ever slept with that I don't know his name.

It was years before I realized what I was doing. I was trying to destroy myself. I was taking boys home because I was lonely and because I was trying to cover up the loneliness, and also because I was self-destructive and masochistic—and horny!

One night I was having dinner with my parents, and I had just told them about a construction worker I'd been screwing, and my father said, "Vanny, why don't you try being chaste for a while?"

I'd never even *thought* of that approach. The idea interested me, because even in my addled state of mind I realized that one-night stands were no good. My father said, "Let's be frank, Vanny. How many men have you slept with this year?" I made the mistake of stopping to count, and he said, "Well, that should tell you something. You're promiscuous. You should try chastity."

So we made a pact. I agreed to be chaste, and I was chaste for four months, except for a college boy and another boy that I'd known for several years. Then I went into a Greenwich Village bar and met Ozark. He was the bartender, and as soon as he saw me he came rushing across the room and zeroed in on me. "Hello," he said, and his eye contact was terrific! He was really coming on strong, and I loved it, because nothing so spontaneous had ever happened to me before. I ate it up! I told my date to get lost, and I talked to Ozark for hours.

A few nights later he called me, and he said, "Let's go to the movies," which surprised me. I'd expected him to call up and say, "Let's sleep together," which I'd been used to people saying, "Come on, let's screw," like the construction worker; we just screwed, we never talked or anything. But Ozark was different. He had such style, such taste. He called for me in a taxi, and I was so impressed! He took me to dinner first and then to a movie, and then we went back to his pad and ended my period of chastity. I was so impressed it was pitiful. He had this wonderful apartment with wonderful Mexican furniture and a black rug on the floor and a mattress for a bed. It was divine, and the sex was divine!

Ozark taught me so many things. He was my first real romantic relationship, the first person I ever went to bed with that I really liked. He put me into things: poetry, music, art, politics, vocabulary, pot. I got stoned with Ozark and I adored it, Ozark and the pot and the sex. These were experiences I'd never had, and I was on a crazy mad trip and loving it. He taught me new concepts. He taught me how to take a bath. He would run the water for me while I took off my clothes, and then I'd get into the tub and he'd give me a drink and a cigarette and show me how to enjoy myself in the hot water, letting it take over my body and my mind. And he taught me how to have fun in bed, to have *body* fun, which I'd never known about. He loved his own body, and he had a wonderful way of using it, both bartending and screwing, all style and strong legs. He made me feel feminine, as if I could move like a woman, which I'd never known before. I thought the woman just laid there and let the man do it to her. My mother had told me all my life to pretend that I'm enjoying sex, whether I'm enjoying it or not. But Ozark's advice was better, because I *was* enjoying it with him, and I didn't have to pretend.

We went together for one divine month. I would go to his bar at about two in the morning and when he got off at four we'd drop around and close some of the other bars on Fourth Street and then we'd go to a couple of after-hours places and go home to bed. We did this two or three times a week. But with all his virtues Ozark turned out to be a very selfish and cool person who didn't want to get involved. Probably he was screwing other women at the same time he was seeing me; I don't know. But when I got kind of clingy, he began saying, "Fuck you!" One night I went to the bar and he wouldn't even talk to me. So that was the end of the first affair I ever had where I was really getting something out of it myself, instead of just giving some stud a thrill. It was funny; Ozark and I had agreed that I should start taking the pill, and the night I took my first pill we broke up for good. Wow!

· 3 ·

SUMMER CAME, and I began another period of chastity, and I felt great about it. Altogether I slept with six guys during that particular chastity period, but they were *the right guys*. There were no *bad* guys, and I felt good about sleeping with them. Three of them were one-night stands; the others lasted a little longer. I was working hard and feeling terribly pure that summer, and the period of chastity did me a lot of good mentally. But I suppose I'd better explain what chastity means to me, because my definition is a little different from the dictionary's. To me the point of chastity is to sleep with nobody until *I* meet a guy *I* want to sleep with. In other words, being chaste is sleeping only with people you choose yourself, not just having sex for the sake of sex, or having sex because some guy asks you for it. I can seem to be chaste and promiscuous at the same time, but there's no contradiction in my own mind. Once I've made up my mind to be chaste, then I feel good and pure and I say to myself, "You're a basically good and chaste and pure person." But my actions may not seem so. My first solution to anxiety is to sleep, and my second solution to anxiety is to sleep with a man. So if I'm anxious, I want somebody to hold me and save me from myself, and I might have a sexual relationship for this reason and still remain chaste—at least in my own mind.

Anyway, that summer was the most successful period of my life. I got over Ozark, I was chaste, and I slept with six men because I wanted to and for no other reason. I lost a lot of weight, I worked hard, and I began to look terrific. When my summer vacation was over and I was back at The Company, I met a man who was so different from the others that it was as though he'd just stepped out of a spaceship from Mars. Listen to this: His name was Casimir, he was a poet *and* a master plumber, he was six-six and built proportionately, he had the body of a Greek statue, and he knew more about Shakespeare and Proust and Gogol and Turgenev and Ezra Pound and practically every writer who'd ever lived than the average college professor knew. In fact, he knew *everything*, and in six different languages! Like wow! He was the last Renaissance man! He could explain Newton's laws, the theory of Pythagoras, Keynesian economics, Marxism, Adam Smith and absolutely anything you asked him. Once I told him that I loved home-made mayonnaise, and he pulled out a pen and wrote out a terrific mayo recipe on the back of a napkin. It was fantastic!

So naturally Casimir ended up in my bedroom, and we had a lovely love affair. It surprised me that he was not a very imaginative man in bed, but he was receptive whenever I did anything special. He explained to me that French whores always suck guys before they make love, and he told me he enjoyed it. After that, he'd always want me to do it. He turned me on fantastically. I think he turned *everyone* on. He told me he had had a virgin campaign when he was twelve and living in Kentucky, and he deflowered just about every virgin in the state! I believed him! He smelled so *good*, like sex, like musk, like a wild animal. And he *took* me, like an animal, and that's what every woman wants. Once we were in his apartment and one of his friends was sleeping on another bed in the corner and Caz began to make love to me. I said, "No, no, no, your friend's here," and he said, "Shut up!" And before I could say another word he was in me. Well, that's what an animal would do, right? You never knew when he was going to start. Like I'd drop a pencil and bend over to pick it up, and he'd come over and grab me and we'd be fucking in the middle of the floor. Wow!

One night he told me that he'd found a girl in his apartment. "What did you do with her?" I said.

"I fucked her," he said.

"Why?"

"Well, she let herself in with the landlord's key and she was lying in my bed when I got home. What else can you do with a naked girl in your bed except fuck her?"

I was furious. It was the first time I'd ever felt such jealousy. And I was terrified that I might lose him. I said, "I thought you were just sleeping with me and nobody else."

He said, "Are you kidding?"

"No," I said. "I've only been sleeping with you—when you've been in town."

"How many men have you slept with since you met me?"

"Six or seven, but only when you haven't been available. Those men don't count. When you're in New York, I'm true to you."

He laughed, and not long after that he moved away to Virginia. I still see him about once a year, and we always go to bed. We'll be going to bed once a year for the rest of our lives. If I ever get married, it will have to be written into the marriage contract that I can screw Casimir at least once a year. He is the loveliest man, and he has the loveliest body.

After Caz left, I went into another period of chastity, my third, and then I began to get bored with New York and The Company and I asked for a three-month leave of absence to go to Paris. I stayed chaste, except for one night when this charming Frenchman said to me, "Vanny, *ma chère*, you are the epitome of intellectuality and sexuality," and I fell into his arms and said, "I'm yours!" I slept with another guy because I got drunk and he challenged my femininity. But those two were all, until I met this silly-looking, pug-nosed, towheaded, sawed-off shrimp of a boy and fell madly in love with him. His name was Hamilton Bauers and he was studying art at the Sorbonne and hacking around Paris and the main reason I loved him was that he fell instantly and madly in love with me, and love was all I wanted in the world. I realized how much he loved me when I started to leave his loft after our first night together, and he began to cry. "Don't leave, Vanny!" he said. "I can't stand the idea of spending a single day without you."

We lived together for six months, and during that time I never slept with anyone else or even looked at anyone else. I can be very loyal. The sex with Hammy was good, for just one reason: He loved me. I had the first climaxes of my life, because I loved him, too, and I could give myself to him completely. We slept together morning, noon and night, and we had sex all the time.

But when that *rouge* period wore off, we found that we had much less in common than we'd thought. I didn't like housekeeping, I never will, and I hated washing pots and pans. Hammy was darling and sweet, but he was also lower middle class, and he expected me to take care of the house without complaint, and after a while I just couldn't face one more goddam dirty dish. Besides, New York was still in my blood. I began to miss it terribly, and one night I just took a taxi to Orly and flew home.

I was in a terrible state. I had overstayed my leave of absence, and I didn't even know if I had a job. I had no place to stay, so I did a desperate thing: I went to the YMCA and lived there. And I loved it! Did I say YMCA? I meant YWCA. Wow! What a Freudian slip! Anyway, the rent was low, the place was conveniently located in the middle of Manhattan, I had total freedom, I didn't have to make my bed in the morning, I didn't have to keep house, and I couldn't bring men to my room. Since I was in another period of chastity, I liked this rule. It gave me an excuse not to sleep around. I stayed there for three weeks, and then I went back to work at The Company and got an apartment of my own and began having some rebound relationships. I fell in love with a young Bolivian count, a wonderful man with a British-Spanish accent and the most charming style. He took me to lunch and just seduced the pants off me! I'd never been so eager to go to bed with anyone as I was with him. He just took over. He made every decision. He was *so* masculine. He told me he'd only slept with two other women in his life, his wife and a French whore, and he was wonderful in bed, because he was so assertive. He just went ahead and did what he wanted. You might as well have tried to stop an express train.

Then I ran into a boy who shall forever exist in my memory as "The Awful Boy," because there's simply no other way to describe him. He put such terror into me that I'm *still* afraid even to mention his name. The first time I saw him was at a party, and all I did was argue with him. He came from a family that arrived on the *Mayflower*, and naturally that gave him the right to lord it all over me, and I just told him that he might have good antecedents but he was horribly lower middle class and he should take better care of his teeth. Except for his teeth, he wasn't bad-looking, in an angry sort of way, with a compact build and black-black beetle eyebrows and dark wavy hair and brown eyes. I argued with him for about an hour and then forgot all about him.

A few weeks later I ran into The Awful Boy at a party, and he had now become the respectable Dr. Jekyll. He was charming and shy and modest, as sweet as he could be, and we wound up in bed at my new apartment. But nothing happened. He didn't lay a hand on me. In the morning he was all apologies. He said he was so sorry that he'd had the effrontery to stay with me all night, and he wouldn't let it happen again, and all that sort of abject crap. I couldn't believe my ears! I didn't think there were any naïve boys like him left in New York City, let alone one of my own age, which was twenty-four at the time. I realized later that he was playing it cool, that he was just trying to get me into his clutches before he struck.

We went out three or four more times, and each time he was polite and courteous, and he never made the slightest suggestion about going to bed. He loved to dance, and we went dancing three times in one week. I loved it! Then he began calling me at the office and telling me how much he adored me, and that was just what I needed, perpetually. I was panting to sleep with him by now, and the next time he was at my apartment I just put him on top of me and began kissing him. Wow! Then I got up and took off all my clothes and his clothes and made him fuck me. Even then he was saying, "No, no, we shouldn't be doing this! This shouldn't be happening!" Wow! What an operator! He gave me a totally different picture than what he really was, which was a woman-killer.

After two or three weeks of going out together, he moved in with me, and that's when I realized for the first time that he was a terribly heavy drinker. He started each day with a triple shot of vodka, and if he didn't have to go to work he just kept that stuff flowing through his system till he fell into bed at night. The sex was okay, but nothing special. Then he began making special demands. He'd make me striptease in front of him, and he'd lie in bed and watch and play with himself. I was so dumb, so naïve! It took me a long time to realize that there was nothing loving about this, that he was just using me, exploiting me for his own needs, which were sick. I used to drink a lot just to be able to do things like that for him. He liked nothing better than wild, abandoned sex scenes, where his only obligation was to play the part of an animal, and never mind whether I was enjoying it or not. He would fuck me all night long, on the floor and on the rug, and it was not loving sex, but animal sex, *sick* sex.

Then one night we went to a party at the home of some of my friends, and I saw an old boy friend and went over and kissed him. That was a mistake. The Awful Boy was already drunk, and he took me aside and he said, "Have you ever fucked that boy?"

I said, "Yes," and he threw my drink at me, right in front of everybody. Then he led me out to the middle of the dance floor and kept grabbing at my crotch all through the dance. I said, "I'm leaving!"

He said, "You don't leave without me."

When I said, "Yes, I do," he slapped me as hard as he could.

At home, he told me to take off my clothes and lie on the bed on my stomach, and he began fucking me in my asshole. I screamed. It was horrible. But he wouldn't stop. I said, "Get out! You've *got* to get out! You're killing me!" But he just pushed it further in. I was in agony! Then he began hitting me, and I realized that he wasn't making love, he was making hate. Buggery is a terrible thing for a woman. There's not enough room there, and it just plain hurts. Sometimes it might feel nice when you're making love if the man just puts his finger up your ass while you're fucking, and that can be very sexy, but ordinary buggery just plain hurts.

After he stopped, I lay on the bed crying for an hour or so, and then I fell asleep. But he woke me up and buggered me again, and again I screamed my head off and again it didn't make any difference to him. That was the most horrible night of my life.

The next morning he warned me not to say a word to anybody, and just to make sure I understood, he knocked me down. Then he stood over me with his foot raised over my face and asked me if I understood. I said I did. A few minutes later when I picked up the phone to call the deli for some breakfast, he wrenched the phone out of my hand and said, "No calls! No calls till you straighten yourself out!"

He went to work and I called in sick and stayed home all day, terrified. He phoned four or five times, "just to see if the line is busy," and he came home very early demanding his supper. For the next several days he kept busy slapping me, punching me, kicking me and abusing me sexually. I was beside myself. One night when he was in the bathtub I picked up the telephone and called my friend Peggy Kern. "Listen," I said, "I'm terrified! I'm trapped in my own apartment." Just then I saw the bathroom door open a slit, and then it opened all the way and The Awful Boy came out. He slammed the phone out of my hand and punched me nearly unconscious.

The terrible days went on. He kept me in a constant state of threat. I couldn't talk to anybody about him. He said he'd kill me if I did. I couldn't tell my psychiatrist, I couldn't tell my therapy group, I couldn't tell my mother or my father or my twin brothers. I needed to scream and say "Help! Help! Help!" but I was afraid.

One night I got up my courage and decided to lock him out for good. I asked him if he'd go for cigarettes, and he said, "Sure," and when he shut the door I ran over to lock it. But he flung it open from the outside and he said, "You whore! I knew you were gonna try that!" and he beat me till every part of my body was black and blue, and then he made me do all sorts of sexual things to him, while I was still in great pain. Another time I got out of the apartment on a pretext and I called him from a telephone booth. I said, "I can't stand this any more! Either you get out of there and take your things, or I'll get the police."

He answered in such a sweet and gentle voice. He said he was sorry about all that had happened, that he enjoyed hitting people and hurting them and he thought that I was a masochist who enjoyed getting hurt—which may have been slightly true. He said he'd be glad to get out, and not to worry about him, and once again he apologized.

I let about six hours go by, and then I went back to the apartment. It was all quiet and dark inside, but his clothes were still there and a half empty bottle of vodka was on the table. I shut the door and stepped inside and he came leaping halfway across the room at me. He'd been behind the curtains, and he had a leather strap in his hands, and he hit me with it until I was dying of pain. Then he fucked me everyplace he could.

Finally I decided that the only way out was to placate him. I was invited to a party at the home of some good friends, and I suggested real sweetly that he go with me. He said fine, he would enjoy meeting my friends. When we got to the party, I took one of my friends aside and I said, "Quick, go to the bedroom and find his coat and get the fucking keys out of it." I was shaking. My friend came back a few minutes later *with the wrong keys*, and I almost collapsed. The Awful Boy had thought of everything; I knew that the keys to my apartment must be in his suitcoat pocket.

That night I refused to leave my friend's apartment. I told The Awful Boy, "Go on home without me. I'm sick. I can't leave here. I'm too sick." He couldn't make a scene right there in front of my friends, so he left. The next afternoon I had a friend make a call to

The Awful Boy's office and make sure he was at work, and then I quickly went home to see if I could get a locksmith to change the locks.

My apartment was a mess. All my clothes had been ripped off their hangars and puked on. They were lying in a smelly mess on the floor. Then he had taken a large felt-tip pen and written all over everything. He wrote a lot of lovely expressions: "Fuck You." "I hate you." "You cunt." "You cocksucker." It was written on the walls, on the chairs, on my clothes, on my lamps, everyplace!

I called the cops. A cop came and he heard my story and he said, "Listen, lady, we don't *have* to do this. You let this man come in here and live with you, now the law says it's your responsibility to get him out. But I'll see what I can do for you. Maybe I can scare him."

I left the apartment and waited across the street in the restaurant. Around six o'clock The Awful Boy came home from work, and I alerted the cop right away. He came over and knocked on the door and The Awful Boy had changed back to Dr. Jekyll again. He was all humble and contrite. He *couldn't* understand what this was all about. Why, there'd never been a harsh word between us! "I don't know about that," the cop said, "but I do know this lady wants you out of here."

The Awful Boy left, and I called an emergency locksmith and had my old lock removed and three new ones put in its place. But I was still scared shitless. I knew The Awful Boy too well; I knew his rage and his hatred, and it wouldn't have surprised me if he had come through my brick wall to get me. I waited in fear. I waited for three days. Then I picked up a *Daily News* and found that he had been arrested in Greenwich Village for rape. I followed the case closely. He beat it on a technicality, and then he left the state. At least that's what some friends told me. I still have awful nightmares about him. I still wake up screaming, imagining that he is coming for me. They say he left, and I hope to God they're right, because wherever The Awful Boy is, I don't want to be.

Well, that's life in the big city. You can't make an omelet without breaking eggs, and all that tripe. You can't sleep around without running into an occasional loony. The Awful Boy taught me to be on my guard more, to watch for the first sign of aberration, and then cut out quickly. But how can you tell? The Awful Boy came on like Little Lord Fauntleroy at first, and not just for a night or two, but for *weeks*, and even after we'd started screwing. He didn't make his sadistic move till he had moved in with me, and by then it was too late.

The truth is, there are lots of awful boys in New York City, and lots of boys who are not quite as bad but are all fucked up in the head in some other way. And some of them are real charmers, as charming as pit vipers. One night I was struggling home with an armful of packages, as usual, and this terribly handsome boy appeared and asked if he could help. After we got the packages upstairs, he asked if we could have a drink together, and I said okay, but it would have to be later that night, because I had to go to a meeting till about eleven.

At eleven he was waiting for me, and we went to a little Mexican restaurant down the street. He told me that his name was Ted Cohn and he was from Milwaukee and his family had lots of money and owned half the city. I said, "Oh, then you must know my friend Jayne Gouldtharpe."

He said, "Yes," but in a very low-key voice, as though he was not particularly interested in talking about Goldie. He quickly shifted the conversation to other subjects, like what was my favorite color in nightgowns. I said, "Oh, there was a new pink nightgown in one of those packages you carried for me today."

"Oh, there *was!*" he said. He sounded excited. He said, "Maybe you'll model it for me someday. I'll buy you another nice one at Saks Fifth Avenue."

I said, "Fine. By the time you're ready to buy me a new one, I'll be ready to model it for you."

But apart from a tendency to want to talk about things like that, he seemed to be a perfectly urbane and intelligent and interesting companion, and on the whole I enjoyed my hour or so with him over drinks. He wanted to come up, but of course I wouldn't let him, and as soon as I got inside the door, I dialed Jayne and told her whom I'd met.

"Ted Cohn from Milwaukee?" she said. "Why, Vanny, where did you meet that creep?"

I told her, and she said, "Oh, Vanny! That man is a raving maniac, a sex maniac! Why, he sleeps with more people in a week than you and I will sleep with forever!" She went on and on. She said, "If ever you see him again, don't let him in your apartment, whatever you do." I didn't tell her, but I already had a date to see him again. The next night, for dinner. And he was to pick me up at my apartment.

He arrived early, and I was nowheres near ready. I said, "I talked to Jayne Gouldtharpe about you."

He acted nonchalant. He said, "Did she tell you anything you didn't already know?"

"Not particularly," I said. "Give me a few minutes and I'll be ready."

I went into the bathroom and put on a beautiful orange dress and the only hose I had: a pair of loud, shocking tie-dyed stockings. I walked out, spun around, and said in my most musical voice, "I'm ready! Let's go!"

He pointed to my legs, and he said, "What are they? Take them off!"

I said, "Well, I'm sorry if you don't like them, but they're the only pair I can find."

He said, "I will not go out with *anybody* wearing stockings like those!"

I said, "Then you're not going out with me, because they're all I have in the house. And anyway I *want* to wear them. If you hate them so much, why don't you run out and get me a new pair? You're always talking about how rich you are."

The argument went on and on. He absolutely would not budge till I did something about the stockings, so I rummaged around in the laundry bag and finally found an acceptable pair. *Anything* was better than arguing all night. When I presented myself for inspection, he said the stockings were all right, but he berated me for being so slow about everything and for not being ready when he arrived. The complaining went on and on, and finally I cut in and I said sarcastically, "Look, let's go across the street for a drink, because we're having *such* a good time."

We sat down in the farthest corner of my favorite bar and we argued royally, on and on and on. Finally he said, "Look, I'd get up and walk right out of here now, except that I don't want to embarrass you."

I said, "So walk! It wouldn't embarrass me at all. It would be a relief." He stayed on a few more minutes, and then *I* got up and walked out. *Up his!* I never saw him again, and that's fine with me. Looking back, I don't think I would have liked sleeping with a yo-yo like that anyway, because I didn't like his attitude in the first place and I didn't want to become just another statistic in the second. But if he'd been nice and we'd have gotten along, I suppose it would have happened. Why not?

If ever I was going to have a lasting relationship, it would have been with the most important man in my life, the great love of my life, Marv Quinley. There are just six problems: his wife and his five children. Marv is fifty-one years old, but I don't regard that as a problem, because I love him, and I would marry him if he was a hundred and fifty-one years old. Our love affair goes back three years, to a morning when I delivered a release from The Company to Marv's office on Wall Street. We struck up a conversation—I always did like father figures—and he asked me to lunch, and we enjoyed each other enormously. For a whole year we went to lunches together at the Gloucester House and Keen's Chop House and the Artist and Writers bar and places like that, and the intellectual feedback was fantastic. We never saw each other at night, and we never crossed the line of simple conversation and the pleasure that we took in each other. Then one day at lunch Marv said, "If I came to you cold and hungry and tired at three o'clock some morning, would you let me in?"

I took the question literally, the way I take most things, and I said, "Sure," and three nights later there he was. He admitted that he had been with another woman, and he was tired and didn't want to take the commuter train all the way to Scarsdale, and could he stay with me? What could I do? Besides, I was thrilled, in a funny way, that he'd been with another woman that night. He said he just wanted to lay his head on my lap and let me stroke it for him. But then I began to think of him with the other woman, and somehow it seemed perfectly all right to go to bed with him, since he'd already been to bed with *her*. That was the beginning of it, and it was great. He acted so relieved. He said, "All that time wasted! I thought it'd never happen!"

We began going out at night, and I taught him to dance, and we went dancing all over town and he loved it. Later he said that dancing was the most important thing anyone had ever taught him; it had changed his whole outlook on life. Then one night we were lying in my bed and he said, "Look, Vanny, I didn't plan for this to happen, I didn't *want* this to happen, but I'm in love with you." My first reaction was misery. I felt responsible. He said, "I'm in love with you, and I want to marry you and give you a baby."

I didn't answer, but after a few more months I realized that I was just as deeply in love with him, and I told him so. He began doing things for me that no man had ever done. He bought me clothes and took me to hundred-dollar-a-plate restaurants and even took me on a few trips with him to places like Nassau and Hamilton, Bermuda. But he didn't mention marriage again, and I realized that he was quite content with things as they were. But of course I wasn't. He had begun taking me for granted, snapping at me once in a while, the way husbands do to wives. And when I mentioned marriage, he turned the subject off.

One night I did the worst thing you can do to a man. We were about to make love, fooling around the apartment, naked, drinking, when the phone rang. To me, the telephone spells excitement; I love it, and I love to talk on it. My new boss was calling, a little bit drunk, and he just wanted to bullshit while he waited for his commuter train. We talked for about ten minutes, and I was my usual flirty, loud, childish self on the phone. When I finally hung up, Marvin was up the wall! He was furious! So he did the worst thing he could do to me, which was to remind me of all he had bought for me and how much I was in his debt. He said, "I've bought you lock, stock and barrel, and don't you forget it!" He said, "When I want to fuck you, I fuck you!" I began crying, and he kept on shouting, and I cried some more, and nobody wound up fucking *anybody*. Jayne Gouldtharpe was a friend of his, and she'd told me that he made a pass at her once, and naturally I brought that information out of the woodwork. "Why would I want to screw Jayne Gouldtharpe?" he said.

"I don't know," I said. "Maybe you're getting tired of me."

"Well maybe I am," he said, "but that doesn't make me interested in Jayne Gouldtharpe." And so it went on till dawn.

Now I'm afraid to say it, but I think Marvin and I have reached the final hours of our affair. I don't think he'll marry me, and I think I have to begin looking elsewhere. A month or so ago I told him that my intention for the year of nineteen seventy-one was to fall in love with somebody, and he said, "Well, if you fall in love with somebody, I'll go out and do the same thing." I was furious! I said, "If you do, I'll go straight to your house with a forty-five-caliber pistol and kill you and your wife and finish you both off!" I said, "*You're not gonna fall in love with anybody!*" That's the way it's been lately, all screaming and hollering and misunderstanding. I recognize the terminal stages. I've been through this before.

· 4 ·

Wow! I've been screwing for the last four days. It's been lovely, but I'm exhausted. I hadn't gone to bed with anybody in a few weeks, and I sure made up for it. Wow! I'm a Gemini, and you know what that means: on and off. Dr. Jekyll and Mrs. Hyde, that's me.

Oh, what a lovely time! Four nights ago it was Dominick. I will tell you about Dominick. A couple of months ago I was delivering a press release in the Seagram Building, and there was this beauti-

ful boy sitting out in front, just loitering, like a beautiful young
boy on the Adriatic seacoast. He said something clever to me, and
we struck up a conversation, and later we had a drink. I knew from
the beginning that I wanted to go to bed with him. He was twenty-
two years old, and a student at NYU, and a beauty! So a few days
later, at lunchtime, we went to bed. He was the first person I ever
took to my bed by design solely because he was beautiful. It was
lovely in bed, and then we made a date to go dancing, and four
days ago he showed up to go dancing again. He had his dancing
shoes under his arm, but by the time he reached my apartment I
just wanted to go to bed, so we did.

Two nights ago Marv called. I hadn't seen him in a few weeks,
and I was dying to get into bed with him. We were supposed to
meet at my place at nine, but he got here at eight, he was so anxious,
and we both went running around the place ripping clothes off and
jumped into bed. "Quick!" I said. "Fuck me! We'll make love
later!" We kept it up till one A.M., when Marv had to go home.
That's the trouble with married men.

Yesterday morning I had a good supportive session with my analyst, and afterwards I went into a coffee shop and I saw a beautiful
boy. And immediately I knew what I was going to do with *that*
beautiful boy.

I sipped my coffee and beamed at the boy, and he beamed back.
Pretty soon I said, "Well, shall we sit here and beam at each other
all day, or shall we do something else?"

He said, "I've got to go to work, but you can come watch me if
you like."

He worked in an artist's shop matting pictures, and I went
and watched him for an hour or so. Then I gave him my address
and telephone number and went home. At seven P.M. he showed
up, and I spent a lot of time on the telephone talking to friends
because I don't always know how to handle a situation like that,
and I could sit on the phone and talk to others and still make good
eye contact with this beautiful boy. Pretty soon I got off the phone
and we went to bed and he continued the terrific eye contact. He
had a terrific way of saying yes, like yes yes yes yes yes, a *total*

acceptance of me, and we had a full night of it. Wow! Eight times! It reminded me of the Benzedrine poppers that we used to take for a quick rush, only this rush was better because it wasn't from drugs.

Well, that's the story of my last four days, and you can see why I'm exhausted. Of course, I'm smart enough to realize that this sort of thing doesn't represent a satisfactory life style. Fun, maybe, but not satisfactory. But I've reached the point where I know a little about myself, and one of the things I know is that I've always tried to fulfill my needs through men, only now I do it consciously. If I'm horny, or if I have other needs, I'll take a man to bed. At least I know why I'm doing it.

I also know that I'm still screwed up on the subject of sex. Like for instance even to this very hour, to this very minute, I think that sex is dirty. That's the way I was brought up. I can't seem to shake it. I'd like to get over that stupid attitude, but so far I haven't been able to. And yet I've come so far in understanding myself. In the old days I didn't realize that I was always walking around looking for a father. It's only lately that I've been able to face that truth. The only thing I ever wanted out of life was a father, and I also had these sexual cravings involving my own father. But I've worked all that out. This morning after the beautiful boy left, I was able to say to myself aloud, "Well, you're well fed and you're happy and you feel real good, and what you want is to screw somebody. Now who do you want to screw? *You want to screw your daddy!*" And I really felt it! It's not that I necessarily feel like having a big sex scene, but I want a comfortable scene, I want somebody to hold onto me, to love me. I want love, but I want *my daddy's love*. I think it's real progress psychologically when you can admit something like that to yourself.

I'm still having my one-night stands, sure, but that's just because I'm acting like a man. I'm saying to myself frankly, "All right, I have sexual needs that have to be met, so I do like Montaigne." He said, "I want an intelligent woman at my table and a beautiful woman in bed." So I find beautiful men to sleep with, and it's sensational! And everybody's happy! It may not be what I *really* want, but it's a very good way to pass the time and take care of your immediate needs in a relatively short, short, unemotional, uninvolved sort of way. The difference between my one-night stands and an average man's one-night stands is that I'm always conscious of wanting a bigger involvement, or finding a husband. That's why I still do the chastity bit from time to time, because I think it helps me toward finding a husband; it helps me to get clear about myself and makes me feel unguilty and pure.

I've always had to face the fact that I consciously seduce men. I used to think of myself as Anna Karenina. *Anna Karenina* is my favorite book. I've read it every year since I was fifteen. I always *was* Anna Karenina. I mean, isn't that okay? I always wanted to be like her—the beautiful woman who is sought after and has marvelous love affairs and goes on trips and wears beautiful clothes. I put it out of my mind that she had an unhappy marriage and a lot of disastrous love affairs and that she killed herself at the end.

But I saw Anna Karenina in a movie the other night and the movie reminded me that there's another character in there I'd like to be. Her name is Kitty and she's a nice little girl and she finds a man who adores her and gives her a nice baby and a farm and Kitty turns out to be an ordinary, nice, lovely, little girl. And I told myself that I'm a lovely little girl, too, and I'm not so fucking extraordinary that I have to go out and prove that I'm the world's greatest seducer. So now I'm trying to be Kitty and not Anna Karenina any more.

I'll tell you how my whole life is going to work out, now that I'm getting my head straight. In about a month or so, good old Vanessa's going to have two or three steady boy friends that are terrific guys, each sensational in his own way, and they're going to call me up all the time and we're going to have long conversations on the phone and we're going to go out on dates, and then we're going to have very conventional and ordinary affairs, and then one of them will ask me to marry him and I'll ask one of the others to marry me, and *I'll get married!* Because I'm sick of people leaving me! And I'll make a hell of a good wife, too, because I can love and I can be totally loyal and I can be the most supportive person I know.

One other thing: I'm getting off the New York cocktail-party circuit. I don't meet the right kind of guys at cocktail parties. I don't know exactly *where* to meet the right guys, but I'll learn! I'll find them! One thing that's against me finding a husband, though, is I know nothing about how to play hard to get. Nothing! If I love, I love! So when I find the man I intend to marry, I might use a younger man to help me to stay satisfied sexually. I'll go to bed with the younger man, and that will keep me from throwing myself at the older man, and it'll all work out nicely. You have to *plan* these things.

Another thing I want to do before I settle down into marriage is have a lesbian relationship. And I know who with, too. But she's away on a trip right now. I already warned her about it. I told her I wanted to have a lesbian relationship with her, not for sex but for intimacy. I found out I had feelings for her when she came here one night with a boy friend and they were very tactile with each other and I found myself getting jealous of him, not her. I was very upset about it, and I told my analyst, and he said it was nothing to worry about, that it had to do with intimacy, not with sex. So when my girl friend comes back, I plan to get on with that little lesbian affair.

I also want to have at least one group grope, with three or more people, all down on the floor together, but in a cozy way, just for the feelings, to see what it's like. A real orgy! But without any sadistic overtones. I'd like to screw somebody other than the boy I'm with at the time, and I'd like to feel up the women, too. I'd like to have the whole scene, for the ecstasy and joy that you get out of association with more than one person at a time. Like Woodstock. Like joining the human race and *loving* the whole human race. That's where my head is at right now.

· 5 ·

TONIGHT I'M upset and sad. Excuse me. I can't help it. I just broke up with Marv this morning. It's over. It's *completely* over. We talked about it all night long, and we decided never to see each other again. Beautiful, wonderful Marvin will never be in my life again! I can feel the loss way down in the pit of my stomach.

We went all around during the night. We agreed that we're having more and more fights and that the sex is not as good as it used to be. We talked about what it would be like to be married, and everything was fine till we got to the subject of the fucking kids. Then he said, "What about the children?" I said, "I can't solve that, Marvin. I can't offer your children anything. I'd be a lousy stepmother. I can offer you some brand-new children, but that's all."

He said that didn't sound like a very healthy attitude toward the kids, and he didn't see how we could marry under those circumstances. So I put it to him bluntly: Did he intend to marry me or not? And he said, "No, not under the circumstances."

So then I did a vicious thing. I told him I wouldn't sleep with him, and I didn't, and it made him suffer masculine pains. I told him that I still thought he was the best lay in town, and the reason was that he loves me, and that makes *any* man the best lay in town. But I told him that I couldn't let him screw me because I'd spent the whole last week screwing—a cruel thing to say. But I had to say it because I was a little ripped and aggravated inside, and I had cystitis. I explained to him that the doctor had told me cystitis comes from screwing upside down, that the penis rubs against the bladder and irritates it and causes irritation. And I told Marv that one of the boys I'd been screwing all week liked to do it upside down. All Marv said was "Oh, I see." He's always been very patient about things like that.

Well, when the sun came up we'd talked everything out and a year and a half of my life were over and lost. No matter how we approached it, we couldn't see any point in going on this way, and he kissed me and we both cried and he left. He must have run down the street, because as soon as he went down the steps I ran out on the balcony to say goodbye to him one more time, but he was already out of sight.

I cried and cried. I picked up a hammer and I smashed my Picasso print, and I hammered away at the bricks on my wall until one of them split. I was still hammering when the phone rang. It was Jayne Gouldtharpe chirping away in her phony good-morning voice. "Hi!" she said. "This is Goldie!"

I said, "Jayne, I've just broken up with Marv."

She said, "Well, the reason I called is to ask you how you liked the blouse I lent you."

I said, "Goldie, *I just broke up with Marv!* He just left here for the last time."

She said in a kind of bored way, "Oh, Vanny, we all expected that, didn't we? I mean, it was long overdue. Your relationship wasn't good anyway."

So I got annoyed, and I told her off. I told her she had a hell of a nerve to talk to me that way when I had just suffered the worst loss of my life and I was still traumatized and upset. She said, "Oh, Vanny, calm down, will you? Now listen. The real reason I called was to ask you if you'd introduce me to that new sculptor."

I was sobbing and sniffling, but I was also mad, and I told her off for good. "Jayne Gouldtharpe," I said, "you are the most annoying person I know! You are the *typical* Freudian analysand. You wouldn't care if I was lying in my deathbed! All you've ever been interested in is my friends and my connections and who I could introduce you to. You always come to my parties and the first thing you say is 'Who should I know here?' " and I went on and on.

At the end there was a silence on the line. Then she said very coldly, "Vanessa Van Durant, you are the rudest person I have ever known!"

"Well, hang up, then!" I said.

"I will," she said, and she did. I halfway expected her to call back and apologize, but she hasn't yet.

At noontime I was still crying and I called my analyst and asked for some extra time. He told me to come right over, and I figured he'd help me through the crisis. But he's such a fucker! He lacks understanding, he lacks feeling. Here I was at death's door, suffering through the worst trauma of my whole life, and he was about as supportive as a fucking jellyfish. I went in there and I said, "Look, I'm feeling weak today, and I'm going through a lot of shit, and I want you to help me." He didn't say a word. He just let me rave on. But he should have known how I felt, if he's so fucking sensitive. And he should have given me some support. Instead he just sat there and blew his nose. What a fucker!

Well, I met an old boy friend on the street coming home from the doctor, a terrific-looking guy, a beautiful body. He was with a girl, but he said he'd call me. I think he will. That's what I'm waiting for now. I'm surprised he hasn't called yet. Not that it's all *that* important. But I *would* like to see him. He *said* he'd call. Of course, people say things like that and don't mean it. I'll just wait here by the telephone.

Mary Adams, 27

————•————

Mary is a lonely girl. She doesn't fit in with the one crowd, and she doesn't fit in with the other. She hates New York, and she's not particularly turned on by her job. She's looking for a husband, but she's beginning to realize this is a poor place to look. I think Mary will go back to Ohio pretty soon, and she'll be bitter for the rest of her life.—Peg Kern

• I •

MEN! MEN drive me up a wall! And New York men are the absolute worst! They are emasculated and unnatural and plastic and strange and compulsive and unreal, and any girl who comes here with the idea of finding a husband should go right down to the Greyhound station and buy a return ticket to Twin Falls, Idaho. I'll go even further than that. *Any* girl who comes here—period—no matter *what* she comes here for—should go buy that return ticket. This is no place for a nice young girl.

Of course you could not have told me that when I came here on vacation in my senior year of college. I was majoring in education at Ohio State, that big factory, and if you've been to Columbus, Ohio, you can understand how New York looked to me in nineteen sixty-two. It was the Crystal Palace! It was magic! Why, I could get high just walking down Fifth Avenue! New York looked like the capital of the universe, sin city, the world's center of hip people, the hub of creation. Everything was humming, everything was happening, and I just wanted to stand there and take it all in. I would have settled for just hanging around New York and being a *voyeuse*.

I went back to Columbus and got my degree and skedaddled back to New York as fast as an airplane could carry me, and the first person I went to see was an old friend of the family, Thomas Lexington Abney III, vice president of The Company and also a man who owed my poor peasant father a favor that would take forever to explain here. Tom Abney talked to me for about thirty minutes and then sent me to Personnel, where I was interviewed by a gimlet-eyed broad of about forty-eight long years who looked at me as though I was dirt. *Now* I understand why. Seven or eight years ago The Company wasn't looking for girls like me from middle-class and lower-class families and big mass-production state universities. They were looking for sweet young chicks from Skidmore and Sarah Lawrence, swirling their suede skirts and swinging their Mark Cross traveling bags at two hundred and twenty-five dollars the copy. Seven or eight years ago The Company was more interested in image than anything else, and these Ivy League chicks were *the* image. No wonder the Personnel lady didn't seem impressed by me! I didn't even know how to use makeup in those days, and I must have looked like the all-time champion Irish washerwoman type.

Nevertheless, I was hired. Thomas Lexington Abney III was not without his usefulness. I went right to work as an assistant, at a hundred and twelve dollars a week, and I was given to understand that I was a very lucky girl, that most assistants earned their jobs by serving as messengers or clerks or typists for at least a year. I said thanks. I didn't care *how* I got the job or what ordeals I had avoided. Anything to get situated in the big city, anything to become that most magic of all humans: a New Yorker!

The second day I was on the job an assistant named Alicia Nemerow came back from lunch and passed out on the floor. I thought, Oh, wow! What have I gotten into? Quickly I learned that the girls in the office were divided into two groups: the lushes and the squares. The lushes were Peg Kern—who became a good friend of mine—Alicia, Samantha Havercroft, Phyllis Brown, Gloria Rolstin and a few others, and the squares were Stephanie Grant, Cordy Simkens, Florence DuValle and a few others. Not that the lushes were falling-down drunks or the squares were living lives of total abstinence. But the lushes plainly were very interested in drinking as a way of life, and the others weren't. The lushes were girls who had every chance to become hard-core alcoholics some day. They would come back from lunch wiped out and fall asleep on their typewriters. I thought, These girls must be miserable to drink like that. I thought, That's not for me. I looked at some of the lushes over thirty and I swore I would *never* let this happen to me. Why, they were finished! They had the puffy look around the eyes and the bloated look around the cheeks that comes from drinking too much and sleeping too little. I thought, How pathetic! How sad! And these were bright women, too! My own IQ is a hundred and thirty, and some of these women were smarter than I was, by a long shot, and still they were sloshing away their lives day by day, coming back drunk from lunch with lecherous supervisors, being used up like cattle in a slaughterhouse, serving other people's purposes and not their own.

In the first few weeks on this strange new job I didn't have much time for any further study of the girls in the office, because the girls in the office were busy slashing my throat. They ganged up on me, and in a way I can't blame them. I had gotten my job through pull, and most of them had had to earn their titles the hard way. Some of them had close pals who were still running messages and clacking away in the typing pool, waiting for a chance to become an assistant, and I had jumped right over them.

You could cut the resentment with a knife. When I had to find something in the general files, the assistant in charge would give me the wrong file, or tell me to look it up myself. I'd leave in tears, and I'd be late with the work. Anyone who has ever worked in an office knows that you have to depend on your fellow workers in your first few weeks, or you're dead. My God, I didn't know *anything* about The Company's procedures. On the first day I asked one of the assistants where the ladies' room was, and she waved her hand vaguely and said, "I don't know. Somewhere down there," and turned away.

This went on for weeks. I was working so hard that I went home aching. Projects that should have taken me a few minutes would take me an hour, an hour of scurrying around, up and down blind trails, repeating myself, making mistakes and having to start over, and all because nobody would help me. Then I got sick of it. I had marked Peg Kern as a decent person, underneath her boozing tendencies, and I went right into her office and braced her. "Listen," I said, "this is goddam foolishness. Now why don't you just tell me what's eating you?"

We had a long talk, and it came out that they were all certain I was sleeping with Thomas Lexington Abney III and that *that* was how I got my job. I said, "Well, for Christ's sake!" I told her the whole story, and I emphasized that I was *not* on intimate terms with the elderly vice-president but that he owed the family a favor and had repaid it by helping me get hired. "I didn't ask to be hired as an assistant," I said. "I'd have been glad to start in the typing pool. Don't blame me!"

Peg was decent about it, and she sort of took me under her wing for a while. But the other girls kept up their campaign, until a supervisor named Alexandra Oats found out about it and banged a few heads. Alex had asked me to work up a report one day, and when I was an hour late with it she came into my office and asked me why. "Because it took me three hours to find a description of the patent in our files," I said.

"Why?" she said.

I blurted it out. "Because that son of a bitch of an assistant in there kept sending me to the wrong files."

Alexandra Oats went down that hallway at about eighty miles an hour, and people in Jersey City could hear her laying out that assistant. After that, everybody was very helpful. When I became close friends with Peg, she explained frankly to me what they had been trying to do. "We were trying to get you fired," she said, "but not because of anything *you* did. There's a lot of that preferential hiring around here, and we wanted to show the brass that they couldn't get away with it. If *we* all had to go through the initiation rites, then so did everybody else."

I felt, How childish! But I didn't say anything. I felt, These people are supposed to be adults. That was before I read books like Desmond Morris's *The Naked Ape* and found out that people spend most of their time acting like wild animals and don't even know it.

Later on I realized that another reason for such petty behavior was that the assistants didn't have enough to do. There were far too many of them—there *still* are—for the available work. And the job was mindless. Within six months I knew everything there was to know about it. So where was the challenge? Well, the challenge lay in playing games like treating new girls with contempt, or gossiping about the affairs that were going on all over the place, or having an affair of your own. The human organism can stand anything but systematic boredom.

Before I went to The Company I had heard a lot about the brilliant, sophisticated men who worked there, and I was told that the way to meet them was to go to company parties. So I went to the first big one, expecting to hear all these brilliant people saying all these brilliant things. Ha ha! How soon we learn! They don't say brilliant things at those cocktail parties. They say *stupid* things. They smile at each other and goose the girls and try to pretend that they're human beings. I took one look around that big party room and I said to myself, "They all look alike! I don't belong here." Nobody seemed to object when I just turned around and walked out. Later I figured I had been too hasty, and I figured it was my own fault they had seemed so dull. Who was I to judge? I was just a country hick from Xenia, Ohio. I told myself that maybe these people do have brilliant minds and fascinating things to say, but why should they say them around a country hick like me? I took all the blame myself. That was six years ago. Now I realize that my first impression was correct. But I'm not blaming The Company, I'm blaming the whole New York setting. It only takes a few months to convert an honest, interesting, intelligent male human being into just another plastic New Yorker. There are too many pressures on men in New York, and the pressures keep them from feeling like *men*. That's one of the reasons I don't get active in Women's Lib. I mean, I endorse the economic side of Women's Lib completely, but I don't go around marching or burning my bra, because I think that things like that only tend to emasculate men, and the New York male has already been emasculated beyond all recognition. That's the number-one problem between the sexes in New York, and Women's Lib only aggravates it.

I spend a lot of time in my apartment, and sometimes I cry from sheer loneliness. It's hard, really *hard*, to meet genuine males in New York City. You certainly are not going to meet them at singles bars, and anyway I loathe the very idea of singles bars. Meat racks! So you sit home, or you go out on a date with a man you really don't want to go out with. And you take your chances! I mean literally. *Anything* can happen to you on a date with these weird, sick New York creatures.

A few months ago I went to an office party and struck up a conversation with an eccentric young man who worked on another floor. I had seen him around the building and once or twice at Santana's Bar, and I had marked him as a weirdo. He never seemed to say anything; he just hung along the fringes of whatever group he was in and listened. He seemed disoriented and alienated, fearful and detached. Well, he wasn't much different at the party, but I had to talk to *somebody*, and he happened to be there. I'd babble away and he'd nod his head, or in a burst of conversational enthusiasm he'd say something like, "Oh, really?" I thought, How weird! And I also thought, Gee, I must really be a dull person to listen to.

But then, after many drinks, he asked me if I wanted to leave the party and have dinner with him, and I thought, Why not? Maybe he'll prove to be a human being, and anyway I hadn't been out on a date in a month or two. Well, we went to dinner, and we had hardly sat down before he reached over and put his hand on my knee, which I thought was a very sophomoric thing to do. I removed the hand gently, and about five minutes later it was back and I removed it again. I thought, *Really!* A man of thirty years! A *big* boy! I thought, I've never met so *many* stupid men as I have in this town. Don't they know how to seduce women? At one point I thought I'd like to conduct classes for New York men in how to seduce women. Because *they just don't know!* Granted, there might be a few degenerate and stupid girls in the world who'd get turned on by a hand on the knee, but they're such a minority! As a technique, it's nowhere. But these New York men have no technique. It's all clutch and grab, and let's strip, baby. They act desperate, terribly desperate. Grope, grope, grope!

But strange as it may seem the dinner wasn't all that bad. He began to talk and got progressively drunker, and I tried to mother the poor thing, to make him feel like somebody. He took me home in a taxi, and I invited him up for a brandy, and no sooner had we walked into my apartment than he made the big grab for me. Now don't misunderstand—I don't mind necking. Necking is a fact of life, a normal thing, and you have to start somewhere. But *before you get your coats off? Before you've locked the door?*

I pulled myself loose and he came reeling across the floor at me. He actually knocked me down and jumped on me!

I wriggled away and jumped up and ran into the kitchen to pour some drinks, trying to gain time and cool him down. But he was hot on the trail. He came after me again and wrestled me down to the floor, and this time I really got mad. I said, "Stop it! I'm *serious!*" and then I saw a certain look in his eye, and I got scared. He looked maniacal.

I felt like crying. I'm not a crier, but this was too much. I thought, Jesus Christ, not this again! I was so weary of this New York City strong-arm stuff at the end of every date. I started sniffling, throwing myself on his mercy, and trying to talk to him. I said, "Look, relax!" and I slowly circled around him to get to the door of my apartment. As I did, he grabbed my skirt and yanked, and about ten of the snaps unpopped. Now I was really scared! He came roaring across the room at me and shoved me up against the wall. I said, "Please! Stop doing that! You're upsetting me! Start acting like a human being!" When I said that, he put his hands around my neck and began pounding my head against the wall. He was halfway strangling me and halfway trying to break my skull.

I had enough sense to go limp, and maybe that's what saved my life. The most incredible things went through my head as I tried to stay conscious. I thought for sure I was being murdered, and I thought how my mother back in Xenia would never forgive me for letting myself get murdered so luridly, with headlines in the *Daily News*. I thought, This is freaky! I thought, I *know* this guy! He won't murder me! Then I realized that he had let me go, and he was raving over and over, "You don't understand! You don't understand! I need you! I need you!" What he meant, of course, was that he needed sex.

I slid slowly away from him, and I said coldly, "If sex is what you want, you can always go out and buy it."

"It's not the same," he said.

"No," I said. "It isn't love, is it? But neither is pounding my head against the wall."

He sat on the couch, and beckoned me to sit next to him. I just stood there. He began begging and pleading, and I circled toward the door. But he was too clever for that. He jumped up and stood between me and the door, and I could see that violent look in his eyes, the same look that I had seen earlier. "Just sit down," I said. "Just take it easy."

He began begging and pleading again, and I tried to stay as cold and calm as I could. He tried everything. He said, "Let's just go and lie down in the bedroom and put our arms around each other and be close. That's all I want."

I thought, This guy is beyond help. He's so bottled up and frustrated and emasculated and lonely, but I can't cure him by lying down and letting him hold me. So after an hour of this kind of talk—by now it was about four in the morning—I just said, "Look, tell me one thing. Are you gonna kill me?"

That seemed to stop him. He said, "No, of course I'm not." He sat down again and put his head in his hands. I ran to the door and yanked it open and stood with my back to it. "Leave!" I said, as loud as I could. "Just *leave!*"

He began whining and wheedling again. Couldn't we just talk? That's all he wanted. "Please!" he said. "You don't understand me!"

"I don't *want* to understand you!" I said. "Now get out before I call the neighbors!"

I stood in that doorway for another half hour before I finally got him to leave, and I slammed the door and locked it with relief. Then I heard him come back up the stairs and knock on the door again. "Please!" he said. "I just want to talk to you!"

"I'll talk to you on the phone!" I said. My phone rang every fifteen minutes till dawn, but I didn't answer it.

You'll say that was an extreme case; I'll say that it was not at all extreme. In a typically extreme New York case, the outcome is far less happy. The New York girl becomes accustomed to extreme cases. She becomes accustomed to dealing with infantile men with hangups in their brains like spider webs. The saddest thing is when you fall in love with one of them. That happened to me once, and I'm still in love with the man, and I still think that there's some hope for him. But not with *me* as his girl friend. I came on too strong with him, and he rushed right out of my life. You can't do that with these men; they have to be mothered and babied.

This man and I had been sleeping together for weeks when I made my mistake. We were talking in my living room, and I began a character analysis of him, a sort of half-ass psychiatric profile, just for fun. I thought he'd enjoy it. I thought we knew each other well enough to exchange some realities. And not everything in my analysis of him was bad—in fact, most of it was good. But before I was finished, he jumped up with this panicky look in his eyes and he said, "Stop! I don't *like* this! You make me feel like you can see right through me! You make me feel like I have no secrets from you!"

I said, "Brad, I wouldn't *presume* to look through anybody!"

But he was raving and stalking around the apartment, acting terribly upset, and I didn't know what to do. I thought, here I am reaching out, reaching out toward somebody I have real feelings for, trying to relate to him as a human being, and he's scared to death! He can't stand it!

Well, I guess there were things inside himself that he didn't want to reveal, because he left and he never came back, and I went around with a broken heart for a couple of months. What was eating him? Emasculation? I don't know, but I'm sure it was related to emasculation. That's the old New York problem. First they're emasculated by their mommies, then they're emasculated by their jobs and their anxieties and their insecurities, they're emasculated by the oppressive atmosphere and the overpowering buildings and the dangers that surround everybody in New York, they're emasculated by the tough broads that they have to deal with, they're even emasculated by their lack of touch with nature. I mean, a young man back in Twin Falls, Idaho, can go out and cut a tree and bring back some logs and say to himself, "Look at me! I'm a man, doing mannish things. I'm bringing back three cords of wood for my family!" But what does a man in New York do to feel masculine? He goes to the Sixth Avenue Deli and brings back a couple of blintzes and a Danish! So then he has to go out and try to convince himself that he's still a man doing mannish things. In the case of my lover, he went and told several of his close friends that he had knocked off a couple of pieces with me. That must have made him feel like a man! I know he did it, because there was an instant change in the way some of his close male friends began to treat me. One of them was a specialist named Red Johnson, and the week after Brad and I broke up Red Johnson stopped me in the hall and grabbed my hand and gave me that finger-in-the-palm bit. Ugh! Sophomoric! And right away I knew that Brad must have been mouthing off about me, because there wasn't a reason in the world for Red Johnson to do this all of a sudden. God, I was depressed! I ran back to my office and shut the door and cried. I thought I was marked as the office whore, when all I'd done was fall in love with a man and sleep with him.

· 2 ·

WELL, IT only takes a few incidents like that to make you wonder what you're doing here, what's your true role on earth. I've long since realized that New York and I have to have a parting of the ways, and the sooner the better, but I can't seem to get myself off my backside to do something about it. One of these days it's going to be too late; and I'll end up as an item on the police blotter. You think I'm kidding? Listen, I live only a few blocks from the slums, and it's more like a battlefield than a neighborhood. I never used to worry about walking the streets—I mean, there are ten million people here—but lately it hasn't made any difference how many people are here, they just go about their business and ignore what's going on a few feet away from them. Last month I was walking along Broadway and I came on this little group of kids, maybe four or five of them, eleven or twelve years old. Well, who worries about kids? But as I walked past them one of them came darting up behind me and goosed me! Wholesome-looking kids, normal-looking kids, one of them wearing horn-rimmed glasses like the Little Rascals cast! I went to pieces! I was absolutely hysterical! I whirled around and the kid was running away, laughing. I went after him. I thought, Why, you little monster! It freaked me out to have a little kid do something like that, at an age when kids are supposed to be smoking corn silk behind the barn.

I knew I couldn't catch the kid, but I wanted to scare him. He went down an alley and I went after him, screaming and hollering. When he reached the end he climbed up and over a wooden wall, and I was so mad to see him getting away that I shouted, "Just keep on running, you little bastard!" and he said, "Don't worry, lady, I will!"

So I pulled myself together and walked back to Broadway, looking over my shoulder toward the alley, and at the same time looking around for a cop. Naturally, there was no cop around. I stood there at the corner, and then I heard a childish voice saying, "What's wrong, lady?"

I turned and saw another small boy, and I decided to ignore him. "What wrong, lady?" he insisted. "Did dat bad boy try to goose yeh, lady?" And as I started to walk away, this one ran up and grabbed for me!

I went right up a wall! I felt panicked, ganged up on. It was just little kids, and that made it worse! It was *Lord of the Flies* all over again, and I was Piggy. I screamed. I went completely off my trolley. I hollered, "You fucking little bastards!" Then the terror set in, and I rushed away, sobbing hysterically. I ran past several people, but nobody even asked me what was wrong. I went to my apartment and I barricaded myself inside and I cried for the rest of the night. I realized that if I had caught one of those kids, I'd have killed him! And I wondered what was happening to me in this awful place, what kind of a monster I was turning into.

Two weeks later I was in the same neighborhood around midnight, and as I walked along I saw this black guy coming toward me. I could tell that he was jockeying for position, and as he passed me he reached out for my crotch. I did a little sidestep and began to walk faster. He said very sarcastically, "Oh, excuse *me!*" as though I'd been a prude to resist his gallant overture. We were the only two people on the block, and I tried not to set him off. I just walked away and looked back over my shoulder, and I was relieved to see that he was doing the same thing and weaving a little. Probably he was drunk or turned on. Most of the people in this neighborhood are drunk or turned on.

When I told the girls in the office what had happened, they just laughed. "Count your blessings," Peg said. "All he did was try to cop a feel."

I said, "But I don't *want* to be felt by strange men!"

She said, "Well, you better get used to it if you want to live in New York."

Lately I've installed burglar alarms and extra locks in my apartment, but what's the use? They'll still find some way to get at you.

You can't stay barricaded in your own apartment forever. The other night I had my window open, and I was walking around in a nightgown, and I heard a rustle from the direction of the open window. I peeked out and saw a flash of white, like a shirt or skin or something. I doused the lights and stuck my head out, and when I turned my head there was a trouser leg a foot away! A man was standing on the fire escape, flattened against the wall! I didn't have time to be scared. I just said, "What are you doing here? Who *are* you?" and I slammed the window down. I heard him run up the escape and over the rooftops. A few days later I saw the same person going through the garbage cans in front of the apartment. He looked like a Puerto Rican, maybe eighteen or twenty years old, kinky hair, very dark, and as I watched him I realized that he wasn't all there, he was retarded or something. And I thought, My God, that's what walks on my rooftop at night! After that, I got in the habit of checking the fire escape when I came home, and three nights ago when I checked I saw a head ducking around the corner of the building. It must have been a burglar, casing the joint, because last night the girl next door was robbed—while she was sleeping in her bed. So I'm getting window gates installed on both my windows, to add to my three door locks and my chains and my burglar alarm. Pretty soon I'll be as safe in here as any prisoner in solitary. And just as contented!

There's no real safety in New York. How safe am I when I go out on the streets? Two of my girl friends were raped *when they were together*. They came home late at night and opened the downstairs door to their apartment building, and a hand came from behind the door and encircled one of them with a knife. A masked man came out of the shadows and said, "Don't move, or I'll kill her!"

He ordered my friends to take him to their apartment. He bound them and gagged them, and then he spent five hours raping them. To add insult to injury, he robbed them before he left. That happened to be one of the rare cases that are solved by the police. The man was caught trying to do the same thing, and he turned out to be a faggot. Talk about emasculation! That's why it had taken five hours to rape the girls. He couldn't get it up! The poor slob. He's now serving fifty-five years in Sing Sing.

Well, in my opinion this sort of thing is going to get far worse before it gets any better. In my opinion, New York is going to become a ghost town. There won't be the very rich and the very poor any more, but just the very poor, plus the demented and the twisted and the insane. As far as I'm concerned, the trend is already well under way, except that a few of us victims are still hanging around, getting our masochistic kicks. The hares are still here for the hounds, but we won't last much longer. It won't be long before the rapists are raping each other, and the muggers will only have other muggers to work on. I told my psychiatrist about my theory, and he said, "Well, that's quite a fantasy."

I said, "Fantasy, hell! It's here!"

He just laughed. But he didn't sound like he meant it.

Well, this one won't be around to see the "fantasy" come true. I'm twenty-seven, nearly twenty-eight, and not a husband in sight. If I'm going to be lonely, I'm going to be lonely someplace else, not in this rat's nest. I couldn't *imagine* growing old here. What a perfectly horrible place to grow old!

Florence DuValle, 40

———•———

*Florence DuValle is getting bitter. Marriage is always on her mind.
and she's about forty, and the souring process is in full bloom. A
few more days will pass, and she'll look in the mirror and discover
that she's an old lady. It seems to me that her big mistake lies in
fighting it. What's wrong with being an old lady?*—Stephanie
Grant

*Florence DuValle seems to move from man to man at the parties.
I think she's looking for a husband, whether she'll admit it or not.
She once told me that she was going to transfer to another depart-
ment because she had met all the men in our department. She seems
to devote all her time and energy to charming the men.*—Samantha
Havercroft

• I •

By the time I came to The Company for my first tour of duty, I'd
been in girls' schools for seven straight years, and I knew from
nothing. I came from one of those upper-middle-class families—
Merion, Pennsylvania, a suburb of Philadelphia—where there was
lots of money, lots of creature comforts, and very few of the
things that really mattered. In our family we had no love and
barely any communication at all. My father wanted a son when I
came along, and he tried his best to make me into one. Thank God
it didn't work. I had to spend five years and twenty-five thousand

dollars on psychiatry to make myself into a genuine girl. That was the biggest fight of my life, and I won. My father lost.

In the early nineteen fifties, when I was at Skidmore, I don't think there was any doubt that The Company was regarded as just about the most desirable place to work in the United States. At least that's the impression everyone had at school. There was an attitude that an office girl at The Company was superior to a top executive in the garment district or anyplace else. Certainly The Company was glamorous. The men thought nothing of hopping on a plane for Paris, and more often than not they took one of the women with them. Everybody was so intelligent, so well dressed, so talented. The Company's *building* was even ultra-handsome! The only problem was that they had no openings.

I had made up my childish mind that it was going to be The Company or nothing, and I padded around New York for about two months sort of halfway pretending to be looking for another job. Then a personnel clerk at The Company called me and said there was an opening as messenger, at forty dollars a week. It was a silly job for a girl with an A.B. and high honors, but I'd been conditioned to think that *no* job was silly if it got you in The Company.

I can't describe how naïve I was when I first went to work. I had had no sexual experience, and—strange as it may seem in the fast age we live in—I barely even knew the facts of life. It was possible to be that way back in the nineteen fifties, especially if you were brought up as cloistered as I was. At first, nothing happened to shake me up at The Company, but then I began to meet some of these tough women, the Alexandra Oats types, and I was repelled by them. Wow! Ugh! *Tough* women! I knew I could never make it the way they'd made it. I could never be that hard in a man's world. And I was right. I had my chance and I didn't make it. Some of those women would eat you up and spit you out and keep smiling all through the process.

Another shock came when I discovered what a free and easy place it was. One afternoon an assistant rode down on the elevator with me and told me she had a heavy date, and there in the lobby waiting for her was this big Negro. I mean, I'd think nothing of it now, but this was nineteen fifty-three, and it seemed so *shocking* at the time. You came to The Company expecting it to be the last place in the world for goings-on like that.

But still it seemed so fulfilling to be working for The Company, even as a messenger. I went to all the parties, and once in a while I'd wind up in a hansom cab in Central Park with a salesman or a junior executive. Now this didn't happen in other companies, I was sure. We called everybody by his first name, and this encouraged the office liaisons that sprang up. Of course, little Miss DuValle from Skidmore wasn't having any naughty relationships in her life! I turned them all away at the door. I wasn't even sure what they were after, but whatever it was I wanted nothing to do with it. So I just rolled along in the hansom cabs, enjoying the parties, soaking up the glamor of delivering messages to fifty-thousand-dollar-a-year men who called me "Flo" and offered to buy me lunch. I had father figures all over the place! They'd talk to me by the hours. And there were several men I wouldn't have minded marrying. Exciting, creative men! And all of them telling me, "You're going to have a great career here. You're going to be terrific!" Mentally I was about twelve and a half, and I sopped it all up.

It was about six months before I had my first hard look right at what was going on. I was promoted to secretary to an executive secretary, and my new boss was one of those brittle hard women. She was having a flaming affair with *her* boss, and at first I was terribly confused by all this. I had been taught that this kind of thing was wrong, that affairs were conducted only by low-life immoral types, and yet these two seemed to be fairly ordinary, fairly decent middle-class people. He didn't seem like Jack the Ripper and she didn't seem like a prostitute, and yet they were carrying on in front of everybody. I didn't know what to make of it. I was so *dumb* about sex. Office affairs happened only in fiction.

It also disturbed me that everyone pretended that nothing was going on. I was struck by the phoniness of it. Their affair dominated the whole life of our office, and yet you were never allowed to mention it or even allude to it. They went off on trips together and we all had to pretend that we didn't notice they were both booked into the same hotel in the same city time after time. I think I'd have been able to handle the whole thing better in my own mind if it hadn't been for the hypocrisy.

My lady boss was not the most popular person in the office. She was totally oriented to *him*, and to hell with the rest of us. As for the man, he turned out to be a psychopath. He was driven, compulsive-obsessive. He worked terribly long hours—and I mean really *worked!* He had a powerful drive to get ahead and absolutely no tact or diplomacy to go with it. He was nothing but pure drive! He *had* to control people. He liked to take out his frustrations on us hirelings, the little snips. And he was so obvious about it. He had this power over my boss, his mistress, and he'd scream hysterically at her in the middle of the office. Then one of the executives would walk in and he'd fall at the man's feet, practically embracing his knees. It was disgusting.

When the affair began to go sour, the whole thing became a scene from Havelock-Ellis, even for those of us who weren't involved. Again my naïveté showed through. My boss would arrive at work all puffy-eyed and sick, and she'd have to leave early. Then we entered a period where she was having these terrible hemorrhages, right in the office, and once she had to be rushed to the hospital. I couldn't understand. Why would this attractive thirty-year-old healthy woman suddenly start having problems with her insides? Well, there was a secretary named Phyllis Brown, and she finally took me aside and spelled it all out one day. "Don't you see what's going on, you dummy?" she said. "It's *him* that's causing this! It's obvious! He must be doing it to her all night long and with everything in the room. He's tearing her up, he's lacerating her! The man is a woman-killer, everybody knows that." At first the idea didn't register, but eventually I had to admit that Phyllis Brown was right. It was just a hopelessly sick affair, and whether the man knew it or not, he was slowly killing her.

I suppose it was inevitable that he would try to destroy her psychologically as well as physically, and he began this phase of his attack by flirting outrageously with some of the rest of us. I turned him completely off—I was terrified of men like him—but some of the others enjoyed the game. Once in a while he'd waltz a girl right out of our office and down to the Santana, for all the world to see, and my boss would sit at her desk and bawl, and only I would know it. Gradually she lost all control of him, and one night she cracked wide open. He was flirting with some busty young assistant at a party, and my boss picked up a heavy glass ashtray and threw it against the wall. Then she began screaming, and she wouldn't stop. At first she was railing against him, but gradually we could see that she was just babbling, that she had broken down. She was taken away in an ambulance, under heavy sedation, and she stayed away for about two months.

Then the whole thing collapsed. We were reorganizing our department, and the executives announced that the reorganization would *not* include my boss's lover. He could take a demotion, or he could quit. He quit, and so did my boss. Luckily they went in different directions. He got another job, and she moved clear out of the state, met a normal man and married and produced normal children. She is one of the lucky ones. Too bad he didn't go someplace and take up a normal existence, too, but instead he stayed in New York with his wife and five children and managed to interfere in my own life. But that was later.

By the time I had been with The Company a year I realized that I was in over my head, and I went around trembling like the pure-white virginal thing that I was. My sexual attitude at that time was that an affair was unthinkable, that I'd get married and have sex with my husband on our wedding night—and absolutely nothing would happen till then! I was like that woman in Peter de Vries who regarded sexual intercourse as an unnatural act. Well, I managed to keep myself pure, but at some price! The men simply bombarded me, and I kept wondering, What can I do, how can I handle these approaches? The men calling up from the bar, picking you up at parties, pestering you at your apartment. I just wasn't prepared for anything like this. What do you do when the chief of foreign sales asks you to go to bed with him, and you're twenty-two years old and dumb? That happened to me, and I escaped him with a fast shuffle at the front door, and the next morning when I came to work I said to myself, Well, I got out of that one, but I hope I'm not out of a job. But he was nice. He phoned me later in the morning and asked me to come around to his office.

"Look," he said, "forget what happened last night. I had a few drinks, that's all. And you're a lovely girl."

"Thank you," I said. I was literally trembling.

"I hope you're not upset," he said.

"Oh, no, I'm not," I said. I was almost crying.

"Tell you what I'm gonna do," he said. "I'm gonna take you out for dinner and a drink tonight, by way of apology. Okay?" The amazing thing is that he did exactly that: took me out for dinner and a drink and never pestered me again. But how confusing it all was! Now instead of wondering if I'd lost my job by turning him down, I began to wonder if I'd said the wrong thing at dinner. I wondered why he'd suddenly dropped me so cold. You can see the situation: I was twenty-two years old and fourteen mentally.

I also began to discover that I was having a hard time getting interested in men of my own age, the typical men I met outside the office. The hot shots at The Company were so glamorous. How could I get interested in a fifth assistant teller at a bank in the Bronx, when the man in the next cubicle at the office had just got back from Hong Kong and was itching to take me out for a drink and tell me all about his trip? Of course, the man in the next cubicle was married, but then we were all supposed to be pals at The Company, first names only, remember? Nobody else seemed to care who was married and who wasn't, so why should I? You work side by side all day with the most stimulating men in the world, and by the time five-thirty came around you were too excited to want to go home and shift gears and go out on a date with some primary-school teacher. So you fell into the bar and had some drinks and maybe dinner later, and for many of the girls it ended in bed.

I try to explain to my friends in other companies, but they can't understand it: how your schedule is so flexible at The Company, how the whole atmosphere is so free and easy, how it's so easy to pull the wool over people's eyes. Why, I knew girls who had flourishing sexual activities just in the early afternoons—matinees, they

called them—while everybody else was at lunch! So in a sense The
Company was a blackboard on which you could write whatever
you wanted, on which you could act out all your weaknesses and
strengths. Personally, judging from what I saw, it's a bad set-up.
Blake said something about the paths of excess leading to wisdom,
but he forgot to mention the ruined lives and the nervous break-
downs en route. You may wind up a wise old lady, but what a
price to pay!

Actually, I hadn't thought all this out in the early phase, but
after a little more than a year with The Company I realized intui-
tively that there was something very, very wrong, and I wanted
out. I was still so immature, and the pressures from the men around
me were tremendous, and I simply did not know how to cope. On
the outside, I had met a few super-solid people, good candidates for
marriage, and they bored me. But inside The Company I felt inadequate and out of step. I was fascinated, but I felt insufficient. It was
like the cobra and the bird, and I knew that the cobra would swal-
low me whole if I didn't make a sudden move to escape.

· 2 ·

WHEN MY grandmother died and left me some money, I saw a way
out. I took the money and opened up a boutique in the old home
town. At first it was a joy to be back in the Philadelphia area. They
were having a big urban-renewal project downtown, and they
were turning blocks of slums into an attractive area called Center
City. My shop and I grew along with the project, and there never
was a year when I didn't show a profit—never anything huge, but
enough to feel that I was becoming the successful mature young
adult. Then Mr. Trouble arrived. My boss's old boss, the lady-
killer. He popped down on the Pennsylvania Railroad and called
me up and insisted that we have drinks together. I hardly remembered him; two years had gone by, and I wondered why he was
calling me at this late stage of the game. It was the cobra and the

bird again. The cobra said he had never been able to get me out of his mind and he just *had* to see me. So we began an inter-city affair, and if you don't mind I would rather not go into the sordid details. It's not easy for me to talk about such things in the first place. Until now, I've never told a single soul that I'd ever gone to bed with *any* man, let alone with a beast like this one. So I'll draw the curtain. No, he did not injure me physically the way he had injured my old boss, but it wasn't for lack of trying. He was the complete sadist looking for the complete masochist, and it took him the better part of a year to realize that I did not qualify. As for what I saw in him, I haven't the slightest idea, and five years of therapy haven't provided the answer. It's funny: he showed up again a few months ago, without warning, and he said, "Let's have dinner, for old times' sake." So we went to dinner and by the time I'd finished the hors d'oeuvres I was so bored I could hardly stand him. He invited himself to my apartment and had a few drinks, and then he began pacing the floor and telling me how wonderful I was and how far I would go in the business world, and then he said, "Come on, let's go to bed. You're the sexiest dame I've ever seen in my life!" What an utter, colossal, smashing bore! But I'd been young when he dropped down to Philadelphia. Nowadays men like him disgust me.

As the years went by in Philadelphia—and there were ten very long years—I discovered that there was never a day when I didn't miss my old job at the glamorous company. If you are saying that I am crazy, you may be right. What did I miss? I missed the whirligig. The parties. The crazy, brilliant people. I missed the challenges, the interplay of personalities and skills in putting out important products. I missed the hubbub of New York—God, what a thing to miss! I missed the way people envied me when they found out I worked at The Company. I felt alone; I felt that I'd let a big chance go by when I'd taken up this lonely life in my boutique, spending weekends with the family in Merion, going to boring social events in that quiet City of Brotherly Love.

To my credit, there was a part of me that also knew I was better off where I was. I wanted to get married in the worst way—I still do—and I knew I had a far better chance of meeting eligible men if I stayed in Philadelphia. I said to myself, "If you go back to that enclosed atmosphere at The Company you'll get all involved and gung-ho about the people again, and you'll *never* get married." And I wrote in my diary, "In order to get married and keep an open mind and meet people and stay relaxed and normal, you're staying right here!"

But the pull was too strong. It was in my blood. I sold the shop and went back to New York and took an apartment and decided to try a final compromise. Although I was back in the glamorous big city, I would not look for work at The Company. Surely there must be something rewarding somewhere else in New York. One day I went to another building for an interview, and the inside of the place completely turned me off. I was used to The Company's building: spacious and fresh and airy, modern and shining, radiating a respect for the people inside—but this other building represented architectual concepts that went back to an era when people were just ciphers, machines, lucky to have a job in the first place. I didn't even ride up on the elevator. I went for an interview at another company that turns out products similar to The Company's, but once again it was a let-down. The atmosphere was wrong. The building smelled old and musty; the people looked bored and listless. Whatever my problems ten years before at The Company, I could never have said that the people were dull. If anything, they were *too* lively! They were so alert and intelligent, including the receptionists. The longer I stayed away, the more I realized that The Company was my kind of place. The men didn't wear white ankle socks and the girls didn't wear garter belts. Everybody was correct, right, *au courant*. I began to see The Company as a haven, as a protection from all those other demoralizing places in the rest of the city. By the time I had finished brainwashing myself, I would have taken a job as a janitress to get back inside that building. But I was lucky. Some of the girls I had worked with ten years before were still there; they put in a good word for me and I got a job as a secretary at a hundred and eleven dollars a week. I was back where I belonged!

Now I was thirty-three, but I still looked good, and I was no longer so stupid about sex and morality. I was perfectly willing to enjoy myself, within reason, and the beaux came along in quantity. It soon began to matter less and less to me that most of them were married. This is a fact of life that almost all New York girls become accustomed to. You simply cannot have much of a dating life in New York unless you date married men. Of course the married men at The Company were the most fascinating men around, and that helped to make up for the fact that a girl had no long-term prospects with them. I was still hoping to get married, and somehow I was convinced that the right man would pop up out of a top hat some night, and in the meantime I was on a crazy round of parties, dinners, openings and—yes—a few affairs, discreet and intriguing. The total environment was exhilarating, as I had expected. It was all fun and games. When there was no formal party scheduled, somebody would always pull a bottle of Scotch out of his desk and offer drinks. It was flirt, flirt, flirt, and laugh, laugh, laugh —an insane whirl. I was going out with good-looking men, sophisticated, knowledgeable men with *savoir faire* and taste, and they were buying me fine wines and taking me to the best shows. Wonder of wonders, I was promoted to assistant, and I began doing a lot of traveling for The Company and not always alone. Sometimes I would have to pinch myself to believe it. One night I was sitting in the bar of the Berlin Hilton with one of The Company's biggest executives, and he was complaining about having to spend so much time in foreign countries. I couldn't understand him. I was bedazzled by the schnapps and the caviar and the foreign languages and the jet-setting around. It was the high period of my life.

Then suddenly I became middle-aged, and I began to notice changes around me. Younger assistants began getting the foreign assignments. Somebody turned off the partying, at least for me, and on Friday afternoons I would walk past gatherings of younger people who would say nothing as I went by, except maybe "Have a nice weekend, Flo!" They were going to the Santana or Twenty-One or Toots Shor's place; I was going home. The merry-go-round hadn't slowed down; it had just gone *clunk* and stopped. My final

years of eligibility had been spent whirling around; now I was un-
wanted. It sounds overdramatic, but it is literally true. You're not
welcome around some places as soon as you stop being one of the
beautiful people. You can stay on the payroll practically forever,
but nothing is going to happen. You're not going to be promoted,
you're not going to be wined and dined, and you're not going to be
welcomed into the big happy family. The luncheon groups form,
and you're left on the sidelines, ordering sandwiches from the take-
out place. I'm not talking about the men. They remain beautiful
people by definition—by *their own* definition. The men run the
show in New York; the men make up the rules. They say they're
beautiful people, and so they are, and they're accepted as part of
the "in" crowd no matter how old or stupid they get, and these
poor subservient dumb women continue idolizing them, looking up
to them, playing their game.

Now I'm just hanging on. I'm treated as the grandmother of the
group. I look around and I see all these beautiful young assistants
with the travel stickers on their luggage, and I say to myself,
"What am I *doing* here?" If I were truthful to myself, I'd go away.
The fun and games have ended. Nowadays, office parties are rare,
and it's even rarer for me to get an invitation to one. So I wonder:
What am I doing? *What am I doing?* The girls aren't friendly to
me, and the men take less interest. For me, it's unisex around here,
and I try to tell myself, "Well, you're going to be working another
twenty years, so you'd better make the best of it." And then I
look at my face in the mirror, forty years old and showing
every month of it, and I say, "Why? Where's the fun? Where are
the parties? What happened?" And I conclude that The Company
is a web, and I'm hopelessly caught in it.

I still want to get married, but what chance is there? I keep looking and hoping, but *nobody* comes along. And I have to admit:
Maybe the last eighteen years have been a mistake, maybe I blew
the whole bit. But on the other hand I could have gotten married
and lived in Merion, Pennsylvania, and been divorced and been terribly neurotic because of getting married. Who knows? Professionally I'm nowhere. I've made a heck of a lot of mistakes, but

who knows if I'd have made more if I'd have married and settled down?

So I hang on, a fossil, the world's oldest living assistant. I don't know when I'll retire, but I do know that it won't be in New York. I used to think that New York was the alpha and the omega. But now it's getting too much even for me. Everything's dirty and noisy, and the cab drivers are *so* rude. The whole city is becoming unattractive and unappetizing. During those first few years back here, when everybody was escorting me around Manhattan, I was having fun in New York, but that's over now. The city is senile; its arteries are clogged. I used to love going to museums and the theater in New York, but now you have to walk through filth to get there. And on the way home you might get mugged or raped—if you're lucky—or murdered if you're not.

To tell the truth, I really haven't figured out what I'll do with my future. I just keep hoping that everything will change back to the way it used to be: New York will become a fascinating place all over again, and The Company will change back to the nice old ways. I think I could adjust to that. I have to revitalize myself, build up my energy again.

I think I'll try to change departments.

Callia Bartucci, about 50

————•————

Callia's getting a bit long in the tooth now, but I would imagine that ten or fifteen years ago she must have been one of the most sought-after women in New York City. Sophisticated, talented, and beautiful—the absolute paragon of the glossy New York beauty. But she also has brains, or she wouldn't have made it for so long at so high a level. The man who finally dragged her down is a master at office politicking, and of course Callia always figured that office politics were beneath her dignity. She wasn't going to play a man's game—she often said that to me. Well, she'll have a long time to think about it.—Samantha Havercroft

As soon as Callia Bartucci was demoted, she disappeared from town for about a month. When she came back she had taken twenty years off her face! Her face had always been her best feature—she had an Elizabeth Taylor look to her—but now her face looked like Elizabeth Taylor's at the age of twenty. All the puffiness was gone, all the lines, all the loose skin. Well, Callia never admitted it, but we suspect she had a face-lift. The trouble is, now her body doesn't match her face. She's fifty years old, and she's got the body that you would expect her to have: thickening around the middle, sagging in the bust, and bony in the legs. Some dark night she's going to meet a young playboy in those jet-set circles of hers, and he's going to wine and dine her by candlelight, and then he's going to take her home and—oh, God! It's all too pitiful to think about.
—Faith Stronberg

· I ·

WHEN I first came here twenty-five years ago, I lived in a continuous state of excitement—theater, ballet, movies, luncheons at the Algonquin, sparkling wit and conversation, and parties galore! I even liked the looks of New York. When I finally saw Paris and London, I *still* rated New York first, even in appearance. Nothing in Paris or London could compare with the clean architectural lines of Rockefeller Center; the view along Riverside Drive was ten times prettier than any view along the Seine; and Central Park made Hyde Park and the Serpentine look silly. Of course, most of this was a state of mind. I had been brought up in a small town in West Virginia, but now I considered myself a New Yorker through and through, even *talked* like one! I started out as a model, and I soon found myself doing radio spots and taking an occasional small role in the theater. It was heaven! I gradually moved into a world peopled by celebrities like David Susskind and David Merrick, Charles Goren, Hunt Hartford, Kitty Carlisle, S. J. Perelman, Jack Kahn, the most *brilliant* people in the country, and the most hep. I'm not bright—I mean I'm bright, but not *that* bright; my IQ is around a hundred thirty or forty—but these people accepted me and made me part of their group. There was a glitter about them, an intellectual vitality and effervescence and kookiness that I'd never seen anywhere else in the world. It sharpened people to live here, sharpened the mental processes and the sense of direction. The people you met here were interested in the world, interested in ideas, in abstractions, in art and culture and politics. You didn't just sit around talking about children and gardens and the country club, the way people in small towns do.

Oh, the parties we had! One of the wealthier men in our group had a penthouse done in a nautical motif, and we used to dance up there till dawn. He had his terrace decorated to look like the deck of a ship, with funnels and ventilators and a bridge with a real steering wheel, and we'd take turns piloting that whole apartment building all over the world. Later on I began giving parties of my own, and my parties became famous in our crowd. Even the most sophisticated New Yorkers were bowled over by my parties. I'd have a famous jazz musician, a very well-known painter, some writers, a famous athlete or two, a few famous politicians, a sculptor, some actors, and maybe a well-known director. I used to blend the guest list like a master chef, and the result was the most magnificent parties. I filled the place with flowers, bought the best liquors, hired the most expensive caterers. Inevitably people would call me up later and say, "I've *never* had such a good time at a party!" Look here, I saved a note from a foreign gentleman. He says, "Thank you very much for inviting me to the cocktail party last Sunday. It was such a refined and sophisticated gathering with many educated and fascinating people that I felt as if I were watching a movie scene." The point is that he was bowled over, they *all* were bowled over. That particular party was about a year and a half or two years ago. No, I don't give parties any more. It's different now.

Not only have I stopped giving parties, I've cut off just about everything else. I don't go to the theater any more, or to concerts. I almost never go to a movie unless it's in the middle of the afternoon. I used to go to an occasional hockey game or a fight at the Garden, but now it's too much bother. I'm just like so many of the beautiful people in New York. We've just stopped functioning. The city has paralyzed us. The humanity is gone. This city is not *working* for people any more. It's too hard just to get across the street, too hard to do shopping, too hard to go to the office, and too hard to get a decent lunch and too hard to make a telephone call. It's too hard to *breathe!* Why, they talk about the decline and fall of Greece and Rome and the last days of Pompeii, but that's exactly what New Yorkers are living through right now! It's all around us: the last days. Within the next fifty years the city will be abandoned. I'm *certain* of it. Gangs will run each part of town, and they'll fight and leave corpses all over town for the rats. The rats are there right now, millions of them, waiting. Sometimes just to keep from getting bored the rats gang up on some poor little black child in Harlem and bite it to death. That's how life has changed in the greatest city on earth.

I'm not the only one who feels this way. Almost all my friends have dropped out, as I have. They don't give parties, and on those rare occasions when somebody else gives one, they don't attend. It's just too much trouble, too dangerous. Why, men are getting mugged by prostitutes in front of the Hilton Hotel these days! Imagine the old days when we went out partying in our gowns and minks till dawn, and then wandered through the streets singing and dancing and cutting up. If we did that now we'd be mugged before we went a block. So we stay home in our apartments, our fortresses, and we wait for the gangs to come over the rooftops and through our windows. That day isn't far off, either.

There is simply no level on which this city is livable. The simplest things are a problem. *Nothing* works. I have to drink bottled water; the water that comes out of the tap is positively orange. You practically have to know somebody to make a telephone call. I had a friend who kept getting a busy signal on a call to Greenwich Village, and when he finally asked the operator for help, she said, "All our circuits to Greenwich Village are busy, but I have an open circuit to the Bronx. Would you like to speak to someone in the Bronx?" Insanity! Lunacy! Things that we have taken for granted for fifty years have stopped working. There are certain telephone numbers that will positively *wreck* your phone if you call them. For a while it was Watkins numbers. You dialed a Watkins number and you got no answer, but your phone went dead and stayed dead for several hours. Watkins numbers did that to my home phone and they did it to my office phone, so it was no accident. People would try to reach me for days, and they'd get a notice that the phone was out of order, or they'd get a busy signal, which is worse. I finally hired an answering service, because I was missing so many calls, but that wasn't much of an improvement. Why, the whole telephone network in New York is a disgrace! And the billings are fantastic! I get thirty- and forty-dollar bills for calls to Alaska and Honolulu. Some of them are made by maids when I'm out of the apartment, but most of them are just plain incorrect. It takes six months to get each mistake untangled, and in the meantime you've had several warnings that they're going to turn your service off. Don't ever let *that* happen! Once your phone is off, you won't get it reconnected for at least a month. I used to have my phone temporarily disconnected whenever I went on a long vacation or a trip, but I don't dare try that now.

I live on the twenty-first floor of a large apartment building, a co-op, in an apartment that I was able to buy years ago for twenty-five thousand dollars, and I pay three hundred dollars a month in "maintenance," which includes taxes and the doormen and the supers and so forth. Theoretically, the supers are there to keep the place in shape and to perform small maintenance tasks in the apartment. Listen to this: I told our super I was getting a new air-conditioning unit for my bedroom and asked him to install it. A month went by and there was no sign of the super. Finally I asked him face to face, and he said he was busy, that I would have to wait my turn. I waited another month and then had one of my gentleman friends install the thing. It took exactly fifteen minutes from start to finish. Summertime came, and I decided to install another new unit in my living room, but the super said he would not put it in for me because I had bypassed him on the other one; it was as though I had employed a scab. I argued and begged and pleaded and he arrived and said grumpily, "All right, where is it?"

He spent two hours installing that simple air-conditioner, and when he was finished he acted like he'd just built me a new house. Three months later I awoke one morning to a chill breeze coming from my living room. The unit had shaken loose of its moorings and dropped twenty-one floors to the street! Thank God no one was hurt. I told the super and he said it was my fault for not noticing that it was working loose. Two weeks before Christmas he sent me a cheap card, which is every super's way of reminding you that you owe him twenty or fifty dollars for a Christmas tip. What could I do? I came across. A friend swore that one of the supers in his building sent him a card that said, "Merry Christmas. Second notice!"

For a while I tried to fight all these little rudenesses and discourtesies in New York. I even enlisted my friends in the fight, and I went to the head of The Company and suggested that we should start a campaign to revive old-fashioned courtesy in the city. He just laughed. He was smarter than I was. There's *no* campaign that would work among these bitter, angry, frustrated people. For a while I would say "Good morning" whenever I got into a cab. Then the driver would say, "Where to, lady?" I'd repeat, "Good morning!" hoping he'd get the hint and say good morning back, and maybe one out of ten would do it. The rest would say, "Okay, lady, where to?" One morning I made up my mind I was going to keep repeating "Good morning" until I got a "Good morning" in return. I said, "Good morning" to the driver, and he said, "Where to, lady?" I said very broadly, "Good morning," and he said, "Where ye goin', lady?" I said, "*Good morning!*" and he turned and gave me this fierce look and said, "Okay already, lady. Now where to!" I said, "Bonwit Teller's, please." There was nothing on earth that could have made that driver carry out the simple social amenity of returning my "good morning" with a courteous response of his own. The truth was he probably didn't think it was a good morning at all, and he wasn't going to be a hypocrite. Maybe he's right. Maybe anyone who says "good morning" in New York City is a two-faced hypocrite.

But it isn't only the cab drivers. The other night I had dinner at the most expensive restaurant in town, and the waiter was awful! He wound up spilling a half bottle of Piper Heidsieck on our tablecloth and not even bothering to wipe it up. He just brought a napkin and covered the stain, glowering all the time, as though it was our fault. Why, in the old days they'd have reset the whole table, brought a new bottle of wine and complimented the bill. But that was long ago.

The big event nowadays is when somebody acts courteously. The other day I got on a bus and two girls asked the driver how to get to Radio City Music Hall. At the time, we were at Sixth Avenue and Forty-seventh Street, within sight of the place, and when he told them how close they were, they all laughed. Then they talked for three blocks and the driver gave them some tips about getting around in New York and when they got off he said, "Nice speakin' wit' you, goils. Have a good day!" Why, I dined out on that story for two weeks! When I'd tell people about it, they'd accuse me of exaggerating, or making the whole thing up! It didn't take long for New York to get even, though. My mother came to visit me from West Virginia, and the first day she was here she took a walk in Central Park and had her purse snatched! When I told that story around, my friends said, "Yeah, that's more like it."

Now I ask you: What kind of person is going to subject himself to an atmosphere like this? Why, the very air stinks! I take drives out in the country just so I can breathe! The other day I walked about six blocks in midtown and by the time I got home I had walked through so much blue-gray "dead" air that I actually felt I could take my lungs and wring them out, like a washcloth. They were full of pollution, and I was wheezing like an asthmatic. I thought I was going to fall down dead! Most of the time you can *see* the air in New York, and who wants to breathe air you can see? I've always loved flowers, but lately I've been buying so many flowers that the florists do a little jig when they see me coming. I buy flowers for the same reason that other people buy Airwick, to get the city stink out of my apartment. Sometimes I'll come home with four dozen roses, just because I can't stand the smell of my own place. I'll *fill* my apartment with flowers.

Who in his right mind will put up with a situation like this for long? The good people are leaving in droves. The no-talents are taking over, running the show, simply because the talented people will not stay here any more. They would rather make a hundred dollars a week in Missoula, Montana, than a thousand dollars a week here. So the quality of the "quality people" is going down, the beauty of the "beautiful people" is going down, and the whole city has sunk to a new low of intellectuality. The trend was symbolized by Sid Perelman's abandoning New York for London. The day he sailed, *The National Observer* bawled him out in an editorial. How ridiculous! I guess he's supposed to stay in New York forever, risking death and disease and God knows what, just because he's made a few dollars here. My city right or wrong! Well, people are just not going to accept that. Those of us who had great loyalty to New York are bailing out by the dozens. Within the last year I've had close personal friends move to London, to Paris, to Gstaad, to Hilo, Hawaii, and even to San Antonio and Taos and Bakersfield, California. These were some of the *best* people in New York, some of the people who made it *run*, commercially and culturally. They were all fond of quoting Yeats: "The center cannot hold." Well, they're right. *The center is not holding.* And the rough beasts are slouching toward Bethlehem by the millions.

· 2 ·

You can see the result right in our office, in what a lot of people regard as the greatest company in the world. Why, when I first went to work here fourteen years ago, I could walk down Fifth Avenue and pick out the people who worked for The Company and those who didn't. They were *that* much sharper! They were *that* much more sophisticated. We were all very excited to be working at The Company, and we were thrilled to be producing some of the finest products on the market. That's why The Company made so much money—it had people bursting to do their jobs better and better, glad to be here, excited to be in New York with all the other big successful people.

Now that's all changed. Nowadays it's all status, prestige, territorial imperative. The motive is not to make the best product; the motive is to sink the knife into the guy in the next office, to enlarge your own territory, to *win out* over the others. The game is to get a better title, a larger office, an extra secretary, a receptionist with an English accent. I don't know exactly what caused the change. Is it because New York City has become so much of a jungle that only people who think like animals can survive here? Is that why the big companies are moving away, because they're finding that they're attracting the wrong kind of personnel to their

New York operations? I suspect so. I'm not so dumb as to think that every businessman in New York used to be altruistic and generous about his fellow workers, but there's been a tremendous upswing in the amount of throat-cutting and back-stabbing. I should know. I'm still losing blood over the back-stabbing that was given to me.

Of course, I was a pigeon for an operator like Montee Hamford. When I quit my career as a model and TV personality to go to work for The Company, I didn't know a thing about office life. I honestly didn't know whether you brought a pencil or they gave you one! Office politics was totally new to me, and it bored me. I simply refused to compete, because I was a woman. It's the man's role to enlarge his territory, to shoo away intruders and protect his own empire. But I'm a woman, not a fake woman, not an imitation woman, but a *real* woman, and I behave like one. For example, I've always preferred to work with a dominant male. I feel natural that way. And I refuse to compete with other men who are trying to enlarge their own territories. Office politics is a strange land to me. I was always too active in my outside life to get all het up about how to get the better of somebody in the office. And when somebody began a campaign to get the better of me, I didn't even see it coming. If the situation were to repeat itself tomorrow, I *still* wouldn't see it coming. My mind just doesn't function that way.

In essence, what happened was classically simple. I was hired to start a new, rather small department in The Company in nineteen fifty-six. I started the department and I did a good job. Two years later, Montee Hamford was hired to start a similar small department, and he also did a good job, but for different motivations. From the beginning, he was a dolt, a stupid, tasteless, dumb, rutting stag, with the most awesome and terrifying territorial-imperative instincts I have ever seen in a man. He would bristle if anyone even *looked* at one of his subordinates. He would run hysterically to his favorite vice-president if anyone made the slightest attempt to take over any of the responsibilities of his department. He was obsessed with protecting his territory, with enlarging it, and with absorbing everyone around him. He operated exactly like a male elephant. After five or six years he began to realize that I could be had, businesswise, and he began an office political campaign to absorb my department.

First he arranged for a glowing article about himself in The Company's house organ, and the article credited him with responsibilities that were my department's and not his. It was as though my department didn't even exist, that everything was being done by Montee Hamford. I just laughed! But a good friend of mine in the executive suite blew his top on my behalf, and he called in the poor young kid who had written the piece. The kid insisted that he had gotten all his information from Montee and that Montee had insisted on reading proof to make sure that everything was reported exactly as he wanted it. The executive called Montee in, and Montee said that he had not even known about the article till it ran. He said the kid was a liar and should be fired.

For his next number, Montee went on a big swing through all our branch offices throughout the country, and word began to trickle back to me that he was doing the same thing all over again —attributing responsibilities to his department that were really mine. Not only that, but he was taking credit for good ideas developed by my department and putting the blame on me for some goof-ups that he had committed himself! It was the big lie again, and no one was wise enough to realize it.

I had no real way of knowing what he was saying upstairs, but soon I began to notice that a lot of my old friends in the executive suite were giving me the cold shoulder. Samantha Havercroft got drunk at a party one night and told me that Montee had made a pass at her and told her that I was really a closet lesbian! Yes! Absolutely! It sounds insane, but he said it. If he would say something like that to a junior assistant, what would he say to the supervisors and the managers?

There was absolutely no limit to how low he would stoop. One day a vice-president brought me a personnel report marked "confidential" and told me to read it and make an evaluation. The instant the veep left, Montee Hamford came storming into my office demanding to know what had gone on. When I told him, he insisted on seeing the report, and under a lot of pressure and swearing and heaving and sighing and threatening, I showed him the report. Then he went upstairs and told another vice-president that I had broken security by spreading a secret report all over the place.

His final ploy was a masterpiece, although I was still too dumb to see it coming. Little by little he had chipped away at my responsibilities and assignments, taking them over himself, but I still had a nucleus of my old staff left and I still had a few responsibilities that belonged entirely to my department. Then word came down that they were thinking about opening a department similar to mine in Rome, and since I spoke Italian from childhood I would be a logical choice to head the new operation. I fell head over heels! I was *ecstatic* about the idea. The new operation would be smaller than the one I headed in New York, but who could resist the opportunity to live in Rome on an American salary?

I jumped at the chance, and Montee Hamford's favorite vice-president told me that the first step would be to allow my New York operation to be integrated into Montee's. That was fine with me. *Anything* to get to Rome! So I turned over all my assignments to Montee and even retrained some of his girls in the work that my girls had been doing. It took about a month, and then Montee Hamford was firmly in charge. I went to Rome and opened the new department, and two months later the operation was shut down and I was brought back to New York and placed in charge of a messenger pool. Was it all a masculine plot? I wouldn't be the least bit surprised.

That was two years ago, and I'm still at The Company, although I'm not going to be here long. All my friends said that Montee Hamford should be fired and I should be given his responsibilities, but of course that will never happen. It is the Montee Hamfords who will take over The Company, take over New York, and maybe take over the whole United States. They have the strength and the determination and mostly the motivation to do it, and poor petty people like me will be swept aside. He's already making a move on Alexandra Oats, and she doesn't know it.

The Montee Hamfords will *never* leave this deteriorating city, not so long as there's the tiniest bit left for them to add to their power. So New York will become Hamfordville, and the talented and sensitive will be gone forever. We're more interested in trees and grass and pure air; Montee is more interested in power and territory. He'll stay, like the rats. Certain organisms adjust readily to garbage.

Sometimes it seems like utter disaster, what happened to me. And *so* unfair! But deep inside I know it's not really a disaster. I never wanted a corporate career anyhow; it was sort of thrust upon me, and I've been aware for years that it was wrong for me. The day I was told I was going to be in charge of a messenger pool I asked for a one-month leave, and I went to a health spa in Arizona. I decided to change my life completely. I gave up smoking and drinking; I lost ten pounds; people said I looked *marvelous*. I've been back in New York for six months now, and I've passed the word that I'll be leaving The Company soon. The job offers have come in, two of them already, and one was a very tempting one that I had to look long and hard at.

But I'm not accepting any new job here. I'm getting financial support for a business of my own, a sort of combination health-food shop and self-improvement center. The money is coming in, although the state of the economy held things back for a while. I expect to be able to give The Company notice within another six months and then go into business for myself, which will be a lot more pleasant than fighting it out with the Montee Hamfords. My shop won't be in New York; I can guarantee you that. Right now I'm thinking of Los Angeles, but I may also open in Phoenix or Denver or San Francisco; I haven't decided yet.

I keep reminding myself that I'm doing all this by choice, that I let Montee Hamford ease me out by choice, at least subconsciously. I'm certainly not leaving New York in shame or chagrin. I'm leaving it because I want to, because it isn't New York any more; it's some new kind of jungle made out of bricks and stone and hatred. Not for me!

Some of my friends say that I should never have been in the business world at all. They say I was born in the wrong century, that I should have been a courtesan in France in the eighteenth century and had an intellectual salon of my own. Maybe there's a message there. Maybe I should find a rich man and become his mistress. God knows there've been enough rich men in my life, but I've turned them all down. They bored me after a while. Maybe I *should* have been a courtesan, living for love, changing lovers often, using up the rich and the talented men, going to museums and art studios and learning to play the piano. Maybe it's still not too late!

I have to admit that the pace of my life has slowed down since I became a certain age. No, I do *not* reveal my age, I let people guess, and I guarantee you'll guess on the *young* side.

Thank God I still have a few glamorous friends left. Some have died, of course, and a lot have moved away, but I keep in touch. There've always been men in my life, and there always will be. Once in a while I go out to lunch and have an interesting conversation. But it's been a year since I gave a party and months since I've been to one. Nobody seems to be giving them any more. I still have dates, and I expect to be having them for a long time. I still seem to overwhelm certain men. In fact, here's a letter from one boy who viewed me from afar and begged a friend of mine to introduce him to me. He told my friend, "I can't eat, I can't sleep. Won't you please at least introduce me?" So he was brought up here for an introduction, and for months afterward he would telephone me and beg me to chat with him. Look here. He wrote: "You have a magical smile and a voice that never fails to cast a spell on me. Not only me, but many people are under your spell." And he closes with "Thank you again. So deeply under your spell. . . ." He was so overwhelmed he brought his sister to be introduced to me!

Some people still think of me as a glossy, sophisticated, glamorous woman just brimming with self-assurance, but of course I'm not. Nobody is. I'll bet that even Jackie Onassis has stopped thinking of herself as the cat's pajamas, now that she's reached a certain age. We're all just aging women when we look into our personal mirrors, and we have a woman's problems and a woman's insecurities. The completely self-assured professional New York woman simply just doesn't exist any more, if she ever did.

I would *hate* to lose my looks. My looks are part of my security. I may overrate their importance, but that's just how I'm put together. In some ways, being physically attractive is a disadvantage to a woman, because you tend to rely too much on your looks and you lose confidence in your other assets. That's happened to me since my demotion. Now I go around caring too much about looking my best, and when I'm not looking my best I won't even go *near* the office. Now that's pretty silly, isn't it? Other people tell me that I *always* look good, but sometimes I don't look up to my own personal par, and then I refuse to compete.

One thing that is not going to happen to me: I absolutely refuse to age! *I'm not going to age!* I take vitamins and minerals and special medicines and I drink bottled water and I exercise and do all kinds of things, and I'm not going to grow old! A few months ago I discovered KH3, and now I have all my friends bring it over to me from London, because you can't get it here. KH3 is mostly made of novocain and vitamins, and it works *wonders* on aging cells. It was discovered in Rumania by a Dr. Anna somebody, and she gave it by injection. My doctor kids me about it, but he's always kidding anyway. He says, "Three of my patients are trying it. If they don't die, I'll try it!" I tell him there are lots of authenticated cases in Rumania, but he says he's not too certain about the Rumanian Medical Association's accuracy. He says, "You go ahead and take it, it won't hurt you. But if this novocain's so great, why do I always feel lousy when I leave the dentist?"

I've been taking the capsules for a month now, and so far I can't tell much difference. But you have to take them for five months before the big difference shows up—that's what the bottle says. People *do* tell me that I look marvelous, so maybe it's working already. Or maybe they're trying to buoy me up. Most of my friends in the office think I'm even more upset about the demotion than I am, and they're always trying to console me. That's another reason I'm anxious to get out of The Company and open my own business, so I can get out of this sea of sympathy that I'm drowning in. I don't *need* sympathy, and I don't *want* it, but I accept it because I know that my friends are just trying to be kind.

KH3 is just one of the things I'll be selling in my shop, if I can get permission, and I'll also be selling some of the other medicines I read about in Pat McGrady's wonderful book *The Youth Doctors*. Generally I prefer books like *Jane Eyre* and *The French Lieutenant's Woman* and *The Possessed*, but I was entranced by *The Youth Doctors*. I've read it six times; it's full of good advice on how to keep from aging. I've practically memorized parts of that book!

Right now I'm studying something called colonal vegetation, which has to do with the exact dupliction of individual cells. When they get it all worked out, they'll be able to produce carbon copies of individual humans, and people will be able to live forever—when their first body wears out, colonal vegetation will produce an exact duplicate, and the exact duplicate can take over the other's life and go right on living in the same apartment and all. It's fascinating! Why, if they develop that system they'll be able to make as many Einsteins as they want, as many Cary Grants, as many Yves Montands. But I'd be happy if they could make just one more Callia Bartucci! I discuss it with my scientist friends, and they laugh at me. And I tell them, "Go ahead and laugh, but I will *not* age! I will *not* slow down! I will *not* die! *Something* will come along to save me." And I'm convinced it will.

Lately I've thought about joining that cryogenic society that arranges for you to stay frozen until science learns how to bring people back to life and cure certain diseases. Walt Disney is frozen like that, and so are a lot of people you don't know about. They're keeping it quiet. But I don't plan to do it the way Walt Disney and the other people did it. I have this questing intellect, you see, and I can hardly bear the idea that life will go on without me for centuries and centuries to come, and I won't be there to see what's going on! It kills me, *I can't stand to think about it!* So my idea is to get frozen and then be thawed out in other eras, *but only for a year at a time,* just long enough to see what's happening in the year

2050, 2200, 2600, *way out* into the future. That may sound spooky, but some day it'll be possible, and when that day comes, I'll be the very first in line. What a dream—to live your life forever, but in pleasant little spans of time. That's a dream worth waiting for. I just hope they hurry.

Samantha Havercroft, 37

———•———

Samantha Havercroft is getting kind of pathetic. She's still a pretty girl, but she's losing that creamy, translucent English skin that she used to have, and she's becoming a little worn around the edges. She has a very wild reputation. When one of our new specialists went on a foreign trip with her and a supervisor, he came back to New York in a state of shock. They had had adjoining bedrooms, and Samantha and the supervisor had moved into one of the bedrooms right in front of the young man's eyes. He came back and told everybody about it. He said, "I was so embarrassed." I'd heard other things like that about her. But now she's beginning to lose out. I'm told that she stands to one side at office parties and nobody pays attention to her. It's partially because she's older and partially because New York men don't have much interest in a girl who's so easy.—Stephanie Grant

• I •

LAST WEEK I was on a working trip with an executive named Jim Smith. It was the first time we'd ever traveled together, and to be perfectly honest I was more than willing to like him and maybe even to have an affair with him. I've had my portion of affairs at The Company, and I've long since tried to leave off moralizing about what's right and what's wrong about sleeping with married men. When the proper occasion arises, one does it, that's all. And when one of the married men makes a pass, you don't get all righteous about it. You accept or you reject, and you try to be courteous whichever choice you make. That has always been my policy, at least since the early days, and I didn't intend to change it on this short trip with Jim Smith. So I wasn't the least offended when we checked into our Baltimore hotel rooms and he rang me up and proposed that we have dinner and drinks together. Fine, why not? We met at the cocktail bar, and he selected a dark table in the corner. We talked through two martinis, and the third round had just been delivered when I became aware of this absolutely petrifying sensation. I shifted my position, but the sensation continued. Jim Smith, a man I barely knew, was massaging my crotch! "Really, Jim!" I said, and I lifted his hand away. He laughed and waited a few more minutes to place his hand squarely and frankly in the same place. When I complained again, he opened this absolutely puerile conversation about how he hated hypocrisy, he knew I'd slept with so-and-so and so-and-so and what was all this prissy stuff about, anyway? I got up and went to my room and spent the rest of the night in tears. I wasn't crying because an inflated sod like Jim Smith had taken liberties with me in a public bar. Not at all. I was upset over what it all *symbolized*. The very idea that he would think that I would be amenable to such a direct approach! The contempt that it showed for me! The utter lack of respect! Do I deserve respect after a long string of affairs? Why, *of course!* Any girl deserves respect. I lay in bed till very late that night trying to figure out how a perfectly respectable girl like Samantha Havercroft had managed to get herself into such a position.

I was brought up in one of those dreary East Anglian villages where every aspect of life is constipated and restricted and compressed into old folkways. I shudder even to remember those early years. I went to London as fast as my legs could carry me, and then I became interested in languages, and soon I found myself living and working in Paris and getting by on my small salary as a secretary, although not putting anything aside. When a job opened in the Paris office of The Company, I jumped at the chance, and I must say I quickly became a super-secretary, fluent in French and English and spending three nights a week studying Italian and Spanish at the interpreters' school. I was a language nut; I even *thought* in three or four languages, and soon The Company began putting my language skills to use. I found myself making business trips around Europe with various supervisors, and within a short time I was transferred to the big office in New York City and assigned as secretary to an important and well-traveled man in the international department of The Company. By now I was twenty-eight and no longer a little farm girl. I knew my way around London and Paris and Madrid, and I knew what I wanted out of life. Success at The Company was my goal; I couldn't imagine a better goal for a girl with my skills. But I must say I was appalled by New York, at least early on. Paris and London are dirty, but compared to New York they are absolutely super-hygienic. Why, New York is the filthiest place I have ever seen! It's like Bombay! I thought I'd bumbled into the city dump when I first went into a subway station. Thank God I had learned to walk long distances as a child. Even today I think nothing of walking fifty or sixty blocks in New York City. It keeps my legs in shape, and it keeps me out of those filthy subways.

When I first went to work in the New York office, I felt like a busy little mouse. I was set up! The men around me seemed like gods, bright, talented, cosmopolitan. I felt so excited when I could contribute something to them, when I could perform some small task that would help to make the wheels of this giant corporation turn more smoothly. I would type up a report and offer it to my boss like a jewel, and if he complimented me, my week was made. If he expressed the tiniest annoyance, I was a ruin! In those days my whole life turned on a trace of a boss's smile, or a minor downturn of the lips. How dependent I was on these glamorous creatures in New York! But I was wise enough to keep them at arm's length on the social level, at least during my years as a secretary. Something told me it would be a bad idea to accept advances, and it wasn't until several years later, when I realized that there was *no* other social life for a single girl in New York, that I began to date married men and officemates.

I soon learned that I was regarded as the top secretary on the staff and that there was a keen competition for my services. I had three or four bosses in a row, and little by little they managed to blunt that terrific enthusiasm of mine. Some of them tried to turn me into a maid. They'd use me to get them coffee, drinks, clean shirts when they'd stayed out all night. One boss expected me to get his car out of the garage each afternoon and wait for him to come down and drive away in it. If it was snowing, I was expected to brush the snow off! Soon he had me performing various favors for his friends, until I didn't know whom I was working for. He expected me to awaken him in the morning and get him home at night when he was taken drunk. I didn't realize till later that he was just showing his power, pushing and pushing in some kind of infantile drive to find out how much he could get away with. Some men are like that.

Four years went by before I landed the job I'd been looking for. I'd coveted that job from the beginning. The title was "assistant," and everyone knew that the assistants turned out the product at The Company. The specialists and supervisors and managers got the credit, but the assistants did the work. I'll tell you how vital the assistants are. If there is a major mistake, the assistant gets the blame. Never the superior! Somebody once wrote that The Company was the only place in the world where responsibility sifts *downward*. It makes a lovely arrangement for the superiors, most of whom are men. When something turns out right, they get the credit. When it turns out wrong, an assistant gets the blame.

Well, I'd waited four years to get this job and when I got it, it was a big let-down. I found out that anybody can do the job. The assistants run around pretending how difficult it is, but it's really very simple, unchallenging and boring. To make matters worse, The Company operates strictly on Parkinson's Law and there are about three times as many assistants as necessary. The reason is simple: The more assistants a supervisor has, the more important his department looks. Therefore he is always pressing for more and more assistants, pushing up the "head count," until the assistants are running around bumping into each other and dying of the worst disease on earth: ennui. To combat the ennui, we come in later and later, take more and more time for lunch, attend movies in the afternoon, and sneak home at four-thirty. Why not? What else is there to do? We become masters at shuffling papers, reading magazines and newspapers, playing bridge. When we do get a meaningful assignment, our skills have become so blunted that we take three times too long to do it, and even then we make mistakes. But nobody ever gets fired. That is another unwritten law at The Company. If a supervisor has three assistants and he fires one of them, his job looks only two-thirds as important. So he keeps girls on no matter what they do. I can think of one assistant who does nothing whatever. *Literally nothing!* She buggered up her last three or four assignments and ever since then she's just been left alone to read the newspapers. It's been about a year now, and personally I doubt if she'll ever get another assignment. Or get fired. Another girl made a huge mistake on top of a long history of huge mistakes, and the manager said to the supervisor, "Well, if she makes one more mistake like that, fire her!" So the supervisor sent her off on a long foreign trip to get her out of the way for a while. You can imagine how this heightened morale around the office! You only have to see inefficiency rewarded once or twice to get the message.

With all this laxity there's too much time for mischief-making, for petty bickerings and jealousies. Somebody gets an office that is a half inch longer than somebody else's, and there's a huge fight, and the Women's Lib marchers take to the halls with their banners and placards. Everyone is especially touchy about the peck order, because *they have no other order to become involved in.* They *create* problems, involvements, and they wallow in gossip and office politicking for the sheer fun of sticking knives in others. I attribute this to the lack of a challenging job, a lack of obstacles to be surmounted. The Company makes it too easy for you, and other companies are beginning to do the same. They think they're doing you a favor by giving you shorter hours and less and less to do in those hours. But the most difficult thing in the world for a human being is a lack of limits. Adults are just like children. They need to have challenges to confront, obstacles to surmount, *something to be proud of at the end of the day.* In the modern American company, you do very little that you can be proud of.

In a situation like this, can it surprise anyone that sex becomes vastly overrated, that it begins to become larger than life and cause all sorts of additional problems? When I first came to New York I couldn't believe that so much energy was being expended on sex. Those who weren't taking part in the extramarital sex involvements were busily keeping score on the others. The biggest discussions every Monday morning revolved around who left Santana's Bar with whom on Friday night and what new couple were pairing off for intimate luncheons, and what supervisor had shared a cab with what assistant that morning, and had they spent the whole weekend together, and what would his wife say?

· 2 ·

I HAD a perfect record as a secretary, never engaging in a single extramarital affair, but my record came to a quick halt as an assistant. I make no apologies, except for taking the job in the first place. There was something about the assistant-supervisor relationship, or the assistant-specialist relationship, that made intimacies almost inevitable. The supervisors used to like to come to my apartment and talk about work, about the office and the pressures. They would rather talk to me about the office than to their wives, because they had a community of interest with me, whereas at home they'd have to make long explanations before their wives would know what they were talking about. We spoke the same language; we were playing in the same game. I don't look on the executives of The Company as villains at all; in fact, I'm highly sympathetic toward them. I've seen them crying their eyes out over some pathetic office rivalry or some imagined slight. It always seemed that on nights of greatest tension they would ring me up and want to come to my apartment to spill it all out. The ultimate catharsis would come in bed. At first I hated myself for this, but how long can such self-hatred continue when everyone else seems to be living the same kind of life?

Once in a while one of the executives would do something unpleasant or gauche. I'd been seeing a specialist named Red Johnson off and on, but obviously we weren't going steady—his wife would have objected—so I didn't think it amiss to leave an office party on the arm of another man. Red quickly spread the word around the office that it didn't bother him at all that I'd left with another, that he'd been to bed with me every night for a week and he was frankly worn out. He said that I was becoming tedious, that he needed someone who would be less demanding night after night. Men! Such fragile egos! I thought it absolutely dreadful of him to go around telling lies like that, and confronted him about it, but of course he denied saying a word. He didn't even have the courage to admit what he had done.

After a long succession of such affairs, you begin to realize that these substitute miniature marriages are crucifying in the end, that they're nothing but traps that leave you alone and lost. And yet so many of our girls in the office settle for them. They only see the present, the thrills and the intrigue. They're producing a product in close conjunction with brilliant men, just as married couples produce children. They lunch together, they share good expense accounts, they drink together, they gossip and vilify together, they fight and win and lose battles and wars together. Is it any wonder that all of this seems so fulfilling for a naïve young woman in her twenties or her early thirties? But in the long run these liaisons only make you unhappy. I dread the thought that one day I'll look back and know that I have spent twenty years like that and I have become one more empty spot in the society. If you accept such a life, you will be alone in the end. If you build substitute marriages out of office affairs, you're reliving the legend of Faust, selling your soul to the devil. You're sacrificing the second half of your life for a bit of glamor and false joy in the first half, and you wind up with nothing.

That's why I say all this intimacy around the office is wrong. The parties are wrong. The first-name basis is wrong. The office should *not* be one big happy family. It should be a place to work. Things were better back in England, where we addressed each other as Miss and Mister, kept long hours, worked hard. At least we didn't get our business and personal lives intertwined and mixed up. There is a wisdom in the old-world impersonal ways.

It is so sad when one of these affairs goes on for years and years and then suddenly it's over. The man has taken up with someone else, or decided to stay at home with his wife. Some of the girls have staked so much on the ersatz relationship that they can't cope with the ending. Gloria Rolstin's affair with Tom Lantini was one of the worst. She became absolutely unbalanced. She started calling up wives to tell them that their husbands were out with somebody else. She was so bitter! She'd call up a wife and she'd say, "He's going to lunch with Jane Jones. They just left. I think they're going to Mama Leone's. If you leave right now, you can catch 'em!" God, the trouble that poor girl caused! Because usually she was right. The wives sit home and have no idea what's going on, at least until a Gloria Rolstin comes along to slap them with reality. She was driving the men around the office crazy. Their wives were waiting to pounce on them. They'd say, "Who'd you have lunch with today? No, you didn't! I *know* who you went with, I *know* where you went!"

Whenever she'd see Tom look at another girl, there would be trouble. At every office party there would be a big, loud, screaming, public fight. Once I danced with him, and she came over and whispered in my ear, "If you dance with him one more time, you'll get it from me!" Once he got into a cab with two other assistants—he was going to drop them off—and she stood outside beating the window and screaming at him, "Get out of there! Get out of there!" The cab pulled away and she fell down, but she kept right on screaming. She caught up with him at lunch the next day, and she dumped a plate of spaghetti over his head, and he hit her with his fist.

I think that Gloria must have seen the whole dismal rest of her life flash before her eyes the night Tom Lantini told her they were through. It's funny that none of us ever think much about the end of the affair when we begin. You wake up one morning and you're thirty-five years old, and all at once you've slipped out of the mainstream at The Company. When you cease to decorate, when you cease to be one of the beautiful, lithe, young people, you're on your way out. I can see it happening to Gloria Rolstin right now.

She staked everything on that miserable Lantini, and now he's three thousand miles away, and nobody else is glancing Glo's way. It's happened to so many. Peg Kern's great affair ended last year when the guy took his wife and children off to live in Europe, and Peg's been putting on about ten pounds a month ever since. She can stay on with The Company as long as she wants, but she'll never again be in the main flow of things. Maybe she'll quit, like so many others. They see their old age beginning before they reach forty, and they leave The Company and take their savings and open up a boutique or a small store, and as often as not they come running back begging for their old jobs. They miss the bright lights, but they don't stop to think that there's a whole new group of beautiful people now, and now they're on the outside looking in. Or they spin around in a succession of jobs with other companies, trying to rebuild from nothing. It seldom works. The Company is the kiss of death. Once you've been here, you're pretty much spoiled for everywhere else. No other company will treat you so nicely, or give you a chance to destroy your future so effectively.

Well, now that I'm approaching forty myself I'm happy to find that the men in the office seem less interesting to me. I find no one who really interests me, except as a friend. It's like marriage. When you see the same face every day for years, it gets boring. The men must feel the same way. My telephone rang off the hook when I first came to New York, but in the last year there's been a marked change. I used to be able to depend on at least one call per evening, from one of the men who'd had a drink or two at the Santana and suddenly been stricken amorous. But in the last year I've had exactly one call like that, from a pipsqueak of a guy whom I detest anyway. He came over and poured himself a couple of drinks of my Scotch, and then he said, "Well, shall we have an adventure?" I said no thanks and sent him home.

I have to face the fact that my old age is going to be a disaster. Financially I'll have nothing. Emotionally I'll have nothing. I try not to think about it. The little bit of extra money I have went into an automobile, my lifeline to the beach and the woods on week-ends. Without it, living in this horrible, dirty city, I would go crazy. But the car is breaking me. I have to pay ninety dollars a month just to garage it, and I can see the day coming when I'll just have to sell it and be damned. That's the day my old age will begin.

I can't look back on many accomplishments in my life; I don't have very much to be proud of. I'm still so terribly unread and physically so unskilled. And I say such dumb things. Stupid! How I must have bored people in my lifetime! I keep telling myself to say less and less to people. And then I lie in bed and tell myself what I *should* have said and cringe over what I *did* say.

I suppose it's some small accomplishment that I escaped my na-tive England, that I saw some of the world and learned to speak a few languages. When I go home to the little village of my child-hood and see that everybody is still there, that so little has changed, I think how lucky I was. It is my ambition that just before I die all the places that I have seen will flash before my eyes—Paris, Lon-don, New York, Lisbon, Madrid, Rome—all of them. That's *one* small thing I've accomplished. I've traveled. I've seen things. And there's still a spot of beauty in my life, even in New York. The com-ing of spring. The park. Walking to the office. I always try to go by a different route. Once in a while I'll take Madison Avenue, and maybe I'll get my reward: an original Miró or Chagall in a gal-lery window. How exciting! It delights me when this happens. You may say that isn't very much, and I will say that it's what I have, and I must make it do. It's too much for me to wish for more, to hope that somewhere there's a middle-aged gentleman who is lonely like me and wants to get married. I've long since given up on finding him, and now I am forced to see my future in different terms. Maybe I'll stay around The Company for a few more years and then try to find some small place in Europe in some unimpor-tant country and try somehow to get by, maybe take a position as a shop lady and draw my social security and sit around my room at night and drink *vin ordinaire* and remember what I had with The Company. I'll remember those good old days. I wonder if they really were *good* old days.

Gloria Rolstin, 38

———•———

*Poor, poor Gloria Rolstin! She had the affair of affairs, six or seven
long years of it, with that woman-killer Tom Lantini. God, it was
horrible! Toward the end we didn't know whether she would kill
him or he would kill her. Maybe they both killed each other—in
certain ways. I know Glo isn't the same Glo any more. She keeps
up the old smiling front, but there's a bitterness there. And she's
the last person you'd have expected to get mixed up in something
like this. She doesn't talk about it, but I happen to know she comes
from Mormon stock—someplace in Idaho, I think—and she gave
the church a year or two of her life, working as some kind of
Mormon missionary. Then she comes to New York and gets involved in the most sordid affair you can imagine. Well, nobody's
exempt, I guess. Not even Mormons.—Peg Kern*

• I •

WHEN I first came here, back in the early Sixties, the livin' was *so*
easy. New York was still a pleasant place, and The Company
treated you like Queen Farouk. There were two-hour lunch
periods, or three hours, if you preferred. You could always get time
off, and there were lots of holidays and the longest regular vacations in the industry. If you managed it right, you could figure on
working about ten months for your full year's pay. And not working very hard, either, unless you were eager, like me, or super-
honest, like one or two of the girls. Most of us were happy to allow
ourselves to be corrupted. The money was good, and most of the

men treated us nicely—because we were doing a lot of their work, and they were getting the credit. As an assistant, I worked longer and longer hours; I was thrown in with the men on late nights, and I grew to enjoy the company of some of them. Sometimes we'd work till midnight or one A.M. and rush downstairs to the Italian restaurant for a quick couple of Scotches, or we'd pile into my Corvair with the top down and drive all over the city waiting for the sun to come up. At dawn we'd find ourselves on Wall Street, giggling and laughing. The Fulton fish market was a favorite stop, because there was always action there, or we'd drive down to the Battery and look out at the filthy, oily New York Bay. One morning we went to Jones Beach for a skinny-dip, and another time we nearly closed a village nightclub by whistling along with the pianist until she stomped off.

I knew it was silly and stupid to spend so much time with the others in The Company. It was the classic mistake, and even while my outside social life was dwindling I knew I was being short-sighted. But it was so easy. Every once in a while there'd be a business trip, to some *glamorous* city like Cleveland or Buffalo, and I'd be thrown in the company of one or two of the supervisors for almost twenty-four hours a day. I learned to drink like a trooper, to swear like the rest of them. There was an awful lot of screwing going on, as always, but that's where I drew the line. I'd had a few affairs, but I was keeping them out of the office. I had *that* much sense. But I didn't have enough sense to cut off this total involvement with The Company. My friends were there, I saw them all day and drank with them and played with them all night. We went to parties and movies together; we lunched together, and pretty soon my outside social life was dead. But I figured that good old Glo could handle the problem. Good old Glo had things under control. Now how in God's name could I think like that! I saw my mistake, I saw it coming, I looked it right in the face. And then I let it happen!

On Friday nights we carried out a ritual. In most New York offices, Friday is a day to get away early and start your weekend, but in our business Friday is a big, busy event that sometimes car-

ries on into the evening, till seven or eight o'clock, and after that
we'd all run downstairs to the Santana, The Company's watering
hole. Some of the people would just quietly get sloshed. Some
would have a few drinks to round off the week and then take the
8:05 straight to New Rochelle. And some would make a night of
it, pairing off with whoever seemed attractive. For a long time I
was in the middle group, having a drink or two and then going to
the Village to meet Laddie Owens, a young newspaperman that I
was seeing kind of steady. I thought I was in love but I couldn't be
sure. Laddie and his friends were my last contact with the outside
world. Every other aspect of my life was built around The Company.

One Friday night I was sitting at a table in Santana's with Mary
Rizzo, who was an assistant like me, and Lars Sorenson, a moon-
struck young supervisor who liked me. I noticed that one of the
glamor figures of The Company was sitting at the bar. He was an
assistant manager, one of the genuine brains of the operation, a creative and imaginative man in his early forties. I'd been with The
Company for going on two years now, and I hadn't said three
words to this man, except in the line of duty, but every time I saw
him in the hall I thought, God, what a really interesting, masculine,
fascinating kind of guy. He had slightly simian features, which I
found appealing. He was compact and built like a fireplug, with
muscles rippling under his shirt, and he had the brownest of brown
eyes and silver-flecked dark-brown hair to match, in tight curls
that reminded me of a Greek statue. He was everything I'd always
admired in a man, and now he was sitting there at the bar staring
at me. I got a little flustered.

I said to Mary, "Hey, isn't that Tom Lantini? He's staring at me.
I think he's terribly handsome. Hey, I wonder why he's staring at
me. I've never really met him." I must have sounded like a school-
girl, and Lars kept giving me these dirty looks and telling me what
a jerk Lantini was to sit at a public bar and stare and what a jerk I
was to be so interested.

After a while Lantini came over and asked politely if he could
join us. He was slightly loaded, but he managed to retain a certain

reticence and low key that I'd noticed around the office. He bought three or four more rounds of drinks, and around ten o'clock he said, "Hey, you guys want to go hear some jazz?"

I said, "Sure, love to!" and off we all went to the Cafe a Go Go to hear Miles Davis and have a great old time. We got thoroughly drunk and wandered around the Village. I'll never forget Sorenson and Tom playing leapfrog over the fire hydrants and Mary and me pretending to get scared. We'd shout, "Oh, my God, you're gonna miss one, you're gonna mortgage your future," and Tom would say, "Protect the family jools at all times!" People rapped on windows for us to shut up and get off the streets, but we leaped around town till dawn. Then we stopped and bought eggs and salmon and Tom said he'd fix breakfast. We took everything back to my apartment and he went to work in my tiny Pullman kitchen and I kept going in and out on some pretext or other, bringing him dishes and trying to be as near to him as possible. Sorenson knew that sparks were flying, and he just sat in the corner pretending to make conversation with Mary, but at that point I couldn't have cared less what Sorenson was doing or thinking. I was fascinated by Tom Lantini! Here was a man who could step in and run an important business, produce these brilliant flashes of inspiration that helped to keep The Company going and still manage to be interested in Miles Davis and egg piperade and jumping over fire hydrants, and all this at forty-two or forty-three years old! An astonishing blend of maturity and energy. Later I thought that was what he'd probably been trying to prove on the street—showing that he could handle the fire hydrants as well as Sorenson, who was fifteen years younger. He and Sorenson had been having a little competition in the street, for my benefit, but I hadn't realized it.

When I came into the kitchen for about the tenth time, Tom just slid from behind the oven, kicked the door shut and grabbed me all in one smooth motion. He kissed me for what seemed like hours, and I kissed him back, loving his smell and his taste and the feel of his body. It was a very dangerous thing to do, because Sorenson was jealous. All through the kiss, I could hear him outside the door, talking excitedly to Mary. "What's he doing to her in there?

What're they *doing* in there?" I heard Mary say, "Lars, there's not room enough to be doing much of anything." "Yes, there is. He's got her on the floor!" "Don't be silly, there's not enough room for that." "Oh, yes, there is!" Finally Tom pulled back from me and opened the door and laughed, as though to tell Sorenson that it was all in fun.

After we ate, the sun came up, and Tom said he had to go to his townhouse and shave and get ready for a tennis date, and he said, "Would you like to go with me?" I said, "No, I'm kind of tired. I think I'll just get some sleep." So they all left and I dreamed about Tom Lantini for the rest of the morning.

All through the next week, I had trouble concentrating on my work. I made up a thousand excuses to walk the halls near Tom's office, and two or three times we bumped into each other, but he was all business. I thought about him constantly. I was charmed by him. I found some special meaning in every move he made. He had great taste, he was cool, patient, understated. Whenever I thought that we might not get together again, I felt a little undigestible lump in my stomach. But I had absolutely no way of telling if he had any feelings about me, and when we saw each other in the office, he indicated nothing.

That Friday night I had a date with Laddie Owens, and I kept it. Later Mary called me and said, "You really set Tom Lantini on his ear tonight."

I said, "How'd I do that?"

"Well, he thought we were all gonna get together at Santana's again. He just assumed it. And when you didn't show up, he went looking for you. He kept saying, 'Where's Glo? Where's Glo?' and he sounded almost frantic. Very unusual for him."

"So what happened?"

"Oh, we went out and listened to some jazz."

"You and Tom?"

"Sure. Why not?"

I was furious, but I kept it to myself. "Sure," I repeated. "Why not?"

He took no chances the next week. He called me on Wednesday

and asked if I'd meet him in the bar Friday evening. For the first time we were alone for a while, and after a few drinks he began telling me his troubles. He'd been married and divorced ten years before. He never intended to marry again. His mother lived with him in a townhouse in the Village, and she was suffering from a combination of liver trouble and arthritis, and he loved her very much and spent his free time trying to make her comfortable. My God, he had me bawling at the table! Such dedication! Such love and devotion! I melted right in my seat, and I said to myself, Glo, you're insane! You're falling in love with this man. He's twenty years older than you are and he has a crazy life and you can't possibly fit into it.

The next week was hell on my office work. All I could do was sit and brood about him. I'd never felt this way before in my entire life. I'd close my door and light a cigarette and tell the smoke, "You're crazy! You're in real trouble! If you let this happen to you, there goes the whole ball game." But that Friday night I broke a date with Laddie Owens—the last one I would ever have with him—and went down to Santana's to wait. Tom showed up about a half an hour later, as though it was an automatic date, as though nothing had had to be said. And that's the way it was from then on. We were an automatic on Friday nights. The rest of the week I'd brood and wonder. I'd sit home at night and wonder what he was doing. I turned down all dates. I couldn't bear to go out with anybody else, couldn't stand to have somebody else touch me. I couldn't even stand to look at another man. Other men seemed weak and pathetic to me.

After about three weeks we began sleeping together. It seemed right and natural. But first I'd sit and listen for hours to his troubles, all the problems of his life, and how heroically he bore it all and tried to do the right thing. There was his mother. There was his ex-wife, still nagging at him after all the years. There was an assistant manager who was trying to knife him. I admired his courage, and I felt sorry for him at the same time. There was this big awful combination of things happening to him, and still he carried on. How noble, how brave! Soon I found myself worrying more about his life than about my own, and soon I began to realize that I was changing. I had changed from a happy-go-lucky type, leaping merrily around New York, to a somber, serious, uptight, *involved* human being, entirely dependent on another person's whims and neuroses and problems. That was bad, and I knew it, but there *wasn't a thing in the world I could do about it.* I loved this man, and my own wants and needs didn't matter any more. I made a few stabs at combining my old life with my new life, but Tom didn't like my old friends, and he made it clear that he didn't want me to see them. He called them "too giddy." I didn't realize it then—he seemed so much younger than his years in many ways—but those people on the East Side were just plain too youthful for him. They had started taking up rock and roll, and he was still listening to Miles Davis and John Coltrane. There was nothing in the world wrong with Davis and Coltrane and the great jazz musicians, but there was nothing wrong with the Beatles and some of the new rock groups, either. Tom couldn't see it that way. He told me he was satisfied with what he enjoyed; he didn't have to go running around trying to find new kicks or new experiences. The old jazz-men were good enough for him, and he would sit and interpret their work to me by the hour.

· 2 ·

FROM THE beginning, I wanted to marry Tom, but I could tell it was going to be a sore subject. We'd been seeing each other for six months and saying nothing about love and marriage, and then one night I blurted out, "I love you, I can't help it, I love you." He said, "I don't know if I love you or not, Glo. I just don't know. It's too soon." I said, "Well, I can understand that." And so we went on. For a long time he didn't say that he loved me, but then one night it came out. And then the next week he acted as though he was sorry he'd said it. "I don't know what it is," he said, "but there's something that's not quite right about us."

"But you do love me?" I said.

"Sometimes I do, and sometimes I wonder."

After we'd been seeing each other for a year or so, I began to bring up marriage again, but he always put me off. He said he had too many problems. He said his marriage experience had been horrible, and now he was gun-shy, and he asked me to be patient and not bring the subject up. So we continued to see each other, to get drunk together, to go to the movies together, and to screw. With all that going for him, why did he have to marry me? I listened to his troubles by the hour, gave him a shoulder to lean on and made myself entirely subservient to his needs. I gave him every advantage of marriage and none of the disadvantages.

But we had moments. We'd been seeing each other for two years when we worked it out so that we'd both be in Europe at the same time, me on a vacation trip with Mary and him on a business trip. I called him at Lyon, France, and he said, "God, am I gonna be glad to see you! I haven't had a conversation with anybody in three weeks." We agreed to meet in Bologna. The train ride from Rome to Bologna was unforgettable, on a fast train called "The Seven Bells," through tunnels and valleys where little terra-cotta villages were perched above streams and rivers and cliffs. I love trains anyway, and I sat in the nose of The Seven Bells, in a special observation area under the engineer's cabin, and watched Italy pass in front of my nose. I got off the train with my usual mess of packages—Tom says I'm always carrying things; he says I always look like somebody's old Polish aunt because I buy stuff at the last minute and then haul it around in shopping bags. There I was, carrying two shopping bags, an air flight bag and a suitcase, staggering up the platform, and I had a raincoat on and a scarf around my head, and I saw Tom long before he saw me. He was standing at the far end of the platform, and I looked so different that I walked right up under his nose and he didn't recognize me, and I said, "Hey, don't you remember me?" He took me in his arms and he said, "Oh, My God, you look like all the rest of us dagoes!"

We went to this wonderful hotel near the railroad station and into an enormous room, with a bathroom almost as big. The bed was wide and fluffy, and I could have drowned in the tub. Tom drew a bubble bath with some German stuff called Badedas and I kept slipping under the bubbles.

Rain? I never saw it rain so hard. Day after day. But we didn't care. We sent down for room service. *Gnocchi* and *tagliatelle* and thick steaks and wild mushrooms, *funghi*. We walked over to a little restaurant called Annello's, where they had game hanging in the window above wild boars, and displays of fennel and endive and truffles, and Annello himself standing behind the food bar, slicing carrots and scallions faster than the eye could see, sending up little fountains of sliced vegetables with his knife. We shared an umbrella and wandered up and down those narrow, twisting little streets, down to the two medieval towers that they call "The Donkey Ears," and into the tiny shops where you could get all kinds of treasures. Tom had two pairs of boots hand made, and the bootmaker traced his foot size on a piece of paper and made each boot to fit his exact size. Where else in the world could you get something like that for fourteen dollars a pair? Then we rented a Fiat 1100 and drove high up into the cool mountains and ordered *tortellini* at a favorite *trattoria* and drank *grappa* and *vino lombrusco*, and tried to talk to the grizzled old stunted natives, and parked and made love on the hilltops. Once we made love inside the ruins of an old church—the war had swept back and forth in this valley—under a statue of the Virgin still hanging near the shattered altar. She was armless and legless, and Tom christened her "The Virgin de Milo."

That lasted for one gorgeous week, the best week of my life, the best week I will *ever* have, and then we both went our separate ways back to New York. Somehow things were different when we got back. Don't ask me why. One night Tom just came out and said, "I don't love you. No I don't love you."

I just said, "I don't believe you," and let the subject drop. And soon we entered a new phase. He had been keeping me away from his mother—later I couldn't figure out whether he was ashamed of her or ashamed of me—but now he took me to the house and introduced me as "a friend." I could see that his mother had been beautiful, but I could also see that she was a very sick old lady. "How do you do, my dear?" she said, sticking out this arching hand, and it was like holding a dry bone. We sat and talked for an hour or so, and I could feel the emotions crackling back and forth between mother and son. They obviously idolized each other, almost to the sickening point, and I wound up the total outsider. But that wasn't what Tom wanted, and he brought me back to the townhouse several times. "I want you to get to know Mother," he said. "I want you to help her." The way I was to help her was to take some of the chores off Tom's back: to help him wage the constant fight against his mother's poor health, to take her to the doctor, to help her change her clothes, to steer her in and out of the bathroom. All the awful things that a nurse's aide has to do in a hospital. The old lady hated me from the start. "Who is this woman?" she said to Tom one night when he brought me home. By this time I was practically living there, meeting the old woman's demands night after night, and sleeping by myself on a couch downstairs in the living room, while Tom and his mother slept in adjoining bedrooms upstairs, their heads separated only by about six inches of wall. "It's Glo," Tom said. "You know Glo. She's your friend."

"Oh, yes," the old lady said in this senile haze. "I know the woman."

I began plotting to get him to my apartment on weekends. He'd always claim that he couldn't be away from his mother, but if I wanted to come along and help out I could sleep on the couch in the townhouse. By this time he had become acutely aware of how much I needed him sexually, and he used the sexual attraction to his own advantage. My God, how I loved that man's body! Just looking at him across a room turned me on, and if he touched me or felt me then didn't go the whole route with me—I'd be miserable. Now that I knew him better, I realized that he wasn't the complete physical Adonis I'd once thought; no one is at forty-four. Even in the few years we'd been going together I had noticed a lessening in his capabilities. In my franker moments, I used to say to myself, What would happen if we got married? What would it be like when he's tired of sex and I still want it? There were nights when he'd fall asleep on me and I'd be about to tear my hair out with passion for this man, and I'd sit and think, Jesus Christ, what's it gonna be like ten years from now if he's falling asleep now? Is he that tired? Doesn't it work any more? Can't he keep up with me? Because I could still run around all night and drink and carry on and screw and still get up the next morning and want to screw again, and he wouldn't. He didn't even want to think about it.

When we were at his place, which was just about every weekend now, sex was strictly out. His mother dominated the house just by sleeping there. She was a very light sleeper, and if there was the slightest noise during the night, she'd be up and around, banging into things, turning on lights. She thought nothing of coming into Tom's room at three in the morning and turning on the lights and asking him to check on the noise.

I'd make my little bed downstairs on the sofa, and then I'd sneak upstairs to say good night to him and I'd clutch him and want him so badly. If I didn't cry I'd consider it a great triumph. And if I did cry, he'd feel bad and I'd feel bad and he'd whisper, "Well, Glo, you know we can't do this. Mother's in the next room," and I'd whisper back, "I know it." It was so frustrating! One night we did make love in his bed, but we might just as well not have. I'd come up to kiss him good night, and we began stroking each other, and both of us got horny at the same time. So finally he said, "Oh, I don't care. Fuck my mother! Let's do it." He went off like a gun, long before I even got started. I felt worse. It messed me up more than ever. I went into the bathroom and straightened myself up and went downstairs and sat up all night smoking cigarettes and crying. We never did it like that again, and I'm just as glad.

I guess we'd been seeing each other for about two years—and I was practically doing *everything* for his mother by now, and running his house to boot, while he was taking more and more trips not only out of town but out of the country, and for weeks and weeks at a time—when one night he got mad at me and said he was not going to touch me that night. That was nothing new—he'd always used sex as a sword over my head, and he knew I'd jump through a hoop for it, because I loved him so much. But now he added something new: He was mad about some little thing and he called me a Friday-night whore! On Friday nights we used to have some drinks at Santana's and fool around town a little and then went to my apartment to make love. I didn't see how that made me a Friday-night whore, but I was hurt just the same. I looked up "whore" in the dictionary; I didn't seem to qualify. But I had to convince myself that I wasn't one. It bothered me terribly! This man that I loved so much, this man that monopolized my entire life and put me to good use acting as the perpetual hostess and nursemaid at his house, this man was calling me a dirty name! It bothered me then, and it bothers me now.

The years went by, and he still used that phrase whenever I made him mad. I'd long since become used to the idea of running two households: his and mine. His mother, despite her various ailments, hung onto life. There were nights when I could have strangled her with my bare hands. She still pulled that old trick of pretending not to recognize me once in a while. But I was wise to her. She recognized me, all right—as the enemy! As for my own personal life, I had almost none. Everything of my own suffered. As far as I was concerned, Tom Lantini was the only thing in the whole world. Gloria Rolstin didn't matter any more. At the office, I went through the motions. I stopped dreaming about becoming a specialist, or a supervisor, or any of those other jobs that women almost never got anyway. I did an adequate job, but I no longer threw myself into my work. There was only so much Gloria to go around, and Tom and his mother were getting most of it. I was enabling her to stay alive and him to spend all his spare energy trying to find himself. He'd go from one interest to the next. When he found out there was a top limit on how far he could go at the office, he began looking for ways out. He thought he'd become a composer, and he'd sit in his study for hours scribbling on music paper and telling me to shut up and play honeymoon bridge with his mother. How many of those dull, dreary games I must have played! And the old lady barely able to tell what was trump! I had to make outlandish mistakes even to keep her interested in the game, to give her any chance at all to win. And I had to jump up every five minutes to get her something, or lead her to the john, or get her medicine. Once in a while I'd hear piano notes from the study, and I'd know that Tom was trying out a melody. Much as I loved him, he never wrote anything that impressed me. If I would try to join him, to suggest something, he'd lose his temper and tell me I was butting in. He said that the whole history of music was that only men made good composers. So *his* music was all that mattered. When I think about that period now, I get kind of tired, really weary. I did all his shopping, his house cleaning, his planning, his cooking—and *everything* involving his mother. If I brought up the subject of marriage, he turned it off instantly and told me how much of my time I was already getting, and how well off I was. "Why, we're as good as married now," he said, and if I suggested that we make it official, he'd tell me to wait a while, things just weren't right at the moment.

· 3 ·

AFTER ABOUT four years, we had a very bad scene about marriage one night, and he called me a Friday-night whore again, and I began to get the idea that I was strictly a convenience to him, that he didn't really love me at all but found me useful. I had become almost indispensable to him, but *I was not loved*. But even this realization had no effect on my own feelings. I was madly in love with him. He was the only man in the world I had ever loved and I desperately wanted to marry him.

Until then, jealousy had never been a part of my makeup. I had a terrible temper, yes. I could get angry and pop off at anyone, the Pope of Rome included, but I just didn't seem to get jealous. But now that awful emotion began to consume me. I think he was already running around with other girls, but at the time I was blissfully unaware of it. What I was jealous of was Tom himself. I used to sit and say to myself, "I'm not anything any more; it's all Tom. Tom for everything, and everything for Tom. It's Tom's job,

Tom's music, Tom's trips, Tom's house, Tom's mother. I'm nothing." That's all I thought about. We got into an argument about it one night. I began having the feeling that my life was being drowned in his, and when I mentioned it to him he said, "Well, don't let *me* hold you back. Go make a fortune, go write a hit play, go do anything you want." And I said, "I can't, I'm so caught up in your life. I can't do anything on my own any more. I've totally lost my identity. I'm not a person. I'm not anything any more, except somebody to take the weight off you so you can be somebody."

His answer was a loud "Hummmph!" and a quick retreat to his study.

I told Mary a few days later, "I'm desperate. I don't know what to do. I'm nothing now. I'm gone! I look in the mirror and I don't even see myself. I don't even look the same. Look at me. Tom always wants me to cut my hair, and now I look like I've got a crewcut. All that shiny black hair: gone. I'm getting so thin I can hardly see myself when I turn sideways. I look bad, but I don't have time for *my* appearance. It's all *his* appearance, *his* life. Nothing matters but him."

Tom and I had more screaming fights about it, and he would taunt me, tell me to go out and make something out of myself, do something on my own for a change instead of hanging around him, and all the time he knew I couldn't. He'd beaten me into what he wanted, and he knew it.

Mary was giving me a lot of advice, and so were my other friends at the office, and all the advice added up to one thing: Drop him. I knew I couldn't do it, but Mary talked me into making a pretense to shake him up. So I told him I loved him but that I was moving out of his life. He looked shocked. His chin dropped a foot. I avoided him for about a week, and then he asked me to have a drink with him at Santana's. He sat there peeping over the top of his fourth Scotch mist and told me that he didn't understand why I had left him. I said, "I couldn't take it any more, Tom. You were driving me crazy. I was absolutely convinced that I'd wind up in a mental hospital. Either I'm gonna have to be your wife and live with you all the time, or not see you at all."

He said, "No, I can't do it."

I said, "Why can't you do it? Do you love me?"

"Yes. I think I love you."

"Well, I love you, so what's the problem?"

He told me that it was family problems and this and that and the whole scene. And I said, "Do you notice that when you talk about *us* you always talk about *you?*" And I told him how I felt about being his handmaiden, doing the dirty work with his mother, acting as his punching bag, his Friday-night whore. We had a few more drinks, and I could see that for one of the first times in our relationship I seemed to be reaching him. He almost looked as though he was going to cry. I reached out and took his hand, and he put both his hands on mine, and he said, "Well, Glo, I suppose you're right."

I said, "What do you mean by that?"

He said, "I suppose you're right—that we ought to get married. Yes—we *will* get married."

I was ecstatic. I said, "Goody!" How silly it sounds now, but that's exactly what I said when the dream of my life came true— "Goody!" Then I said, "When? How about tomorrow?"

He laughed. I knew that he was leaving on a business trip the next evening. I said, "When?"

He said, "As soon as I get back."

I said, "No, no good. We'll get married *before* you go." I didn't want him to have time to change his mind. The whole thing was too important, too *important.*

He said, "No, there's not enough time. We have to get blood tests and all that."

I made the mistake. I gave in. I said, "All right, fine, we'll get married as soon as you get back. We'll get blood tests and do the whole bit."

We went to my apartment and made love, and as soon as he left I called up Mary Rizzo and told her, "Mary! I want you to be the first to know. Tom and I are gonna get married." And then I added: "I think."

Mary said, "What do you mean, 'I think'?"

I said, "Well, I think he means it, but with Tom you can never be sure. I want you to stand up with me, Mary. You've been through this whole thing with me. You're my best friend. But don't tell anybody, on account of he just might not mean it."

Tom came back a week later, and I met him at the airport to drive him home in my Corvair. I said, "Well, I've been thinking about it for seven days and I think I've got everything worked out."

He said, "About what?"

I said, "About our marriage."

He said, "I can't do it."

I said, "What do you mean you can't do it?"

He said, "I can't do it, Glo. There's just something wrong. It's not you, it's me. There's something wrong with me. I can't go through with it."

I was in shock. I said, "Well, Tom, I don't know how I can go on this way."

He said very gently, "Well, try. Try it for a while. Let it go for a while, will you? Let me try and straighten myself out."

What do you say to a man you love? You say okay, and you go on for three more years.

My own mother—that dear old country girl from Podunk—finally joined the ranks of people telling me to cut this thing off, to stop losing my best years, from twenty to thirty, in a hopeless cause. She said, "Glo, if you've gone on like this for all these years, he's never gonna marry you." I said, "Mother, how can you say that? We're practically married now." She said, "That's the trouble." She was very bright about it. She said, "Look, you ran into Tom at a bad time in his life, when he was in the throes of a lot of personal problems, and on top of that he had a sick mother to take care of. You came along just then and you helped to pull him through. But he'll never marry. He'll keep you around as long as you can be of any help at all. And then he'll dump you. Because I'll bet you a hundred dollars he doesn't love you." I laughed, and I said, "Mother, how can you say a thing like that?" I took it all very lightly. I thought she was absolutely wrong. I said, "Mother, he's just confused and mixed up. He'll marry me when he's got his head straight." And Mother just shrugged and said, "It seems pretty futile to me, sitting around waiting for a fifty-year-old man to get his head straight."

My troubles with Tom's mother grew worse. Once Tom had to haul her off to her room and lock her in to keep her from carrying on about me. I told him she'd be better off in a home, and he told me that a Friday-night whore had no right to make such remarks. A few days later he told me that his mother now referred to me only as "that woman" and insisted to him that I was a "street slut." One night when Tom and I had a few close friends to his house, she came sneaking out of her bedroom and announced, "I will *not* have that woman in my house," pointing a quavering finger at me. When she called me "that whore" in front of another group, I fled into the street and cried and cried. Buckets of tears! I didn't feel I could fight back. Whatever I said, Tom shrugged it off and reminded me that I was talking about his mother. He wouldn't hear a word against her! Finally I said, "You and your goddam mother! You'll never leave her! You're sick! It's a sick relationship!" He lashed out at me with his fist, and I took the blow in the side of the head. But I got back up. I always do.

It wasn't long after that two things happened: Tom told me I didn't have to help out with his mother any more, and he took a tiny *pied-à-terre* in midtown. I had mixed emotions about both moves. At first, I was glad to be relieved of the dirty work with the old lady, but soon it became obvious that Tom didn't want me near his townhouse at all; that was why he told me not to help his mother any more. And I couldn't understand his reason for renting a midtown apartment. "What in the world do you need that for?" I asked him. "We can always go to my place."

"I just need a place of my own," he said. "I need to get away." That wasn't what he really needed the place for, but I was too dumb to catch on at first.

Now the fights began to get bloodier, more physical. In our years together, Tom had grown from a handsome, tasteful, mature man into a spiteful grownup baby, and I was taking the brunt of his

childishness. He used to like nothing more than to tell me to meet
him at the Santana or some other bar and then let me sit there for
hours waiting. It gave him some sense of power, I suppose. One
night I waited for three hours, and when I realized that I'd been
stood up I walked over to his *pied-à-terre*. There he was back-
lighted in the front window. He'd just walked in, and he was staggering around drunk. I knocked on the window and he said in this
sloppy voice, "Get out of here! I don't want to see you!" I saw red.
I'd been sitting in that bar for three hours, and now his royal high-
ness didn't want to see me. I said, "You open this door, God damn
you! Nobody is doing this to me!"

He said, "Get the fuck out of here!"

I said, "You son of a bitch!" and I kicked in the stained-glass
window. There was glass all over the place! He came out and
dragged me inside and tried to calm me down; I suppose he was
embarrassed, in his drunken stupor, about the neighbors. Then he
fell on the little bed, and I could see he was just about out cold
from drink. I went over and shook him and I said, "Listen, you
drunken son of a bitch, how dare you treat me like this!"

He opened his eyes and said, "You're gonna pay for that window."

I said, "You're just a drunk. And you're disgusting. And I'm not
paying for any window."

The argument went on for hours, there among the shards of
glass, and at last he said, "Why don't you fuck off! I'm getting
undressed!" He started taking off his clothes and then he said again,
"I'm getting undressed."

I said, "What do you want me to do, jump up and down?"

He said, "Well, I don't know why you'd want to sit there and
watch me get undressed."

I said, "For Christ's sake, I've been watching you get undressed
for years. What is that gonna do to me?"

He said, "I don't think it's very nice for you to sit there and
watch me undress, that's all."

I said, "I don't care what you think. I'm gonna sit right here and watch. I'm gonna sit right here for years. I don't care *what* you do."

He said, "Well, it's not right."

I said, "Listen, you have walked about in absolute nothing in front of me. You have screwed me. You have done just about everything possible to me, and there you sit, you drunken bastard, and you tell me that you don't think it's nice for me to watch you undress!"

It went on like that for more hours, and finally I began to feel sorry for him. He was still so drunk and pathetic. I hung up his clothes, took off my own dress, and jumped in bed with him. I'd hardly fallen asleep when I felt this clutch. I rolled over and said, "What the hell do you want?"

He sat upright and said, "Where'd you come from?"

I said, "Don't you remember? I kicked out the window."

He said, "That's right, you bitch! You kicked out the window!"

By now the whole thing had grown so ludicrous that I began a laughing jag, and pretty soon he started to laugh, and that's the way we finished the night, screwing and laughing till the sun came up. Honest to God! It was so totally beyond belief, all we could do was laugh. An Italian movie! It was like being married. I told Mary later, "If I never marry anybody, I'll feel that I've been married once."

· 4 ·

HE BEGAN playing around with other women, secretly at first, and then right out in the open. He knew that I desperately loved to sleep with him, and so long as he had this power over me he figured he could get away with anything. He was the first man I'd ever known that I desperately loved to sleep with. He felt beautiful. I never looked at another man through all the years with him, not until he practically begged me to go out with others. I never gave him any cause to be jealous. If I was sent out of town, I'd call him each night. But then I began to notice that he was seldom home when I was out of town.

After he played around with other women, he'd come and tell me about them. He'd never say he screwed them, but he'd give me just enough information to kill myself with jealousy, just enough to make me cry and carry on and scream at him. He'd say, "I went down to Philly while you were on your trip, and I met an interesting girl. Valerie was her name." He told me that Valerie invited him over for a drink after a business meeting, and how they played this Sinatra hit, "Strangers in the Night," on her hi-fi, but it was all in fun. All in fun! Did you ever hear the lyrics to "Strangers in the Night"? The *do-be-do-be-do* is the least of it. The song talks about these two people meeting for the first time, "exchanging glances," "wondering what the chances," and "sharing love before the night is through." How the hell could you go to some strange broad's apartment and make a big fuss over a song like that and then claim that the whole evening was all innocent fun? Then when he had planted that idea in my head, he began comparing Valerie's apartment with mine. Hers was tastefully decorated; mine was "a garbage collector's paradise." He actually used that phrase! She had a Marantz hi-fi system; mine was by Philco. He chopped and chopped at the differences between Valerie and me and between just about every other girl and me. I couldn't understand his purpose. I'm not sure *he* could.

As the months went on I began to realize that both of us were making more and more trips away from each other. When I'd ask him if I could go with him—like the old days—he'd say that was impossible. When I had to go on one of my glamorous trips to Pittsburgh or Akron, he'd positively brighten, and then I'd come back home and hear about another one of his "innocent" adventures while I'd been gone.

Now the superfights began. He cut my nose. I sprained his wrist. He blackened my eye. I pulled out about five square inches of his curls. Both of us were coming to work like the walking wounded, and my girl friends were saying, "Glo, Glo, you better get out of this. Get out of it while you're alive!" I was irritable, mean, snappy. I was smoking three packs a day and eating almost nothing, and I was down to about ninety-nine pounds. Ninety-nine pounds of hatred for humanity. Once I'd been able to drink. Now four or five Scotches and I was out. And for the first time in my life I began to get mean when I drank. Tom had always been like that, but I had always been the opposite. After three drinks, it was kisses for everybody! Now I was arguing with my best friends—and over nothing. One night I argued for hours with Mary and a couple other girls from the office, and when Tom showed up at my apartment at midnight, drunk and demanding, ordering me to strip and lean over and things like that without the slightest preamble, I told him to go fuck himself. He smashed me so hard on the side of my head that he knocked me down, and my ear was ripped open from his ring. I still have the scar. I grabbed a knife and went after him. I said, "You son of a bitch, I'm gonna kill you!" and I was! I ripped open his suit and I would have ripped open his chest, but he was strong enough to wrestle the knife away and get out of there.

Don't ask me why he kept coming back after scenes like that. I know why I took *him* back: I loved him. Simple as that. But I don't think he loved me, not at that stage of the game. And yet he'd come back, and we'd screw—there's no use calling it "making love" or "sleeping together" any more; it was just plain screwing, or fucking, or whatever word you want to use. Then he'd do some vicious, cruel thing and the fighting would start again.

St. Patrick's came on a Friday that year, and Tom had been un-usually sweet about asking me out. In New York, St. Patrick's is one of the biggest holidays, and there's a very good reason. It is so agonizing to live in New York City that everyone is looking for a way out of the pain, and since St. Patrick's Day is a license for even the most temperate people to go out and get drunk, it's em-braced as a big holiday by everybody. Bars on Second and Third Avenue are so full on St. Patrick's night that there are lines out on the street, and around midnight the sidewalks look like a battlefield, and you can hear the ambulances going up and down the avenues till dawn. Personally, I'd just as soon have stayed home and had a few quiet drinks, but he didn't want it that way. He came to me earlier in the week and he said, "Say, hon, I've been invited to a fancy dinner and St. Patrick's-night party. How about going with me?"

I was flabbergasted. It had been months since he had taken me out publicly. I bought a new dress and a new hat, and I looked pretty good around the office as the work hours passed on Friday. Late in the afternoon I passed by his office and I saw one of the girls from the typing pool sitting there all dolled up. She looked exactly the way I'd looked for years—sitting on a little bench outside Tom's office waiting to go out with him. I came back about ten minutes later, and she was still there, reading a magazine and sipping a drink. Everybody was drinking around the office that day, including me. You'd have looked like a genuine square not to take a few drinks on such an important occasion as St. Patrick's Day.

At six o'clock the office party was in full swing, but Tom's secretary told me he was still working, putting some project to bed. I drifted around with a glass of Scotch in my hand, and whenever I went past his office the girl was there. I'd always had a short fuse about Tom and other girls, and I went back to my office and dialed him. "What time are we going to the party?" I said.

"We're not going," he said. Right away I could tell he was drunk. "It's off."

I stewed for a while, and then I marched around to his office. I walked in just as he was telling the girl from the typing pool, "Go ahead. I'll meet you there." I marched right over to his desk, picked up a framed picture of his mother, and smashed it into a million pieces. The girl ran, and Tom grabbed me and wrestled me to the floor. I was trying to kick him in the crotch, but he's powerful, and he kept me pinned. I began screaming, and he let go. I jumped up in a blind rage, and I raked my nails down the side of his face and drew blood. He grabbed me again, and I kicked him as hard as I could in the shins. "You son of a bitch!" I screamed. "You son of a bitch!" The wonder is that nobody came into his office to break us up; it must have sounded like somebody was getting killed. But by now I guess the office was getting used to me and Tom and our battles, and they decided to let us fight it out. By the time it was over, my new dress was ripped down the side, and every button was torn off Tom's shirt, and he looked like he'd been in a fight with a wild animal—which he had.

I dragged myself back to my office and lit a cigarette and bolted my drink. There was a knock on the door, and who should enter but a woman executive from upstairs, a genuine brass-hat big shot. She was as drunk as anybody. "There, there, honey," she said, patting my back. It was like being soothed by a Tyrannosaurus. I was still shaking and sniffling, and this old broad was going on, "That man's wrecked your life, honey. Now you just break off with him for good! That man is thoroughly rotten, honey. Now you get rid of him!" I whirled around and said, "Listen, you, how dare you try to meddle in my personal affairs! Just go fuck yourself!" She disappeared fast when I grabbed an ashtray. A few minutes later she came back with an honor guard of her flunkies and stood at my door spouting this long speech. I couldn't understand a word she was saying—she was so drunk and angry—and furthermore I didn't care. It developed later that she was saying I was fired, but she was too drunk to get it out and too hung over the next day to remember.

If you think that my behavior was insane at this point, I was thinking the same thing, drunk as I was. I stormed out the office and walked the streets for hours, half out of my mind. It was raining hard, one of the worst rainstorms of the year, but I couldn't even feel it. Cars drove by and sloshed water on me, and I stepped into deep puddles where the sewer water had backed up, and I just kept on walking, walking, around and around the blocks. After three or four hours of this aimless staggering around, I decided what I'd better do is go over to Bellevue and commit myself. I figured I'd be better off in somebody else's hands, because I was crazy. I headed east along Fifty-second Street toward the hospital and I hadn't gone a half block when I saw Tom and the girl from the typing pool walking out of a bar, arm in arm and giggling and looking as if they were the last two human beings on earth. I lost all control of myself. I ran up to them and called her a whore, and I said, "Lady, you'd better get your ass out of here, because if you don't, I'll finish *you* after I finish *him!*"

Tom put his body between her and me, and just then a taxi pulled up and he shoved her inside. He told her, "I'll see you later," and I said, "You son of a bitch, you'll *never* see her later!" The taxi pulled away, and we had a screaming battle on the street. I was crying, and he was calling me all kinds of names and saying I was insane. He was right. For the moment, I was as insane as the wildest nut in Bellevue, and he had made me that way.

He began walking fast down the street, and I chased after him. "Tom," I said, "you can't do this to me. You really can't!" He kept on going. "We've had too much together," I said. "You can't run away from me now."

He turned and stopped. "We've had *nothing* together," he said. "You just get the fuck out of my life!"

"Where are you going?" I said. "It's late. It's raining." As if that had anything to do with anything.

"I'm going to my apartment," he said. "I'm gonna meet somebody there, and we're gonna fuck all night."

I grabbed him by the arm, and he flung me to the sidewalk. Another seam opened up in my new dress, and my coat was soaked with muddy water. By the time I scrambled to my feet, he was halfway down the block, almost running, and I knew I'd never catch him. So I walked toward his apartment, the little one where I'd broken the stained-glass window, and when I got there it was dark inside. I knew what was going on. Once it had been me in there in the dark. "Open up that door, you dirty, rotten bastard!" I shouted. There was no answer. I stood outside for ten or fifteen minutes, screaming things. "Get that whore out of there!" I said. "Let her go back and hustle the streets!" Everything was quiet. Then the police drove up. "Ma'am," this polite cop said, taking my arm, "move along now. You're disturbing the peace."

I started to cry. The cop was so nice. "I'm sorry, lady," he said. "But you'll have to go someplace else. The neighbors are complaining."

I leaned back against the doorway, and I looked at the two cops, and I thought to myself, This is a movie I'm seeing. I'm not really in this. This can't be happening to me. I'll wake up and it'll all be a dream, a movie. The two cops took my arms and led me to the corner, and the nice one said, "That's a good girl. Run along now. You'll feel better in the morning."

I walked sixty blocks to my apartment, through the driving rain and all, and when I got there I found Mary already inside. Somehow she'd gotten wind of what was happening, and she knew that I'd need help when I got home. "Oh, Mary," I said as I took off my drenched, ripped clothes. "It's over. It's really over! All I can think of is to commit myself."

"It's him that should be committed," Mary said as she helped me out of my wet clothes and bundled me into a robe. "Look at you! Do you know you have a black eye? What else did he do? One of these days he's gonna kill you."

"Or I'm gonna kill him," I said.

"You've got to let it drop," Mary said. "It's got to end for good."

"I *can't* let it drop. I know I'm a total idiot. But I can't. I still love the man. Look what he's done to me. He's made me a mess, but I still love him."

The upshot of the big St. Patrick's-night battle was that one of the more benevolent supervisors called me up at home and told me to go some place and lie around a beach for a few weeks, *all expenses paid*. I accepted gratefully. I hauled myself off to Key West and thought and thought and thought. When I came back, I walked straight into Tom's office. He gave me the kind of look you give to a kid that's just come home from burning down the schoolhouse.

"Knock it off!" I said. "You didn't behave any better than I did."

He said, "I've never been through such a night in my life."

I said, "Oh, you haven't? Well, do you think it was any better for me? Cops bawling me out, walking all the way home in the flood. Do you think that was so terrific? You could have shown a little humanity, but not you! You could have just patted me on the head and taken me home, but not you!"

We began seeing each other again, but after about a month Tom said, "Look, what we both need is a little freedom. We're getting so we can't even talk sanely together." He suggested that we start dating others. When I put up an argument, he refused to listen. Finally he said, "Either we date others, or we don't see each other at all. It's up to you." What could I do? I was grasping for straws. I knew the whole thing was winding down. I said, "I don't see how I can date others, Tom, but I'll give it a try."

It was laughable. I hereby apologize to the men I went out with in the next few months. Those poor miserable creatures! I must have been the cause of more cold showers than any other girl in New York. The only time I could be any good at all was when I was raging drunk, and then it was purely physical. But if I was sober, I'd just go to sleep and leave the guy lying there wondering about his masculinity. Oh, I was terrific! I feel sorry for a couple of very nice guys who were really good people. They tried to turn me on, and they must think I'm the biggest dud in the world. But I still loved Tom. If you can't screw, you can't screw.

All this time he was dating Jeanne, the girl from the typing pool. He'd meet her every Friday night, the same as he used to meet me. It was history repeating itself, and I could sit back and see it, and I still loved the son of a bitch. Once every week or two he'd take me out for a few drinks, and once every month or so he'd drop over to my apartment for a quick lay. He never said anything about love or affection or much of anything. It seemed like he'd have his fly unzipped before he walked through my door. And I took it. It was all I had.

One night there was a big office party, and he was there with Jeanne, and I was spending my time talking to other men and trying to pretend I didn't care whether I was with Tom or not. At one point I looked across the big room and I could see that Tom was in a violent rage with Jeanne, and I remembered so well how he'd acted that way with me, and I said to myself, He's drunk, and he's as screwed up as ever.

A little later I went into the john, and Jeanne came in crying copious tears. She said, "Oh, Glo, I have to talk to you." I turned around and I said with all the contempt I could muster, "What the hell do *you* have to say to *me?*"

She said, "You're the only person around here who understands him. You're the only one in the whole world! And you're the only person he really loves. He keeps talking about you. All the time he talks about you. It's Glo this and Glo that." Isn't it funny, but in that instant, standing there in the ladies' room, I realized for the first time that Tom Lantini hated women, and that was all there was to it? And if he hated women, if that's the way his mind worked, then he'd be only too happy to hurt *me* and then use *me* to hurt Jeanne. It was sick, but it was obvious. He was *making* it obvious. I said, "Jeanne, I'll tell you something. Unless I'm dreadfully wrong, the man doesn't love *anybody*. The man is not capable of honest-to-God love."

She said, "How can you say that? You're all he talks about. Every time we go out he talks about you."

I said, "What happened between you two tonight? What made you come running in here crying?"

"He called me a whore."

I shook my head. I said, "Honey, that's par for the course. He called me that, too, and years ago he called his wife the same thing."

Jeanne wiped her eyes. "You're kidding," she said.

"No, I'm not kidding," I said. "It's the sad truth. Basically he thinks all women are whores. That's just the way he feels. I doubt if he realizes it himself. The trouble with me is, I'm still in love with him. I can stand here and tell you exactly what's the matter with that man, because I know him practically inside out, but I still love him. And I know that he doesn't love me or you or anybody else, Jeanne. He's not capable of it."

After a while he stopped seeing Jeanne and began seeing me more often. For a few final months we rolled and muddled, muddled and rolled. We usually had a good time together, but not always, and we usually went to bed, but not always, and sometimes he'd just come over to the apartment and screw me and hardly say a word. I minded it, but I adjusted to it. A few times he would stay

334 · *The Girls in the Office*

late, and then he'd wake up in the middle of the night and berate me for making him stay. I'd say, "I didn't make you stay! I didn't take your pants off, for God's sake!" Then he'd tell me that we were wrong, all wrong, and pull on his clothes and get out.

At the office, I began working hard to help get myself together. People had started avoiding me, or passing me in the halls and giving me that dying-cow look, as though they felt so sorry for me. I was sick and tired of that, so I began throwing myself into my work. I even took on some outside jobs, little free-lance jobs that filled the hours. I was killing myself with work so I wouldn't have to think about Tom. At the same time, I began seeing more of my old friends. For some reason, they flocked around eagerly. Hands reached out to save me. Tom was still around, but I began to get a vague premonition that I'd be able to make it someday without him, that all this help would get me through. I had the feeling that *whether I liked it or not, I was going to be saved.*

· 5 ·

THANKSGIVING WAS approaching, a day that I used to spend with him and his mother, cooking turkey and pretending that we were a nice, cozy group. I hadn't been in his townhouse for two years, and I had no reason in the world to expect an invitation this year, so I planned a dinner of my own for some of the newer people in the office, the lost souls. The day before Thanksgiving, Tom called on the interoffice phone and said, "Of course you're coming down to cook dinner for Mother and me?" And when I told him of course I was *not*, that I had my own plans for Thanksgiving, he acted disturbed and annoyed. Later I pieced out his mental process. He must have realized that I had regenerated enough of my old spunk to do a few things without him, that I was bouncing back. He must have said to himself, "Well, I haven't *entirely* destroyed this person. *So I'll try again.*"

That's why he invited me for Christmas a few weeks later. I was talking to my mother by long distance one night, and I mentioned to her that I was going to Tom's townhouse for Christmas dinner. She said I was crazy. I said, "Mother, I'm going, because this is the last Christmas I'll ever spend with Tom, and he's been a part of my life and he'll always be a part of my life."

On Christmas day, at Tom's, it was like old times, as though I was still a part of the property down there. His mother was nicer to me than she'd ever been—though that's not saying much—and Tom was attentive and affectionate, the same sophisticated, warm, mature person I'd imagined him to be long before I met him. If they planned it this way, to hurt me the most, it couldn't have worked out better. As I puttered about the kitchen helping Tom roast an enormous Christmas goose, I got that old feeling that no one else would ever do, that I would somehow have to spend the rest of my life with Tom, and that deep down inside his neuroses he felt the same about me. Then I found the letter. It was right on the top of his desk, in his study. You only had to read about two lines to realize that this letter was from a typical Southern belle and that she and Tom were thick as thieves. The letter gushed on about how much she missed him and how beautiful the magnolias were but how nothing could be the same without dear Tom around. I'd never read anybody else's mail in my life, but this letter just jumped up and begged to be read. The ending is stamped on my memory: "Darling, soon we'll be together again—forever."

Well, I thought, he's laying that terrific charm of his on another victim. Thank God she's way down yonder in the land of cotton. I went back to the kitchen and worked on the dinner some more, and then the phone rang. It rang and rang, and I thought Tom must have stepped out for cigarettes or something, so I picked it up. "Ready on your call to New Orleans," the operator said.

I said, "Just a minute." I heard the toilet flush, and I called out coldly, "The operator's ready on your call to New Orleans."

He took the call in his study, making an elaborate show of closing the door, and about fifteen minutes later he came out all red in the face and said, "How dare you answer my telephone!" And I said, "How dare *you* call *another* woman when you've invited me here for Christmas?" We had a big fight, and I stomped out the door. A few weeks later I got word from a mutual friend that a woman had moved in with Tom and his mother. I confronted him and he denied it, but I knew it was true, and I knew who the woman was. You could smell the camellias on him when he came to work each morning. But I figured either he'd get over her or she'd get sick of him and his mother both. Nobody else would put up with what I had put up with. So I just kept going, seeing him once in a while, having a quick physical event with him maybe once every four or five weeks, usually after he got drunk at an office party or at Santana's. I went on loving him, knowing that the girl was with him night after night. I leaned on my friends more and more. I was just trying to get through each night, to survive till morning without doing something drastic. One night I was having a drink with Lars Sorenson and he blurted out, "Glo, Glo, I can't stand seeing you like this. Get out of it! Forget about Tom. I can't stand what he's doing to you, I can't stand what's happening to you." I looked across at him and tears were streaming down his face, and I realized that there *were* people in the world who cared deeply about me; there were people who could cry for me and my pain.

Tom and I had a few short conversations, over drinks or in the halls, but I never mentioned the girl in his house. I was afraid it would end things forever. One day he said, "You know, I like you —as a friend. You're really a fine human being. What we should really be is friends, just damned good friends."

I said, "Tom, there's no way possible for us to be just friends. We *were* friends, but we can never be friends again."

One night I went into a bar in the East Village and there he was with the girl, and she was exactly as I had imagined: dainty, fragile, wearing a hat, smelling like a mortuary, smiling and giggling every time he took a deep breath. "Jesus Christ," I said to myself, "if that's what he wants he's welcome to her." When they got up to leave, he tried to brush by me and my date without saying anything, but I made a big point of saying, "Hi, Tom, how are you?" He said, "Oh, hello, Gloria," and kept on going.

A few days later he called me into his office. "How dare you spy on me?" he said. I laughed. He said, "You're *never* in the East Village. You were spying on me." I almost went into hysterics. The whole idea of me spying on him was so ridiculous. Finally I said, "No, I'm never in the East Village, you're right, but I was this time. It was a coincidence, a nine-million-to-one shot. But as far as spying on you is concerned, you're not worth it! I would never stoop to that because you're really not worth it. There was a time when I thought you were—but you're not!" He was still accusing me of spying when I turned and walked out.

After that he didn't talk to me for two or three weeks. Finally I got him over to my apartment on the pretext of fixing something for me, and I fed him some chicken and gave him some drinks and we wound up in bed. I remember lying there still caring so much about this man and knowing there was no hope, no future for us, that whatever we'd had was gone, and I was just getting fucked. He didn't seem to care whether I enjoyed the act or not. He went ahead and got his rocks off. I felt very sad, and I started to cry. He said, "What's the matter with you?" I said, "There's something awfully wrong." And he said, "Why? I don't think there's anything wrong." And even while he was saying that, he was getting up to start putting on his clothes and get out of my sight.

The girl kept on living in his house. I knew that from friends. But in the office Tom was cordial and warm to me and I resurrected my hopes one more time. Then I ran into his mother on West Tenth Street. She was being wheeled by a black woman in a nurse's uniform, but the old lady seemed full of vitality and more friendly than I'd ever seen her before. I couldn't understand this. She seemed to be taking a superior attitude toward me, a gloating attitude, but smiling all the while and telling me how much they all missed me around the house and how it was a shame I couldn't come back again. I told myself to ignore her.

A few days later the manager called me in and told me he wanted me to be part of a small task force that was going to Chicago to make a very important presentation. Nothing like this had happened in months, and I was excited about the idea. I asked him who else was going, and he named Mary and three or four others—and Tom. I figured I had nothing to lose, and I accepted with thanks.

During those four days in Chicago, Tom treated me like Queen Farouk! And in front of the others, too. He took me to dinner almost every night, showed me around the Loop and the other sights of the city—where he'd lived during his marriage—and in general made me feel that we were together again—a unit, a pair. I told Mary, "I can't believe it! The whole nightmare's over! I don't know how I did it, but I won him back!" Mary said, "Excuse my cynicism, Glo, but watch out! Keep your guard up!"

"Whatever for?" I said. "What in the world could he gain by faking affection toward me?"

"I don't know what he could gain, but I know he's a mean man, and he's working on something."

"He's not working on anything, silly. He really does care for me."

On the airplane flying home that weekend, Tom sat with me, and we talked all the way. The last thing he said when he dropped me off at my apartment was "Be sure to keep next Friday night open, Glo. We'll have a nice long dinner and a nice long talk." He left me on cloud nine, and I stayed on it till the next Thursday afternoon. Then I walked into Stacy Krupp's office just as she was saying on the telephone, "Yes, I understand Tom's getting married tomorrow and transferring to Los Angeles." When the conversation was over, I couldn't wait to say, "Tom who?"

"Why, you know Tom who," she said, laughing. "Tom Lantini."

"Oh, yes," I said, "Oh, yes, Tom Lantini. Oh, yes, I knew about that." I was floored. I was shocked. I don't know how I kept from showing it, but I rushed around to my office and sat down before I fell down. I felt like I'd been hit by a railroad train. I was sitting there with my head in my hands, crying to myself, when Mary walked in. I said, "Oh, Mary, Tom's getting married and leaving here."

She put her arms around me and she said, "Oh, Glo. Poor, poor Glo."

"Mary, I've got to know for sure," I said. "I've got to find out."
"Who can we ask?" Mary said. "I know. We'll ask his pal,
Buddy Bowers. He's bound to know."

By now I was close to hysterics. "Go ask him, will you, Mary?" I
said. "I can't do it. I'd only make an ass out of myself." Mary was
back a few minutes later, and the second she walked into the office
I knew for sure. She was crying, and the two of us just stood there
in the middle of the office, holding onto each other and bawling
away. At last I pulled myself together and I said, "Mary, I'm gonna
go confront Tom myself." She begged me not to go, and she asked
me what I could gain. I said, "It's not whether I have something to
gain or not. It's just something I've *got* to know from him." I said,
"You know me, you know how I am. This is the end of something
very large in my life, Mary. I want to know from him, because this
is the last, final blow."

I went around to the ladies' room and bathed my face and put on
some eye makeup. When most of the wreckage was repaired, I
walked straight to Tom's office. It was about four in the afternoon,
and he had his coat on. I said, "I hope you had a nice day."

He said, "Thank you. I hope you had a nice day, too. I'll see you
tomorrow."

For a minute I just stood there looking out the window, trying
to get up my courage. It was as though my whole life would go
down the drain if I asked one question, but I had to ask it anyway.
"Tom," I said, in a choking, strangled voice, "I understand you're
getting married tomorrow."

He laughed, and he said, "Glo, don't be ridiculous."

I said, "Tom, tell the truth for once in your life. Just once!"

"Me getting married tomorrow?" he said, and he laughed a big
ho-ho-ho, like a department-store Santa Claus and just about as sincere. "Glo," he said, "don't be ridiculous. You must be out of your
mind."

I looked at him, and I knew he was lying. I *knew.* "I don't believe you, Tom," I said.

He said, "Oh, for Christ's sake, Glo! You come in here with
these damned awful stupid questions. For Christ's sake—" and he

changed his tone from derision to deep sarcasm— "*of course I'm getting married tomorrow,*" and he laughed again, as though to show how ridiculous the very idea was.

"Okay, yeah," I said. "That's all I wanted to know," and I left.

He got married the next morning, and half the people in the office went to the wedding. He hung around for two weeks, and neither of us said a word to the other. Then he transferred to our Los Angeles office, and that was the end of it. I never spoke to him again. I never intend to. Don't ask me what happened to his mother. I suppose she went to Los Angeles with the happy couple. They deserve each other.

· 6 ·

A FEW years have gone by, and I've done a lot of thinking and analyzing. A long time ago I realized that Tom Lantini hated women, but it took a while for me to figure out what it was about me that attracted him and kept him interested for so long. The reason was that I was a strong person, much stronger than he was. For a woman-hater like Tom Lantini, it's no big kick to break down a weak, petty woman. But to take somebody even stronger than yourself, and then break them completely—that's an achievement. That's what men like Tom live their miserable lives for. He spent seven years trying to make me feel worthless. He broke me in many ways, at least for a long time to come. And he took the most important years away from me and made me a beaten person. If you could go through an experience like that and come out of it at the age of twenty-two or twenty-three, well, fine, you'd have learned something valuable. But it's different when you come out of it at thirty-two. Too much of your life is gone. Too much has been lost.

I look back on all that lost time, and I realize that the unknown person I might have married and lived a happy life with—why, I might have walked right by him and never taken a second look. Or

some eligible young man might have looked at me and said to himself, I could really love that girl, and then asked few questions
around the office and realized the idea was hopeless. That's the
price I paid.

Well, the hell with it. I'm better off than some few girls I know
who have *nothing* to remember. I have all the heartbreak, but I also
have the memory of the beautiful, lovely things. It's a beautiful
thing to love somebody and have it work—even for a week, a day,
an hour. To be in love with somebody and have them love you
back, and have all the lost and lovely things to remember—I
wouldn't give that up for all the awful days and all the awful times.
I'm sorry it lasted so long, that I gave away so much time, but I
wouldn't have missed it.

And I still love Tom. I'll always love him. I also feel sympathy
toward him. He's a sad man. Anyone who lives to inflict harm on
others is sad, because they can never be satisfied. They can never sit
back and say, "Well, now I've achieved my goal, now I can rest
and be happy." For personalities like that, there's never any rest,
because they can never get rid of the negative impulses that drive
them. If they humiliate ten girls, they push on to humiliate ten
more. The need never goes away.

I learned my own strength, too. I've had some blows since Tom
left, and I've ridden right through them. My mother died. Once
there was a time when I doubted that I could survive without that
dear lady, but here I am. I survived. I've had other problems, and
I've handled them with strength and—if I do say so—courage. I
learned that getting over a tragic event is simply a matter of getting
through the first night. Getting through the first night makes it
easier to get through the second, and so on. Each one becomes
easier. Before I learned that, I was ready for Bellevue. I was so
close. At my worst, I was stark, staring crazy. I didn't even know
what time it was. But as that song goes, "I'm wise, and I know what
time it is now."

Faith Stronberg, 36

———•———

*I never liked Faith Stronberg. I think she's a fake, and she's got a lot of fake problems, too. She's always having boy-friend trouble, but she's too gutless to do anything to solve her own problems. She never says, "This is what I want and I'm going out and get it!" She just sits around and waits for it to come to her. Instead of making the guy marry her, she stays home and bakes cookies and roasts chickens and makes gourmet meals and stuff. Around the office she's very brisk and cool and efficient, and she has wonderful hips and breasts. That's what my boss was always pointing out to me. Personally I thought she was kind of cold-looking.—*Vanessa Van Durant

*Faith used to come to me with tears in her eyes and tell me the things that Montee Hamford was doing to her and to others in The Company. Innocent as she was, she couldn't comprehend animalistic behavior like this. But at least she had more sense than I did—she got as far away from Montee Hamford as she possibly could and still be in the same company. I'll give her credit for that.—*Callia Bartucci

• I •

WHEN I was small I lived in a strait jacket. My parents were strict fundamentalists, members of a sect that had started in Germany, and they practiced a paranoid approach to religion and life. God was a constant threat. God was going to "get" you if you danced,

343

drank, looked at a Sunday newspaper, went to the movies. When I became a teener, I was permitted one movie a month, but I was also made to feel like a terrible sinner when I went. So I seldom exercised my movie-a-month option. I offered up my rare monthly pleasure as a sacrifice to my parents and that strict old fellow, God. And of course if I did the least thing wrong, the movie was the first pleasure taken away from me. So between giving it up and having it taken away from me, I saw a movie about four times a year. As a result, I'm now an inveterate moviegoer, and goodness knows New York can fulfill *that* need. That's a big plus for New York— one of the few plusses for the awful place.

I wish I could look back on a happy childhood. I hate whiners and I hate complainers. But honestly my childhood was grim. Do you know that Andrew Wyeth painting called, I think, "Christina's World"? The one that shows a girl lying in the tall grass looking at a bleak, stark farmhouse a few hundred yards away? That's a perfect picture of my childhood. There was nothing to warm the heart. My parents worked like frontiersmen. They went around acting as though they were going to be struck down at any second. We had a fireplace but no fire; we had a family but no love. That is the great tragedy of my life. Even now, when I'm nearly forty years old, I know they both look down on me; they both think I live a "fast" and sinful life. Deep down inside, I probably think the same thing about myself, because when you have sternly moralistic parents like mine, you tend to carry them on your shoulders for the rest of your life. They sit up there sermonizing to you, and they won't let you rest.

I have to laugh when I read about the generation gap, as though it's something brand new. Why, it's hard to imagine a bigger gap than the one between my parents and me back in southern Illinois. The modern parents are shocked to find their son smoking marijuana; believe me, my parents were equally shocked to find me walking home from school with a boy—in my senior year of high school! Modern parents think it's terrible the way the kids neck and "make out"; my parents were ready to send me to reform school because they found me reading *Tom Jones,* a book assigned by my teacher! No wider gap was possible. Nor was there any chance of reconciliation. My parents were rigid, unbending, fundamental, and when I was eighteen years old and a high-school graduate, I was cast out for my evil ways. I fled to St. Louis, the nearest big town, and went to work as a clerk in the sinful beer town.

I liked St. Louis, and I did well there. After a while my boss helped me get started at night secretarial school, and I took a liking to the work. The detail pleased me; I liked the idea of filing, putting things in their place, typing faster and faster, and sharpening up my shorthand until I was so fast that I could almost have been a court reporter. I got better jobs, too, and when I was twenty-one I was on my way to becoming a useful, competent young woman. I was secretary to a vice-president of a middle-sized corporation. I had a few handsome boy friends, including a dashing grad student from Washington University, and I was going to more movies in a month than I'd gone to in five years at home. Also, I am a modest person and I dislike saying things like this, but I seemed to attract men. It has always been that way, and it's still that way. I suppose you could say that I'm not bad-looking, and I've kept my figure, and I have a very soft, low voice that men seem to find appealing. Whatever the reason, I have never lacked for men. More often, they've been a problem.

I'd been working for the vice-president of my company for about six months when he called me in one morning and asked me if I'd do him a favor. The president of the company—a nattily dressed Napoleonic little sawed-off monster—had asked to borrow me for a trip to New York. He had to attend a few meetings and wanted me to take notes. What could I say but yes? I was too naïve to recognize what he intended, and I was thrilled by the idea of a free trip to the biggest town of all. Before we left St. Louis my boy friend made me promise not to take a single drink on the trip. "That's what he'll try first," he told me. "That's the way guys like that operate." I told him he had a dirty mind.

But my boy friend was right. The boss spent a whole weekend trying to get liquor into me. We went everyplace, from the Rainbow Room to Greenwich Village, and I wouldn't even take a sip.

He ordered Chateaubriand for lunch, everything! He took me to a place in the Village that had Flamenco dancing, and in between the performances I looked up at the stage and saw a young girl dancing with a bald-headed man who must have been three times her age. That was the first time I'd ever seen anything like that, and it turned my stomach. I saw myself in that same role, and all of a sudden I realized this wasn't a business trip. Oh, yes, there were meetings, but we weren't attending them. There was a valid reason for coming, but in the excitement of shepherding an attractive young thing around town, the boss had worked up a whole new set of aims.

After a while, he asked me if I wanted to dance, and I said no. He kept after me, and I kept on sipping my Shirley Temple and turning him down. I was an absolute stick about it, and I sat there saying to myself that my days with this company were certainly over. When we got back to St. Louis on a Sunday-night plane, he told me to take a few days off, and I did. I went right down to the kiosk where they sold out-of-town newspapers, and I began studying the want-ad pages of a few big-city newspapers. New York had looked good to me—no wonder, it had just been a two-day succession of shrimp cocktails, steak, nightclub acts, rides through Central Park, and all the surface things—and I found myself drawn to it. Two months later I was the secretary to the manager of a small department in the most glamorous place of them all: The Company. I felt real proud of myself.

My new boss's name was Montee Hamford, and he was the laugh riot of The Company. He went up and down the halls smacking people on the back and exchanging dirty jokes and fondling the women, and everybody loved him. At least, that was the cliché about him. In truth—but I didn't find this out for a while—quite a few of the people hated his guts. They had found out, by osmosis or something, that Montee Hamford wasn't all that met the eye. If he didn't like you, or if he felt competitive with you, he would pump your hand even harder and almost break his jaw smiling at you, and then in one quick motion—zip!—he would cut your throat. But if you were his superior, or you could help him some-how in his ambition, he would bow down before you.

Well, I was the little girl from the farm, from Bend-in-the-Road, Illinois, and I noticed none of this at first. I went spinning on a merry-go-round. I had a different date every night of the week, which was good, because it kept me from having too many respon-sibilities with any one of them. I could escape from each one by knowing that the next night I'd be with another. I went with a stockbroker, a song writer, a trumpet player from the Village; I had dates with a rich playboy, a famous disk jockey, and a man who brokered steamships for a living. I had a heavy four-month romance with a social worker, just long enough to lose my virgin-ity and to hear some scathing attacks from those two martinets perched on my shoulders, but then we broke up and I returned to the dating. One night I was at the Stork Club with my millionaire playboy, and about midnight Montee Hamford strolled in with a beautiful blonde, not his wife, on his arm. We were at ringside, and Montee and the girl were ushered to a corner table. He couldn't miss seeing us, and I knew it must have disturbed him to see his daytime slave sitting ringside with one of the richest bachelors in New York.

It wasn't long after that incident that Montee Hamford began to apply the screws. He called me in and said I'd finished my appren-ticeship with him and now he was ready to use me to the fullest. He pumped me full of that rah-rah stuff about how The Company was making some of the most important products in the world, and our little department was a key to The Company's success, and how we'd all climb together until we had the finest operation in New York. He painted rosy pictures of promotions and raises and hosannas for all, and of course I bought it. I didn't realize that in his own smiling, enthusiastic way, he was about to make his move.

Somehow I had known instinctively to keep office and social life separate, even to the point of turning down dates with a few hand-some and eligible young men from The Company. Montee must have noticed this, and he worked out a subtle campaign. He began assigning me important customers to shepherd around town, or meet at the airport, or take to lunch or dinner. "It's all work," he explained. "Sometimes it might seem like play, but keeping those people happy is important." There were times when I had to get up at five in the morning to meet some big customer's plane and escort him to his hotel, and there were times when I was up till two or three in the morning, fending off the passes of some Casanova from out of town who mistook my professional charm for a personal interest in his body.

At first, Montee was meticulous about keeping his own desires out of the picture. He must have realized with that animal cunning of his that I'd have spooked right back to St. Louis if he had raised a finger toward me. He kept pushing The Company's clients on me, and he even arranged a few out-of-town trips for me, doing simple errands like delivering a package that had to go "by hand," or performing some silly chore for one of the customers. I realized that I was spending less and less time in my New York apartment and seeing less and less of my old boy friends, but I put it all down to the normal pressures of the business world. Montee worked night and day; the office was his life, and I couldn't get too mad at him for trying to make the office my life, too, especially since The Company was paying both of us good salaries.

Then the frontal attack began. I was sleeping in my apartment one morning at six when the telephone rang and it was Montee. "Say," he said in that overconfident voice of his, "I'm at the airport. I just got back from Phoenix, and I was wondering if I could come over to your place and take a shower."

I was flabbergasted. "A shower?" I said.

"Yeah, well, I don't want to have to go all the way up to Brewster just to take a shower."

Brewster was thirty or forty miles away on the New York Central. He lived there with his wife and six children and another on the way, and I knew it would be silly for him to try to go all the way to Brewster before coming to work. What he should have done, of course, was take the day off, but that wouldn't have been like Montee. He slept on planes all the time and went to work as usual.

"Well, I guess it's all right," I said. I didn't know what else to say.

I dressed hurriedly and straightened things up and put on some coffee, but I didn't make any breakfast because I had had a little time to think and I wanted it perfectly clear in his mind that this was a business arrangement and nothing more. I didn't want him to think that he could come down to good old Faithie's apartment for a shower and breakfast any time he wanted to.

But he was smart. If anything, he acted *more* businesslike than I did that morning. I realized later that he must have figured it was a major step forward to come to my apartment and take a shower like this. He would settle for that for the time being. So things stayed cool.

Two weeks went by, and then the telephone rang again. This time it was a Sunday morning, and he'd just flown in from Los Angeles, and the next train wasn't for four hours. Could he come and take a shower and kill some time at my apartment?

This time I said no. I said I didn't think it was right. I said I'd be willing to do anything within reason to make our department the best one in The Company, but I didn't think this should include his showering at my apartment early in the morning. He argued and cajoled, and finally he threatened, but I insisted. "Well, I'm coming anyway!" he said, and he hung up.

I dressed and waited, and an hour later my buzzer rang. I ignored it. It rang some more, and then it stopped, and I heard a heavy footfall on the stairs. Somebody had let him in! There was a knock on my door, and I said grouchily, "Yes?"

"It's me!" he said.

"Well, you're not coming in!" I said. I don't know where I got the courage.

"Come on!" he said. "Let me in!" he began knocking insistently.

Pretty soon I realized that this drumming on my door was going to wake up the neighbors, and there was one neighbor I definitely didn't want to wake up. She was an old lady who missed nothing and told all, and her approach to morals was about on a par with my parents'. So after Montee began to shout and redouble his pounding, I opened the door. He stumbled in, leering. He was drunk, that was obvious, and it was also obvious that he wasn't here to take a shower. I walked down the stairs and out of the apartment. By the time he realized what was happening, I was around the corner and out of sight, and I stayed out of sight for several hours. When I came back the apartment was empty, and there was a little note: "Sorry. Montee."

Well, of course that was the beginning of the end of it. I tried staying on for a few more months, and he kept his distance, but he never stopped trying to involve me in more and more of his nighttime and weekend assignments. I began to get a sick feeling about it, because in my naïve dumb farm-girl way I realized that he was acting in response to deep dark animal drives that he didn't even understand himself. He was trying to possess me and my attributes and absorb them himself. Everyone in The Company looks for power in different ways, and one of Montee's ways was to take over total control of those around him, like a jellyfish completely surrounding a sea urchin and digesting it until it ceases to exist as a sea urchin and just becomes part of the jellyfish. Montee Hamford was consumed with impulses like that.

That last straw came one evening after work. I was getting ready to go down the block and do my laundry at the laundromat when my buzzer rang, and it was one of the middle-aged business executives that Montee had assigned me to shepherd around from time to time. More than once this man had tried to cross the line with me, but I had always called him "Mr. Jagoe" and kept things on a business level. This time Mr. Jagoe was drunk and disorderly and ready for trouble. He pushed his way into the apartment and grabbed me and tried to kiss me. "Why, Mr. Jagoe!" I said. "What are you doing here?"

His answer was to slobber and grunt and grab me all the harder. I broke loose and ran down the stairs with one of our most important customers chasing me, and I wondered what all the step-sitters must be thinking as I fled out into the street with this old man in pursuit. I still had my laundry under my arm, and I figured the laundromat was as good a place as any to calm him down. I went inside and he followed. He leaned over and breathed his pungent breath on me as I put the clothes in the machine. When I went outside to sit on the front step and wait for the clothes, he followed. He began trying to kiss me again, and I pushed him away. Then he began acting kittenish and cute. "One kiss and I'll go!" he said. "One kiss and I'll be out of your life forever!" I knew better. I told him to go home, and he said that he lived in northern Connecticut and the last train had left. He had no place to go, poor fellow! He took long pulls at a flask, and I began to worry. I said to myself, "You can't go back to that apartment!" but I wondered what I *could* do. Finally I pulled the laundry out of the drier and packed it and began to walk briskly home, with Mr. Jagoe following.

I smiled grimly at the step-sitters and went inside, and he stayed right with me. As I climbed the stairs, he kept trying to push me into corners and kiss me, and once he grabbed at my breast. I decided to try to beat him up the stairs, but the laundry slowed me down and he reached the top landing as fast as I did. I didn't dare take out my key, but I wasn't all that safe in the hall either. By this time he had warmed to the whole idea of a chase, cat and mouse, and he was no longer acting gentle about it. He jerked the laundry out of my hand and slammed me against the wall, and I did something that I've never done before or since. I smacked him in the face as hard as I could, and then I went down those stairs three at a time and around the corner to the all-night bookstore. "Quick, I've got to hide!" I told the young proprietor. He knew me from the neighborhood, and he hid me behind a stack of books and supplies. Mr. Jagoe came in a few minutes later huffing and puffing and asked the proprietor if he'd seen me, and he said no. I stayed for two hours, and then I returned home by a back route. It was nearly midnight when I got there, and the front steps were empty. I was scared to death as I let myself in, but there was nobody there. The next morning I told Montee Hamford that I was through, that he had turned my job into an impossible blend of personal and business life and I didn't want five more minutes of it.

• 2 •

THE ONLY good thing about my six months as Montee Hamford's assistant was that I had been spared some of the other goings-on at The Company. When you worked for Montee Hamford, you were Montee Hamford's! Everyone else had to keep his distance. This was no idle misunderstanding, either. A couple of young male assistants were now walking the streets looking for work because they had made the mistake of trying to break into Montee Hamford's private harem. He was a bull seal.

But now I had a normal secretarial job in a normal department—I thought. My new boss was a man that everybody called "steady Eddie," because he did absolutely everything by the numbers and according to the book. If steady Eddie Brinkling never brought any world-smashing ideas into the creative conferences, he never turned in a late report, either, and if one of the big executives gave steady Eddie an assignment that had to be finished by March fifteenth, the assignment would be on the big executive's desk at nine on the morning of March fifteenth, and you could set your watch by it.

I was excited by this. Now I was seeing the kind of business office I had imagined when I first came to New York. I called Eddie "Mr. Brinkling" and he called me "Miss Stronberg," even though company policy suggested first names all the way up to the executive suite. Our department hummed like a well-oiled motor; nobody took the customary two- or three-hour lunch hours and nobody waltzed in at ten-thirty in the morning or sneaked out at four. I was in my element here, and for a long time I was very happy with my work. The only discordant notes came from men in other departments. There is such a free-and-easy style in The

Company that people get to know you very easily, much too easily, and then they begin to make assumptions. One of the assumptions was that since I'd worked with Montee Hamford I'd slept with him, certainly not an illogical assumption. I'd long since crystallized my feeling that my office life and my social life had to be kept completely separate, and I had to beat off some of these men with clubs. I hate to remember all the afternoons at three-thirty or four when my telephone would ring and some married supervisor would come on with a big hello and a raucous laugh and try to get me to join the party going on at the Santana or some other nearby bar. Of course, I never went, but the pressure never stopped. At parties, all the employes seemed to put on their stupid clothes and do the most asinine, childish things. It was the alcohol that did it, and thank God alcohol was never a problem with me. Maybe that was the only good result of my dreary childhood: There'd never been any liquor around my house or even around my neighborhood, and I'd never developed a taste for it.

So I'd go to the parties—and even occasionally have to arrange one—and stand on the sidelines and watch the animals. Only seldom did I get involved. One night a high executive absolutely insisted that he take me to dinner, and after the martinis and the wine and the after-dinner brandy he told me that he was madly in love with me and fully intended leaving his wife and children for me. At one time I might have been impressed, but by now I'd learned how things like that worked. With all his inhibitions released by the liquor, the executive had one motive in mind: to get into my bed. The same liquor that dulled his inhibitions also dulled his sense of proportion, and so he was making lavish promises that were entirely inconsistent with his real intentions. I practically had to throw him out of my apartment. The next morning he called and apologized. He had some grace and style; maybe that's why he's an executive. A few years later I had a chance to work for him, and it would have been a golden opportunity. But of course I couldn't take it, not after he had revealed himself so thoroughly. That's another reason I detest playing around in the office: It leaves hangovers that last for years and interfere with normal working relationships.

You had to learn early in the game that most of the men at The Company had extremely fragile egos, that very few of them felt truly qualified for all the privileges they had, and that the combination could be volatile, especially when mixed with alcohol. They did the strangest things. One of them kept eying me at a party one night and finally asked me to accompany him to his office down the hall. I knew that he was a married man with kids, but I didn't see what harm could come from sitting with him in his office. He said, "Sit down, sit down," and began telling me what was going to happen that night. We were going to go to the Forum of the Twelve Caesars and have a beautiful dinner; we were going dancing in Greenwich Village; we were going to ride through the park in a hansom cab; and then we were going to go back to a little apartment that he had in town and light a fire and enjoy some cognac. After that—*heh heh!*—we would see what developed.

When I told him that I had to help clean up the dishes from the party and then meet my boy friend, he hit the ceiling. It was as though the slave girl had refused the pasha! When I insisted, he picked up his telephone and began dialing a number. I got up to leave, and he said, "Stay there! I want you to hear this." Then right before my eyes—and ears—he made a late date with another girl in my office. As if I cared one way or the other! But his fractured ego had made him prove that he could get a girl anytime he wanted one. That was fine with me. I just wanted to be left alone. When he finally put the phone down he said, "All right, get out of here! I don't want to see you again." And ever after that he's cut me dead in the halls. A grown man! An executive!

There's really no end to what goes on in this city, and no end to how far some of these sick, neurotic men will go to achieve their aims. The problem is not unique to The Company. I'm always hearing from outside friends about similar things that go on. It's just New York, I guess. There's so little normal life here that some people engage in crazy behavior, like rats in a frustration maze. I mean, you can't take a long walk in the woods or go chop down a tree or pick a flower. You're trapped, and so you flail around till you find a way to get your mind off things. Sex is a great aspirin. For millions of years girls have been on men's minds, and vice versa, but some of the New York men have girls on their minds morning, noon and night. And some of them go completely berserk on the subject. I know of one case where an executive of a company had a short affair with a very young, very pretty girl, and when she broke it off he actually became mental. One day the girl got a package in the mail; when she opened it, hot pepper exploded in her face. Her telephone began ringing at all hours of the night, but there would be no one on the other end. She shook salt on her meat one night and almost choked when she ate it. The salt turned out to be crushed Drano. She slipped into a pair of loafers one morning and broke a vial of acid that burned her toes seriously. She knew who must be doing all these things. No one had a key to her apartment except the old boy friend. A private investigator set a trap and caught the man trying to get into her apartment with a bottle of hydrochloric acid. He broke down on the spot, and he was confined to a sanitarium for several months. But when he got out he began pestering her again, and the girl was so afraid that she quit her job and went to another city and left no forwarding address. She had to pay for her small indiscretion by losing everything she had in New York—her apartment, her friends, her job— *and now the guy is riding high!* I hear that he doesn't bother girls any more, but then you never can tell about a man like that.

I avoided all such entanglements, but I didn't know that a bad situation was developing right in my own office and without my suspecting a thing. For almost two years I had worked efficiently with Mr. Brinkling, and there was never a trace of a personal relationship. That's the way I wanted it, and that's the way steady Eddie—Mr. Brinkling—seemed to want it. But then I noticed a slight change. Mr. Brinkling began to put me under pressure, far more than was necessary. He began to berate me and insist that I work harder, which was kind of ridiculous, since I was already working hard. He began arranging his work so that it would extend into the evening, and then I'd have to stay to help him finish up and in a tense, unreasoning atmosphere. He'd snap at me and compare me to other women who'd worked for him. It seemed that all of them were superior to me.

Well, I still didn't see what was happening. Then came the night of the famous New York City blackout, and who should be stuck in their office high above the city but me and Mr. Brinkling? It was a weird evening for everybody. Strange vibrations went back and forth between people; there were people stuck in total darkness in elevators for four or five hours; there were people who had to walk down fifty or sixty flights of stairs to get out; there were neighbors who'd lived side by side for years and had never known each other till this weird blackout; and there were all sorts of personal relationships that sprang up among total strangers. One of the personal relationships was between steady Eddie Brinkling and steady Faith Stronberg. I certainly wasn't the one who started it. Somebody down the hall pulled out a bottle, and a little office party developed by candlelight. We were all thrown together, and we decided to make the best of it. Down in the street, total darkness fell, and the only light came from automobile headlights. Somebody got out a camera and took a picture of the whole bizarre panorama, and after a few more drinks Mr. Brinkling announced that we couldn't stay in the building all night; we'd have to get a flashlight and make our way down to street level.

It took forty minutes, but we made it, and as we walked out to the sidewalk Mr. Brinkling said, "Where do you go from here?"

I told him that I usually walked home. I lived about thirty blocks away, but New York blocks are short, and I'd rather walk than risk my life on the public transportation. "Good!" he said. "I'll walk you."

The problems began the next day. He called me in and suggested that I stop calling him Mr. Brinkling.

"Oh, I couldn't do that, Mr. Brinkling," I said. "It's just my training. It wouldn't seem right to call you anything else."

"No, no, I insist!" he said. "From now on it's Faith and Eddie."

I never gave an inch. I had an idea what was coming, and I became more careful than ever to keep our relationship on a formal, businesslike basis. A few days went by, and then came the note. It was long and flowery. It said that he loved me, that he respected me too much to try to enter into an affair with me, and that he intended to divorce his wife and marry me. There was a P.S.: "Will you go to dinner with me tonight so that we can talk this over?"

I walked around in a daze all day. I didn't know *what* to do. I didn't have any loving feelings whatever about Mr. Brinkling. All I wanted to do was continue in my job and keep my social life apart. All day long I avoided the subject of dinner, and when he brought it up just before quitting time I quickly changed the subject and left.

The next few weeks were pure hell. When I kept on calling him Mr. Brinkling he acted hurt. More notes followed, all of them just begging me to give our love a chance. When no one was looking, he'd reach out and take my hand, or touch me on the shoulder. I'd say, "Excuse me, Mr. Brinkling," and run, and he'd look stricken. Flowers began to appear on my desk every morning, and when I took a day's sick leave, three dozen deep-red roses showed up in the morning and a half a ton of marguerites arrived in the afternoon.

I went to the company doctor and without mentioning any names told him about the problem. He sent me to a psychiatrist, and when I laid out the whole story the psychiatrist told me to go on home, that the real trouble was not with me but with steady Eddie Brinkling. He also suggested that I lay it on the line with Mr. Brinkling before matters became completely out of hand.

The next afternoon I went into his office and asked him if I could close the door, and then I let it all out in one breath: "Mr. Brinkling I'm terribly terribly sorry but I just can't handle this Mr. Brinkling I'm not sleeping at night and the whole thing's driving me crazy Mr. Brinkling I have enough troubles in my personal life already and I never did believe in mixing business and pleasure anyway and I don't love you Mr. Brinkling you're a nice person and a nice boss but there's got to be more than that and I'm sorry to have to tell you this Mr. Brinkling but please cut it out because if you don't I'm sorry but I'm gonna have to quit and I hope I don't have to do that and we can stay friends," and I was out the door before he even had a chance to reply.

Things cooled after that, and we went back to the old relationship, and I had some time to figure things out. Like most of the men in The Company, steady Eddie Brinkling was looking for power to ease his own insecurities, to prove to him that he was adequate to his great fancy office and his fancy title and his fancy responsibilities. One form of power was to take me over, to make me work hard, to treat me sadistically. People like Eddie Brinkling are really nervous and insecure in this world of oaken board rooms and towering glass skyscrapers, and without knowing it they're continually looking around for ways to increase their power in little ways, to add to their flimsy security. So Mr. Brinkling had made more and more demands on me—come in earlier, work later —and when none of this broke me down, when none of this changed me from the impersonal person that I was, he made the ultimate demand: He said he loved me. Later on I found out that this wasn't the first time he'd worked this routine. There were several other girls around The Company who'd had to leave him for the same reason.

For a short time I thought I might be able to survive in Eddie Brinkling's office, but soon I could see that it wouldn't work. If I remained exaggeratedly cold and formal, everything was okay, but the minute I let up and acted personal or friendly, he would begin again. The flowers would start to arrive and the reaching-out would begin, and I'd feel so stupid and inadequate. Then I'd call him Mr. Brinkling and he'd accuse me of being stuffy and ill-humored, and when I'd relax he'd make the pass. So I got out. There was nothing else for me to do.

Now I'd been with The Company four years—two with Montee Hamford and two with Eddie Brinkling—and once again I had to start at the bottom. I caught on as secretary to a new man in The Company, a hotshot brought in from the outside to bring new life to a sagging division. At first it was the most thrilling job in The Company. Everybody said that John Grambling was headed for big things, else why would he have been brought in from the out-side to head a department, something that almost never happened at The Company? There's no feeling quite like being hitched to the tail of one of these fast-rising comets, and for a while I was thrilled. Not only was I Mr. Grambling's secretary, but soon he began giv-ing me more and more responsibility, and within a few months I was office manager in everything but name. It was only then that the horrible truth began to set in on me and everybody else in the department. Mr. Grambling was hopelessly inadequate. Bringing him in from the outside was one of those master strokes of insanity that all companies sometimes pull to the confusion of everybody, including the stockholders. Mr. Grambling hardly had the intelli-gence to get to and from the men's room. He issued frantic orders, then countermanded them and issued more, then tried to enforce the original orders while the new orders were still in effect. We all went spinning around the office like Teddy bears in the ten-cent shooting galleries.

The others in the department could pool their misery, but re-member, I was Mr. Grambling's secretary, and a secretary doesn't go around discussing what a jerk her boss is. So I had to keep my mouth shut and pretend I didn't know, and that made me look stupid in the eyes of the others. I could have stood that, but one day he called me in and he said, "Faith, the heads have to roll. We're thirty percent over the head count. I want you to pick out the losers."

He wanted me to pick out the losers. When that ordeal was over, he told me to tell everybody one by one that expenses would have to be cut fifty percent, that the party days were over and that he was sick and tired of the way some of them were coming to work ten and fifteen minutes late each day. Once again I did my job, and once again I made enemies. Now the office had become like two pitched encampments: Mr. Grambling and me on the one side, and a group of employees headed by an old battle-ax on the other. The old battle-ax was practically unfireable, and she knew it. She had so many hot lines to the executive suite that not even an imbecile like Mr. Grambling dared to push her. Little by little the situation became intolerable. He kept making me do his dirty work, and he kept putting more and more pressure on me, until I had to return to the psychiatrist for more assistance. The old battle-ax would spend the whole day gossiping about me and giving me the evil eye, and some of my best friends had stopped talking to me.

After a few months the situation had become so grim that even the old battle-ax was beginning to show some signs of tension. She had always been a heavy drinker, but now she was drinking even more than *she* could handle and fouling up her work pathetically. For a long time nobody would admit what was happening. This is a tradition at The Company. They pretend that everybody's doing a great job, no matter how poorly they're doing, and when they finally do sidetrack somebody into another job, they always announce it as a promotion. But this woman had already been sidetracked into our department, and she couldn't be moved again, and she had become the acting head of a little *cosa nostra* that was fouling things up as badly as she was. There was no chance for our sick department to recover so long as she was there, and a few of us knew this and felt angry about it. In another company she'd have been fired, to everybody's benefit. It would have been cheaper to retire her at full pay than to have her around, but nobody wanted to admit that.

I tried to take up what slack I could, but I had so much to do, and there were so many foul-ups out on the floor that I just couldn't handle it. I used to go home every night and cry. At the height of her drinking period the old hag tried to get her hooks into me, tried to turn me into her own errand girl, but I had come too far to be subjected to this. I went straight in to Mr. Grambling and I said, "Look, I have to leave. Things have become impossible around here." He made me promise not to leave, and he took the matter to the men above him.

The result was that in a rare stroke they were both fired, and once again I had to look around for another boss, my fourth in five years. I began to feel like a misfit, and yet I couldn't see where it had been my fault on any of the occasions.

Well, I came into my fourth and final job with The Company

seven years ago, and I'm proud to say I still have it. I'm not proud of some of the other things that have happened in those years, but at least I've managed to stay in the same department. I'm an assistant supervisor now, but sometimes I think I'd have been better off if I had stayed a secretary. A secretary can stay out of most of the personal relationships, or at least give it a good try. But a supervisor has to take a larger part, and that's where I made my mistake. I violated my fundamental premise of never mixing business and pleasure, and I will be paying for the rest of my life.

· 3 ·

THE REAL problem—or is it an excuse?—was the nature of my job. When I moved into the department that I'm now in, I was just a secretary, and there were no problems, but then the boss decided that I had potential for conciliation, public relations and morale-building. He noted that I was a natural office manager, and in fact I'd been an office manager before, but in name only. He promoted me and gave me a long rah-rah speech about morale in the department being low and the need for better personnel relations. I was touched, inspired, excited. I went home and laid my plans, and for the next year or so our department was as gay and cheerful a department as there was in the whole Company. I organized parties, contests, ski trips, personal incentives, business luncheons, all sorts of "together" activities. I kept schedules of everybody's anniversary dates, birthdays, children's birthdays, and saw to it that the boss sent cards and gifts. I turned that office into one big happy family—which was stupid. Families are one thing and offices are another. Now I know.

One of my first morale-builders was a suggestion box, and one morning I opened it and found the following suggestion: "A very important step forward in this department would be for Miss Stronberg to go to lunch with Mr. Sarris." I laughed. Will Sarris was a handsome specialist, with dark black curly hair and brown-black eyes and deeply tanned skin. He was of Greek extraction, and he was always showing one of the girls or another how to lock arms and do the Greek folk dances that were shown in *Zorba the Greek*. He was energy and vitality personified and a good worker. He was also married.

"I got your note," I said when he came in. "I think you're talking about a very important step *backwards*."

We both laughed, and he didn't press the subject. But for a year or so he made goo-goo eyes at me, seemed to show off like a male bird around me, and in general let it be known that his interest had not waned. Then we all began to notice a gradual change in Will Sarris. The enthusiasm and energy seemed to go out of him like a pricked balloon. He began moping around the office, taking a lot of sick leave and showing up late or not at all. The boss called me in and asked me what I thought, and I said, "I know less than nothing about Will's private life, but he's showing all the symptoms of alcoholism."

"I agree," the boss said. "There's just one thing wrong with that idea. Will Sarris doesn't drink."

Before long Will's production had dropped so low that he was going to have to be fired. Something *had* to be done. "Look," the boss said, "why don't you take him to lunch, just the two of you? Sit down and find out what this is all about."

That day I had a three-hour lunch with Will Sarris. The boss was right. Will didn't drink, unless you count two or three sips on a ritual martini as drinking. But he looked decidedly hung over, and when I asked him what was the matter, he launched into a long diatribe against his wife, how she was destroying him, how he couldn't sleep, how his life was falling apart. He was very literary and poetic, and he kept throwing out lines. He made a lot of references to *Hamlet* and passages like "How weary, stale, flat and unprofitable seem to me all the uses of this world." I was impressed and touched and also a little nervous. I could feel a strong attraction toward this Greek waif sitting across from me spouting poetry and letting his *boeuf bourguignon* get cold. I told myself to remember that he was married and that this was strictly business.

The luncheon had no visible effect on his manner around the office, although it did start him hanging around my desk a lot and calling me up and telling me his troubles. For a very short time I thought I might have accomplished something, but then he took a week's sick leave, claiming that he had the flu, and when he came back to the office he looked like a candidate for the graveyard. His deep brown Greek eyes were sunk far back into his head; he had lost weight, and he moved about the office like a man under water, as though every step gave him pain. I called him in. "Will," I said, "what's the matter?"

"What do you mean, what's the matter?" he said in a listless, hollow voice. "I had flu, but I'm better now."

"Will," I said, "let's have lunch together."

We had another three-hour lunch, and once again he talked about his wife. He said she had left him, that she had moved back to her parents' home in San Rafael, California, and that he was ecstatic over the departure.

"You don't look ecstatic," I said.

"Greeks are funny," he said. "Sometimes we look bad when we feel best." And he rolled off a couple of lines of poetry about being free and having a whole new life before him. "Grow old along with me," he said. "The best is yet to be," and he lapsed into a long coughing spell.

That night he walked me home and came in for a drink, and the affair was on. At first, I didn't think of it as an affair but as a humanitarian gesture. Something had to be done to help this poor frail man who seemed to be dying by the inch. We saw each other for several weeks, but whenever I brought up the subject of his physical condition he turned it off. "Will," I said, "it's obvious there's something physically wrong with you. Why don't you get a checkup?"

"I'm physically fine," he said. "Never felt better." Five minutes would go by and then he'd start this awful coughing, or he'd walk across the room and have to stop and steady himself against the furniture, or he'd sit down and close his eyes and utter a long sigh that sounded as though it was coming right from the center of his heart. Still, I had no idea what was the matter. Even when he arrived at the apartment one night babbling and giddy and acting like a silly five-year-old, I didn't catch on. But I did find out that night—through his babbling—that his wife had *not* left home at all. She was right there in the apartment, living with Will. I felt terrible. I cried and cried, and Will kept saying, "It's only a technicality. We're not *doing* anything. She's leaving soon." After an hour or two the vitality seemed to ebb out of him again, and he lay on the couch breathing heavily. I sat alongside him and I said, "Will, this is silly, this is ridiculous. I can't see you again while you're living with your wife."

"All right," he said in a weary voice. "Then I'll leave her."

He was so physically run down that the chore of finding an apartment was too much for him, so I found him a little place down the block from me, and some of the men from the office helped him move in. We continued seeing each other for several months. He was a strange, compelling force in my life, an inexcusable indulgence, perhaps, but something that I had no control over. I actually had the feeling that I was keeping him alive, that if I turned him out like a whipped puppy dog no one would ever see him alive again. But it was also apparent that my assistance would not be enough in the long run. He continued to look worse, and he continued to deny that he needed any help. Just before my three-week vacation came up we had a long talk at my apartment. At first he denied that there was anything wrong—"Ah, I just smoke too much," he said, "and I don't eat right." God knows he didn't eat right. I prided myself on making gourmet meals for the two of us, and I can't remember a time when he would do more than pick at his food. But there had to be more to his problem than that.

"Will," I said, "you're holding something back from me."

He argued for a while, but late that night he made a concession. "You're going on vacation," he said. "I'll give you some of my personal stuff to read while you're gone."

On vacation I found out about Will Sarris. He was hopelessly hooked on drugs. It was all there in his writings, in his poetry, in the continued references to Timothy Leary and William Burroughs and Jean Gênet and some of the others. There was a long, disorganized section apparently based on Will's own sufferings. It told how he had been hospitalized, how he'd been fed intravenously, and how the doctors had had to perform a tracheotomy on him. I remembered his long periods of sick leave.

I don't know why it was, but something about letting me in on his secret seemed to break Will's spirit almost completely. When I came back from my vacation he was already on extended sick leave, and when I went to see him at his apartment he was lying in bed staring at the ceiling, almost incoherent. "Will! Will!" I said. "What's the matter?"

"Go away, little girl," he said. "Just let me rest."

The weeks went by, and he stayed in bed. Then he made a few halfhearted attempts to come back to work, but he just couldn't function. His hands trembled, and he dropped things. He disappeared again, and soon I stopped seeing him altogether. I was prepared to help out a fellow human being, but not if the fellow human being didn't make a slight effort to help himself.

Then my attention was turned completely to another office problem. The most talented specialist on the staff, Ed Wilson, had handed in his resignation. "My God, Faith," the boss said, "this is terrible. We just can't lose this guy. He's half the department."

It was typical of The Company that in any given department two or three people did the work, while the rest went along for the ride. Ed Wilson was one of the two or three hard workers in our department, and we just plain couldn't survive his loss. "See what you can do, Faith," the boss said.

"Me?" I said.

"Yes, you, sweetheart," the boss said. "You're the vice-president in charge of morale around here, aren't you? Talk to the man. Let him know we're interested in him. Let him know he's not just one of the Nubian slaves around here."

"But he's not that easy to know," I said. "He puts in his day and goes home to Teaneck and his wife and children. As far as I know, he's never even gone to lunch with anybody on the staff."

"Well, do *something*," the boss said. "Use your charm."

From the beginning I thought that my efforts to keep Ed Wilson on the staff would be futile, a time-wasting exercise, but how wrong I was! He just seemed to spring to life when I began flirting lightly. Around the office, he had always seemed so cold, so austere, so thoroughly wedded to his job, but I quickly found him to be a fascinating, charming man, full of zest and life. We went to lunch several times in the first weeks of my campaign to keep him from quitting, and soon I'd won a concession: He agreed to withdraw his resignation and think about it some more. "But on one condition," he said.

"What's that?" I asked.

"Lunch with you once a week."

I laughed. There had been a time when I would have bridled at a suggestion like that, but Ed made me feel different. We saw eye to eye on a whole community of interests, and he was exciting to be with, and anyway I was accomplishing something by agreeing to his demand—I was keeping our most valuable player on the team.

After a few weeks our department had to make an important presentation before a committee in Washington, and Ed asked me if I'd help him with it. "I don't know anything about preparing a presentation," I said.

"That isn't what I meant," he said. "I meant fly down to Washington and help me keep my knees from shaking."

The idea seemed innocent enough; we would leave in the morning and be back that night. The boss said I should go; he still wasn't certain that Ed was going to stay on. So off I went to Capitol Hill with Ed Wilson, and I never had a lovelier time. He made the presentation in the morning, and we spent the rest of the day sightseeing in Washington. We taxied through Georgetown and saw all the quaint houses, and we did the quick tour of the Washington Monument and the Lincoln Memorial and Tomb of the Unknown Soldier, and we ate a lobster dinner at a delightful place called O'Donnell's, where they serve rum rolls with the seafood. It was lovely. We were back in New York at midnight, and Ed saw me to my door in a taxicab. When I opened the front door of the building and turned to whisper good night to him, he took me in his arms.

"Ed," I said. "I don't want to cause any problems. Let's keep this cool." I went inside and shut the door.

A couple of weeks went by, and all I could think of was Ed Wilson. He was on my mind whatever I did, wherever I was, and I couldn't shake him loose. We halfway avoided each other in the office; he was embarrassed about the scene in my foyer and I was stricken with confused feelings about him. Then one night about nine my phone rang, and it was Ed. "Faith," he said, "I've just got to see you. I've just got to come over."

"Yes," I said, and that was it. From that night on we saw each other constantly. We were *immersed* in each other. He would take an early bus for work just so he could rush up to my apartment and walk me to the office. We had every available lunch together and an occasional dinner, and once in a while we went out of town and stayed together at some lovely country inn. Inevitably the subject of marriage came up, introduced by him. "I want you," he said. "Do you want me?"

Of course I wanted him, but I was stricken by the fact that he had never strayed before, that he seemed to have very real feelings for his wife, and that he was totally attached to his three young sons. "Ed," I said, "I could never be the cause of your breaking up your home. It would be on my mind the rest of my life. It would always come between us."

He didn't disagree, and he didn't pursue the subject. But from time to time he would bring it up almost casually, and always I would tell him that as much as I loved him, I could not break up his home. We went along on that basis for a year.

Then Will Sarris telephoned. "Will!" I said excitedly. "Where've you been?"

"Never mind that," he said. "I'm in town, and I never felt better. Can I come over?"

I had to tell him no, and he insisted on an explanation. "What's different?" he said.

"What's *different?*" I said. "Will, I haven't seen you in ages. You just dropped out, disappeared. And now you expect to come right back into my life?"

"Sure," he said. "Why not?"

I tried to fend him off. Ed and another couple were coming to dinner that night, and the last thing I needed was a voice out of the past to disrupt my already disrupted life. "Will," I said, "just stay away, please!"

We were all seated around my table that evening when the front-door buzzer rang. I pretended to ignore it. "Your buzzer rang," one of the guests said.

"Yeah, I know," I said, and I pushed the button that opened the door. Will Sarris came into the room, and he looked better at first glance, but his eyes were gleaming and his words were slightly slurred.

"Oh," he said, "friendly little group, eh?"

Ed got up and shook hands; they had known each other in the office. "How've you been, Will?" Ed said.

"Around," Will said and turned to me. He seemed to tilt slightly to one side as he stood in front of me and began talking. "How long has this been going on?" he said. "What's happening here?" When I tried to answer, he kept right on. "A fellow turns his back and look what happens!" he said, his voice rising. "It's not fair, it's damned indecent!" he said, and then he drew back his hand and slapped me. I fell back across the floor, and Ed and the other man jumped up, but Will was already out the door and down the stairs.

"Let him go!" I said. "He doesn't know what he's doing." I cried and cried. The poor man! He was running completely out of control.

My guests left soon after dinner. No one felt like talking, and Ed had a train to catch. At three o'clock in the morning my telephone rang again, and I was still awake, trying to put all the pieces together. I picked up the phone and heard Will Sarris's voice, completely composed, completely level and normal. "Faithie," he said, "this is Will. I called to tell you I'm sorry, *truly* sorry. I don't know what got into me."

"Okay, Will," I said, trying to sound friendly but also trying to keep him at a proper distance.

"Faithie," he said, "there's another thing I want to tell you. The minute I walked in there tonight, I knew you were in trouble. It was written all over your face. I know you've got terrible problems on your mind, and I want you to know you can always count on me."

"Oh, Will," I said, trying not to cry again. "I appreciate that." I hung up the phone and considered the irony of the situation. Imagine Will Sarris helping me! The poor, sick man!

But he tried, in his own helpless way. He called me at the office now and then, and he sent flowers once or twice. Nothing fancy, and nothing signed, but I knew who they were from and what they signified. Then I ran into him on the street one night. He had moved back into the old apartment down the street from mine, and he looked worse than ever. He was hunched over, and coughing, and at the age of twenty-five or twenty-six he looked at least forty. We stopped and talked for a few minutes, right there in the rain and the street, and he seemed to find it difficult to bring up words. He said something that I didn't get, and I asked him to repeat. He said, "Promise me one thing."

"Yes, of course," I said.

"Go to my funeral," he said. "I want to be sure *somebody'll* be there."

"Oh, Will," I said, "what a silly thing! You won't be having any funeral for a long time to come."

"Promise, that's all!" he said, reaching out and grabbing my arms. I wrenched away and ran home.

A few weeks later I was walking to work when I saw two police cars and a fire-department truck pulled up in front of Will's building. "What's the matter?" I asked somebody in the crowd. "What happened?"

"Nothing much," the man said. "Somebody found dead, that's all." A few minutes later the body went past me on a litter, all covered up with gray tarpaulin. I ran inside to the landlady, and I asked her who had died, and she said it was Will Sarris.

Will's death hit me like a visitation. I ran back home and began sobbing and sobbing. I could see that dark, sweet face, that poor *loser's* face, reciting lines from Shakespeare. I called in sick, and all day long I saw Will's face in front of me, blaming me for letting so helpless a human being go to his death alone. The most gentle person I'd ever know. A person you wanted to do things for, and I turned away from him. The funeral was two days later. I took four tranquilizers and went with Ed and a couple of the people from the office. I struggled to keep my composure. I didn't know any of the relatives at the funeral—dark, Mediterranean-looking people who huddled to one side—and I didn't want to have to explain what I was doing there, why I was so upset. After the funeral I walked fifty blocks home, trying to shake off the depression. Still, I kept seeing him in my mind. A man came by on a bicycle, and I was convinced it was Will, and I ran after him and he turned out to be somebody else. Of course! He *had* to be somebody else. Will was lying dead in his coffin. I got a chilled feeling later when we found out that the coffin had been empty. Will's body was being autopsied at the coroner's office while the funeral was going on. "Poor Will," Ed said. "He didn't even make it to his own funeral."

I still see Will wherever I go; I still think of his death as a visitation, as a punishment, for everything I did and keep on doing. My life has turned into a living hell, and I think back to what I was taught by my fundamentalist parents, and I wonder if they were so wrong after all.

· 4 ·

ED AND I grew closer after the funeral, and within a few months he became very outspoken about our relationship. I don't suppose you can carry on an affair with somebody from your office without the whole world finding out, but at least I thought we should try to be a bit more decorous, not flaunt our illicit love in everybody's faces. But then Ed told me that there was no need for secrecy; he had already told his wife, and they were trying to work something out. I was shocked. Then I began to hear from my close friends around the office that Ed had told a few people he was going to leave home and marry me.

I said, "Ed, you're gonna get us both in trouble. Remember, the boss is Catholic. I don't think he minds our seeing each other, but he won't like any talk about divorce."

"The hell with the boss," Ed said. "He won't care. This isn't the kind of company that pries into your private life." And he was right. To this day there's never been a word of criticism to me or Ed over our affair. I suppose it's just standard behavior.

One night Ed said to me, "Look, Carrie and I decided to give our marriage six months, to see if we can work it out."

"Well, fine," I said, slightly hurt that he was making intimate plans with his wife.

"And a condition of the six months is I have to stop seeing you," he went on.

"Oh?"

"Let's at least give it a try. Let's try to be fair."

I agreed to be fair, but by now Ed and I were too deeply in love for any such arrangement to work out. He lasted two weeks, and then he asked me to go on a trip with him. "Won't Carrie find out?" I said.

"I've already told her," Ed said.

We saw each other constantly for a few more months, and then he announced that he and Carrie had made another decision. "I told her that I would have to leave her and the boys," Ed said, and I could see he was holding back tears. "God, I hate to think of leaving my boys, Faith, but I hate to think of not marrying you, too."

For the next few weeks he suffered, sometimes silently, sometimes sobbing his soul out in my arms. It was pure hell for both of us. I couldn't sleep; my work suffered, and for the first time in memory, Ed wasn't pulling his load at the office. "I don't know what I'm gonna do, Faithie," he said. "I don't know *what* I'm gonna do. I know I have to leave the boys, and I just can't bring myself to do it, and Carrie's putting all this pressure on me, and I don't know how to handle it."

Then he got a brilliant, design-for-living idea. He talked it over with Carrie, and then he talked it over with me. "Carrie and I decided that there's no sense in breaking up the family," he said. "We've been together fifteen years, we have three beautiful boys, we have a *life* together. But you and I have a love together, and that's just as important. Somehow we've got to blend the two, make them both possible."

I told him to go on.

"She's agreed to let me stay a few nights a week with you and the rest with her and the boys."

I gasped. "You can't be serious," I said.

"Why not?"

"Nothing like that would ever work out, Ed," I said. "You know that."

"No, I *don't* know that," he said. "But I do know that leaving the boys would never work out, either. We can't base our own marriage on something that destroys three fine boys."

"No, we can't," I said. I didn't mention that leaving his boys might also destroy Ed. He was already a nervous wreck just from thinking about it.

"Look," he said, "why can't we talk this over? The three of us. Modern people. There's a solution to every problem, and I'm sure the three of us can work it out together."

So the plans were laid: Carrie and Ed and I would sit down together and work it all out. How naïve it all seems now! *The manipulators.* What we didn't realize was that it was human lives that we were trying to manipulate, and human lives don't manipulate so easily.

Ed didn't help matters by impulsively driving Carrie into town and ringing my buzzer without any warning. We had planned the three-way negotiating session for weeks, and now he was doing it on impulse!

I opened my door and there they were, the loving couple, Ed and Carrie, bearing gifts of two large, soggy pizzas and a bottle of Chianti. I could hardly believe my eyes. We were going to have a pleasant meal together while we split up Ed's body. We were going to be *modern*.

From the beginning I felt at a terrible disadvantage. I was in jeans, my customary at-home attire, and I made a fine contrast to Mrs. Ed Wilson, all decked out in fur coat and pillbox fur hat and a suit that I recognized as a Christian Dior. At first she was stiffly formal, and I concluded from her dress and her manner that her aim was to show me the sanctity of marriage: the wife in her fancy clothes and the little home-wrecker in her patched and mended jeans. She sat on a chair with her ankles neatly crossed in front of her, and she lit a cigarette at the end of a foot-long rhinestone holder, and I said to myself, My God, how am I supposed to discuss anything with this woman? I looked at Ed. He was busily distributing the pizza, making homey remarks, smiling and acting like a man in the dentist's waiting room. The atmosphere was *charged*. Without being asked, Carrie began a long monologue about their marriage, how they had met in high school, how their sons had been born, how faithful Ed had always been—here her voice cracked a little, and I could have sworn it was for effect. Everything that she said and did seemed to be aimed at showing me her role and the institution she represented: the wife, the mother of his children. She was trying to show that the institution was so sacred that she couldn't even dress informally for a meeting like this. She wanted me to realize that I was attacking a formidable foe. I got the message.

When she finished her speech, wiping at her eyes with a handkerchief, Ed took over as moderator. He said he saw no reason why we should not be discussing our relationships together, that we were all part of one big emotional package and we should face up to it. He tried to inject a few light one-liners, but the laughter was forced. He went on to say that he loved Carrie, but he also loved me, and for different reasons. He said that since I'd come into his life his whole attitude had changed, that he had been relaxing into stolid middle age when I came along and I had revitalized his whole way of living. I had improved his health; I had trimmed his figure; I had given him a new outlook on life. On the other hand, Carrie had stood by him faithfully for fifteen years. She was a wonderful wife; she kept a wonderful home and she had helped him bring up three wonderful sons.

Carrie looked up at him all through these remarks, giving him that sickly saccharine look that Pat Nixon gives her husband, and I kept right on feeling like the outsider, the home-wrecker. Then she began to speak again. "You've been a wonderful husband, too, Ed," she said. "This is the first time you've ever slipped, and I want you to know I forgive you for it." I said to myself that any minute now they were going to fall into a big clinch and walk into the sunset together, leaving me behind in my blue jeans.

"We've had fifteen years of happy marriage," she was droning on, "and Ed's always told me everything. That's why I thought this meeting might work out, if we were all frank and honest with each other. He's such a marvelous man. He's never given me a second's cause for grief." The message was clear: If Ed was such a paragon, and yet Ed and I were carrying on, then the affair must be *my* fault; I must be the culprit.

We talked for another hour or so, ate the pizza, drank the wine and came to no conclusions. I don't think I said ten words the whole time. When they were leaving I said, "Don't worry, Mrs. Wilson." I patted her on her furry shoulder. "I won't wreck your home."

The next day Ed came in early to walk me to work, and he said, "It's all worked out! We're going to give it a try!"

"What?" I said.

"I'm going to spend two nights a week in town with you and the rest at home. Just as we planned."

"What did Carrie say?"

"She said she'd rather have it that way than break up our home." Ah, the martyr!

The new arrangement was right out of one of those old Doris Day–Jack Lemmon movies, and it lasted just about as long. On Ed's second night with me we had a lovely dinner—escargots, broccoli Hollandaise, steak *au poivre,* all with a gorgeous Pauillac nineteen sixty-two, and we finished off with a chocolate mousse and espresso. We were curled up in front of the fireplace sipping our drinks when the telephone rang. I answered and it was a hysterical Carrie. She couldn't stand this arrangement one more minute! She was going out of her head at home, wondering what we were doing. What *were* we doing? "We're just sitting around, Carrie," I said.

"I'll bet!" she said. I handed the phone to Ed, and he spent fifteen minutes trying to calm her down. Then she put the youngest son on the phone, and I heard Ed say, "All right, son, here's a good-night kiss for you," and when he finally got off the phone he was a wreck.

"God, I don't know!" he said. "Maybe it's not working out."

"Who knows?" I said. "We've barely given it a start."

The rest of the night he was withdrawn and distant. I could tell he was thinking about the three boys, and I could hardly blame him. Especially since Carrie had seen to it that one of their voices was fresh in his mind.

We bumbled along for about two more weeks, and then Ed and I faced reality. It was plain that the arrangement wasn't working; it was plain that his marriage and his three sons meant more to him than I did, and I told him I could understand that and respect him for it, but we were going to have to call the whole thing off and not see each other again. "Well, we've tried everything else," he said. "Might as well try this. It'll kill me, but I'll try."

We didn't see each other—except in the office—for one month. It was agony. Whenever he came near me in the office I couldn't work for the next hour. I'd sit at my desk and wait for the telephone to ring, or slip out into the hall on the hope that he would be on the prowl looking for me. Later he told me that he'd been acting exactly the same way. We two were all that we two thought about for the whole month. But Ed was bright enough to realize that there were no simple solutions, that whatever we did would bring great pain and anguish, and so he was trying with all his strength to stick to the agreement. Above everything else on earth, he loved those boys.

One night I arranged an office party for an important visitor from our London office, and just when things were getting under way Ed walked in with Carrie. He told me later that he was trying to join fractured lives together and he thought he should begin including her in what went on at the office. I thought it was simply cruel and thoughtless. For weeks I had had nothing on my mind but this man I loved, and now he walks into a party that I arranged —and with his wife! When I first spotted them I almost fainted. If he'd only warned me I'd have left earlier. When I saw them I put my drink down and walked straight out the door. He looked over his shoulder as I left and winked at me, as though to reassure me, but I didn't even want to look at him.

Well, the seesaw continued soon afterward. Carrie was making him miserable at home, and he missed me, and pretty soon he just moved into my apartment on Riverside Drive. At first, it was an idyllic arrangement. We were together twenty-four hours a day, and we were going to stay together for life. I had expected him to be anguished about his sons, and he was. Long into the night he would sit in the living room with the lights out, playing those morbid symphonies of Mahler. When I would come in to comfort him, he'd beckon me away, and sometimes I would see the tears in his eyes. Sometimes he would call the boys from the apartment, and talk to them for thirty minutes or an hour at a time, and then say goodbye in this strange, cracking voice. "Ed," I said to him one night, "that can't be good for the boys. Don't you think you're upsetting them when you do that?"

"It's none of your business!" he said almost hysterically. "Don't *you* tell me anything about my boys!"

I tried to understand. I knew his torments, but I wished he'd let me try to soothe him. It wouldn't make up for the loss of his three sons, but it might remind him that the two of us also had something together.

Then he began acting out little love-hate routines. He would

wake up at three or four in the morning and pinch me. "Ed!" I
would say, "I'm sleeping. Let me sleep."

"Why should you sleep when I'm awake?" he would ask, as
though that were logical.

For the first time he began inflicting physical pain on me. It was
nothing out of Krafft-Ebing, but it was annoying just the same.
When I came out of the shower, he'd be standing by with a wet
towel, and he'd laugh and snap it at me, and those things hurt. More
than once he left a livid red mark on me. He also began a program
of ridicule. When I'd be doing my face in the morning he'd say,
"Well, what are we painting on there today? The Mona Lisa?" and
he'd make cruel remarks when I was doing my exercises.

Well, his guilt was showing, and I had enough sense to understand this. Some part of him blamed me for the anguish he was
going through, and so he had to try to punish me. But I thought it
was asking too much when he insisted that I drive over to Teaneck
with him while he visited the boys, and then he'd come stumbling
out to the car crying, and as we drove away I could see the face of
dear Carrie peeking from behind a curtain. "Ed," I said, "I can't do
that again." But he made me do it three or four times.

After two months together, Ed was sent to Europe on an assignment. He would be gone for a week, and I thought the trip would
be helpful. He would be away from the boys and Carrie and me
and he would be able to think things out. I prayed that the trip
would help him, because the situation was only getting worse at
home. Instead of recovering from his losses, he was wallowing in
them, beating himself over the head with them, and sometimes
beating me too, in cruel, subtle ways.

On the night he was supposed to be back, I got a call. "Faithie,"
Ed's voice said. "Faithie, I've been thinking it all through and I've
got to tell you something."

My heart sank. I had the feeling in my stomach that men must
have when they go into battle: empty, tingling, hollow. "Yes, Ed,"
I said. "What is it?"

"Faithie, I'm home, and I'm gonna stay home."

"You're in Teaneck?"

"Yes, Teaneck. It's the only way, Faithie. I know it'll be hard for a while, but things'll sort themselves out."

"Where's Carrie?"

"She's standing right here by the phone."

"Oh," I said.

He came over for his clothes the next evening, and I made a point of being at the movies. But I didn't see anything that was on the screen. I was a wreck! I felt like a Ping-Pong ball, and I felt as though I would completely lose my mind over this loss, just when it had seemed that there was some chance for us together, some chance to solve our problems. I went to an expensive psychiatrist and began using up my thin cash reserves at the rate of forty dollars an hour. I took a leave and went to the Virgin Islands for a few weeks, but everything I saw reminded me of Ed. I went home and visited my parents, trying to regain equilibrium in the scenes of my childhood, but that was the worst mistake of all—the trip to the corn country of southern Illinois only sent me spinning into a worse depression, a depression so deep that I was barely able to function. Friends came to my aid; dinners were cooked for me; girl friends forced me out of my apartment, to movies and parties; my telephone rang all day long with old friends saying with false cheer, "Well, *Faithie!* How the heck are you?"

Usually time heals these things, but time was doing nothing for me. In the first place, Ed was around the office, and I had daily reminders of what I had lost. We tried to keep things on a formal basis with each other, but every now and then I'd catch him looking at me with deep yearning, and then I'd run to the ladies' room and cry, or shut my door and put my head in my hands and tell the girl to hold all calls. One day he passed me in the hall and he said, "Hi, Faithie," and his voice broke. I ran to my office and he came in a few minutes later. "Honey," he said, "I can't live another day without you."

He walked me home that night, and we talked it out. I told him that whatever he did, he had to face the fact that he was going to suffer, and he would have to be a man about it and not keep jumping from one alternative to the other. I told him I'd rather spend the rest of my life missing him than to keep on having him and losing him in alternation.

"You know," he said, "I think I've figured something out. I think part of the problem is your apartment."

"What do you mean?"

"I mean if we're going to get a new life started together, we're gonna have to start it in a new place, one that's just ours together, a place that doesn't have any bad memories."

"Well," I said, "we'll talk about it."

· 5 ·

So WE began seeing each other again, and Ed said there was no use avoiding the issue any further—we would simply have to get married and take it from there. He promised to get everything settled at home. My job was to find the new place. We both decided that we'd like to live in Greenwich Village, in a colorful old loft-type apartment, or in one of those cute little floor-through places on streets like Gay and Horatio and Waverly. We thought we could make it there, build a new life, recover from the old losses. There were times when the logic didn't impress me, but I told myself to stop doubting. I loved Ed totally, and he loved me, and love was going to win the day. That is the oldest formula for human despair: Love conquers all. But people in love are not the brightest.

Ed and Carrie worked out a separation agreement with her lawyer, and Ed moved back with me. I was zeroing in on about three apartments now, but the one place that we really loved presented some problems. The owners wanted more than we could pay, and they insisted on letting the place stay up for sale for another five or six months to see if they could get their price. If not, they'd sell to us for *our* price. The place was a delight! It was a tiny gingerbread house, tucked into a back lot behind a larger house on Charles Street. In Chicago it would have been called a coach house, in New

Orleans a slave quarters. Here it was just a house, a miniature house with four miniature rooms and two fireplaces and a kitchen that had a butcher's block, an old wood-burning stove that had been fitted with an electric cook top, and a full set of old copper cookware that went with the place. It was heavenly, especially for somebody who loved to cook.

Well, if you think there are no avenging angels in heaven, consider what happened. On a Saturday, Ed went home to visit his boys, and I stayed near the telephone waiting for calls from real-estate brokers. I bided my time by reading our copy of the separation agreement with Carrie; it took Ed for *everything*, including his total salary for years to come. He and I would have to live on my income, which was fine with me. It would help to assuage Ed's guilt. If it kept him from crying out in the night about the terrible things he was doing to his sons, then the loss of his salary would be well worth it.

All in all, I was feeling almost optimistic. Considering everything that had happened, and the anguish and terror and agony that we had both gone through, we seemed headed for a happy ending—or at least a bearable one. Then the phone rang. It was the real-estate agent for the lovely place in the Village. The people had decided to sell to us rather than wait out the market. How soon could we come down and sign the papers?

When I finished talking, I was wild with happiness. The most charming doll house in New York City was ours! What a start for the new life of Mr. and Mrs. Ed Wilson of Charles Street!

I couldn't restrain myself. I thought of calling Ed in Teaneck, but that would have been indiscreet. Besides, I didn't want him to be with his wife when he heard the news. It was *our* news, and we deserved to relish it together. So I compromised by calling several of my girl friends and telling them that the last stumbling blocks had been removed and Ed and I were going to be married. I ran downstairs and told the landlord I'd be moving out. I called up all the neighborhood stores and cancelled my charge accounts and asked for final bills. And then I placed a long-distance call to my parents in southern Illinois and told them that their aging spinster daughter was going to be married at last. They asked all the dumb, predictable questions—How long have you known him? What is his religion? He's not Catholic or Jewish, is he?—but I was so high on pure joy that not even questions like that could get my goat.

I had just hung up the phone when it rang again. It was Ed, calling from Teaneck. I don't pretend to remember his exact words, because I went straight into shock. But he told me that he had had a long talk with Carrie, that some of his old friends from the neighborhood had come over to talk sense to him, and that he was staying home for good and all. The pack had banded together and hit him with a load of guilt, and it had done the job.

That was the lowest point of my life. My life was over. Nobody could help me. The psychiatrist was nice; he stood by me on the phone. I told him I couldn't get through the weekend, and he gave me emotional support. He made me promise not to take any drastic steps without calling him back. When I hung up, I thought of suicide. I was beyond crying; there was a jagged piece of ice jammed into my throat, and I ached. I was sick to my stomach, and I vomited over and over. I took a few sleeping pills and went to bed; as soon as the pills wore off and I could feel my awareness returning, I took another, and so it went all through the weekend. I never slept; I stayed in a semi-coma. On Monday morning I called in sick and said I'd probably be out all week, and for seven straight days I did not leave my bed. Too bad I don't have a weight problem, because I lost nine pounds. It must have come out of flesh and bone.

Three weeks later I was up and around, but not yet back at work, when Ed called and said he wanted to come over and see me. We cried together till the sun went down, and then we went to bed together, and then we told each other that we would never love anyone else for the rest of our lives. I have seen him steadily since, but we have never discussed marriage again. He still walks me to work. He takes me to lunch, and sometimes to bed, though not as often as he used to. I've resigned myself to what I am: the permanent "other woman," with no hopes beyond any twenty-four-hour period. We don't make dates or plans; I am at his beck and call, and therefore I don't date anyone else. If Ed announces that he wants to see me, my calendar must be clear. And I keep it that way.

I'm sorry to say that Carrie is not yet completely out of my life, even though she got Ed back. Sometimes when Ed's with me she'll call, and she'll gripe at me. Sometimes he has to lie to her; he'll come to my apartment when he's supposed to be on a business trip or staying late in town to work. If Carrie suspects, I'll get a midnight call. "Is my husband there?" "I *know* he's there! You send him home this minute." One night she started to cry, and she said, "Does he want a divorce?"

"No," I said. "He hasn't mentioned that."

She said, "Oh, I'm so afraid he'll ask for a divorce."

"I doubt it, Mrs. Wilson," I said. "He loves you, and he loves the boys."

"Oh, do you really think so?" she said. She sounded so grateful and so insecure and frightened at the same time that my heart went out to her, and I started to cry myself.

"I'm so sorry," I said, "for all the trouble I've caused."

She whined, "We always had such a happy marriage till you came along."

"I can't talk about it," I said, and I hung up.

A few weeks later she called at eight-thirty on a Sunday morning and said, "Is Ed there?"

I said, "Yes," and when I told Ed, he almost collapsed. Apparently he was supposed to be elsewhere. He jumped into his clothes and raced home to make his explanations. I don't know what he said, and I don't care. What it all means to me is that she doesn't know how often he stays with me. I don't know how he solves the problem, and I don't ask him. Whatever we have, I don't want to risk losing it.

Some of my girl friends ask me, "What future is there in this thing?" And I answer, "No future. Of course there's no future." But then I knew that all along. There's *never* any future in these extramarital office affairs. You take your chances, and you can get split right up the middle, like me. An affair is like fifty percent of a marriage—the *bad* fifty percent. You have all the hardship and misery of a marriage and none of the joy and contentment. Lately I've begun to get crabbier and crabbier with Ed, just like an old fishwife who's been married to a man for twenty years. I'll start to cry, and I'll say, "How much more of this can I take? Do you realize that the only time you can be with me is one or two nights a week and a little bit at the office? I find it hard to sleep alone all the time, and I find it hard to stay at home." Now what does that sound like? *Like the henpecking wife!* That's what I've become, and *I'm not even a wife!* I tell him, "All our relationship means to you is party time. Drink and sex and food, but none of the other satisfactions that come with a relationship. You don't want to go shopping with me; you're not interested in helping me budget, run the household, do the wash—all the little things that people are supposed to enjoy together. How long do you think I can go on like this?" How long? Only forever, I suppose.

Well, it was all light opera, all *Modern Romance* magazine. There was no practical foundation to any of it, from the beginning. We were going to support two homes, his in Teaneck and ours in Greenwich Village, on his salary and mine, which was impossible. There was no practical thinking. It was all dreams, children dreaming about the enormous chocolate marshmallow sundaes they were going to have. We had no realistic daily life together; the first time he saw me down on my knees cleaning the apartment he laughed at me. It never had entered his mind that I did such drudgery. We were supposed to be a couple of cherubs, flying high above that sort of thing. Reality didn't fit into his romantic dreams; he didn't want to see me in my bandana and on my knees with the scrubbrush.

I said to him the other night, "You know, Ed, some of the old things like the Ten Commandments may seem silly, but maybe there's a higher reasoning behind some of them. Like 'Thou shalt not commit adultery.' It seems so old-fashioned and silly when you look around and see that everybody's doing it, but there's a reason for that commandment, and you and I have seen the reason. We've seen the misery, the pain. We would have been much better off if we'd never committed adultery together."

He said, "I don't agree. We would have missed a lot. We've had a lot together."

"Sure," I said, "but far more pain than pleasure, you'll have to admit that. Extramarital relationships are wrong, Ed, and we're the proof. It's natural law. You become too guilty to work out anything sensible. The guilt ruins it."

He put on one of those faces that he uses when he wants to turn me off. "Yeah," he said in a flat monotone. "I guess you're right."

· 6 ·

WELL, AS I told Corey Simkens, a thing like this wouldn't have happened in Cleveland, Ohio. It could only happen in New York, in the city of the geniuses. Geniuses are granted certain rights and privileges that are withheld from ordinary people. The geniuses at The Company, men like Montee Hamford and Tom Lantini and poor Will Sarris, they're authorized to sleep around and make passes at all the new young girls; it's practically in their contracts. They're "special," and they get special privileges. But in Cleveland, Ohio, you leave your office at a certain time and you go home at a certain time and it's a lot harder to get away with a secret life than it is here in the big town. I don't say it doesn't happen—of course it does—but it's abnormal. Here in New York, running around is the norm. I know girls at The Company who have had fifty or a hundred affairs, counting their one-night stands. I know fifty-year-old executives who have spent twenty-five years going from woman to woman in The Company—and they're *still* doing it!—and their colleagues are *still* looking the other way! "That Red Johnson," they'll say admiringly, "he's sure got a way with the ladies."

Well, the trouble is that you can't run a business on this basis. You can't smile down on loose behavior by *some* of your employees and then expect the others to toe the line. The new employees see what's going on, and they begin to adjust their own life-styles accordingly. Instead of working hard, they begin to wander in at eleven, stay home with "headaches," go shopping for two or three hours on company time in the afternoon, and, when they *are* in the office, sit around and talk about their affairs all day long. Look at my own secretary. She came here three years ago as a trainee, and she worked like a trojan. She knew *no* hours. Now she complains if she has to come in at ten and stay till five. She's been corrupted, and if I ever tried to have her fired, the union would be on my neck in a second. Besides, how can I fire her for doing what all the other girls in the office are doing?

The work is done by a nucleus of martyrs, people who see what's going on around here and revel in it because it gives them a chance to act out their secret longings for martyrdom. They do a lot of complaining, but there's no real steam in it. They *like* the system. It lets them go to hell in their own fashion. They've been brought up on the Protestant ethic that hard work pays off, the business of America is business, and all that, and they wouldn't be secure if they weren't working overtime and taking work home and acting all nervous and put-upon. So The Company allows a person to be what he wants. He can drive himself unmercifully, or he can go to the movies on company time five days a week. This has destroyed a lot of our employees. They can't stand to be running their own lives, writing their own tickets. The greatest irony of all is that other companies are becoming more and more like ours—more permissive, more relaxed, less strict about hours and responsibilities, more aware of each person's so-called "rights and privileges." So the whole city and the whole business structure are going to hell. No wonder.

Personally, I'd like to get out of here and get a job in an office where you're expected to hit the time clock at nine on the dot, and everybody is Mr. and Miss, and it's all kept on a businesslike basis. But I wonder if there are any such companies left. I think that might be just another one of my impossible dreams.

The truth is, I'm becoming a grouch, a stereotyped spinster lady with a minor scandal in her background and no future at all. I used to like New York, but now I spend a lot of my time wondering what's happening here. I got along with New York for years, even after it became a very hard place to live. But now I hate the place, everything about it. I hate the rude people, I hate the streets and the dirt and the filth, the thieves and the muggers and the freaks. You can't walk the streets after dark; you can't ride the subways anytime. The other day a girl friend of mine got so disgusted about the feelers in the subways, she just reached down and grabbed the guy's hand and held it straight up and yelled, "Whose hand is this?" Everybody just laughed. Getting goosed and pinched and stroked in the subway has now become regarded as just another New York City normalcy. It will never be normal for me, and I have joined the army of New York girls who'll never ride the subways again.

No, I can't stand it here much longer. I can't stand the noise, I can't stand the smells, I can't stand the dog litter all over the sidewalks. It's a shame that people are allowed to have dogs in New York City, except that most of us are so lonely that we couldn't bear it without something. In the winter the dogs use the snow; their owners don't bother curbing them. Then when the snow melts there's this awful stench in the street. The dogs themselves become filthy, and the people let them sleep with them, love them up, kiss them and hug them: dogs with pieces of excrement attached to their fur, dogs that have been licking and nuzzling everything that's on the streets, including the backsides of other dogs. Disgusting! More than anything else, the dog problem characterizes New York City to me. If you did a word-association test on me, I'd say "cobblestones" for Paris, "flowers" for London, "bullfights" for Madrid and "dog dirt" for New York.

I love life, I've always loved life—that's why I have these tanks of tropical fish and my Siamese cats. But lately I've liked it less and less. It always seemed to me that there was an infinite number of things to do in New York, but now I'm finding none. My life seems so dull and horrible that nothing seems to please me. I don't want to go out to the theater, or walk across the park and see all those godawful people, or walk downtown and get mugged. It seems like a hundred years ago when I used to walk these streets for the joy of looking at other people's faces, or sit in the park and enjoy watching them stroll by, or get excited by the fact that I was in Central Park or at the Battery or the Cloisters or Grant's Tomb, or shopping in one of the funny little districts—Chinatown, Little Italy, or the Fulton fish market. It seems a hundred years since I walked across the Brooklyn Bridge just for the fun of it, the excitement, or took the cruise around Manhattan Island and looked back at all those powerful, tall buildings with a feeling of awe and respect. I've tried doing some of those things lately, but now they just make me feel lonely and sad, and everything seems so ugly to me. I walk into Bloomy's and I see little family groups that are happy together and I feel very alone, and I go home and hope that Ed will call. He doesn't call often. But then he's busier these days, what with his promotions and his work with the PTA and his trips around the country.

Lately, for the first time in my life, I've begun to think about getting away from here for good. On my last vacation I tried to find a job in Miami, but there wasn't time enough. I discussed it with my psychiatrist, and he said that I might find New York more enjoyable if I would just learn to pick my men differently. He said that maybe it wasn't New York's fault; maybe it was my love life that was making me unhappy. It seems that I tend to choose situations that can't result in a normal, healthy relationship—drug users, married men, unstable types. This is my hangup, but I'm getting too old and too weary to do much about it.

A lot of the problem is that we girls from the rest of the country are led to believe that New York is something that it isn't, and that dupes us into coming here and destroying ourselves. I have a book called *The Seducer's Cookbook* and it's written in that same style that's so popular in current writing about urban American life. It tells you what to cook the man before you go to bed and it tells you about the fabulous breakfast you can make him the next morning, and all of this is supposed to make him think you're a wonderful person and lead you straight to the altar. Well, it doesn't. The provincial girl would like to think that New York is one big swinging scene where everybody's equal and emancipated. Well, it isn't. The female swinging life doesn't exist. "J" is crazy. There might be a few nymphomaniacs running around, but who wants to imitate them?

At thirty-six, I still have strong, normal sexual desires, and I regret them deeply. I keep hoping they'll go away. Sex leads to nothing but trouble. I wish I could stop having physical relations with Ed and concentrate on more meaningful things. Then I would be free; then I wouldn't be so anxiety-ridden and have so many psychosomatic disorders like rashes and asthma and muscle spasms that bother me all the time. But I can't. I'm still imprisoned by my flesh. I hope it won't last much longer.

Corey Ann Simkens, 25

Corey Simkens is probably the most professional girl in the office. She's at her desk at nine and she's up and gone at five-oh-five and her lunch hour lasts exactly from noon to one. She doesn't work much overtime because she doesn't have to—she plans her work so well that she gets it done in normal hours and without a lot of wasted motion and hysteria. Nobody knows where she goes when she leaves here; she keeps a sharp separation between her business and social lives. I have never seen her at an office party. She always minds her own business and gets her job done and excites everybody's admiration. She's also a stunner—the best-looking girl in the office—but she's so cool and efficient that she keeps the office Romeos at a distance. All in all, she's probably the most envied girl in the place—happy and well adjusted and sensible. Everyone thinks the world of her.—Faith Stronberg

I don't know what to think about that beautiful blonde, Corey Simkens. Mostly she acts like a prude, but one day I sneaked up on her just as she was saying this terrible oath like a stevedore. I wonder where she learned that!—Alexandra Oats

· I ·

THE SOUTHERN Belle. Yes, that's the perfect way to describe me. I was a Southern belle in almost every way, in my attitudes, in my mannerisms, in my social outlook, even in the way I walked and moved. I hope to God I'm not a Southern belle any more, but then it's hard to be brought up in the Garden District of New Orleans and go to Sophie Newcomb College and not retain a bit of that sick, decaying Southern aroma. Although I *do* think I'm getting over it. I've even begun to get interested in the black culture. Before now, prejudice always kept me from dating black men, but I think I'm loosening up on the subject. I mean, I'd never fuck a black just for the sake of fucking a black—that would be stupid. But if one came along that I liked personally, well, then I might do it. So I guess you can say I'm improving. I'm overcoming my upbringing.

If you're raised in uptown New Orleans, the way I was, you might as well be raised in Pago Pago or a pueblo in New Mexico. The life is so insular. I went to a private school with exactly the same kids from kindergarten through high school, and then a lot of the girls went on with me to Sophie Newcomb. My mother had gone exactly the same route, and so had her mother. There were no Negroes in any of my schools, of course, and there were very few Jews. Those Southern schools don't believe in race mixing; they protect us pure, lily-white types from the evils of miscegenation.

But they don't protect us from the evils of our own race, and they perpetuate the sick, decayed Southern attitudes. I think that the South has never been able to get over the War between the States, and it permeates all our thinking and makes us the distorted people we are. Every Southern home has its bigotries and its skeletons in the closet, its shames and its scandals. Ours was my father. My fucking father! God, how I idolized that man! Now I just hate his guts, and I put him down every chance I get. He was a bastard. Sometimes I get drunk and hysterical alone in my apartment, and I just raise my fist and stomp around and scream about my father. "You fucker! You're the reason I'm like this!" And I really want to *get* him!

And yet when my father died in my junior year of high school, I absolutely did not think I was going to survive! It was the end of the world! Explain that to me. I ask you: *Explain that to me!* My father caused me more grief than anything else in my childhood; he was never a loving father; he wasn't even an especially intelligent father. And yet I loved him with all my soul. I actually thought about killing myself when he died. How can you explain that?

One of my worst memories is my grandmother screaming at my father in the middle of the night. The old bitch lived with us, and I remember hearing this yelling and screaming and I woke up and sat up straight in my canopy bed. I must have been about five or six. Mother and Daddy had been at a party, and Daddy had gotten drunk and sick as usual, and when he stepped into the house Grandmother was waiting for her precious son. I heard her shout, "I will *not* have a drunk in my house!" Because it was her house; Daddy had inherited it from my grandfather, but as long as Grandmother was around she always referred to it as *her* house. She said, "You sicken me! You disgust me! You suck on drink like a baby on a nipple!" I was shocked! I was scared! I jumped out of bed and I ran to the head of the staircase and I cried, "Daddy! Daddy!"

"Yes," Grandmother said sarcastically, "stagger up the stairs and comfort your daughter, you drunken bum! Go on and give her some of your strong manliness, you slimy bum! Go on. Go on! Your daughter wants you."

Those scenes became routine after a while. Sometimes Daddy would go on the wagon, and once it lasted for three or four years and he became a pillar of society and a deacon of the church and a leader of one of the big Mardi Gras clubs. We began living a normal life, at least as normal as anyone lives down there among the pralines. I remember imitating my mother, draping a blanket across my shoulders like a mink cape and stumbling around in her high heels and pretending to have a drink and a cigarette in my hand. I would engage in make-believe conversations with young gentlemen: "Why, Mortimer, I simply cannot attend the Cotillion Ball with you! I'm going with Lord Acton, and I must be ready when his carriage arrives at seven." "No, dahling Freddie, a marriage is simply out of the question. I cannot accept the hand of one who insists on fighting and dueling, no matter how much I may love him." For a while we had a summer home across Lake Pontchartrain in Mandeville, and it was there that I spent the happiest hours of my childhood. I see it in my mind: a dark bungalow, set off the damp black earth on stilts; a cedar roof blackened by years of damp; thick stands of cottonwood and pine, choking in Spanish moss. A narrow boardwalk led to the bayou, and at certain times of the year the water would be full of green trout and speckled trout, sea fish and sweetwater fish, and there were always catfish and needlefish and gars.

A screened-in porch ran all around the house, and there was a boat dock jutting into the lake and crab traps out at the end on permanent station. They were almost always full, and we would pull them out of the water and pick out the soft-shell crabs, "busters," and fry them in butter and eat them whole. The oyster dredgers practically gave oysters away, two or three cents apiece unshucked, and Mother would pound them open and coat them lightly with cornmeal and serve them twice a day. God, how we ate! All Louisianians ate like that, even the poorest folks in Back-of-town or the Irish Channel. I wonder if they still do. I don't know. I don't go back.

I've been keeping notebooks all my life, ever since I was about ten. I found an entry about going to Mandeville: "We packed the car and left in the evening. We made the trip every year, but I always felt excited. I knew the route by heart, around the edge of the lake, through Slidell, along the two-lane roadway. When we reached the north shore of the lake, we entered a swampy forest, and the only lights for miles would be our headlights. It was like drilling a hole through the night. Then finally pulling into the gate: We were back for the summer. The house looked neat and clean, beds made, towels out. It smelled musty and hot, not the tinny screen smell of the city—but the old smell, generations old. Our rooms were tiny—low-ceilinged rooms—hot in summer and chilly in winter—and each one had a name—the blue and pink room, Grandma's room, the playroom. Do people still name rooms? Burglars. Snacks. The stuffy, hot movie in town. Fishing shacks. Driving to Slidell in the mornings. Different kinds of berries. Lafitte Point. Bathroom soap. Porches. My room was light blue, with space for a bed, a bureau, a bedside table. A chair, a rocker by the window, where I used to sit late at night thinking about my fantasies, talking to myself."

My father dominated the scene, either through his temper or through his drunkenness. How I loved him! I had two sisters, but I was Daddy's baby. Always. How I wanted his love! But he didn't have much love to distribute around. He'd get angry all the time. Sometimes when I was very small he'd come up and tuck me in bed and tell plantation stories about his own childhood. The bed I slept in came from the family plantation, lost long ago, and there was a framed picture of the plantation home in our living room, and sometimes I'd see my father standing there in front of it, rocking slightly, staring and staring. The main thing I remember about him is the smell of booze. And his temper! Once I said "damn," and he was drunk at the time, and he slapped me as hard as he could across the face. Once in Mandeville I was playing hide-and-seek with my cousins, and we were all about eight, and I was "it." Daddy was watching, and he was drunk, and he saw me peek when I should have been hiding my eyes. He screamed that he was not going to have a dishonorable daughter, and he came running over and dragged me into the house and hit me with a whip across the back. I still have a scar there. Years later, just before he died, he said to me, "Corey, do you still have that scar I gave you?"

I said, "Yes, Daddy, I do."

He said, "Oh, Corey, I feel so bad about that."

I said, "Don't worry about it." When he walked away, I could see him wiping at his eyes. The poor man! I'm really glad he died.

During my high-school years he was sort of a closet drunk. He'd smell of booze, but I didn't know where he was getting it. He didn't go to bars—as far as I know—but even in the morning he'd have the smell on him. Then one day I was looking for something in the basement and I found this half gallon of sour-mash bourbon in the corner. I thought I would die, I was so upset! For a while I had kidded myself that my father was getting better, just taking a sip once in a while, but here was the proof that he was as bad off as ever. After that I used to wake up and hear footsteps in the middle of the night, and the cellar door opening, and I knew who it was and where he was going. And I was so ashamed! I lived in mortal fear that some of my friends would find out, but I guess they already knew. When friends came over, Daddy would rave about the Colonel Simkens who fought at Runnymede and Manassas and the Major Simkens who was killed when he attacked a cannon emplacement at Gettysburg, and all the other glorious Simkenses of the past. He said he could trace us back to the Magna Carta, and that there was no more illustrious family tree in all of New Orleans. And I wondered why he had to stay half drunk if our family was so illustrious.

In high school I did everything that girls of my station did. I was presented at the debutantes' ball. I went to a lot of balls, but I didn't date. I thought myself fat and ugly. I was busy in society, in meaningless things like charity drives and Mardi Gras and teas. Our group never did anything real, like helping the hungry Negroes. That wasn't our style. We spent our time and energy and money impressing our own peer group, having parties and balls and teas, preparing floats for Mardi Gras, and ignoring the real problems. The system had worked in the South for two hundred years.

Daddy died in my junior year of high school, and I almost died along with him. I stayed in my bed for two weeks after the funeral, and a doctor saw me almost every day. I literally didn't think I could go on. But Mother kept telling me that I was Daddy's girl and he would be ashamed of me acting like this. She said Daddy had always counted on my going to college and I should pull myself together and study hard for the future. Of course, Daddy's dream of having me go to Sophie Newcomb seemed out of the question now. He had always pretended that we were rich, or at least very well off, but it turned out that we had hardly anything. I told mother not to worry, things would work out. We moved into a smaller house still in the Garden District, but five or six blocks closer to where the "Nigras" were slowly taking over, and I spent all my time and energy on my schoolwork. I didn't date, I withdrew from the social scene, I was consumed with a single idea: to fulfill my father's dreams for me. I applied to Sophie Newcomb for a scholarship, and I scored an eight hundred on my college-board exam in English, which nobody'd ever heard of. I was top dog in my class, and Sophie Newcomb strewed roses in my path. They wouldn't tell me my IQ, except to say that it was over a hundred and thirty-five.

The college years turned out to be awful ones, through no fault of Sophie Newcomb. I majored in English literature almost to the exclusion of everything else. I took the required courses, but then I settled into solid English literature, mostly Victorian, eighteenth and nineteenth century, authors like Tennyson and Dickens and Browning, poetry and prose. I was steeped in it! *Too* steeped in it. In those four years I never dated. I can count on both hands the number of social events I attended. I still imagined that I was fat and ugly and that I wasn't the equal of the other Southern ladies. Most of those south Louisiana belles are short and dark, Latin and Creole types with bad complexions and thin pursed lips and thick waists, but I was tall and large and voluptuous and thoroughly ashamed of my curvature. Anyway, the men didn't seem interested. They kept chasing after the ballbreaking Southern belles around me, and I was content to stay to myself. I even dressed the part. I never wore straight skirts; my mother and I regarded them as indecent. I wore full skirts always, and they made me look like a collection of balloons.

The truth was that I was so out of it that I needed psychiatric help even then, but I didn't know and my family didn't know. We had a contempt for psychiatry; it was a sign of weakness. I remember Daddy saying that psychiatry was just a sick self-indulgence. How I got through those college years without help, I'll never know. I had no girl friends, let alone boy friends. I was alone all the time. I cried at night, and my grades slipped from straight A's to a mixture of B's and C's. Those were sick, sick years.

When my grandmother died, there was a provision in her will that I was to have a year abroad, and so I went straight from the Sophie Newcomb graduation ceremony to the Sorbonne, the University of Paris, the most glamorous university in the world. At first, I was terrified, because I didn't have mother to call up if anything went wrong. But slowly I began to find myself. I made friends, the first friends I had ever made on my own. And I fell in love, with Pierre Louis Guy Bernard Rochefort Emery, a boy my own age and with a background much like mine. Louis was the first boy I ever kissed, but I did not allow any other advances. I was a Sophie Newcomb girl! We went together for the whole summer, and when my money ran out and I went home to New Orleans, he promised to come over and marry me and take me back to his family's baronial estates in the south of France. I think Louis really loved me and really wanted to marry me. But it just didn't work out.

After my year in Paris the Garden District of New Orleans left me cold. I felt smothered. I couldn't stand the people, and I couldn't stand the life. To me, it all stank of rotting flowers. One night I spoke to an old friend of the family, a broker, and he told me that his brother worked on Wall Street in New York, and if I was so hell-bent to get out of New Orleans, he would see what he could do for me. The result was that Corey Ann Simkens, twenty-two years old, virginal and provincial and dumb, went away to the big city. It was an absolute awakening! I got a room at the YWCA and every morning I pushed and shoved my way through the hubbub to my job as a file clerk on Wall Street, and I was entranced! When I got out of the subway each morning, I could smell the money in the air! The din and the traffic and the smells—they turned me on from the beginning! New York and I were in love at first sight.

I found the men on Wall Street interesting, but I didn't date. Even then there were indications that I was anything but mentally healthy. When Louis stopped writing, I borrowed money and flew to Paris on a three-day weekend, and I bought a tube of birth-control goo so I could sleep with him. But we were both virgins, and he wouldn't do it. He said he still loved me and still intended to marry me, but he was having difficulty in his personal life, and he hoped I would understand. I went back to New York thinking of suicide.

The men on Wall Street mostly interested me only as father figures. Sometimes I think that *all* men interested me only as father figures. They were straight, square, very conservative. They came from good families, and they were snobby. Most of them had gone to Princeton or Yale, and they all had their pompous little clubs where they shuffled off for lunch. They were lucky, because most of the public eating places around Wall Street are awful. For a girl raised on fried oysters and buster crabs, the Wall Street food was an awful let-down. But the place itself never stopped being exciting. I was there the day the market broke one thousand on the Dow-Jones index, and it was like Mardi Gras. You could tell that something was in the air, because everything began to move faster and faster; everything began to spin like a big electric engine, and then there was this cheering and shouting and everybody ran into the streets congratulating one another. That was the high point of my Wall Street career. After that, things began to get duller, and I got tired of filing A-L and never getting a chance at M-Z, and I ran into an old friend of Mother's and she told me there was only one place in New York City for a girl like me to work. The Company. I said how in the world could I get a job at a big important place like The Company when I couldn't even type or take shorthand, and she said not to worry. She knew the personnel director.

I got the job! Wow! They issued me a distinctive red jacket, and I became a messenger at the most progressive company in New York. I was consumed by the mystique: the terrific products, the cool people, the super-efficiency, the terrific sense of purpose and hurry and importance. Why, people in other companies would stop everything to take care of some little business deal with The Company. They considered it an honor just to be slightly connected!

· 2 ·

WHEN I started, I was told that each newcomer had to work about a year as a messenger before getting promoted upwards. It was like an initiation rite, and it applied even if you had graduated from college with highest honors. At first I didn't mind, but after a while the other messengers and the bosses of the messenger pool began to bug me. They had big smiles on the outside and tremendous hatreds on the inside. They'd say the most devastatingly cruel things to you and be smiling at the same time. Most of them were just mean, frustrated women. I stopped responding to them, and I didn't even talk to them unless I had to. After a year, the boss called me in and said, "I'm giving you a raise, but only because I *have* to, under the contract." I went right upstairs to Personnel and demanded another job! I was so pissed off! I said I'd never work another day for that bag who ran the messengers, and the personnel man said he could understand that, and so I was shifted into another department as a clerk. The job was perfect, and before long I had become a junior assistant, one of the glamor jobs in The Company, and I've been one ever since. If I could get my head together, I could probably be chief of the assistants, but that will come in time. It's an easy job, and you get a lot of prestige, and you start at seven thousand a year, which is a good salary for a girl. And you get regular annual raises, and sometimes merit raises, although they've become rare lately.

From the beginning of my job in the new department, I had to make a decision about dating. I still barely dated at all, still considered myself gross and ungainly and ugly, even though others told me I really wasn't. All around me, office romances were flourishing, and I told myself from the beginning that office romances were bad scenes, and whatever else happened to me, I would not date married men or men from the office.

There was one specialist who was terribly persistent. His name was Ernie Rhoades, Jr., and he absolutely insisted on taking me out to lunch. He was attractive, but it was obvious to me that he was really fucked up. He'd hang around my desk all day and bring me candy and flowers and beg to take me to lunch, so I finally let him. He breathed on me all through the lunch and laid out this big line, and finally he said he knew the one bar in town where you could get genuine Napoleon brandy, and would I go there with him some night? I said no, I wouldn't. I said I didn't believe in going out with officemates, and he got mad and said I was stupid, and I told him I didn't care what he thought, and never talked to him again.

My social life stayed dead. Louis was writing once in a while, but not often enough, and I was going home to my Greenwich Village apartment at night and scribbling for hours in my notebooks. I always tend to do that when I'm depressed: "Well—a year ago exactly I was in Paris, getting acquainted with the city I was eventually to fall in love with. (It is the blight man was born for/it is Margaret you mourned for.) No—the key phrase is 'You will weep and know why.' Yes I do know why I weep. For time that is past and can never return. Oh, what the hell. It doesn't make any difference anyway.

"I am young enough to have joys and sorrows, deep longings and high dreams, and many many problems.

"What have I lost, what have I learned from my experience. Tennyson: 'Yet all experience is an arch wherethrough gleams that untraveled world whose margin fades forever and forever when I move.' I am afraid of being a failure, of being inadequate . . . but I have to face myself."

In the middle of the summer of 1967 I wrote: "I think I'm in one of my suicide moods again. Flashback: 'If you ever start to throw yourself into the Seine, remember that Louis Emery liked you.' Or maybe I am just feeling super sorry for myself. What exactly is the problem? I am jealous of the other more attractive women in the world who have men that adore them. I need someone who loves me for myself. It seems as though I am always apologizing to someone for being the way I am. Maybe I should stop apologizing and start doing something about all my faults. I did behave abominably last night. I must remember never to make such a poor show again. Maybe I am the one who is immature. I always quit: I never take up the challenge and try to win. Well—I'm starting now to change all that. For one thing—I have a pretty face, but I should watch my weight.

"Okay, I can't do anything about some things, but I can try to stand up straight and be graceful and watch my weight. I can do something about my muscle tone. I can take better care of my hair. No more rubber bands, and try to use a creme rinse, and maybe buy a fall, and practice working with my braid. Next Thursday— have my hair cut and shaped. My clothes are so far okay—at least for the most part. I can practice using makeup to better advantage. I guess I do rely too much on what Mom's friends used to think of me. I must see what I can do on my own. I am going to work on looking elegant. I don't think I can manage to look sexy, but I could attain elegance. Am going to concentrate on getting my mind into shape as well. Can read *New York Times* and *Time*, plus some other mag—*Saturday Review*, among others. Take some night courses."

So my self-improvement course began, and it was a whirlwind! The potential had always been there, but I had never utilized it. I slimmed and shaped and coiffed and sunbathed and exercised, and pretty soon they were whistling at me on the streets. I went back to my books, and I kept trying to expand my mind. I took notes feverishly, like a school girl: "Joyce : theme of exile, alienation. Inability to communicate. Urban life. Thinking of Parnell and Christ. Stephen's dichotomy. John Wellington Synge: theater had a purpose, part of literary renaissance. Knew loneliness and despair. Introspective.

"Ulysses. Buck Mulligan: Oliver St. John Gogarty. Stephen: isolating himself, cutting off from friends, home, job. 'Leopold Bloom ate with relish the inner organs of beast and fowl.'

"*Don Giovanni*. Eliot. 'Fear death by water.' Drowning: one of many forms of death."

But interspersed with these notes were scribblings of despair and fear. I told you that I usually wrote in my notebooks when I was depressed, and they reflect it: "Out of the bitterness of our experience, we learn what? Something. Nothing. It doesn't matter anyway.

"I can never listen to the sound of a boat whistle without understanding—knowing—exactly what it means. It speaks for all the lonely souls and faraway places . . . the staccato rhythm of what?

" 'I always wondered what exactly it means to have everything to live for.' "

"Yesterday was so awful. Alice is right. We don't have any communication in our family—never did. Poor Mom—faced with ungrateful children. I could be nice to her if only I would try.

"Sonnet III expresses it: 'When to the sessions of sweet silent thought I summon up remembrance of things past . . .'

"Poignant, pregnant. Out of the depths of what? And tell me why—why why—why what?"

Well, I might have been poignant, but I was definitely not pregnant. I was twenty-three years old, attractive, elegant, and still not dating, or barely dating. And still very much the constipated virgin from Sophie Newcomb. Something was bound to happen, and it did. But I didn't simply fall from virginity. I went all the way down, as far down as you can go. I slopped around in the garbage. I rubbed filth and sawdust in my face, and I almost destroyed myself in the process. I'm not sure I can explain how it happened, because it all ended only a few months ago, and I'm not completely out of the mire yet. I've just taken the first steps, and I don't even know where they'll lead. Maybe back to the muck and the mire.

It started in the middle of the summer of nineteen sixty-eight. I had a halfway girl friend named Sarah, very much a Greenwich Village type, who played this old Village game of pimping prettier girls for the bartenders on West Fourth Street, only I didn't know it at the time. I met her at one of my night classes, and she kept telling me about the fascinating life in the West Village bars and how there was one particular bartender she wanted me to see. She said he was a legend in the Village, girls fell over when they looked at him, and he never had to lift a finger to get a girl. I said, "So what?" I reminded her of my background, and I told her there wasn't anything in the world I *less* wanted to meet than some filthy West Village saloonkeeper. But she persisted; she told me it was a shame for me to waste such a beautiful face and such a sexy body. So one night, out of sheer boredom, I agreed to meet her at the bar called Chandler's Place and take a look at the mythological stud named Steve Drake.

I arrived first, and I felt stupid walking into a bar like Chandler's alone. Everybody turned and watched as I entered, and I looked into a sea of degraded and degenerate types, all turned toward me. I would have walked right out of this cesspool, except that I would have looked stupid. I took a seat at the end of the bar—feeling like the great sinner of all times!—and studied the scene out of the corner of my eyes. Chandler's was long and narrow, like a tunnel, and just as dark. The whole place is maybe ten feet wide, maybe sixty feet long, with the bar running almost to the rear, and a single booth at the back. I couldn't tell what was behind the booth, except that there appeared to be a small service area. I was certain that somebody was using dope back there. Later on I learned that the bathrooms were behind the service area, and every once in a while somebody would slip inside and light up, because the mythical bartender wouldn't tolerate pot-smoking at the bar.

The people in the place were the dregs of humanity. They were right out of *Dead Souls*. Some of them had their heads resting on their arms, getting up the strength for the next round. Some of them were obviously in their last days, their bodies wracked by booze. One man fell off his stool while I was sitting there and had to be helped back into position in front of his boilermaker—whisky and beer on top of it. There were several blacks; they looked like the kind who couldn't make it in Harlem and had to come down to this hole to be accepted. There were a few chicks, painted ladies with loud, strident voices and spiked heels and clothes that were already five years out of style. And there were the hard-hat types, stevedores from the docks, some of them still proudly wearing their orange-painted hats, smelling of sweat and talking about motherfucker this and motherfucker that, and coming on with the sideways leers and the chirps in my direction.

The bartender served me a bourbon and water, and I realized that he was not the mythological creature named Steve Drake; Drake must have been out to dinner or on a break. The bartender who served me was listless and unanimated. He didn't ask me what I wanted; he just came over and stood in front of me till I told him. He didn't say you're welcome when I said thank you, and he didn't say thank you when I paid him. He just moved quietly back and forth behind the bar, as though he was bored shitless by the whole thing. He had a droopy mustache and about six scars on his face, and he was not very tall, and he was forty or fifty years old. I was watching him when Sarah came in and took the seat next to me and said, "Well, little Miss Sophie Newcomb! How do you like him?"

"Like whom?" I said.

"Steve Drake," she said, pointing to the bartender.

"Oh," I said. "*That's* Steve Drake?" I began studying him, trying to associate the man with the legend. It didn't take me long. What I had mistaken for lassitude was simple coolness. Steve Drake was on his own turf when he was behind that bar, and he owned the world. He didn't have to say thank you or you're welcome to anybody, and in fact as the evening went on and I sat there staring goggle-eyed at him I saw him tell two or three guys to fuck off and get out, and once he jumped over the bar and muscled a big guy right out the front door and hit him in the mouth for good measure. It was an impressive show, and I was fascinated. On closer study, Steve Drake's facial scars only improved the image, and his handlebar mustache made him look like Viva Zapata, and he was two hundred percent man, *all man*. I was transfixed. I drank more and more bourbons, and I began to think that Steve Drake was the most gorgeous person I had ever seen. It's hard to explain, but when I walked into that bar I was the total Sophie Newcomb virgin, and by the time midnight arrived I was hot on the chase. I wanted to be screwed, and I wanted Steve Drake to do it.

The bar closed at four, but most Village bars allow a select few to sit around and drink after hours. I had been staring at Steve all night long, and now I moved to the back booth by myself—Sarah had cut out hours before—and waited. Steve ignored me. He counted the money and poured himself a drink and then joined a little group of regulars at the bar. I finally walked up and said, "Excuse me. Remember me?"

"Yeah," he said. "The chick from the South."

"Please," I said. My heart was pounding with girlish anticipation, "May I sit down and talk to you?" It *had* to be that way; I had to hustle *him;* Steve Drake didn't ever move a finger to get his women.

So we sat and talked, and pretty soon the others left, and there was only me and Steve in the place. After a while he reached over and touched my breasts, as though checking me out. Nobody but Louis had ever done that, and it was like an electric shock, only a pleasant one. Then he pulled me to him and kissed me, and he suggested that we have another drink, a double, and pretty soon he was blind drunk and reciting his own poetry. All I remember is something about "The paradox of wildebeest, the coin flips up and down." It sounded wonderful at the time, but I was too drunk and excited to have any critical faculties. At six A.M., after he had felt me and kissed me and recited his poetry, I told him I had to go home. I would have gone straight to his apartment and gone to bed with him, but I had my period, and I had to get to work by nine, and anyway he didn't care one way or the other.

I slept for two hours and then spent a torturous day at the office trying to do my work efficiently while I kept flashing on visions of Steve Drake's scarred face and the whole crazy underworld scene at Chandler's Place. I told myself that the scene was wrong for me, but another part of me knew that there was no use fighting it. I was hooked on the stale smell of booze and a middle-aged man with a scarred face, and I could only fight it so long.

I fought it for one week, to be exact, until the next Saturday night. Then I went to a hen party uptown, and all I could think of was how cool and inviting it was inside Chandler's Place and how Steve had fondled my breasts and recited his poetry and told me I was beautiful, and all of a sudden I just picked up my purse and went right out the door and took a cab to Chandler's. On the way down I said to myself, "Okay, this is the night I'm going to lose my virginity!" I went in the bar and sat down at the end, where I'd sat the Saturday night before, and Steve poured me a drink and didn't say a word. It was as though we'd never met, never seen each other.

Pretty soon it was midnight, and I'd been drinking for three or four hours, and I was drunk. I still didn't know how to handle myself in a bar scene, how to stay cool. Later on another bartender explained to me, "It's like this, baby. You order a tall drink with a lot of fluid, like a Scotch and soda tall. Then you nurse it. You freshen it up with more soda, and that way you can go all night." But now I was blind drunk, out of my head. I began talking to strangers, and I stood up on one of the chairs by the booth and shouted as loud as I could, "I want to fuck Steve Drake! I'm a virgin, and I'm gonna fuck Steve Drake!" If he noticed, he gave no sign. People were always doing crazy, drunken things like that in Chandler's Place. Just before four o'clock, when he would have to lock the doors, he asked me to walk down to the Bistro and get him a hamburger, and like a fool I agreed. When I got back to Chandler's, the doors were locked. I pounded and pounded on the door, and I screamed for him to let me in, but he paid no attention. It was dark inside, and I realized he had closed the joint and cut out while I was gone. Probably he had something going.

That was the end of the world. I couldn't stand it! I raved up and down the streets for a while and then I called my friend and found out where Steve lived and I went and pounded on the door of his apartment. He came to the door all sleepy-eyed and naked, and for the first time I saw that his body was laced with scars, thirty or forty of them. He must have spent his entire life in knife fights. There was that same faded scent of booze about him, and it thrilled me again, and I almost fainted with happiness when he beckoned me inside.

Well, that morning turned out to be one of the most embarrassing experiences of my life. Steve tried to enter me, but it hurt so much that I just couldn't stand it. I said, "Please, Steve, you're hurting me! You're killing me!" He waited awhile and then tried again, and it was just as painful. I jumped up, and I said, "Steve, I don't know what to do! I want you so badly, but I can't stand the pain!"

He was disgusted. He said, "Oh, fuck it," and he pulled the sheet up over his face and went back to sleep. It was horrible. There was blood all over the place, *and I was still a virgin!* I stayed there in bed with him, and when we woke up around noon he took pity on me and poured me some coffee. I told him I was terribly embarrassed and sorry, and he said, "That's okay, honey. Don't worry about it." From then on, I loved Steve Drake madly. I had no idea why, but now it seems like it was just a typical sado-masochistic thing, and a father-figure thing, and a half a dozen things all intermixed. I loved him because he was a rough-looking, virile man, and I loved him because he was wanted by so many others; he was a kind of a stud-god in the Village.

On top of those reasons, it was just my time to rebel. I was tired of being the virginal Corey Ann Simkens; I was tired of being my mother's daughter and wearing the fucking white gloves all the time, and I was tired of being horny and not being able to do anything about it. I'd never been able to masturbate. I came from a society where you were taught that masturbation stunted the growth of boys and made whores out of girls, and even after I had learned that this was bullshit, I was unable to bring myself to a climax alone.

But if I was tremendously attracted to Steve, I was also tremendously ashamed of how I had led him on and then let him down, and for weeks I was afraid to go into Chandler's Place again. I wouldn't have known what to say. In the middle of all this, Louis Emery came to town, and I took one look at him and realized that my romance with him was dead, destroyed by the new life I was finding in the West Village. I went out with Louis about twice, and then I sent him packing.

After a few weeks I went back to Chandler's, and after three drinks I got up the nerve to talk to Steve again. He couldn't have cared less. I said, "Listen, Steve, I just want to tell you one thing. When I learn how to fuck, you owe me a night!"

He said, "Well, cool, we'll do that. I'll teach you some things."

I said, "Great! Terrific!" But he didn't mean it, I guess, because nothing developed after that. Whenever I'd see him, he'd be bored and listless, or with another girl or sometimes two or three, and I began to look around elsewhere. I also went to my gynecologist's and had my hymen ruptured surgically. If another Steve came along, I wanted to be ready.

· 3 ·

DURING THOSE next few weeks I went from Village bar to Village bar, searching but not finding exactly what I wanted. I was hypnotized by the scene, by the fact that all that fascinating underworld life existed right in my own neighborhood, and I had never noticed it before. Somehow I kept up my work at the same time that I was going from bar to bar till four every morning. I've always had tremendous energy and vitality, and through this whole strange abandoned period, my work at the office never suffered. At lunchtime I would get out my notebook and write about the bizarre new world that had opened up to me.

"*The Worldbeaters,* by Corey Ann Simkens.

"First you have to know where the streets go. West Fourth Street is like Main Street of a small town. It links most of the bars. You can start at the corner Bistro and end up at the Fifty-five—with stops at the Riviera, the Lion's Head and Chandler's Place on the way. The Bleecker Street bars and the White Horse and the Cinebar are a little off the beaten path but easily accessible nonetheless. Each bar has a different atmosphere, and you choose your bar according to your mood. The Bistro has tables and wooden benches in the back. There is no privacy at Chandler's Place. You go there only if you can handle it. It's a rough place, a place to go if you are depressed or so high—up—that you can handle the depression around you. A new bar is a challenge—a long polished piece of wood—people there three and four deep, new people, strange people. Can you make it with them? Get to know them? Develop some kind of rapport? Most people want to make it in the 'in' bars—get to know the bartenders—be on a first-name basis."

You can see from the style of that scribbling how impressed I was by the Greenwich Village bar scene. You couldn't *help* but be impressed, at least if you were as unhip as I was. I thought that the bartenders along West Fourth Street were the most glamorous figures I had ever seen in my life. And they were! To begin with,

West Village bartenders are never simply bartenders. They all have other things that they're into—poetry, sculpture, ceramics— although they never seem to quite make it with the other stuff. Like Steve Drake—he wants to be a poet, but he never gets off his ass enough to push it and make it work, and so it's pretty lousy poetry, it's doggerel. Bartending is so easy for people like him, and they get hooked on it. He doesn't have to talk, he doesn't have to work hard, he doesn't have to relate to other people, all he has to do is mix a few drinks and do whatever he goddam feels like.

Most of the West Village bartenders were highly influenced by people like Alan Ginsberg, Brendan Behan, Dylan Thomas, Norman Mailer—big swingers with huge talent and huge carousing tendencies. They try to imitate people like Mailer and Behan, but the only part they end up imitating is the dissolute part, *the wrong part*, the sick part, and they spend so much time in the process that they wind up losing whatever talent they ever had, if they ever had any to begin with. They can never get it together, and they wind up being permanent parts of the Village underworld, the tin gods of West Fourth Street, the top members of the pecking order of a sick society.

The reason they're little tin gods is because they come on so super-masculine. They're like no other men on earth. They can't be pansy types or they couldn't handle a West Village bar. They have billy clubs and blackjacks and they'll swing them if they have to. Plus all those bartenders have lines of chatter, and they can talk with all types, or they can ignore all types, put them down as though they were on the highest level themselves, and they don't need to impress anybody. Steve once told me he liked his job because he could tell people to get the fuck out and never come back. That only made him more attractive to me—that arrogance, that nonchalance.

Underneath all this tough veneer, of course, you find out eventually that the bartenders are dull, that most of their talk is limited to a few subjects that they work to death: horses, professional football, boxing, fucking, movies, "broads"—I *hate* that word!—and they never deviate from those themes. They're enormously shallow as a group, but it takes a long time to realize this. On the face of it they seem like supermen, giants, the most impressive father figures on earth. They have the trappings of masculinity, but underneath I think they're in tremendous doubt as to who they are and what they are. That's why they spend night after night with different women, why they stand in front of the bar mirror getting each hair in place. They're insecure, and a lot of them are masochists as well as sadists. They like to be in a vulnerable position behind a bar, killing themselves staying up till four every morning, looking shitty, ruining their health. They know this, but they pursue it. When they finish their own shifts, they go to other bars to drink, and then for recreation they go home and open a bottle. They live and work in bars that are more like zoos, and they act more like animals.

It was a long time before I gained any insights like these. In the month after I had failed with Steve, I kept crawling from bar to bar, ogling the bartenders and striking up new acquaintances. One night a fascinating creature named Jim Green took me home to my apartment, but he was too drunk and nothing happened. He left the country the next day, and I made up my mind to see him again. I drifted around some more, and if I wasn't as horny as before, it was because I was consumed with interest in the bar scene. It was my passion, my Ph.D. dissertation, and I went home and made notes every chance I got.

"I want to make a record of what I have seen and heard. Today —in the Cinebar—an old woman with a cane walked with a heavy tread—three bracelets—one partly open on her wrist, on the other wrist a name tag where she was from—the nursing home or the hospital? She seemed to enjoy her drink and watching the young people in the place—looked on with a smile at a couple together— what was she remembering?—now the flesh hangs off her arms— and she is old—also had five rolls of coins—like from the bank. Was she going to pay with them?

"I've hung around bars a lot lately, and this kind of life does get to you after a while. The same bars, bartenders, customers, they all understand each other—does the same kind of loneliness and desperation drive all of us to the smoky, dim, anonymous depths of these bars? Sitting on a bar stool with a drink, smiling, talking if you want, or just sitting if you want.

"I think about Steve. I wonder if I ruined everything. We had such a good thing started. Oh well—I'll see what happens."

Later on I added up the pleasures of hanging around bars, and they didn't seem to total a whole lot. The main thing was being accepted as part of a group—but what a group!—to have my own clubs where I was known and admired and wanted sexually, places where I would be told that I was pretty, and places where I wasn't lonely. I had such feelings of inferiority, and I could only be comfortable with people that I knew to be inferior to me, and here they were in the West Village bars by the dozens. *My* people, taking care of me. I've always been a very dependent person.

I was sitting at bars for seven and eight hours every night, listening to a lot of bullshit, smelling bad smells, and some nights I would say to myself, "What the hell am I doing here?" The next night I'd decide to stay home, but the pull would be too strong, and I'd be drawn back to the bars. Then I'd see these women who'd been in this same pattern for ten or fifteen years and God, they looked awful! I'd say to myself, "Man, if you don't get yourself together that's what you're gonna look like." And that thought terrified me. I wrote: "A kid of twenty-two—doing nothing hanging around bars—idolizing older men. Do you know what it's like to suddenly look out the barroom window and see that it is no longer last night, but this morning? To realize that you have spent another night— doing what? Sitting, drinking, rapping, reaching out to touch— physically and mentally—another person, or other people around you. Oh, Steve, don't you remember that you once told me that the reason you liked your job was because you could tell anyone you didn't like to get the fuck out and stay out? You have very mean eyes—and your eyes said that to me once—as plainly as if you had spoken the words. So I did, and I have. I am too young for you, Steve. But I am growing up fast, and there will be many Steve Drakes for me."

At last I took up with a man of my own age and at last I had sexual intercourse. Finally! At the age of twenty-three! Funny, but he wasn't a bartender, even though I was a thoroughgoing bartender groupie by then. He was a hippie-type guy named Bryan Mallory, a bar hanger-on, a tall, skinny, blond-haired beach-boy kind of kid who was hated by the bartenders because he never left a tip. Once he had lived a very straight life, and he still had a job, as a cashier in a Village restaurant, and he was sort of in transition. His wife and two children were at home in Boston, waiting for him to finish the transitional period and come home. Instead he began going with me, and we enjoyed each other, and I felt I really loved him. It was the first time that I ever loved anyone in the true sense of the word. But that didn't mean that I was over the groupie scene. One night Bryan and I went to the Cinebar and a bartender named Myron took one look at me and made a beeline move across the room. He said, "Hey, babe, do you want a job?" Well, by this time my whole head was turned by the bar scene, and it was like a dream come true for a bartender to be asking me to go to work with him. It would be like Bob Dylan walking up to one of his groupies and offering her a job as private secretary. I was *that* excited. Of course, I already had a job with The Company, but I wasn't going to let that stand in the way. We discussed the situation, and I agreed to wait tables at the Cinebar on Saturdays and Sundays.

Bryan was disgusted with me. He couldn't understand this kind of slavishness to the bar scene. "You don't need the money," he said, "and you're just gonna wind up losing your straight job."

"Bryan," I said, "it's something I've *got* to do."

So he cut out of my life, and to console myself I went to bed with another of the bartenders at the Cinebar. Two weeks later I spotted Bryan on the street and I ran and caught up and began seducing him back to me. Later we talked about being in love, and he asked me if I wanted to be his old lady, and I said yes, but I'd have to think about it. A few nights later there was another sex scene with another bartender, and then I went home and said to myself, "You're passing yourself around, and pretty soon the whole Village is gonna know about it. You've got to do something to stop it." So I called Bryan, and I said, "Do you want to move in with me?" He said he did, and I told him to bring his stuff the next day while I was at work. Then I sat down on my sofa and I looked at an old picture of my father and I started to cry. I said to myself, "Well, Corey, your father would *really* be proud of you now! You've been sleeping around, and now you've invited a married man to move in with you." The whole thing seemed so scary—and so *wrong*. But by then I was out of my head with the whole Village scene, and I didn't know what I was doing. I was tired of being hustled by West Village bartenders and I was tired of the way they talked among themselves and I just *knew* that the word was out that there was a nice new hunk of ass in town, so having a steady old man seemed the least of many evils.

Well, it worked fine for a while. Bryan and I laughed a lot together, and he appreciated my housekeeping, and I appreciated the way we shared expenses, and with my income from the work at the Cinebar I was practically getting rich. So for a while it was nice sailing. Bryan was heavy into pot, and he smoked a lot, and he taught me to smoke with him, and it was a pleasant, harmless high. He always called for me at the Cinebar, and word got out that I was his old lady, and the other members of the alcohol underworld began to keep their grubby hands off me. Up to then, they had acted as though I was community property.

Then one snowy weekend Bryan went up to visit his wife and two kids in Boston, and he got back late Sunday night. Part of the reason for the trip was to talk to her about divorce, so he could marry me, but when he got back home he admitted that he hadn't had the courage to bring up the subject. He said maybe they would discuss it some other time. He told me not to be discouraged, that we would surely be married soon. On Tuesday morning he woke up sick and he gave me an envelope with money for his wife and asked me if I'd take it to the mailbox.

Outside, I held the letter up to the light. Some animal instinct took over, I guess. All I could read was something about "love you forever, and soon we'll continue our lives together." When I saw that, I ripped the letter open, and sure enough, it was a long explanation of how he was coming home for good the next weekend.

There was a hundred dollars enclosed. I put the bill in my wallet, and I went back to the apartment.

"Bryan," I said, "here's your letter. I'm sorry you're not feeling well, because you're getting out of here right now. By the way, I've kept the hundred dollars."

He said, "I knew you were going to read that letter."

"Yeah," I said. "Maybe you *wanted* me to." He called up some friends and they hauled him and his stuff away. It turned out he had a slight case of hepatitis. Too bad it wasn't leprosy. I cried that night, and I wrote in my notebook: "When I was a little baby, Daddy had deposited me in the crib and as he turned to go I reached out both hands to try to grab onto him. But I missed and fell on my head. This recent experience with Bryan is somewhat shorter. I reached out again to hold onto somebody—and fell. The fall probably didn't hurt any more than the first time."

I told myself that I would be all right, but actually I was shattered by losing Bryan. I told myself that I could never again return to the bar scene, and I had consecutive dates with a young banker and a young lawyer, but they both turned me completely off, and I went back to the bars and rolled over for the first degenerate alcoholic type that was the least bit nice to me. He was a bartender, a friend of Bryan's, and he had been dying for Bryan to get out of my apartment so he could make a pass. I didn't care; I needed somebody, and when he called me up and said he'd heard what happened and he had just the thing to make me feel better, I told him to come over. He brought cocaine. We sniffed some and we drank some wine and after a while he put some cocaine on his lips and I kissed him and licked it off. Then he put some on his cock and asked me to lick that off, too, so I did it. It wasn't much fun. All it did was make my lips numb. When he left I wrote in my notebook: "I, too, had a summer and burned myself in its flame."

For the next few weeks I worked on myself again, and I came out of it looking great. I felt like an attractive woman, and I was full of confidence. I felt more accomplished sexually, instead of like a dumb young virgin. I felt like a complete woman. I flaunted my figure and I walked into bars as though I owned them. Everybody turned and looked, and later men would ask one another, "Who was that gorgeous chick?" I know, because they would tell me about it later. It was really an up for me.

By now I'd been working at the Cinebar for several months, and I knew the scene backwards, and I dug it. Most of the customers of the Cinebar worked on the docks, or had regular jobs someplace else. Some of the longshoremen would steal stuff from cargos, and they'd come in and sell watches and clothes and TV sets, all hot stuff and very cheap. Then there were the steadies who had no jobs but pretended they did. They'd arrive in the morning and have a couple of straight shots and then they'd disappear for a few hours, pretending to do some work, and then they'd come back in the afternoon and drink till the four A.M. closing. Most of them were phony people, "pretend" people, with all the genuine feelings and emotions burned out of them. I mean, they'd pretend to get irate about what's going on in the world and the way the city's going to the dogs, but it was phony anger, phony talk, just something to say to reach out and touch another human being. They really didn't give much of a shit about anything except alcohol. They lived in stupors. Once in a while there'd be a fight, but usually everybody was too drunk and rundown to care. Sometimes they'd go back into the men's room and smoke a joint.

I fitted into these lower depths as if I'd been born into them. I loved every second of it; I loved being one with the bartenders: a part of the establishment, protected and accepted by everybody on the scene. One night I had a few bourbons and I got up on the bar and danced the whole length without spilling a single drop of anybody's drink. I was so proud and happy! I wound up falling down in the sawdust at the end, but I was laughing. It was a gas, and everybody loved me and applauded me for it.

· 4 ·

ONE DAY the owner hired a new assistant bartender, a very good-looking guy, about thirty years old and very hip and cool. He called himself Ozark, and he always had a half-dozen chicks following him, so at first I just put him down and ignored him. But then he asked me to supper one night and bought me a couple of drinks and took me home and never touched me. We smoked a joint together and then he said, "Well, I think I'd better be going," and he was gone. I was so impressed! Now I know that it was all technique; I'm older and wiser.

A couple of days later we went out and had drinks with friends at another bar, and he laid a hundred-dollar bill on the bar, and I was very impressed by that, too. I was so pleased to be with a bartender and to be his girl. So we slept together that night and for several weeks afterward. He taught me all about fellatio, and to tell you the truth I found it a lot easier than the first time I ever had intercourse. I mean mentally. I will always prefer straight sexual intercourse to sucking, but I really enjoy the beforehand stuff, too, the going down. It's really fun and enjoyable. The first time I sucked a man off I felt like I'd done a degenerate thing, and I was very ashamed. I felt like a sex pervert. But now I feel that it's very natural and very commonplace, and everybody does it. *Everybody* that I know does *everything*.

One night Ozark and his friend Lew came over to my place with some hash, and we went up on the roof of the apartment building to turn on. It was beautiful up there, with the stars and the lights of the city and a huge great moon, and we passed the pipe around and smoked. Later I wrote about what happened: "An awful feeling hit me—I knew I was sick. I knew I had to get downstairs and lie down. But I couldn't move, so I spoke to Ozark and he tried to help me—I must have passed out on the roof because it took a long time to get to the stairs. Then I managed to wake up enough to get downstairs and throw myself on the bed. Ozark stayed a few minutes and then I had what I thought was an attack of diarrhea—but nothing happened, so I left the bathroom and threw myself back down on the bed and lay there with my feet and legs on the floor—dying. I knew so clearly that this was what it is like to die. You keep spinning and twirling farther and farther down into the abyss until there is no end—and that is death. While I was spinning my mind kept wanting to call Ozark and Lew and tell them not to let me die. But I realized they were not there, and I knew that the ability to live had to come from me; no one could help me but me. And that's when I started to pull out of it—to pull myself together.

"Bryan used to say that a bad trip was caused by a bad head. I think—I *hope* I worked out some of my bad paranoia, lack of self-confidence and inferiority complex. I have no reason to panic just because Ozark might get tired of me. I might get tired of him first —and there are people lined up waiting for both of us. How funny. . . . Well, it's better for my head to trust him—and if he proves unworthy of my trust—that is *his* bad head. It doesn't concern me."

It turned out that Ozark did have a bad head, a very bad head, and it wasn't long after that rooftop scene that he began putting me down and doing negative things to piss me off. One night I called him at the bar, and he told me that Jane Fonda and Roger Vadim were drinking there and he started coming on with how much he'd like to fuck her, that she was "quite a woman." I was so angry and paranoid I could hardly sleep, and I stayed awake till three in the morning trying to figure out my own emotions. Finally I wrote: "I feel that things have come to a pretty pass when I get uptight about Ozark saying Jane Fonda is quite a woman. Of course she is. There's no reason for him not to fantasize what it would be like to ball her. It's just the same as me wanting to ball James Taylor or Mick Jagger. My paranoia is reaching huge proportions these days. I am so afraid of being alone. I used not to be afraid to go home alone—I guess I'm still not. But I'm afraid of being made a fool by him coming on to some other chick. There are reasons for him to be uptight, too—getting old, getting bald, getting paunchy. And he said he had an inferiority complex—so I am trying to understand. I was going through all my blessings tonight—and I am really very lucky."

A few days later, after more scenes with Ozark, I wrote: "If only I could recapture the feeling I had this morning. Everything is certainly going better now—I don't feel the compulsion to rush things with Ozark. I can take my time and decide whether I want to become more deeply involved. I still feel uncomfortable about seeing him and being with him—as if something has gone out of our relationship—and something has—my dependence on him—my almost frantic desire to keep him, to hold onto what I know is secure and safe. But there will always be a man around—I hate the way that sounds. I've really worked hard at not getting too dependent on him. . . . *My feelings are just as important as any guy's.* I don't have to allow myself to be talked into anything. I'm worth something as a person too. And I do know people who believe in me, who will back me up and respect me even when they think I'm wrong—not merely tell me how stupid I am."

Then Ozark quit the bar and disappeared for a few days, and my next entry tells what happened: "How naïve all that preceding shit sounds now. It is all over between Ozark and me. I last saw him Tuesday. He was uptight then, said he would come by if his troubles straightened out. Then he said he'd come by Wednesday if his claustrophobia didn't get worse. I left him a note Thursday—no reaction, no call. Friday no word. I kept believing he was hung up with his problems, giving him the benefit of the doubt. Saturday he came into the Cinebar and said he'd been on a bad trip and he wanted to be alone. He said everyone was putting him uptight. The inference was that I was, too. Later we went for a drive together and got beautifully stoned, but then he drove me home and said he couldn't stay. He obviously had no desire to go to bed with me. Don't be uptight, babe. I'm not uptight. I'm just sorry you have to go away from me to work it out. Did I slam the door? I hope so.

"This Wednesday he called me—wanted money and wanted grass. Told me to come down to the Cinebar and leave it for him. Met him and gave him money. No communication, no touching. When I went home, someone was following me. I was frightened."

It went on like this for a few more days, and then came a Sunday when I was working at the bar and he had promised to come in and talk to me. When he didn't show up, I told myself that maybe he'd had another bad attack of claustrophobia or another bad trip, but then I found out from the new bartender that Ozark was around the neighborhood, and that's when it hit me that he was avoiding me deliberately and the whole thing was over. I crashed! I started sipping wine to get through the day, and then I popped three dexxies and felt better. But late in the afternoon I began to realize that I just wasn't going to make it, that I had hit the lowest depth. It wasn't only that Ozark had put me down; most of all, it bothered me that I *could* be put down by a piece of shit like him. I said to myself that I must really be worthless garbage.

So I got my coat on and went out into the street to throw myself in front of a truck. The substitute bartender followed me—what a sweet guy!—and he saw that I was reeling and staggering and he sat me down at the curbside and talked to me for an hour. I cried and cried and cried. I'd hit bottom. I was drunk and crashing at the same time. I started to get up a couple of times, when big trucks were coming down Fourth Street, but he pushed me back down each time. Then he saw to it that I got home and he put me in bed and left. I stayed in bed all night, and the next morning I went to work at The Company bright and early, as usual. I don't know how I kept it up, during this bar-fly time, but I don't think I was ever late to work during the whole two-year period, and I only took off two or three days for sickness. I guess there's just something about me that can compartmentalize two different lives completely, and not let the one interfere with the other.

I composed a couple of maudlin letters to Ozark. I wrote: "Dear Ozark. I want to say some things I'm sure you know. I won't be able to sleep unless you know them. I know that tonight you are worried about a lot of things: your job, your family, your drinking, money, cops, and maybe other things. But I want to tell you that you're my friend, and if I could take any of the burden off your shoulders, I would. And if I could say a few magic words to make all your troubles go away I would. But I'm not very good at

either of these remedies. But anyway—if you want me to do anything—as your old lady or as your friend, I will."

I never mailed that letter. Instead, I got sore and added in the
bottom in red ink: "Just remember! I am your *ex*-old lady, not
your friend. Don't *ever* call me your friend. A friend is someone
who likes you, needs you."

My mood changed again and I wrote him another letter: "I'm
not sorry we had our thing together, and I'm not sorry that it's
over. . . . But I object to the way it was done. You left me nothing. You wouldn't even tell me how you felt. You just led me on—
promising things you never meant to do. I can't stand dishonest
people. You treated me as if I were someone you really hated—and
I can't believe I did anything so awful as to make you hate my guts.
Anyway, we can be friends. I'm not going to make any issue over
it. It's not important enough."

That was another letter I didn't mail. A few days later I got the
letter out and wrote across the bottom: "Just remember one thing:
I'm your ex-old lady, not your friend." Then I wrote in my notebook: "Ozark was really on a big ego trip. That's what's easiest for
him. It really did show me where he's at. Ozark, I could destroy
you! I am not dependent on this saloon society. I need never walk
into another West Village bar as long as I live. But this is your
milieu. You *have* to be here, you *have* to see these people. It would
be so easy to destroy you—too easy."

Well, now I'd been with Ozark and we'd broken up for good,
and everybody in the Village bar scene knew how he'd dumped
me, and I'd slept with a lot of other guys, and they all had big
mouths. I knew the word was out that I was an easy lay. What a
paradox! I had gone to great pains at The Company to avoid getting talked about; I had kept my personal life entirely private, and
as far as they were concerned up at the office, I was the Virgin
Mary on wheels. And then I went into the bowels of the earth,
those West Village bars, and made exactly the mistake that I had
avoided so carefully at the office. The bars were just as organized,
just as integrated, as The Company; it was just another hierarchy
down there, just another close-knit organization. I had allowed my-

self to get into that hierarchy and be passed about from stud to stud, and I hated the very idea. I couldn't stand the people pointing me out and saying, "There she goes. *Anybody* can have her."

So I quit my job at the Cinebar and tried to get it together. One man helped me enormously, and it was ironic because he had been a West Village bartender himself and he was an ex-convict and everything else, but he had a certain nobility underneath it all, and I'll always love him for it. His name was Jim Green—at least that's what he said his name was—and I had met him earlier and always liked him. We had just never gotten together. A few times we had drinks, and he always gave me good advice. He told me that I was a great chick, that if I had an inferiority complex it was *prima facie* evidence that I was nuts. He told me he'd like to walk barefoot through my long blond hair, but out of respect he wouldn't try to do it. He told me not to use such horrible language. He said, "You've got too much class for that. You should watch it." He also told me that I had no business in the bar scene and that I should get out before it destroyed my life. I soon realized that underneath his prison record and his fooling around with drugs and his libertine existence, he was a genuine WASP, with all the WASP's attitudes. He could go out and sniff cocaine for a one-week trip, and then get shocked because he heard me say "shit!" Strange, but refreshing. A Victorian in the jungle.

Through all my boy friends, he kept coming around and never making a move toward me. God, he was handsome! I have some notes from the middle of our affair: "Jim Green—one of the most attractive men I have ever met. Tall, slim, very tight, *together*. No hips, no ass—but very strong arms, and a beautiful lithe back. A man with charisma, *machismo*, both a man's man and a woman's man. A great cocksman. Men envy him and women love him. In and out of prison since teens. Spent a lot of time in solitary. Confused about his masculinity, but doesn't know it. He says he's never had a homosexual experience, but I don't believe him, because with all the time he's spent in prison and with all his sexuality, he's had to. But something about him touches me. He's such a child in so many ways."

One night after I began to get myself together, I ran into Jim Green and we spent a long time drinking together. Then we went home to my pad, but he said he wasn't going to sleep with me because he didn't want to fall into the category of only wanting me for my body. We got undressed and everything, but he wouldn't do it. I'll never forget that night. We sat in my living room naked. Then he wanted to take a piss and insisted that I go into the bathroom while he did it. Then we came back to the living room and talked some more, and he got drunker and drunker. He told me that he was on his fourth wife, and he said, "I love my wife very much, I really do, but I want to fuck you so bad I can taste it."

I said, "Jim, that's the nicest compliment I've ever had."

We drank some more, and he said, "Have you ever seen me drunk?" And before I could answer, he said, "No, wait. Have you ever seen me *not* drunk?" And I really couldn't remember seeing him completely sober in almost two years.

One day in midwinter he was getting ready to make his annual pilgrimage to Mexico City, and he said, "Why don't you come along?"

I had some vacation time coming, so I took off a week and joined him down there. He had an apartment in the slummiest part of Mexico City, with a mattress for a bed and cold water only, and it was heaven on earth. I wouldn't trade that crummy little pad with its two-inch *cucarachas* for the Presidential Suite at the Waldorf. What a marvelous vacation that was! I told Jim about every detail of my life, and I mean *every* detail. And he told me his. We talked for days, and we went to bed together, and it was beautiful. Our fantasies meshed, and everything that he liked to do turned me on, too. He used to like to strip me to the waist and then he'd sit on his kitchen chair and make me kneel in front of him. He'd take out his cock and grab me by my long hair and pull my mouth over him, and we'd both get so wild we'd almost explode. Then we'd fuck till dawn.

· 5 ·

ONE NIGHT he said he was going out to get some cocaine, and I told him not to bother, that I had licked it off a man's cock once and all it had done was deaden my nerve endings. He said I hadn't used it right and he knew a place where he could get it for a hundred and sixty pesos a bag, dirt cheap, and he told me to wait. So we got into cocaine together and it was very nice, the nicest of the drugs. We used to fuck all night on cocaine. We'd be fucking till nine in the morning, and then we'd sleep for a couple more hours, sniff some more cocaine and start over. It was heavenly! But when the vacation time was over, I was on that jet and headed straight back to New York, and I showed up for work an hour early on my first Monday back. I was still going by my old rule that no matter what happened, I would tend to the store. No matter how low I sank, I managed to follow that rule through the whole ordeal.

During my affair with Jim Green I made only one entry in my notebooks, which shows that I was getting less depressed.

"Everything is so cool at last. I really enjoy the beginning of a love affair the most. I like to spend money on bath oil and powder and perfume and makeup. It gives me such pleasure to get ready for a date with Jim—to make myself beautiful for him, running to meet him, knowing he's waiting. . . .

"I can hear my mother saying, 'Oh, Corey, I think that's crazy.' "

"Jim said I should open my head to experiences, let myself fall in love with whoever it is, live through one more number. I can do it—yes—I know I can do it. That's one of my strengths. I find myself consciously telling myself that I am worth *something*—that I count too. It may sound silly, but I think it is working. Also—I don't feel guilty about doing crazy things. But I have to be careful about who I'm with when I do them."

Of course nothing could go on so nicely. Jim and I met and meshed in our fantasies, and his power needs matched my masochistic needs, but deep down we were mismated. When he came back from Mexico and we tried to get it together, the whole thing started to fade. I wanted him to want me, *only* me, but that wasn't his life-style. He had other girl friends, plus his wife. And when he was with me, he wanted to spend the time in bars, never a movie or a dinner or a normal date, just sit and sit and sit around bars. There was a time when I'd thought it was an up to sit around bars, but now I was getting over that stage. When Jim said he wanted to marry me, I told him I wanted a husband who would come home to dinner once in a while and who wouldn't play around. He said, "Well, I'm not quite ready for that. Right now I'll fuck anything that walks."

"Jim!" I said. "Don't talk that way to me! Don't you dare!"

Later I realized that he couldn't really care for me and still talk like that. One night he said, "Let me know when you're ready to make a commitment," and I said, "Well, you're not ready to make a commitment. Why should *I* make one?"

He said, "Yeah, I guess you're right. I'm still looking. And I'm still fucking everything that walks." He used that expression over and over again, and one night I said to him, "Go fuck!" and that was the end of it. I was so broken up about it—and I was so disappointed about every aspect of my life except the business aspect—that I went to a psychiatrist and began trying to figure myself out. I wrote:

"I am having the rebellion that maybe all young people are entitled to, only I'm a few years late with it. Well, get on with it and get it over with. I came from a very straight Protestant Puritan background. My father and mother, but especially my father, expected me to be perfect—and for twenty-two years I really tried to be and do everything they wanted. But now I'm twenty-three—and it's time I started doing what I want—make my own mistakes, and hopefully learn from them.

"My parents would definitely not approve of people like Jim Green and Steve Drake and Ozark—and for such superficial reasons. Because they smoke too much, drink too much, live with women they aren't married to, use what is regarded as 'foul language.' But I think there is more to them than that. I never knew people like them, and I was entitled to.

"Parents are so hypocritical. I can remember my father in a drunken stupor yelling about the Simkens boys at Appomattox and the Simkens boys at Gettysburg and screaming out, 'What has our family fallen to?' And all because one of my sisters had come in from a date at five minutes after midnight. How do you explain or justify that?

"Sarah said I reminded her of a white satin doll. Yeah, that's it. Smooth, unwrinkled, beautiful—but uninteresting. Well, I have my youthful enthusiasm to offer. My sensitivity, my tenderness, my sense of humor."

The beginning of psychiatry was the end of the bar scene for me, and with only a few exceptions I haven't spent another night in a Village bar in a whole year. Not that there haven't been moments when I practically had to chain myself to my bed to keep away. At first, I only saw the doctor once a week; that was all I could afford. But when I saw the potential good that therapy could do me, I asked my mother if she would stake me to one extra visit a week. She hemmed and hawed and said she totally disapproved. She said, "I think that eighty dollars a week is an awful lot of money to spend thinking about yourself!" She just didn't understand! And she didn't want to admit that a total stranger could help untangle the mind that she and my father had tangled. Honestly, sometimes I think parents should be shot at birth. I had to keep after her for weeks, and I finally told her a few of the things I'd been doing, like sleeping with an ex-con, and then she took the attitude that *something* had to be done in such a desperate situation, and she agreed to finance a second session each week. Since then I've added one group-therapy session a week, so I'm getting a lot of psychiatric help, and it seems to be doing me some good.

But of course everybody has his downs when he's in therapy, and I've had my share. Life hasn't all been a bed of roses lately. At one point I felt a terrible need for male companionship, and I went into a singles bar and got picked up by a good-looking young man.

We went out three times, and on the third date he beat me black and blue. Another time I went into a terrible depression, and the doctor gave me some pills and told me to be absolutely sure not to drink with them. I was in a self-destructive phase, and I saw my chance, and I took twice as many of the pills as I should have and drank a bottle of bourbon a day on top of it. The idea was to keep from having to think, to keep from facing life. That was the absolutely *only* time that my mental problems ever interfered with my work at The Company. I'd get to work at ten and be slurring my words, but I still managed to keep my condition from the others. Then one lunchtime I was really out of it, trembling and afraid and alone, and I went to the infirmary to lie down. As soon as I hit the bed I began crying, and I cried and cried. There was a girl in the next bed, and I knew she couldn't rest with me making so much noise, so I went into the bathroom, and the next thing I knew I was out in the corridor crawling on my hands and knees. "Miss Simkens!" the nurse said when she found me. "What's the matter?"

She took me in to the doctor, and I swore him to secrecy and told him the whole story, and he gave me some medication and promised to keep my secret. So my slate is still clean at The Company.

Nowadays drugs scare the hell out of me. I don't even take diet pills any more. I know how drugs can fuck you up something terrible. Instead of depending on drugs, I depend on people. If I get really strung out, I call somebody in my therapy group, or I call the doctor, or I call some close friends. This is a hundred percent better than drugs, believe me. And little by little I'm figuring things out, not that I don't have a long, long way to go. I'm sure that there was a connection between making the bar scene and my memories of my father. The smell of booze still means Daddy to me, I guess. And those bartenders meant Daddy, too. My daddy let me down as a male image, and this subjected me to a lifetime of repeating the pattern, seeking out strong-looking men who would dump me, hurt me, let me down. Plus, there was the fact that I needed to rebel. When I went to bed with the West Village bartenders, I was saying, "Fuck you, Mother! Fuck you, Daddy! You made me ashamed! Now I'm gonna make you twice as ashamed of me!" I think all those points played a part in what happened to me.

Of course, a year of therapy isn't going to change you around completely or protect you from an occasional bad scene, especially in a place like New York. In fact, I just got over my latest bad scene a few weeks ago, and there was a valuable lesson to be learned from it. The lesson is that there's no point in falling at the feet of the famous; they're just as fucked up as the rest of us.

I was walking out of my hair stylist's and in a hurry to get back to the office, when I was conscious of a man running up behind me. I'm approached often on the street like that and I've become pretty tough about it. My immediate reaction is to say, "What the fuck do you want?" and walk away. But this time it was different. This dainty little voice said, "Pardon me, miss, pardon me, but I'm so-and-so, the fashion designer, and you may have heard of me."

Well, I certainly *had* heard of him. He was one of the most famous designers in the world, and I recognized him instantly. He rambled on, "I saw you walking out of Louis Guy d's and you're absolutely perfect for my new campaign, very natural, and I'd like to talk to you about it."

If you knew this man's name and reputation, you could understand why I didn't hesitate to give him my name and telephone number. He called me at the office the next day, and for a few months I hung out with him and his famous friends. Oh, I could tell some stories! One of his friends was one of the richest men in the world—everybody knows him and envies him—and as far as I'm concerned he's exceeded in his wealth only by his total, unbelievable dullness. Talking to him is like talking to a statue. Mr. Fashion Designer himself was a lot more interesting, but in a limited sort of way. He traveled in a pack of "city people," and by that I mean people who are not essentially nice, who lack compassion, sympathy, human interests, any interests except making money and cutting the throats of their competitors. All they talked about was how to screw the guy in the business next door. But models and actresses and beautiful people fell at their feet, because these men could do something for almost anybody. I wouldn't have been human if I hadn't been impressed by their chauffeurs, their butlers, the limousines that they'd send to pick me up and then send me home in, plus the luncheons at Lutèce—a hundred dollars a plate, and nobody even *looking* at the prices—and the flying week-ends to the Bahamas and wherever they felt like buzzing off to. Very early in the game I told the fashion designer that I lived with my boy friend, because I couldn't bear the idea of having him drop in on me and find that I only had a three-room apartment in the Village. So when it came time for the lovemaking, we had to go elsewhere. It started in the back of his chauffeur-driven car, coming back from Lutèce after about three bottles of Dom Perignon and some cognac. Mr. Fashion Designer surprised me by reaching under my blouse and fondling my breasts, and he said, "Oh, my darling! You have things I didn't know you had!"

"What?" I said, "Breasts? I have one on each side."

"No, no, my darling," he said. "I mean your nipples. They are so large and so lovely."

I found myself getting highly interested and I asked him if we were going to his townhouse. He said, "No, my dear, I have sixteen house guests. We are going to my friend so-and-so's house."

His friend so-and-so had a two-story penthouse on Park Avenue, original Cézannes all over the place, Turkish rugs wall to wall in every room, and a liquor cabinet that included several dozen bottles of Glen Livet Scotch and several dozen bottles of a certain Rémy Martin brandy that went for eighty-five dollars a bottle. God, I was floored! The fashion designer led me downstairs to one of the private bedrooms and began undressing me and whispering sweet compliments with each new revelation. I said, "Oh, so-and-so, we can't do that here! People will walk in on us!"

He said, "My darling, if you really love me you'll do it right here."

Then he couldn't get it up. Maybe it was the liquor, but I think it was just the way he was constructed. I'd heard that he was a fag, and although this didn't seem to jibe with his actions all night long, it wasn't entirely inconsistent either, because after a little while he asked me to blow him, and I did, and that's one thing that some fags can enjoy with a woman. They enjoy it more with a man, but they can also do it with a woman. After he had come, he was *so* apologetic. "Oh, my dear, it will be better on another night," he said, and he looked so ridiculous there in his pale little unmuscled frame and his bare feet and his mussed-up hair. I had an awful time keeping a straight face, he looked so pathetic!

There wasn't any encore, of course, because I realized that he'd never been interested in me as a person at all. Jet-set men like him have to have a constant supply of fresh, pretty faces around them. To tell you the truth, I think he really wanted me as a fag-hag, a beautiful woman who attracts men for a fag. I remembered several parties where he showed me off and then sent me home so he could ramble around with the boys. And I remembered the night he said, "Oh, my dear, you're fantastic! Every man adores you! *Most* women adore me, but *every* man adores you!" And he offered to set me up in an apartment on Park Avenue. I thought, "To do what?" But all I said was "Oh, so-and-so, why don't you cut the shit?" The whole thing died a natural death as soon as I got tired of being chauffeured around in Rolls-Royces and I decided that it would be infinitely preferable to get screwed normally instead.

· 6 ·

WHEN I'M completely frank with myself, I have to admit that there are still a few celebrities that I would like to have a chance at, I mean just to fuck. The main three that I think about are James Taylor and Mick Jagger, the rock musicians, and a bartender on West Fourth Street named Evans Richardson. He is regarded as one of the big three of West Village stud-bartenders—Steve Drake and Ozark are the other two—and there are times when I'd like to find out if he deserves his reputation. I think I must have a sado-masochistic streak in me, because I associate all three of these men with roughness toward women, black masks and whips and that sort of thing. I must be a long way from finished with my therapy, because things like that still turn me on. And sadism is very much a part of the bar scene and the super-stud image of the bartenders. When bartenders come on like super-stud with me, I would like to find out if they can really produce. But if I made a habit of this, then I'd wake up the next morning and feel horrible about myself. That's what keeps me from doing it, from running down there and trying to seduce Evans Richardson and all the rest of them. So I must be getting somewhat better, my therapy *must* be working a little.

Another thing I'm getting out of psychiatry is an understanding of my own essential hatred of males. It's there, but it's deep down, and I'm dredging it out. Jim Green was one of the first people wise enough to spot it in me. One night I was drunk and I was saying things like, "Fuck men! They're all like my father!" and stuff like that. Jim told me to shut up. He said I was giving away a secret that I should keep to myself. He said, "If any lesbian ever heard you talk like that, she'd move right in on you." No lesbian ever has, but I see his point, and I'm trying to understand the part of me that hates males. After I understand it, I'll overcome it and treat men normally. That's the way psychiatric therapy works, I hope.

For the moment, I think I'll stay right here in New York and continue at The Company and continue with my therapy. Once in a while I get a wild idea about saving money and moving permanently to Paris, but I know that would never work. I really can't see myself ever living happily any place but New York. The people here have an extra *Je ne sais quoi*, and after you've dealt with them for a while, all others become unbearable. And it's not so hard to live here. There are days in the spring and the fall when the air is clear, and you can even hear birds singing, and you get a feeling of life, of vitality, right in the middle of the city. Sometimes at dusk when I'm going from the subway to my apartment, the sun casts long shadows down these streets, and the patterns are fascinating, like modern art. After a snowfall, everything's hushed and quiet, and the little parks and playgrounds look so beautiful and white. There's *plenty* of beauty here, but you don't find it with your head down looking at the dirt. You find it by *looking* for it and by realizing that beauty comes in many forms. I don't even notice the dirt unless it's really horrible. I don't hear the noise around me. I fit in very well in the city. I even feel safe here, even when I get drunk and have to find my way home. There's always somebody in my neighborhood to see me home, and there are always a lot of people on the streets. I think that safety is a state of mind, and my own state of mind is that this is *my* city, this is *my* neighborhood, and nothing is going to happen to me here.

When I look back on my life, my biggest regret is that I haven't given my mother everything she wanted from me. I'm sorry I didn't marry right after graduation, marry a wealthy lawyer who works on Wall Street. I'm sorry I don't have a home in suburbia and three or four nice grandchildren for my mother to bounce on her knee. But I'm not sure any of that's for me. If I had done all those things, I'm absolutely certain that I'd be divorced right now, at age twenty-five.

My problem is that I'm still trying to find out what *is* for me. Sometimes I think I want to find a normal person, a banker or whatever, with a bit of craziness in him, to match the bit of craziness in me. But so far I haven't found anyone like that. The people I meet in the business world are square and boring, they're entirely straight. And the people I meet in the lower depths are *all* craziness and *no* straightness. Somewhere there must be a man walking around with both qualities. I want to find him, and I want to have children, and I want to please my mother, even though I doubt if she believes it any more.

As for the bars, I think I'm through with them, but I'm honest enough with myself to know that you never can tell. The pull is still there, and I still have to watch myself, because I could get right back in that scene tomorrow. I got a great deal of pleasure out of going into those bars and seeing everybody stop and look at me. That's a real up. And I also enjoy the fact that I could go into one of those bars now and put everybody down. I could say, Fuck you, man, and I could get back for all the times when they put me down. It's like that Bob Dylan line, "When I was down, you just stood there grinnin'.'" Now I'm in a position to do the grinning, and some nights it's hard for me to keep from barging into all the bars, the Cinebar and Chandler's Place and the Fifty-five and Jack Barry's and all the rest, and telling them all to go fuck themselves. The only trouble is if I did that I might *stay* in the bars, and then I'd be right back where I was a year ago.

No, I'm stronger now, I'm going to survive. I feel like it's some kind of a big battle, and I'll win it, maybe not next week, but sooner or later. If I survived my father's death, I can survive the West Fourth Street bartenders.

When my father died I remember praying to God to let me live through his death, because I was so scared that I wouldn't be able to survive without him. I don't even know if I believe in God any more; I just don't think about it. I told my mother the other day that I'm not sure I believe in God, and she said, "Well, you better, 'cause he's done lots of things for you!"

I thought to myself, "Name one!"

Stacy Krupp, 41

———•———

Stacy Krupp does all the work in her department, and she seems to like it that way. She radiates a little of the martyr thing, like my mother. She seems to enjoy being victimized by lazy people on the staff. But maybe she has no choice. I think her job is the only thing she has; it's her whole life. But I'll never know how she put up with that fucker she used to work for. He was without a doubt the biggest prick on the face of the earth. He didn't have one redeeming quality. When he showed up at Santana's, all the other guys would make up excuses and leave, one by one. And yet Stacy worked her ass off for that guy and wouldn't say a bad word about him. Now that's loyalty! Loyalty or lunacy, I don't know which.—Bettye McCluin

Somebody told me that Stacy Krupp's old boss used to sit at his desk and play with himself while he dictated, but that must be a joke. No secretary would put up with a thing like that.—Mary Adams

Jock Harris used to masturbate at his desk, and that told me almost as much about his secretary as it told me about him. If I had been Stacy I'd have hit him over the head with a typewriter.—Alexandra Oats

· I ·

I often sit back and close my eyes and imagine Jock Harris, my old boss, when he was twenty-one or twenty-two: big man on campus, all-around intellectual and *bon vivant*, tall and handsome and witty. He graduates *magna cum laude* from the Wharton School at Penn and he's besieged by job offers. Naturally, he comes to The Company. He's wined and dined in the executive dining room, taken under the wing of several vice-presidents, invited to the board chairman's home for dinner, introduced to the chairman's eligible daughter from Sarah Lawrence, and handed a job that puts him square on the bottom rung of the executive ladder. The year is nineteen forty-nine, business is fantastic, and Jock Harris is going to rise step by step till he takes over the glamor job of them all: president of The Company.

But something goes wrong. It turns out that Jock Harris lacks one essential ingredient—no, *several* essential ingredients. He has no tact, no diplomacy, no flexibility, no adaptability, and he's the worst handler of personnel in the history of The Company. He's fired, of course. But no! Wait! He is *not* fired. Back in The Company's *belle epoque, nobody* was fired. They used to say the only way to get fired was to punch the board chairman in the nose, but not even *that* was a guarantee of dismissal. More likely you'd get a six-week paid vacation in the Bahamas, to help you over your nervousness.

No, Jock Harris was not fired. But the ladder that he had been placed on was an administrative ladder, one on which every promotion involved the ability to handle personnel in large numbers. And that was the one thing on earth that Jock Harris could not do. He chewed up personnel and spit them out; an offhand conversation with Jock Harris could traumatize an employee for a month, and a formal interview with him almost automatically meant that the employee would seek a job elsewhere—voluntarily, and as quick as his legs could carry him. *Nobody* would put up with Jock Harris' cutting tongue and his glib and nasty personal remarks. "How is it,

Jones, that you can keep your skull so shiny and your brain so dull?" "Miss Johnson, it is customary in this business office to end sentences with periods, not with empty white spaces that only serve to show our ignorance." "Hawkins, the next time you write a memo like this, don't waste good bond paper on it. Just tear off three or four feet in the toilet and use that. Then at least it'll be of some practical use."

These sarcasms and cruelties happened to run exactly counter to The Company's philosophies and so Jock Harris had to be transferred. He had worked hard, and he was placed in charge of an unimportant inventory operation that was perfect for him. He would have much less contact with personnel; he would retain his fancy office and his title of supervisor, and most of the real work would be done by subordinates, leaving Jock Harris free to contemplate his sins. It would also leave him free to realize that he was no longer on a ladder that led straight to the top and that there was no real executive future for him at The Company. But Jock was too proud to quit, and he lingered on for sixteen more years. You can imagine how happy and productive those years were for Jock Harris and the people around him, especially after he discovered the sweet uses of vodka.

Do you see Jock Harris clearly? Now switch your view to a little farm community in East Central Texas, and a child—a female —growing up with all the old values. I was the child; my parents were immigrants who had fled the Sudetenland in nineteen twenty-five. Imagine a two-room schoolhouse and a teacher who taught four grades at a time and a high-school graduating class of thirty-four students. Imagine parents teaching respect for others, and not teaching it by rote or by ruler, either, but by example. My father was up at four A.M. to muck out the stalls and milk the cows. My mother was up with him, simply because she was his wife, and the wife was supposed to take care of the husband. My father used to sprawl on the living-room couch at seven o'clock at night, so exhausted that he couldn't get up for dinner, and Mother would have to half drag and half lift him into the kitchen. Then he would shovel down the food and fall into bed with the last ounce of strength he possessed and be up again at four A.M. and *without complaining!* My mother and father were so damned glad to be in the United States of America, they would have shoveled cow dung eighteen hours a day just for the privilege of staying here! And they passed that attitude of thankfulness along to me. They inculcated me with the idea that this was the greatest country on earth, and we were privileged souls to live here, and we owed America a good day's work every day, and what America owed us was opportunity. That's all, just opportunity. Before I was four years old I knew that you did your job properly and that work was the most important thing in the world. If your job was to scrub floors, you scrubbed the hell out of them! You scrubbed them till they shone like mirrors! And you didn't complain. You were lucky to get the opportunity of scrubbing floors.

I had good grades all through school, and I won a scholarship to Barnard College, right in the middle of Manhattan. What a shock for a farm girl from Texas! New York seemed so filthy to me; I couldn't get used to it. On our farm, if you were looking out the window and you saw a piece of paper blowing along the highway, you walked the quarter mile down to the road and picked it up. In New York, people flipped candy wrappers and Kleenexes right into the air, as though the whole place was a dump. Dogs used the sidewalks for their own personal toilets, which would have been fine anyplace else, but sidewalks don't absorb manure; they just hold it, and hold it, and hold it, till the stink becomes unbearable.

I never did get used to the filth of New York; I'm not used to it now. I also had trouble adjusting to the people, starting with my classmates. Most of them had grown up in the city, and they were the most competitive human beings I had ever seen. They were monsters! I'd never been exposed to such a level of cutthroat competition. They'd been competing like this from kindergarten. They would cut your throat for a matzo ball! They were perfect New Yorkers!

At first I wanted to be a social worker, but after one semester my adviser called me in and told me to forget it. I'll never forget her words. "Stacy," she said, "with your bleeding heart you'd never make it as a social worker. You get so involved in other people's problems that you'd just tear yourself apart. If I were you, I'd try something else."

By this time I was thoroughly sick and tired of the competitiveness of college life, and I decided to abandon ship and go to a business school and get a job. I came out of business school four months later with a typing speed of eighty-five words per minute, and I went to work for The Company. It was nineteen forty-nine, and I considered myself the luckiest person alive.

My first job was in a nine-girl pool that serviced The Company's sales offices, and it was a madhouse! There were messages coming in from our offices all over the United States and overseas, and teletypes clucking away, and stock tickers spewing tape all over the floor, and telephones ringing at the rate of about two a minute. A lot of drinking went on among the girls—no wonder—and after a week or two I concluded that I had made a wrong turn someplace and ended up in one of the circles of hell. There was a lesbian in the office, and she used to have long, horrible fights with her mistress over the telephone, right in front of the whole world! She'd slam down the phone and then cry in her cubicle and then we'd hear her call up the florist and arrange for flowers to be sent as though it was the most normal thing in the world for one girl to be sending flowers to another. I often wondered what the florist must have thought when she dictated cards like: "Dearest Dorothy, forgive me! I will be holding you in my arms tonight. Love always, Barbara."

The second week I was there, one of the girls came to work black and blue from head to toe. Her eyes were blackened, and one arm was in a sling. The supervisor explained to me that the girl had been beaten up by her black boy friend and that this was a fairly frequent occurrence. I thought, How *strange!* How *different!* Little did I know that the whole city was different!

There were a lot of office parties in those days, and I found them exciting. The Company attracted brilliant young men, the top-of-the-lists from places like Harvard and Yale and Princeton, and we young girls used to stand and ogle them. Most of them were married, but that didn't seem to keep them from going to the parties

438 · The Girls in the Office

and whisking an occasional young girl out into the night air for a drink or a walk or who knew what else. All these men seemed to want fresh new blossoms. They showed no interest in the older girls—girls of twenty-eight or thirty. There was a constant turn-over of girls like me, fresh and young and innocent, and the parties would serve as a meeting place for the seekers and the sought-after. I refused to become involved in this game, but it was interesting to observe.

Well, two years went by, and I was transferred to the inventory department as a private secretary, and then one day my boss was kicked sideways into our Tokyo operation and I was introduced to my new boss, the handsome young Jock Harris. At that time he was still only about twenty-four or twenty-five, classically tall, dark and handsome, with deep-brown eyes and wavy black hair and a loud, strident voice that commanded attention. I remember his first words to me: "All right, Miss Krupp, let's not take all day shaking hands. There's work to do!"

At first I was really gung-ho for Jock Harris. Not on a personal basis, of course; I've always kept the office entirely separate from my personal life. But our department sadly needed revitalization; it was out of the mainstream of The Company's operation, and the minute I met Jock Harris I could see that he would be the person to move it right back in. But what I didn't know—and didn't learn for a few months—was that he had already made so many enemies that he didn't have a chance to succeed in a large way no matter *what* he did at The Company. He worked hard for a few months, but then all the ambition seemed to ooze right out of him, and as a brilliant young man in his twenties he became a professional has-been. He had no power or authority over anyone of importance, and yet he still seemed to have power needs. He looked around and he found—me. Me and the other inconsequential people of his small staff. He turned our lives into hell on earth. He took that sharp, twisted mind of his and he used it for the sole purpose of torturing us. The others left one by one; the turnover was fantas-tic. But I had been taught a different approach to a job. I stuck. I almost killed myself doing it.

Jock's favorite technique was to make me feel guilty. Within a year of his arrival I was working twelve hours a day and running the whole department, while he sat in his office and read newpapers and magazines, but he still managed to make me feel that I wasn't pulling my load. He would make me feel guilty a hundred different ways and then grind my guilt into me. I never went on a single vacation except in tears, fully convinced that I was deserting him and The Company. Once he took me aside on the day before I was to go away with a girl friend and he said, "You'll be the laughing-stock of the company, Stacy. That girl's a lesbian!" I went off on my vacation red-eyed and scared, and I had a lousy time. He had planned it that way. Making me cry was the supreme pleasure of his life. And he could do it in so many ways. If ever I had to ask him to slow down his dictation, he'd roll his eyes up toward the ceiling and heave a deep sigh, as though he had been saddled with the dumbest, stupidest secretary in the world. *But I wasn't!* I was a *good* secretary! Not only a good secretary, but a good all-around worker, doing my own work and his work and everybody else's work in the department. Somebody had to do it! But God help me if I made a typing error; he would cluck and crow like an old nanny correcting a four-year-old. And if I made a slight grammatical mistake in my speech, I could absolutely depend on him to interrupt me and correct me sarcastically, even before I could correct myself.

Jock Harris was consumed with feelings of inferiority, and the only way he could assuage his feelings was to trample on others. I just happened to be the handiest and the most vulnerable. My psychiatrist and I have talked about him for hours, and we've concluded that he must have been made to feel inferior as a child, and therefore he worked abnormally hard and overachieved in college. But when The Company slapped him in the face later, it revived feelings of inferiority, and now there was no way out for him except to fly into rages and dig his claws as deep into others as they'd allow.

Even if he did something nice, he would exact payment later. Once in a while he would do me a small favor, and for a week he would remind me of it and demand to know why I was so damned ungrateful to such a wonderful boss who did such thoughtful things. He seemed to be saying, "See? I'm a big boy and a *nice* boy! You really ought to like me!" And when somebody does nice things for those kind of reasons, it gets sickening after a while, and you just get colder and colder with him, and the colder you get the more cruelties he inflicts, trying to get you to react and trying to get even with you. It's a horrible, vicious circle.

But if the telephone rang and it was one of *his* bosses, he'd say, "Yes, sir," "Yes, sir," "Yes, sir," till you wanted to puke. He'd be a different person. He'd rush down the hall like a frightened chicken, and he'd change his opinions in a second if he thought one of the big bosses disagreed with him. So underneath the bluster and the bombast and the cruelty he was a real genuine suck and a coward.

From the very beginning, Jock Harris had been an active participant in the three- and four-martini lunches, and I became accustomed to having difficult sessions with him in the afternoons. He would fly off about anything! He would come back from lunch and raise hell and stagger around for an hour or so and then go home. But it wasn't until I had worked for him for seven or eight years that I began to hear the trickle of liquid from inside his office. He was pouring vodka into his coffee cup! That was the beginning of the end, but my God, how long the end was in coming!

After a few more years, his drinking had become so heavy that some of his body functions had become impaired. It's disgusting to talk about, but he'd come back from the men's room with the front of his pants all wet, and he'd sit there amidst that stench and never seem to notice it. One night he went to his train with a stain from his crotch to his knees. He was wearing a beige suit, and it looked two-toned from all the urine. I couldn't say anything to him about it; how could I? He would just have flown off the handle. I said to myself, "He's *so* repulsive! I hope he gets arrested!"

The years went on. It is excruciating to describe them. When he was about thirty-five and still in exactly the same job, he began propositioning me in little repressed ways. The alternating moods were so hard to take. One second he'd be telling me that I was the stupidest, most worthless employee he'd ever seen, and the next he'd be suggesting that we go out for a drink after work. Or he'd eye me up and down and pierce me with those dark-brown eyes and he'd say, "You look pretty good today. Let's get together later!"

He seemed obsessed with my personal life, which I was still careful to keep private. He would say, "Were you up late last night?" or "You look like you've been partying. Who's the lucky man?" This kept up for two or three years, and I finally got sick and tired of it. I have very strong feelings about men—either they're attractive to me or they're not, and he was *not*. But he'd start propositioning me at ten o'clock in the morning and keep it up all day, *every* day, except for brief time-outs to tell me how dumb I was. It reached the point where I felt like smashing him if he so much as touched me, and I realized that something had to be done. I discussed the problem with Alexandra Oats and Samantha Havercroft, two of my best friends, and they said that the only way to turn him off was to call his bluff. Alex said he was a weak, frightened worm and he was all talk and if I ever took him up on his propositions he'd run home to his wife as fast as his legs could carry him.

"Yes, I agree," I said, "but suppose he *doesn't* back down? He's got that terrible temper, you know. He might try to kill me!"

"That slob is scared of his own shadow!" Alex said, and Samantha agreed. They told me to challenge his masculinity.

Well, there was a party a week or two later, and I had just enough drinks to give me some courage. Jock sidled over to me midway in the party and began suggesting that we go to my place and "get together." I put him off, but after a while I said to myself, "Okay, this is the night!" I put on my slinkiest manner and I asked him if he was ready to see me home, and he acted surprised and got our coats. He wasn't inside my apartment for ten minutes before he broke out in a sweat and began nervously pulling my books down from the shelf and leafing through them. When I changed into slacks and a housecoat, he turned fourteen colors and announced that he didn't want to miss the last train and rushed out of there like a skyrocket! That was the end of the propositioning problem. He never approached me again. Except very indirectly.

· 2 ·

JOCK HAD a brownish-yellow overstuffed chair at his desk, and I began to notice a darkening stain in the front of it. At first I thought he had dirty hands and was rubbing them on this one spot, but that didn't make sense. Then one day a young girl assistant came running out of Jock's office with this horrified look and said to me, "Stacy, that chair's wet. I can see it!"

I said, "Bettye, it must be the light," and I shooed her out of there. When she was gone, I took a close look. Something white and frothy, like spit, was drying in that same spot that I had noticed before. I bent over and sniffed, and the stuff had a sharp, acrid smell. I thought I knew what it was, but I couldn't believe it.

A month or so later, right after lunch, one of the messenger girls came out of Jock's office looking absolutely ashen. "Stacy!" she whispered. "He's sitting there with his fly open! He's got it out! He's playing with it!"

"Oh, my God!" I said. "No, you must be imagining things."

"I'm *not* imagining *anything!*" the girl said, and she ran out of the office.

That was the beginning of the worst period. Later on I discussed it with my psychiatrist, and I asked him why in the world a man would sit at his desk and masturbate. If he *had* to do it, why not go into the men's room? The psychiatrist explained that doing it at his desk must have been part of the thrill, part of the reason he masturbated in the first place. I remembered that Jock usually sat up tight to his desk, and *anything* could have been going on underneath while he was talking to people in his office. Apparently his kick was to call a girl in, have a conversation with her, and play with himself all the time. I wondered how many times he'd done this with me. And I wondered what part his propositioning had played in the little game. Maybe he got himself all steamed up by propositioning me and questioning me about my private life, and then went in and masturbated. My psychiatrist said he must have been a terribly repressed man.

Well, it got so bad that his umber chair became an office joke. When Jock was on vacation I called the building-services department and asked them to send a man down for a little cleaning job. But then I was appalled at what I had asked. How could I ask a poor, dumb janitor to scrub somebody's semen off a chair? I asked them to do it once or twice, but then I just couldn't bring myself to ask them again, and finally I called the supply department and I said, "Look, I've got to replace a brown chair with a dark black one," and they did the job. After that, it didn't show so much, and no poor dumb slob had to clean up after him.

One day Jock's wife called up and asked me if there was another woman. I said, "Oh, my goodness, *no*, Mrs. Harris! What ever gave you that idea?" She told me hysterically that their sex life at home had just stopped entirely, and the only conclusion she could reach was that he was seeing somebody else. I thought I knew the answer to her problem, but I couldn't bring myself to say anything. Jock Harris wasn't seeing anybody else. He was seeing his own hand!

The drinking grew steadily worse. It got so that he arrived at work at nine-thirty half drunk, and he kept pouring vodka all morning long until he could get out and drink his lunch. Several times he came back from lunch all beat up and bleeding, and each time he made up an excuse—he had been brushed by a car, or he had been mugged in the park. Probably he had got drunk in a bar and opened that vicious, sarcastic mouth of his to the wrong party —that's what we all concluded. He seemed to revel in not going to the company doctor on these occasions. He'd sit proudly at his desk, with blood dripping from his face, as though to say, "Look at me! I have some value, I deserve some respect. *I come to work when I'm oozing blood!*" God, it was so sick! We used to be embarrassed just to look at him. He was so repulsive! He would have belching spells till we thought he was going to throw up his insides, and you wouldn't dare go in to help him—he'd fly into a rage and belch all the louder. He smoked three packs of cigarettes a day and kept the alcohol flowing through his liver and abused himself with his hands, and by the age of thirty-seven he looked like a dead man.

Sometimes I'm not too fast on the uptake, but after twelve or thirteen years with him I began to realize that he was deliberately, intentionally killing himself—and not only that, but killing our department and killing each of us workers at the same time. I screwed up my courage and asked for an appointment with the big boss. My intention was not to squeal on Jock or to cry and complain; my intention was to ask the boss to help a fellow human being.

That meeting was the most frightening of my life. The boss seemed to know my purpose from the beginning and to oppose it. I had wanted to cite some examples of the horrid things that were going on, but when I walked in the office he was looking at me with this dour expression, as though to say, "Speak up! Get it over with! I have other things to do." He lifted his nose and peered down at me through his glasses as though I was some kind of inanimate object. I tried to state my message, but I just faltered and fumbled and wound up saying that I hadn't been feeling too well lately and wondered if I might have a week of my vacation time. The boss said, "You didn't have to ask *me* for that."

"No, sir," I said, and I left his office, trembling. The feeling he gave me was that Jock could keep on drinking, keep on masturbating, keep on killing himself, and keep on his verbal assaults against all the rest of us underlings, and simply for one reason: He was a man. He could do all these things and get away with them *because he was a man*, and I had to take it all *because I was a woman*. At that point, I think the big boss could have helped Jock, but from the second I entered his office it was obvious he knew what was on my mind and didn't want to hear it. I was intruding in the men's club.

So Jock stayed on. I tried to be civil to him and nothing more. I would say "good morning" and "good night" and not another word, and he'd stay in his office and read—and whatever. I was doing all the dirty work, and he liked that. But he still used me as a punching bag whenever the rage built up inside him. It became a terrible competition to see which of us would outlast the other. He pushed me, *pushed* me. He ridiculed me, turned his most vicious sarcasms on me. Why did I put up with it? I don't know. Maybe there's something wrong with me. All I knew was that I liked The Company and I liked the job, and that son of a bitch wasn't going to shove me out. It practically killed me, but I wasn't going to let him win! I was going to be stronger! I wasn't going to give up everything I'd worked for, just because of this dirty man.

Then I began to lose control of myself, and I began to think that I'd blown it, that he was going to outlast me after all. Things began to happen to me that I had no control over. I developed terrible phobias. I was afraid to ride up in the elevator and I had to get a special key from the building-services department to let myself in the stairwell and walk up to the sixth floor each morning. I could barely enclose myself in the ladies' room, and at night I was scared to lock my apartment door for fear I wouldn't be able to get it unlocked in the morning. I would wake up screaming on dark nights and grope around in a panic to see where I was, and I finally had to sleep with the bathroom light on.

That's when I began seeing the psychiatrist, and I learned that my hysterical reactions were the result of anxiety caused by the situation at the office and certain interlocking neuroses that went back to my childhood. It all went together, and as long as I stayed around there and Jock Harris stayed around there, the situation could only get worse. When I figured this out, I *really* began to hate him, because now I knew I was going to have to leave my job, and except for him I *loved* my work. It all seemed so unfair. But I knew better than to try to reopen the subject with the big boss. I still didn't belong in the men's club!

At last, good old Jock saved the day. Just as I was about to go to Personnel and ask for a transfer, Jock went absolutely classically loony! He began telling people loudly that he would be the president of The Company, and he began reminiscing about the wonderful days when he had been head of our European operation. Actually he'd never even been to Europe. He was just plain hallucinating. One morning his poor wife called to tell me that Jock wouldn't be in, that he had been acting upset and the doctor had been called and Jock was on his way to examination at a nearby hospital. A few days later I got the great news: He had been committed by his wife and the family doctor to a mental hospital upstate. That was a few years ago. He's still there, probably driving the nurses crazy. But at least *I* got a reprieve. The way things were going, I almost beat him into the padded cell myself!

The day that I enjoyed the most of all the days of my life was when I walked into the big boss's office and said, "Jock's been committed."

He really looked flustered, and he asked me to repeat, and I thought to myself, "Well, you cool son of a bitch, I've rocked you at last!" Then he said, "Poor Jock!" and I thought, "Why, you hypocritical bastard! You could have helped Jock, and you deliberately chose not to." But I didn't say anything. A few months went by, and they put a new, older man in Jock's job. The new man was a disaster, and he's still a disaster. But he's a thousand-percent improvement on what we used to have. I mean, I did all the work under Jock and I do all the work under the new man, but at least I don't have to call building-services to have the chair cleaned.

It's really fruitless to try to figure out blame for things like what happened to Jock—psychiatry has taught me that blame is a stupid concept in the first place, and in the second place blame is always very diffused—but I'll never forgive The Company for what it did to that poor, miserable man. The way I look at it is this: There are natural processes in business and in life, and you shouldn't try to defeat them. One natural process is that if you're good you rise to the top, and if you're bad you get dumped and you try something else: survival of the fittest. The Company used to violate that rule all the time, and that's how it killed Jock. Back in the forties and fifties, when The Company was making money every place they turned, a lot of Jock Harrises got put into jobs they couldn't handle. What the hell—we kept on making money, didn't we?

But it would have been so much more intelligent, and so much more humane, just to fire him, the way we're firing people nowadays if they can't cut the mustard. It would have hurt Jock to be fired, but not the way it hurt him to be cast aside and left in the same meaningless job for years and years, living a life of hypocrisy and pretense that finally turned into a life of fantasy. If they'd fired him, maybe he would have become a CPA or a hod carrier or a hard-hat or something like that, something he could handle! It would have been better for everyone, himself included. But that's the trouble with a company that's too humane and generous—it treats people *too* nicely, it offers too much latitude. If a man comes to this company with a minor weakness, he gets every opportunity to turn it into a major weakness. If he drinks a little too much, he can become an alcoholic. If he has an eye for the ladies, he can act like a raving sex maniac. He simply will not be fired. We're modern, up to date. We kill our employees with kindness—or allow them to kill themselves. Thank God times are changing, and we're toughening up at last. Why, the big boss actually *fired* somebody last week, and I just heard today that Florence DuValle has been issued a hunting license. That means she's been put on notice and she can use the time to hunt for a new job. Now *that's* more like it. Florence DuValle is not cut out for this line of work—it's time we got rid of her and others like her.

I enjoy the new professionalism that's creeping back into our office, even under this stupid new boss. There's a quickening in everyone's step, now that a few heads have rolled, and you get the feeling that you're working in a business office again instead of in a social club. I'm about to celebrate my twenty-first anniversary with The Company, and I feel pretty good about the whole thing. Jock is in a ward for the incurably insane, and I'm running the inventory operation as usual, and I don't have any real regrets. I don't look back; I don't *believe* in looking back. I might have become a schoolteacher if I had graduated from Barnard, but I don't have any real regrets. You can spend the rest of your life torturing yourself, regretting what you've done. That's a waste of time. Tomorrow is the important day. I'll be ready for it.